Networking Services

QoS, Signaling, Processes

HARRY PERROS

Networking Services
QoS, Signaling, Processes

BY

HARRY PERROS

COMPUTER SCIENCE DEPARTMENT
NC STATE UNIVERSITY

TO:

HELEN, AS USUAL !

ABOUT THE AUTHOR

Harry G. Perros is a Professor of Computer Science at NC State University, an Alumni Distinguished Graduate Professor, and a Fellow of IEEE. He is also the founder and coordinator of the Master of Science degree in Computer Networks at NC State University.

He received the B.Sc. degree in Mathematics in 1970 from Athens University, Greece, the M.Sc. degree in Operational Research with Computing from Leeds University, England, in 1971, and the Ph.D. degree in Operations Research from Trinity College Dublin, Ireland, in 1975. He has held visiting faculty positions at INRIA, Rocquencourt, France, NORTEL, Research Triangle Park, North Carolina, University of Paris 6, Paris, France, University of Paris 13, Paris, France, University of Versailles, Versailles, France, Victoria University, New Zealand, and Beijing University of Post and Telecommunications., Beijing, China.

He has published extensively in the area of performance modeling of computer and communication systems, and he has organized several national and international conferences. He has also published five print books (*Queueing Networks with Blocking: Exact and Approximate Solutions*, H. Perros, Oxford Press, 1994; *An Introduction to ATM Networks*, H. Perros, Wiley, 2001; *Connection-Oriented Networks: SONET/SDH, ATM, MPLS, and Optical Networks*, H. Perros, Wiley, 2005; *VBR Video Traffic Models*, S. Tanwir and H. Perros, Wiley-ISTE, 2014; and, *Bandwidth Allocation for Video under QoS Constraints*, B. Anjum and H. Perros, Wiley-ISTE, 2014), and an e-book (*Computer Simulation Techniques – The Definitive Introduction*, H. Perros, 2009) that can be downloaded from his web site free of charge.

In 1995, he founded the IFIP Working Group 6.3 on the Performance of Communication Systems, and he was the chairman from 1995 to 2002. He is curently an associate Editor of several Journals including the Performance Evaluation Journal, and the Annals of Telecommunications.

His current research interests are in the area of networking services, QoS, IoT, and queueing theory.

In his free time he likes to play the bouzouki and also go sailing on his beloved sailboat *Aegean*, a Pearson 31.

TABLE OF CONTENTS

PREFACE

This book deals with various aspects of networking services related to signaling and *Quality of Service* (QoS). The term networking services is used in this book to describe multimedia services with real-time and non real-time communications, delivered over the Internet. Examples of such services are: Voice over IP (VoIP), presence, instant messaging, video conferencing, distribution of TV channels over the internet (IPTV), video on demand, and service and device continuity. A networking service may involve two users who have established a video connection, or a group of users participating in a video conferencing, or a user and a server from which the user receives a service, such as IPTV.

The multimedia services considered in this book are not to be confused with data communication services typically used in apps on smartphones and tablets. Data communication services include data retrieval applications, data file transfer, email, web browsing, online sales, sensor network services, and remote control/teleaction services.

A key feature of the networking services examined in this book is that a logical session has to be established between the parties before a service is delivered. For instance, in the case where two users want to establish a video connection, a number of signaling messages have to be exchanged first in order to locate the called party and also make sure that the devices of both parties can communicate using the same codec and transmission speed. The signaling protocols used are SIP and IMS. The latter is a signaling protocol based on SIP that can be used by a service provider to provide multimedia services to subscribers across roaming boundaries and over diverse networking technologies. IMS has been adopted by the operators as the signaling protocol for LTE.

The book has been structured around the *Next Generation Network* (NGN) framework, standardized in the early 2000s, which separates the transport network, services, and signaling protocols into the service stratum and the transport stratum. The service stratum is the control plane for the establishment of multimedia sessions, and the transport stratum is the data plane over which the data of a multimedia service is transported. The transport stratum may also contain a control plane for the establishemnt of QoS connections, such as MPLS connections using RSVP-TE, but this has nothing to do with the service stratum. On top of the service stratum, third party application providers can provide services that use the service and the transport strata.

The main objective of NGN is to consolidate the various networks that exist, i.e., the TDM circuit-switched telephone network, the FDM circuit-switching TV cable network, and the packet-switched Internet, into a single

QoS-enabled IP network that will carry all the services currently offered by these three networks. The IP network currently runs over different transport technologies, such as wireless networks, optical networks, gigabit Ethernet, and SONET/SDH.

There have been other solutions in the past to consolidate these three separate types of networks into a single network, such as the *Asynchronous Transfer Mode* (ATM) architecture introduced in the late 80s. This time round, it seems that achieving this convergence is a reality!

The book is organized in the following five Parts, after an introductory Chapter where some of the basic concepts dealt with in the book are explained.

- Part 1: Processes
- Part 2: Quality of Service and Quality of Experience
- Part 3: Signaling for Establishing a Service
- Part 4: QoS Architecture in the Transport Network
- Part 5: Capacity Planning of Networking Services

Part 1 consists of two Chapters which deal with the general notion of a service, service characteristics, and diagrammatic representations for describing a service. These Chapters are not prerequisite to any of the remaining Chapters in the book and they can be skipped.

Part 2 consists of a single Chapter which deals with various QoS measures, such as, end-to-end delay, jitter and packet loss, and describe how to evaluate the QoE of audio and video streams using subjective and objective means.

Part 3 corresponds to the service stratum of NGN and it consists of four Chapters which deal with SIP and IMS, two protocols used for setting up multimedia services. Examples of the signaling involved in setting up various networking services are also given. In particular, the following services are examined: presence, instant messaging, conferencing, multimedia telephony, IPTV, and multimedia service and device continuity. Service continuity refers to the capability of continuing an ongoing multimedia session while the user roams across different packet-switched and circuit-switched access networks. Device continuity deals with the transfer of media components of an ongoing multimedia session from a user equipment to one or more other user equipment.

Part 4 corresponds to the transport stratum of NGN. It comprises five Chapters which deal with MPLS and DiffServ, two widely employed architectures used to provide QoS guarantees in the IP network. It also deals with congestion control, *Resource and Admission Control Functions* (RACF), and *Virtual Private Networks* (VPNs) based on the MPLS architecture. The RACF is a mechanism introduced in NGN that permits IMS and non-IMS schemes to interact with the underlying transport network in order to guarantee the QoS of a multimedia session that is being established or modified.

Last but not least, the often neglected topic of capacity planning is taken up in the Part 5 of this book. Capacity planning is the process of determining the capacity of a system so that it meets a certain performance criteria for a given demand. This Part consists of three Chapters, in which two different but complimentary modeling techniques, namely, queueing theory and simulation techniques, are described. A more detailed description of simulation techniques can be found in my book, *Computer Simulation Techniques: The Definitive Introduction*, that can be downloaded free from: http://www4.ncsu.edu/~hp//simulation.pdf.

This book has been written as a textbook for graduate and undergraduate students, and also for networking engineers in the field. A prerequisite for this book is the equivalent of an introductory course in networking.

PREFACE version 1.1

This book was first published in February 2014. A revised version, version 1.1, was published in December 2014. The revised version is identical to the original book minus some undesirable typos and formatting errors. Also, in certain cases, the narrative was improved in order to remove ambiguities. My thanks to Dr. Bushra Anjum for pointing out a number of these errors.

Harry Perros

LIST OF ABBREVIATIONS

3GPP	3rd Generation Partnership Project
AC	Attachment Circuit
ADSL	Asymmetric Digital Subscriber Line
AF	Assured Forwarding
ALG	Application Layer Gateway
AMR	Adaptive Multi-Rate
AoR	Address of Record
AP	Application Servers
API	Application Programming Interfaces
AR(1)	Autoregressive Model of Lag 1
ARIB/TTC	Association of Radio Industries and Businesses/ Telecommunication Technology Committee
AS	Application Server
ATM	Asynchronous Transfer Mode
AUC	Authentication Center
B-frame	Bidirectional-Coded Frame
B2BUA	Back-to-Back User Agent
BC	Bandwidth Constraint
BFCP	Binary Floor Control Protocol
BGCF	Breakout Gateway Control Function
BMI DTF	Business Modeling and Integration (BMI) Domain Task Force (DTF)
BP	Business Processes
BPEL	Business Process Execution Language
BPM	Business Process Modeling
BPMI	Business Process Management Initiative
BPMN	Business Process Modeling Notation
BPX	Branch Exchange
BRAS	Broadband Remote Access Aggregation Server
CAA	CS Access Adaptation
CAC	Call (or Connection) Admission Control

CAMEL	Customized Applications for Mobile Network Enhanced Logic
CAP	CAMEL Service Environment
CBS	Committed Burst Size
CBWFQ	Class-Based Weighted Fair Queueing
CDF	Charging Data Function
CDR	Call Detail Record
CDT	Congestive Discard Threshold
CE	Customer Edge
CGF	Charging Gateway Function
CIR	Committed Information Rate
CNPS	Core Network Path Selection
CORBA	Common Object Request Broker Architecture
CoS	Class-of-Service
CR-LDP	Constraint-Based Routing Label Distribution Protocol
CR-LSP	Constrained-Based Routed Label Switched Path
CRLF	Carriage-Return Line-Feed Sequence
CS	Circuit-Switched
CS	Class Selector
CSAF	CS Adaptation Function
CSCF	Call Session Control Function
CSRN	CS Domain Routing Number
CT	Classes of Traffic
DiffServ	Differential Services
DSCP	DiffServ Code Points
DSCQS	Double-Stimulus Continuous Quality Scale
DSF	Domain Selection Function
DSIC	Double Stimulus Impairment Scale Method
DTF	Domain Transfer Function
E-CSCF	Emergency Call Session Control Function
E-UTRAN	Evolved Universal Mobile Telecommunications System Terrestrial Radio Access Network
ECN	Explicit Congestion Notification
ECUR	Event Charging with Unit Reservation
EDF	Early Deadline First
EF	Expedited Forwarding
EFF	Elementary Forwarding Function
EPA	Event Publication Agent
ERC	Element Resource Control

ERO	EXPLICIT_ROUTE Object
ESC	Event State Compositor
ETSI	European Telecommunications Standards Institute
FCS	Frame Check Sequence
FDP	Final Decision Point
FE	Functional Elements
FF	Fixed-Filter Style
FIB	Forward Information Base
FIFO	First In First Out
FWMS	Firewall Working Mode Selection
GC	Gate Control
GERAN	GSM/Edge Radio Access Network
GMPLS	Generalized MPLS
GOP	Group of Pictures
GRUU	Globally Routable User Agent URI
GSM	Global System for Mobile Communications
GUI	Graphical User Interface
HLR	Home Location Register
HSPA	High Speed Downlink Packet Access
HSS	Home Subscriber Server
I-CSCF	Interrogating CSCF
I-frame	Intra-Coded Frame
IAB	Internet Architecture Board
IANA	Internet Assigned Numbers Authority
IBCF	Interconnection Border Control Function
ICS	IMS Centralized Services
ICS UE	IMS Centralized Services UE
ICSI	IMS Communication Service Identification
IEC	International Electronical Commission
IEC	Immediate Event Charging
IEEE	Institute of Electrical and Electronics Engineering
IEEE SA	IEEE Standards Association
IESG	Internet Engineering Steering Group
IETF	Internet Engineering Task Force
iLB	Internet Low Bit Rate Codec
IM	Instant Messaging
IM-SSF	IP Multimedia Service Switching Function
IMPI	IP Multimedia Private Identity

IMPU	IP Multimedia Public Identity
IMRN	IP Multimedia Routing Number
IMS	IP Multimedia Subsystem
IN	Intelligent Network
IntServ	Integrated Service
IP-CAN	IP Connectivity Access Network
IPER	IP Packet Error Ratio
IPLR	IP Packet Loss Ratio
IPMC	IP Packet Marking Control
IPP	Interrupted Poisson Process
ISC	IMS Service Continuity
ISC	IMS Service Control
ISO	The International Organization for Standardization
ISOC	Internet Society
ITIL	IT Infrastructure Library
ITU	International Telecommunication Union
ITU-D	ITU Development Sector
ITU-R	ITU Radiocommunications Sector
ITU-T	ITU Telecommunications Standardization Sector
IUA	ICS User Agent
J2EE	Java2 Enterprise Edition
J2SE	Java2 Standards Edition
JAIN	Java Application Programming Interfaces
JTC 1	Joint Technical Committee 1
LDP	Label Distribution Protocol
LFIB	Label Forward Information Base
LLC	Logical Link Control
LLQ	Low Latency Queueing
LRF	Location Retrieval Information
LSP	Label Switched Path
LSR	Label Switching Router
LTE	Long Term Evolution
LTV	Type-Length-Value
MAM	Maximum Allocated Model
MC	Master Clock
MCF	Media Control Function
MDA	Model Driven Architecture
MDF	Media Delivery Function

MEGACO	Media Gateway Control Protocol
MF	Media Function
MGW	Media Gateway
MIME	Multipurpose Internet Mail Extensions
MMPP	Markov Modulated Poisson Process
MMTel	Multimedia Telephony
MNC	Mobile Node Control
MOS	Mean Opinion Score
MPEG	Moving Picture Experts Group
MPLS	Multi-Protocol Label Switching
MPM	Management of Performance Measurements
MRFC	Media Resource Function Processor
MRFP	Multimedia Resource Function Controller
MSC	Mobile Switching Center
MSRP	Message Session Relay Protocol
NACF	Network Attachment Control Function
NAPT	Network Address and Port Translation
NAPTC	NAPT Control and NAT Traversal
NFS	Network File System
NGN	Next Generation Network
NHLFE	Next Hop Label Forwarding Entry
NHOP	Next Hop
NRM	Network Resource Maintenance
NrtPS	Non-Real-Time Polling Service
NS	Network Selection
NSP	Native Service Processing
NTM	Network Topology Maintenance
NTRD	Network Topology and Resource Database
OASIS	Organization for the Advancement of Structured Information Standards
OCS	Online Charging System
OLA	Operational Level Agreements
OMA	Open Mobile Alliance
OMG	Object Management Group
OPWA	One-Pass with Advertising
OSA	Open Service Architecture
OSA SCS	Open Service Access Service Capability Server
OSI	Open System Interconnection
OSPF	Open Shortest Path First

P-CSCF	Proxy-Call Session Control Function
P-CSCF	Proxy CSCF
P-frame	Predictive-Coded Frame
P-GRUU	Public-GRUU
PA	Presence Agent
PBS	Peak Burst Size
PCE	Path Computational Element
PCM	Pulse Code Modulation
PCRF	Policy and Charging Rules Function
PD-FE	Policy Decision Functional Entity
Pdf	Probability Density Function
PE	Provider Edge
PE-FE	Policy Enforcement Functional Entity
PHB	Per-Hop Behavior
PHOP	Previous Hop
PHP	Penultimum Hop Popping
PIR	Peak Information Rate
POC	Push To Talk Over Cellular
POTS	Plain Old Telephone Service
PPP	Point-to-Point Protocol
PS	Packet-Switched
PSAP	Public Safety Answering Point
PSI	Public Service Identity
PW	Pseudowires
PWE3	Pseudowire Emulation Edge-to-Edge
QMTD	QoS Mapping – Technology Dependent
QMTI	QoS Mapping – Technology Independent
QoE	Quality of Experience
QoS	Quality of Service
RACF	Resource and Admission Control Functions
RACS	Resource and Admission Control Sub-System
RDF	Routing Determination Function
RDM	Russian Dolls Model
RFC	Request for Comments
RLC	Rate Limiting Control
RLS	Resource List Server
RRO	RECORD_ROUTE Object
RSVP	Resource Reservation Protocol

RSVP-TE	Resource Reservation Protocol – Traffic Engineering
RTCP	Real-Time Control Protocol
RTP	Real-Time Transport Protocol
RtPS	Real-Time Polling Service
S-CSCF	Serving-Call Session Control Function
SBC	Session Border Controller
SCC AS	Service Centralization and Continuity Application Server
SCF	Service Control Function
SCS	Service Capability Server
SCTP	Stream Control Transmission Protocol
SDF	Service Discovery Function
SDP	Service Design Package
SDP	Session Description Protocol
SE	Shared Explicit Style
SEG	Security Gateway
SH	Session Handoff
SIMPLE	SIP for Instant Messaging and Presence Leveraging Extensions
SIP	Session Initiation Protocol
SLA	Service Level Agreements
SLEE	Service Logic Execution Environment
SLF	Subscription Locator Function
SLP	Service Level Package
SLP	Service Location Protocol
SOA	Service-Oriented Architecture
SPAN	Switched Port Analyzer
SR-TCM	Single Rate Three Color Marker
SRVCC	Single Radio Voice Call Continuity
SSCQE	Single-Stimulus Continuous Quality Evaluation
SSF	Service Selection Function
SSL	Secure Sockets Layer
SSME	Service Science Management and Engineering
SWOT	Strengths and Weaknesses, External Opportunities and Threats
T-ADS	Terminating Access Domain Selection
T-GRUU	Temporary GRUU
TAS	Telephone Application Server
TCP	Transmission Control Protocol
TDDP	Technology Dependent Decision Point
TDM	Time-Division Multiplexing

TLS	Transport Layer Security
TR-TCM	Two Rate Three Color Marker
TRC-FE	Transport Resource Control Functional Entity
TrGW	Transition Gateway
TTL	Time-to-Live
UA	User Agent
UAC	User Agent Client
UAR	Diameter User Authentication Request
UAS	User Agent Server
UDP	User Datagram Protocol
UE	User Equipment
UGS	Unsolicited Grant Service
UICC	Universal Integrated Circuit Card
UML	Unified Modeling Language
UMTS	Universal Mobile Telecommunications System
UPSF	User Profile Server Function
URI	Uniform Resource Identifier
USSD	Unstructured Supplementary Service Data
UTRAN	UMTS Terrestrial Radio Access Network
VCC	Voice Call Continuity
VCC AS	VCC Application Server
VM	Virtual Machine
VMSC	Visiting MSC
VoIP	Voice over IP
VPLS	Virtual Private LAN Service
VPN	Virtual Private Network
VQ	Video Quality Single Radio Video Call Continuity
vSRVCC	Single Radio Video Call Continuity
WF	Wildcard-Filter Style
WFQ	Weighted Fair Queueing
XCAP	XML Configuration Access Protocol
XDMS	XML Document Management Server

CHAPTER 1: INTRODUCTION

1.1 NETWORKING SERVICES

The term *networking services* is used in this book to describe multimedia services with real-time and non real-time components delivered over the Internet. The wired telephone system was probably the first networking service. In addition to the basic service, the user was offered a variety of extra services, such as, call forwarding, caller id, and voice mailbox. The telephone service has evolved to the wireless telephony which provides services such as, roaming, caller id, mailbox, internet access (browser, email, navigation), instant messaging, and push-to-talk. Another evolution of the telephone system was to use a packet-switched network to transfer voice. This service is known as *Voice over IP* (VoIP) because voice is transferred over the IP network. Other services involving the wired telephone line or the TV cable is the triple play service. A subscriber can have a telephone service including VoIP, Internet access, and also view TV channels using an *Asymmetric Digital Subscriber Line* (ADSL) modem over the telephone twisted pair that connects a subscriber to a telephone network. These services are also offered over the TV cable through a special cable modem. TV content has been traditionally distributed over the air, cable, and satellite. More recently, it is distributed over the IP network, and it is known as IPTV. The same applies also to video on demand. For instance, if we are watching a YouTube video on a computer or a smartphone, the content of the video is delivered in the form of IP packets over the IP network. Finally, video-based communications is expected to become very popular in the near future, whereby in addition to talking to someone it will be also possible to see each other.

Another commonly used service is *presence*. This is information regarding the status of a subscriber, such as "free to chat", "busy", "away", "do not disturb", "out to lunch", "off hook", and "on hook", that is used in conjunction with instant messaging. This information is distributed to other subscribers through a presence server. Current standards also support rich presence, which involves displaying additional attributes, such as mood, location, specification of the subscriber's device and operating system.

There are several services grouped under the term of multimedia *service continuity*. This refers to the capability to continue an ongoing communication session with multiple media across different networks or different *User Equipment* (UE). The main need for this is because UEs with multimedia capabilities may roam across different networks, or the users can move the media of their communication sessions across different UEs to best meet

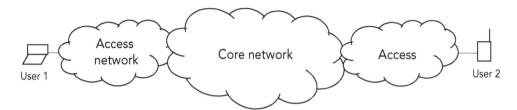

Figure 1.1: The inter-connection between the two UEs

their communication preferences. For instance, let assume that UE 1 has established a multimedia session with voice and data components with UE 2. UE 1 is currently connected to the Internet via a Wi-Fi. UE 1 moves away from the Wi-Fi where only 3G service is available. The ongoing session and its media are transferred seamlessly without the users observing a degradation in the quality of the communication. This change in the network is also known as a *vertical handover*. Moving the media of a communication session from one UE to another is also known as *terminal continuity*. This permits the transfer of some or all the media components of a session from one terminal to another. Assume for instance that an individual who is walking in a street is carrying out a teleconference with two other people using her smartphone. With the terminal continuity service enabled, she can transfer the teleconference to her desktop once she enters her office.

New services will continue to develop since it is a source of revenue for operators, equipment manufacturers, and service providers. Networking services are typically offered by service providers, but it is possible that a user can create his own service using available API functions through a service mashup software.

1.2 SETTING UP A MULTIMEDIA SERVICE SESSION

Let us consider two users, user 1 operates UE 1 and user 2 operates UE 2. The UEs of the two users are attached to two separate access networks as shown in figure 1.1. The two access networks are interconnected via one or more wide area networks, collectively referred to as the *core* network. The access networks can be based on various technologies, such as, Wi-Fi, ADSL, cable modem, WiMAX, and E-UTRAN. The wide area networks in the core are IP-based and they are *Quality of Service* (QoS) capable, that is, they use a QoS scheme such as, *Multi-Protocol Label Switching* (MPLS), *Differential Services* (DiffServ), and DiffServ with MPLS.

Let us now assume that user 1 wants to establish a video conference with user 2. There are several issues that need to be addressed for this to happen, such as, locating user 2's UE 2 and also making sure that the two UEs can communicate with each other. A UE is always attached to an access network, which may be in the user's home network or in a visiting network. The establishment of the video session can be done using a protocol such as the *Session Initiation Protocol* (SIP), see IETF RFC 3261[1], or the *IP Multimedia Subsystem* (IMS), see 3GPP[2]. SIP is a signaling protocol that can be used to establish, modify, and terminate multimedia sessions. It can also invite participants to an already existing session, such as a multicast conference. IMS is also a signaling protocol for setting up multimedia sessions, but it is more versatile than SIP. It uses SIP in conjunction with a collection of

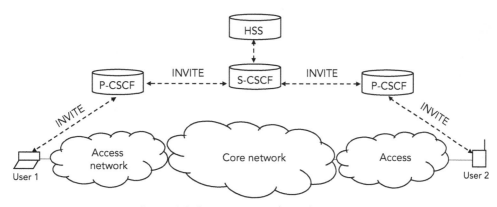

Figure 1.2: Setting up a multimedia session in IMS

servers in order to enable the establishment of multimedia sessions, and to provide a platform for service and content providers through which they can offer a variety of networking services. The IMS servers reside within the network of an operator, and they perform a variety of tasks, such as, authentication, billing, setting up a multimedia session, and mobility. Each operator runs its own IMS signaling protocol, and depending upon the location of the UEs, multiple IMS signaling protocols each belonging to a different operator, may be involved in order to set up a multimedia session. IMS has been adopted by the operators as the signaling protocol for LTE.

In our example in figure 1.1, we assume that the two access networks and the core network are owned by the same operator, and it is the home network of the two users. Also, we assume that the operator uses IMS to set up multimedia sessions. When user 1 initiates a request to set up a video conference session with user 2, UE 1 sends an INVITE message to the *Proxy Call Session Control Function* (P-CSCF), as shown in figure 1.2. This server is the first contact point with IMS, and it performs a variety of tasks, such as security, authentication, and verification of the correctness of IMS messages. After P-CSCF processes user 1's INVITE message, it forwards it to the *Serving Call Session Control Function* (S-CSCF), which is the main control point of the IMS. The S-CSCF processes the INVITE message and it then accesses the *Home Subscriber Server* (HSS) to locate UE 2. This is a database that contains user-related information, such as, user profile, security and current user location. The S-CSCF subsequently forwards it to the P-CSCF that serves UE 2. Assuming that user 2 accepts the invitation to establish a video conference with user 1, several messages are exchanged subsequently between the two UEs via the IMS servers in order to deter-mine the type of codec that will be used for the video conference and acknowledge the establishment of the session. After that, the two UEs can communicate directly with each other without the presence of the IMS, which is only used to enable the establishment of the session. The IMS is described in detail in Chapter 6. We also note that this multimedia session can also be set up using SIP, as explained in Chapter 5.

The SIP signaling messages and the data packets from the audio and video streams are all transported over the ubiquitous IP network. Yet, we make a distinction between the IMS messages and the data packets. The IMS/SIP messages are said to be in the *control plane* and the data packets in the *data plane*. The control plane is concerned with the signaling necessary to enable the transport of packets that contain data from an application other than signaling, whereas the data plane is concerned with the transport of these data packets. This distinction may not be

	Conversational voice and video	Voice mail	Streaming Audio & video	Fax
Tolerant	Remote app., command & control games	E-commerce Web browsing	IM FTP (foreground)	FTP (background email)

| | *Interactive* *Delay << 1 s* | *Responsive* *Delay ~ 1 s* | *Timely* *Delay ~ 10s* | *Background* *Delay >> 10 s* |

Tolerance for packet loss (vertical axis: Intolerant / Tolerant)

Tolerance for delay

Table 1.1: QoS metrics for common networking services

very obvious since both control and data planes run over the same IP network. However, in the telephone system, the signaling messages that have to be exchanged in order to set up and tear down a telephone conversation are transported over a packet-switched network which is different to the circuit-switched network used to transport voice. In the case of the telephone system, we say that the signaling is *out-of-band*, whereas in the SIP and IMS case described above it is *in-band*.

1.3. QUALITY OF EXPERIENCE (QOE) AND QUALITY OF SERVICE (QOS)

Let us now consider the quality of the video communication as experienced by users 1 and 2. *Quality of Experience* (QoE) is a term used to describe the experience of a user with a particular service. If we call someone over the Internet using a VoIP service, it is possible that we may not be able to hear the other person very well. In this case, our experience may not be satisfactory. This is in contrast to using the regular telephone system where the quality of the voice is always very good. In general, our experience with the use of a service is subjective. In the case of networking services, QoE depends on the easiness of using a device to access a service, and on the *Quality of Service* (QoS) provided by the underlying network that transports the packets related to the service.

QoS is a well understood and studied topic within the networking community. It is typically expressed in term of three metrics, namely the *end-to-end delay*, the *jitter*, and the *packet loss rate*. The end-to-end delay is the amount of time it takes to transfer a packet from the transmitter to the receiver, and it consists of the end-to-end propagation delay and delays induced by transmission systems and switch processing times plus the sum of all the delays a packet encounters due to queueing in the buffers of the routers through which it travels. Jitter refers to the variability of the inter-arrival times of the packets at the destination, and the packet loss rate is the percent of packets that are lost end-to-end. Different applications have different tolerance to these QoS metrics. Table 1.1 relates various common networking services to the end-to-end delay and packet loss. For instance, for conversational voice and video it is important that packets should be delivered to the destination in less than 150 msec in order to maintain user satisfaction. (Studies have showed that in fact up to 220 msec end-to-end delay can be tolerated.) On the other hand, a packet loss of about 1 in 100 can be tolerated. So, this type of service is packet loss tolerant, but delay intolerant. Now, we can contrast this to an FTP service, which is delay tolerant but packet loss intolerant. Typically, we do not expect a file to be delivered immediately, but the integrity of the file is important, and any lost packets have to be retransmitted. Packets can also be delivered with erroneous payload, in which case they will be retransmitted. The rate of erroneous packets delivered to the destination is another QoS metric that is used to monitor the quality of a network.

1.4 CONNECTION-ORIENTED NETWORKS

One of the questions that arises from the above discussion on QoS, is how can the network provide the necessary QoS to various services. Let us first take a look at how an IP network routes packets. Each IP packet consists of a header and a payload, and the header contains different fields one of which is the destination IP address. When a packet arrives at an IP router, the header is examined and the destination address is used in a *forwarding routing table* in order to find out the next IP router to which the IP packet has to be forwarded. The forwarding routing table in each IP router is constructed using a routing protocol, such as the *Open Shortest Path First* (OSPF). This forwarding operation is carried out at each router along the path followed by the packet, until the packet reaches its destination. The advantage of this type of routing is that it is simple. However, since it minimizes the number of hops, it is difficult to guarantee any QoS measures such as end-to-end delay, jitter, and packet loss rate. For instance, the fact that the path that a packet follows has the smallest number of hops does not necessarily mean that it has the shortest delay, or that jitter is bounded. On the other hand, if all routers have approximately the same packet loss rate, then the shortest path will result to a low end-to-end packet loss rate. Another problem is that a router cannot distinguish packets and therefore it cannot give packets from delay intolerant applications a higher priority for transmission out of an output port. (As will be seen later on, using priorities at the output ports of a router is important in providing QoS guarantees.) In view of this, the only way that delay sensitive applications can be served satisfactorily is to under-utilize the network so that the queues of packets waiting for transmission in the output ports are never too long. This is known as *over-engineering* the network. As a result the delay to transmit a packet out of an output port is typically negligible. This solution is expensive since the links are under-utilized (less than 20% on the average), and it does not prevent the occurrence of transient traffic congestion. Another advantage of over-engineering the network, is that when a link failure occurs, traffic can be redirected over other links without saturating these links.

In order for the IP network to provide QoS guarantees without having to operate it at very low utilizations, we need a scheme that can satisfy the following constraints. First, the network has sufficient bandwidth to carry a new traffic flow. Secondly, the network satisfies the QoS metrics associated with a flow. Thirdly, the packets associated with each flow can be identified within a router so that they can be scheduled for transmission out of an output port, according to their requested QoS. Such a solution can be provided by using the *connection-based* scheme Multi-Protocol Label Switching (MPLS), see IETF RFC 3031[3].

A connection is a path from the sender to the destination which is set up before the sender starts transmitting packets. In MPLS parlance, a connection is referred to as a *Label Switched Path* (LSP), and it is established using a signaling protocol, such as RSVP-TE. Some of the steps involved in setting up a connection are: a) calculation of a path from the sender to the destination, b) allocating resources, such as bandwidth on the outgoing link of each router along the path, to the connection, and c) tearing down the connection and releasing the resources allocated on each router. An MPLS-ready IP router, known as *Label Switching Router* (LSR), is aware of all the connections that pass through it, and therefore, it can decide whether to accept a new connection or not based on the amount of traffic that will be transmitted and the requested quality of service.

In MPLS, IP packets are not forwarded based on the destination address in the header. Rather, they are forwarded based on a label that is associated with a connection. This label is carried in an MPLS header which is between the LLC and IP headers. Each LSR maintains a table with labels and other relevant information for all active connections. When an IP packet arrives at the router, the label carried in the MPLS header is used in the table of labels to determine the next hop. The IP packet is then switched to the appropriate destination output port of the LSR that connects to the next hop LSR. In addition, since the IP packets are now identified by their label, they can be associated with different scheduling priorities for transmission out of an output port. In this way, the packets from a delay-sensitive application can be given higher priority for transmission over packets belonging to a delay-insensitive application.

We note that the notion of a connection is also used in the *Transmission Control Protocol* (TCP), but this type of connection is a logical one and its purpose is to synchronize the two TCP peers. The IP routers are not aware of TCP connections and they do not allocate physical resources to them as in the case of MPLS.

In general, a connection may or may not be set up in order to transfer data for a networking service. For instance, when we use Skype for a video conference, the video stream is not delivered over a connection, which means that there are no QoS guarantees and which explains why often the quality of the video suffers. On the other hand, Cisco's telepresence running over an enterprise network requires the provisioning of a connection in order to provide the necessary QoS for thr delivery of the high-definition video.

Finally, we note that there are other schemes, such as IntServ which can be used to allocate bandwidth to a connection. Also, DiffServ is a very popular scheme, but it allocates bandwidth for a group of flows, rather than for each specific flow. DiffServ can also be used in combination with MPLS. DiffServ and MPLS are examined in detail in Chapter 9.

1.5 THE RESOURCE AND ADMISSION CONTROL FUNCTIONS

The *Resource and Admission Control Functions* (RACF), ITU-T Y.2111[4], is a mechanism that sits in-between IMS, and the underlying network, as shown in figure 1.3, and its purpose is to set up a connection with QoS guarantees for a multimedia session. The RACF can also interact with non-IMS schemes.

As mentioned above, when user 1 initiates a request to establish a video connection with user 2, UE 1 sends an INVITE message to its P-CSCF. Subsequently, the P-CSCF sends the message to its S-CSCF which forwards it to the P-CSCF that currently serves UE 2. Several messages are then exchanged between the two UEs via their IMS

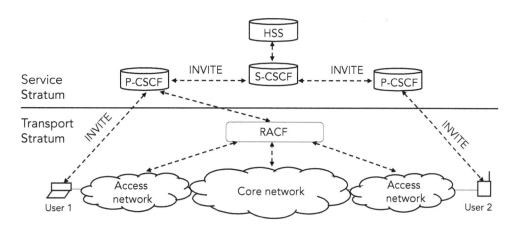

Figure 1.3: The RACF in relation with IMS and transport network

servers, and when the session parameters have been negotiated and before the two UEs can start transmitting in the data plane, IMS instructs the RACF to establish a connection through the underlying transport network. The RACF monitors the utilization of the resources of the underlying network, such as, the utilization of the links of the network, and it can determine whether there are sufficient resources for the connection so that the requested QoS for the multimedia session is guaranteed. If there are sufficient resources, then it instructs the transport network to establish a connection and informs the IMS. Otherwise, it sends a rejection back to the IMS. If the transport network is MPLS-enabled, then the connection is set up using the RSVP-TE signaling protocol. The RACF consists of several entities and it can be implemented in many different ways. It is described in detail in Chapter 12.

1.6 NEXT GENERATION NETWORKS

We note that figure 1.3 is divided into the *service stratum* and the *transport stratum*. The service stratum is the control plane for the establishment of multimedia sessions, and the transport stratum is the data plane over which the data of a multimedia service is transported. We note that the transport stratum may also contain a control plane for the establishment of QoS connections, such as MPLS LSPs using RSVP-TE, but this has nothing to do with the service stratum. This division between the service and the transport stratum was introduced in the *Next Generation Network* (NGN) architecture which was standardized in the early 2000s, see ITU-T[5, 6]. The main objective of NGN is to consolidate the various networks that exist into a single IP-based network that will carry all services. Traditionally, networking services have been provided by different vertically integrated networks, as shown in figure 1.4. Telephone services have been provided by the telephone network, which is a SONET/SDH circuit-switched network. Likewise, data services have been provided by a separate network, the Internet, which is based on packet switching. Finally, the distribution of TV services is done over yet another network which uses different technologies, such as FDM circuit-switching in the case of cable TV. In the last few years, we have seen that the services provided by a vertically integrated network have been expanded into services offered by other vertically integrated networks, as operators are deploying triple play services. Internet and TV services are now provided over the telephone system using ADSL modems, and telephony and Internet are provided over the TV cable network using a cable modem.

NGN is a concept developed in the early 2000s with a view to unifying all vertically integrated networks into a single IP-based network that will carry all services. The IP network should run over different transport technologies, such as wireless networks, optical networks, gigabit Ethernet, and SONET/SDH, which should be able to provide quality-of-service (QoS) assurances. Users should have access to existing services offered by competing service providers, which should be enhanced with the introduction of some key features, such as, service continuity, integration of multimedia and multi-party connections, and end-to-end quality of service. Service continuity permits a user to roam seamlessly in heterogeneous networks. For instance, a user can move from Wi-Fi to LTE to 3G without service interruption. Also, quality of service can be typically guaranteed within a networking technology and networking domain. The new integrated multimedia services should provide guarantees between two users or a group of users and it may involve multiple networking domains and technologies.

NGN services are classified as follows: *multimedia services, data communication services, telephone services,* and *public services.*

- Multimedia services involve both real-time and non real-time communications, such as, conversational real-time voice, point-to-point interactive multimedia (voice, text, video), multimedia conferencing, content delivery (radio, video streaming, video on demand, professional and medical image distribution, electronic publishing), push-based services, messaging, location-based services, and presence services.
- Data communication services include virtual private networks (VPN), data retrieval applications, data communication services (data file transfer, email, web browsing), online services (online sales, e-commerce, and online procurement for commerce), sensor network services, remote control/teleaction services (home application control, telemetry, alarms), and over the network device management.
- NGN-based telephone services should provide telecommunication services to both legacy and NGN telephone terminals with a quality of experience identical to the one provided by legacy telephone networks.
- NGN should provide public services in compliance with regional regulations and international treaties, such as, lawful interception, malicious call traces, user identity presentation and privacy, emergency communications, access to users with disabilities, and service provider selection.

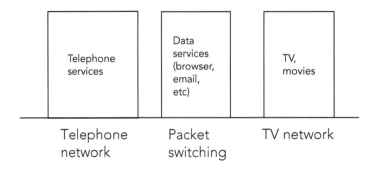

Figure 1.4: Vertically integrated services

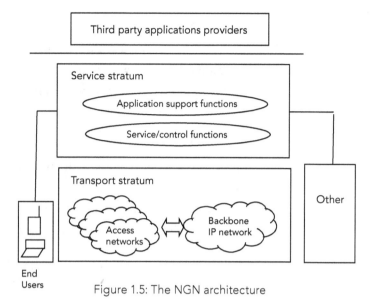

Figure 1.5: The NGN architecture

An overview of the NGN architecture is given in figure 1.5. As can be seen, it is divided into the *service stratum* and the *transport stratum*. On top of the service stratum, third party application providers can provide services that use the service and the transport strata. The service stratum is divided into *services/control functions* and *application support functions*. The service/control functions enable a user to set up session-based and non session-based services. Typical session-based services are IP telephony, and video conferencing. These services require a number of functions in order to be offered, such as registration, authentication, authorization, session initiation, and end-to-end quality of service. Non-session based services, such as video streaming and broadcasting do not require complex service functions. The application support functions are entities, such as *Application Programming Interfaces* (APIs), that enable third-party service providers to use the NGN capabilities in order to create enhanced services.

The transport stratum is completely independent of the service stratum and it typically consists of access and core networks. An access network could be, for instance, a set of ADSL users served by a metro Ethernet network which is connected to a core network via a router, known as the *Broadband Remote Access Aggregation Server* (BRAS). QoS schemes such as DiffServ and MPLS are part of the transport stratum, since they provide control functions used by the transport network to provide QoS. These control functions a re independent o f the service/control functions in the service stratum. Support for network management is also part of NGN. Services can be established using signaling protocols such as SIP and IMS.

1.7 STRUCTURE OF THE BOOK

The book is organized into the following five parts:

- Part 1: *Processes*
- Part 2: *Quality of Service and Quality of Experience*
- Part 3: *Signaling for Establishing a Service*
- Part 4: *QoS Architecture in the Transport Network*
- Part 5: *Capacity Planning of Networking Services*

Part 1 consists of two chapters: Chapter 2 - Services: Definition, Characteristics, and Frameworks, and Chapter 3 - Process Modeling. All services have the same characteristics whether they are in health, transportation, government, entertainment, education, or telecommunications. Consequently, understanding what is a service in general will help to better understand what is a networking service. In Chapter 2, we examine the notion of a service and its characteristics, and we also give a broad description of the framework for creating a service.

A networking service, and in general a service, consists of a set of different processes that have to be executed in some order so that to provide the service. A process is a set of activities that are undertaken in order to generate an output. In Chapter 3, we provide a set of diagrammatic representations for describing a process. Readers familiar with computer programming will recognize most of the constructs presented in this Chapter. Both Chapters 2 and 3 are not prerequisite to the remaining Chapters in the book and they can be skipped.

Part 2 consists of a single chapter, Chapter 4 - Quality of Service and Quality of Experience, in which we discuss various QoS measures, such as, delay, jitter and packet loss, and describe how to evaluate the QoE of audio and video streams using subjective and objective means.

In Part 3, we describe two signaling protocols for setting up services and give examples of the signaling for various networking services. Part 3 comprises the following four Chapters: Chapter 5 - The Session Initiation Protocol (SIP), Chapter 6 - The IP Multimedia Subsystem (IMS), Chapter 7 - Networking Services over IMS, and Chapter 8 – Multimedia Service Continuity. In Chapter 5, we describe SIP, the well-known signaling protocol used for establishing, modifying and terminating sessions in an IP network. SIP is also used in IMS, described in the following Chapter. IMS is a signaling system that can be used by a service provider to provide multimedia services across roaming boundaries and over diverse networking technologies to subscribers. It is used as the signaling protocol for LTE. A networking service is implemented using an application server which runs on top of IMS. An application server is not considered to be part of the core IMS functions, and it may be owned by the subscriber's operator or by a third-party provider. In Chapter 7, we give a high-level description of the networking services: presence, instant messaging, conferencing, multimedia telephony, and IPTV. In addition, in Chapter 8, we describe additional networking services related to multimedia service and device continuity. Service continuity refers to the capability of continuing an ongoing multimedia session while the user moves across different packet-switched and circuit-switched access networks. Device continuity deals with the transfer of media components of an ongoing multimedia session from a UE to one or more other UEs.

In Part 4, we describe various architectures used in the IP network to guarantee QoS. It comprises the following five Chapters: Chapter 9 - The MPLS and DiffServ Architectures, Chapter 10 - Label Distribution Protocols, Chapter 11 - Congestion Control, Chapter 12- The Resource Admission Control Functions (RACF), and Chapter 13: MPLS Virtual Private Networks. In Chapter 9, we describe the MPLS and DiffServ architectures, two widely used schemes that can be employed to provide QoS guarantees in an IP network. MPLS requires a set of procedures for setting up a connection. In view of this, various schemes have been proposed for the distribution of labels, of which the *Label Distribution Protocol* (LDP) and the *Resource Reservation Protocol – Traffic Engineering* (RSVP–TE) are widely used. These two protocols are described in Chapter 10.

Congestion control is an important component of networking, as it permits a network operator to carry as much traffic as possible, so that revenues are maximized, without affecting the quality of service offered to the users. This subject is taken up in Chapter 11, where we discuss the preventive congestion control scheme and various other relevant topics. In Chapter 12, we describe a mechanism that permits IMS and also non-IMS schemes to interact with the underlying transport network in order to guarantee the QoS of a multimedia session that is being established or modified. The underlying transport network is assumed to be QoS-enabled, that is, it runs a QoS architecture, such as MPLS or DiffServ, or DiffServ over MPLS. This mechanism, known as the Resource and Admission Control Functions (RACF), is a concept introduced in NGN to ensure QoS for multimedia sessions. Finally, in Chapter 13, we present layer 2 solutions for a *Virtual Private Network* (VPN) based on the MPLS architecture.

Part 5 focuses on capacity planning, the process of determining the capacity of a system so that it meets a certain performance criteria for a given demand. Part 5 consists of the following three Chapters: Chapter 14 - Capacity Planning of Networking Services, Chapter 15 - Queueing Models, and Chapter 15 - Simulation Techniques. In Chapter 14, we first give an example of how the response time of an existing system can be measured, and then present various types of models that can be used to study the performance of a system, and motivate the next two Chapters that deal with two different but complimentary modeling techniques, namely, queueing theory and simulation techniques. In Chapter 15 we describe a number of queueing systems and show how they can be used to model networking services. This is not an in-depth presentation and the interested reader is referred to books on queueing theory for further details. A rudimentary knowledge of probability theory is required in order to understand the basic concepts. The main objective of this Chapter is to help the reader develop an intuitive feel about queueing theory and how it is used to model networking services. Finally, in Chapter 16, the basic simulation techniques are introduced. Simulation is a popular modeling technique since it is easy to use, unlike the queueing models presented in the previous Chapter that require a more in-depth knowledge.

1.8 STANDARDS ORGANIZATIONS

We conclude this introductory Chapter with a description of some of the standards organizations. Standards allow vendors to develop equipment to a common set of specifications. As a result of the standardization process, one can purchase equipment from different vendors without being bound to the offerings of a single vendor. There are two types of standards, namely *de facto* and *de jure*. De facto standards are those which are first developed by a single vendor or a consortium, and then they are accepted by the standards bodies. De jure standards are those generated through consensus within national or international standards bodies. Several national and international standards bodies are involved with the standardization process in telecommunication. Below, we describe some of them that are referred to in this book.

THE INTERNATIONAL TELECOMMUNICATION UNION (ITU)

ITU is a United Nations specialized agency whose job is to standardize international telecommunications. ITU consists of the following three main sections: the *ITU Radiocommunications Sector* (ITU-R), the *ITU Telecommunications Standardization Sector* (ITU-T), and the *ITU Development Sector* (ITU-D). The ITU-T's objective is the telecommunications standardization on a worldwide basis. This is achieved by studying technical, operating and traffic questions, and adopting recommendations on them. ITU-T was created in March 1993, and replaced the former well-known standards committee *International Telegraph and Telephone Consultative Committee*, whose origins are over 100 years old. This committee was commonly referred to as CCITT, which are the initials of its name in French.

ITU-T is formed by representatives from standards organizations, service providers, and representatives from vendors and end users. Contributions to standards are generated by companies, and they are first submitted to national technical coordination groups, resulting to national standards. These national coordinating bodies may also pass on contributions to regional organizations or directly to ITU-T, resulting in regional or world standards. ITU also recommends and references standards adopted by the other groups, instead of re-writing them.

ITU-T standards are published as *recommendations*, and they are organized into series. Each series of recommendations is referred to by a letter of the alphabet. For instance, recommendations H are for audiovisual and multimedia systems, recommendations I are for integrated services digital networks, recommendations M are for telecommunications management and network maintenance, recommendations Q are for switching and signaling, and recommendations X are for data networks and open system communication. Currently, there are well over 3000 Recommendations in force on topics from service definition to network architecture and security, from broadband DSL to optical transmission systems to next-generation networks and IP-related issues.

EUROPEAN TELECOMMUNICATIONS STANDARDS INSTITUTE (ETSI)

The European Telecommunications Standards Institute (ETSI) is an independent, non-profit, standardization organization in the telecommunications industry (equipment makers and network operators) in Europe, with worldwide projection. It was created in 1988 and is officially recognized by the European Commission. It is responsible for standardization of information and communication technologies within Europe. These technologies include telecommunications, broadcasting and related areas such as intelligent transportation and medical electronics. ETSI has 740 members from 62 countries/provinces inside and outside Europe, including manufacturers, network operators, administrations, service providers, research bodies and users. Significant ETSI standardization bodies include TISPAN (for fixed networks and Internet convergence). ETSI has been successful in standardizing the GSM cell phone system and the TETRA professional mobile radio system.

THE INTERNATIONAL ORGANIZATION FOR STANDARDIZATION (ISO)

ISO is a worldwide federation of national standards bodies from some 130 countries, one from each country. It is a non-governmental organization established in 1947. Its mission is to promote the development of standardization and related activities in the world with a view to facilitating the international exchange of goods and services, and to developing cooperation in the spheres of intellectual, scientific, technological and economic activity.

It is interesting to note, that the name ISO does not stand for the initials of the name of this organization, which should have been IOS! In fact, ISO is a word derived from the Greek word *isos*, which means "equal". From "equal" to " standard", was the line of thinking that led to the choice of ISO. In addition, the name ISO is used around the world to denote the organization, thus avoiding a plethora of acronyms resulting from the translation of "International Organization for Standards" into the different national languages of the ISO members, such as IOS in English, and OIN in French (Organization International de Normalization).

ISO's standards covers all technical fields. Well-known examples of ISO standards are: the ISO film speed code, the standardized format of telephone and banking cards, ISO 9000 which provides a framework for quality management and quality assurance, paper sizes, safety wire ropes, ISO metric screw threads, and the ISO international codes for country names, currencies and languages. In telecommunications, the *Open System Interconnection* (OSI) reference model is a well-known ISO standard.

ISO has co-operated with the *International Electronical Commission* (IEC) to develop standards in computer networks. IEC emphasizes hardware while ISO emphasizes software. In 1987 the two groups formed the IOS/IEC *Joint Technical Committee 1* (JTC 1). This committee developed documents that became ISO and IEC standards in the area of information technology. A well-known standard brought about by this committee is the *Moving Picture Experts Group* (MPEG), pronounced m-peg, used to encode video and audio.

THE INSTITUTE OF ELECTRICAL AND ELECTRONICS ENGINEERING (IEEE)

IEEE is the largest technical professional society in the world, and it has been active in developing standards in the area of electrical engineering and computing through its *IEEE Standards Association* (IEEE-SA). This is an international organization with a complete portfolio of standards. The IEEE-SA has two governing bodies: the Board of Governors, and the Standards Board. The Board of Governors is responsible for the policy, financial oversight, and strategic direction of the Association. The Standards Board has the charge to implement and manage the standards process, such as approving projects.

One of the most well-known IEEE standards body in the networking community is the *LAN/MAN Standards Committee,* or otherwise known as the *IEEE project 802*. They are responsible for several well-known standards, such as the 802.11b Wireless LAN, the CSMA/CD, token bus, token ring, and the Logical Link Control (LLC) layer.

THE INTERNET ENGINEERING TASK FORCE (IETF)

The IETF is part of a hierarchical structure that consists of the *Internet Society* (ISOC), the *Internet Architecture Board* (IAB), the *Internet Engineering Steering Group* (IESG), and the *Internet Engineering Task Force* (IETF) itself.

The ISOC is a non-profit society that is concerned with the growth and evolution of the Internet worldwide. The IAB is a technical advisory group of the ISOC, and its charter is to provide oversight of the Internet and its protocols, and to resolves appeals regarding the decisions of the IESG. The IESG is responsible for the technical management of IETF activities and the Internet standards process. It administers the standardization process according to the rules and procedures which have been ratified by the ISOC Trustees. The IETF is a large open international community of network designers, operators, vendors, and researchers concerned with the evolution of the Internet architecture and the smooth operation of the Internet. The actual technical work of IETF is done in working groups, which are organized into several areas, such as routing, transport, security, etc.

Each area has one or two area directors, who are members of IESG. A working group is made-up of a group of people who work under a charter in order to achieve a certain goal. Most working groups have a finite lifetime, and a working group is dissolved once it has achieved its goal. Much of the work of IETF is handled via mailing lists, which anyone can join.

The IETF standards are known as *Request for Comments* (RFC), and each of them is associated with a different number. For instance, RFC 791 describes the internet protocol (IP), and RFC 793 the transmission control protocol (TCP). Originally, an RFC was just what the name implies, that is, a request for comments. Early RFCs were messages between the ARPANET architects about how to resolve certain procedures. Over the years RFCs have become more formal and currently RFCs are IETF's official standards. Another type of Internet document is the *Internet draft*. This is a work-in progress document of the IETF, submitted by any group or individual. Internet drafts are valid for six months, and they may be updated, replaced, or become obsolete.

Finally, ISOC has also chartered the *Internet Assigned Numbers Authority* (IANA) as the central coordinator for the assignment of "unique parameters" on the Internet including IP addresses.

THE BROADBAND FORUM

The Broadband Forum is a global consortium of leading industry players covering telecom equipment, computing, networking and service provider companies. Established in 1994 originally as the ADSL Forum and later the DSL Forum, the Broadband Forum united with the IP/MPLS Forum.

The IP/MPLS Forum started initially as three distinct Forums, namely the *Asynchronous Transfer Mode* (ATM) Forum, the Frame Relay Forum, and the MPLS Forum. The ATM Forum started in 1991, and they were focused on developing the solution set for ATM provisioning, management, and applications. Key deliverables from this period were the 1996 Anchorage Accord, and more than 200 specifications, many of which are still referenced today. The Frame Relay Forum also commenced in 1991 and until recently, provided the most chosen solution for wide-area packet transport, evolving from X.25 and serving primarily the business market. Finally the MPLS Forum begun in 2000 and focused on MPLS. The key development from this organization was the development of global standard implementation agreements, industry-wide educational programs, and multi-vendor interoperability testing. In 2003, the MPLS Forum and Frame Relay Forum merged to create the MPLS and Frame Relay Alliance. They were known for strong interoperability initiatives and driving multi-service implementation agreements. In 2005, the ATM Forum and the Alliance merged to form the MFA Forum, which was later re-named to IP/MPLS Forum.

The Broadband Forum's mission is to develop multi-service broadband packet networking specifications addressing interoperability, architecture and management.

THE 3RD GENERATION PARTNERSHIP PROJECT (3GPP)

The 3rd Generation Partnership Project (3GPP) was created in December 1998, and it is a collaboration between groups of telecommunications associations to make a globally applicable third-generation (3G) mobile phone system specification within the scope of the International Mobile Telecommunications-2000 project of the International Telecommunication Union (ITU). The groups are the *European Telecommunications Standards Institute* (ETSI), the *Association of Radio Industries and Businesses/Telecommunication Technology Committee* (ARIB/ TTC) (Japan), China Communications Standards Association, Alliance for Telecommunications Industry Solutions (North America), and Telecommunications Technology Association (South Korea). 3GPP should not be confused with the *3rd Generation Partnership Project* 2 (3GPP2), which specified the standards for another 3G technology based on IS-95 (CDMA), commonly known as CDMA2000.

3GPP specifications are based on evolved *Global System for Mobile Communications* (GSM) specifications, and they encompasses radio, core network and service architectures. The IMS architecture described in this book was standardized by 3GPP.

ORGANIZATION FOR THE ADVANCEMENT OF STRUCTURED INFORMATION STANDARDS (OASIS)

OASIS is a not-for-profit consortium that drives the development, convergence and adoption of open standards for the global information society. OASIS was founded in 1993, and currently it has more than 5,000 participants representing over 600 organizations and individual members in 100 countries. The consortium produces more web services standards than any other organization along with standards for security, e-business, and standardization efforts in the public sector and for application-specific markets. The Consortium hosts two of the most widely respected information portals on XML and web services standards: Cover Pages and XML-org.

OASIS is distinguished by its transparent governance and operating procedures. Members themselves set the OASIS technical agenda using a lightweight process expressly designed to promote industry consensus and unite disparate efforts. Completed work is ratified by open ballot. Consortium leadership is based on individual merit and is not tied to financial contribution, corporate standing, or special appointment.

OBJECT MANAGEMENT GROUP (OMG)

OMG has been an international, open membership, not-for-profit computer industry consortium since 1989. Its membership includes hundreds of organizations, half of which are software end-users in over two dozen vertical markets, and the other half represent virtually every large organization in the computer industry and many smaller ones. Its mission is to develop enterprise integration standards that provide real-world value.

OMG Task Forces develop enterprise integration standards for a wide range of technologies, including: real-time, embedded and specialized systems, analysis and design, architecture-driven modernization and middleware and an even wider range of industries, including: business modeling and integration, C4I, finance, government, healthcare, legal compliance, life sciences research, manufacturing technology, robotics, software-based communications and space. Some of the most well-known OMG's modeling standards, are: the *Unified Modeling Language* (UML), the *Model Driven Architecture* (MDA), and the *Common Object Request Broker Architecture* (CORBA).

BUSINESS MODELING AND INTEGRATION (BMI) DOMAIN TASK FORCE (DTF)

In June of 2005, the Business *Process Management Initiative* (BPMI), responsible for the well-known standard *Business Process Modeling Notation* (BPMN), and OMG announced the merger of their business process management activities to provide thought leadership and industry standards for this vital and growing industry. The combined group has named itself the *Business Modeling & Integration* (BMI) *Domain Task Force* (DTF). The mission of this group is to develop specifications of integrated models to support management of an enterprise. These specifications will promote inter- and intra-enterprise integration and collaboration of people, systems, processes, and information.

PROBLEMS

1. Identify a new networking service that will become popular within the next five years. Discuss where it fits in terms of QoS in table 1.1. Discuss whether a QoS-enabled IP network is required for the delivery of the service.

2. Let us assume that the routing tables in an IP administrative domain remain unchanged for a long period of time. In this case, the path between any two computers, say A and B, within the same domain will not change. Therefore, all the packets sent from A to B will follow the same path. Can we say that during that period of time, the IP network behaves like a connection-oriented packet-switched network? Why?

3. Visit the web sites of some of the Standards bodies and familiarize yourself with their organizational structure, and the type of standards that are available on these web sites.

4. Many networking and service providers offer access to their networking services that can be used by a third-party to develop a new application. Search the web to find a list of services offered by a provider.

REFERENCES

[1]   IETF RFC 3261, "SIP: Session Initiation Protocol".
[2]   3GPP - ETSI Mobile Competence Centre, "Overview of 3GPP release 5 - Summary of all release 5 features", 2003.
[3]   IETF RFC 3031, "Multiprotocol Label Switching Architecture".
[4]   ITU-T Recommendation Y.2111, "Resource and Admission Control Functions in NGN".
[5]   ITU-T Rec. Y.2001, "General Overview of NGN".
[6]   ITU-T Rec. Y.2011, "General Principles and General Reference Model for Next Generation Network".

PART 1:
PROCESSES

CHAPTER 2: SERVICES: DEFINITION, CHARACTERISTICS, FRAMEWORKS

2.1 INTRODUCTION

USA and many other countries with advanced economies are service-oriented economies with about three-fourths of the economic output coming from service-related business. Services not only dominate the output of developed nations, but also absorb much of the inputs of production, such as labor and capital. In this Chapter, we examine the notion of a service and its characteristics, and we also give a broad description of the framework for creating a service. All services have the same characteristics whether they are in health, transportation, government, entertainment, education, or telecommunications. Consequently, understanding what is a service in general will help to better understand what is a networking service. This Chapter is not a prerequisite to any of the remaining Chapters and it can be skipped.

2.2 DEFINITION OF A SERVICE

There are many definitions of a service. In Computer Science, a service is often understood as being a software designed to support a certain set of functions such as, a software that allows the creation of a document, a web service, and SIP. In this book, we take a broader view of a service, which in simple terms can be defined as work done by one person or a group for the benefit of another person or group. When defining what is a service, we distinguish the following two cases: *business-to-customer* and *business-to-business* services. We are mostly familiar with business-to-customer services since these are part of our daily life. These are services offered by businesses and government to individuals. Examples of such services abound, such as, accounting, transportation, auto repair, banking, education, entertainment, medical, government services, real estate, restaurant, entertainment, and retail. Some of these services are obvious, such as accounting, retail, and auto repair. Other services, such as, education and entertainment are less obvious.

A service is often offered to enhance the value of technical and manufactured products. That is, when we buy a product, it often comes with additional services, which enhance the usefulness of the product while at the same time generates additional revenues of the company offering the product. For instance, when we buy a laptop, we may also buy additional options, such as automatic backup of files, customer support, and warranty. Also, a customer service is another form of service that enhances an organization's manufactured products and other offerings.

The business-to-business services involve the application of scientific, management, and engineering disciplines to tasks that one organization beneficially performs for another organization. The following is a list of examples from the IT sector.

- *Call centers*: These are centers manned by operators which are geared to handle service calls for other businesses. For instance, when we call the support service of a computer manufacturer, this may not necessarily be handled by the manufacturer itself. Rather, it is more likely that it is outsourced to an onshore or offshore company which specializes in handling service support calls. In this case, the call center provides a business to business service to the computer manufacturer, preferably at a cost which is lower than what it would have cost the manufacturer to run the customer support service.

- *Applications on Demand*: Hosting and managing applications of an enterprise (SAP, Oracle, PeopleSoft) on a pay-as-you-go basis. This is another good example of a business-to-business service. A company has determined that it has to use SAP for its business. Instead of buying, installing, and maintaining the software product, the company hires another company to run it for them. Cost is a factor in the decision to outsource this operation; it should be less to outsource it than to do it in-house. This notion of outsourcing software can also be found in business-to-customer services. A very nice example of this is a software used to prepare tax returns. Instead of buying every year a software package, one can access a web site which provides the same software, stores the data from year to year, and electronically files the tax returns. Thin clients is another example of this type of service, where application software resides in some central server and it is downloaded on demand.

- *Web hosting*: This is a very popular service offered by web hosting companies which maintain a large number of servers with automatic backup, electric generators in case of a power failure, and a high-speed access network to the servers. A web hosting company develops a customer's web site based on content provided by the customer and it maintains a quality of service negotiated with the customer, which is typically measured by metrics such as percent availability, response time, and quality of experience with the web site.

- *Data center outsourcing*: This is a large scale project whereby the entire data center of a company is outsourced to another company. This is popular among companies, such as banks, which want to focus on their business and do not want to have to deal with IT infrastructure, personnel, and other issues related to providing the necessary IT services.

- *Managed storage services*: This is similar to data center outsourcing, but at a smaller scale. A service company provides storage space with backup and guarantees the necessary quality of service for business clients. This relieves a company from having to buy and maintain disk farms. Again cost is a factor, as this service should be provided at a cost which is less than what it would cost the client to run an in-house operation.

- *Output management services*: Install, maintain, and provide supplies for fax machines, copiers, scanners and multi-function devices.

- *End-to-end IT relocation services:* Companies offering this service undertake to relocate computers, servers, and whole IT centers.

- *Planning, design, and management of Service-Oriented Architecture (SOA) solutions:* Service oriented architectures provide a structured way to implement enterprise software and integrate it with legacy software packages.

Such activities can be done in-house or they can be outsourced. Companies that provide such services may also have their own SOA software packages that they can sell to the client. This is an example of enhancing a product, in this case SOA related software, with services related to planning, design, and management of SOA solutions.

Examples of business-to-customer and business-to-business from the telecommunications sector also abound. One of the oldest business-to-customer service is the telephone service, or otherwise known as POTS (*Plain Old Telephone Service*). This is a highly reliable service that has evolved to the triple play service. Technology has improved dramatically so that it is possible to provide Internet access, TV channels, and POTS over the same twisted pair that connects the regular wireline telephone to the central office of the telephone provider. In addition, a *Voice over IP* (VoIP) service can also be provided since it runs over the Internet. VoIP is an important service that has undermined the regular telephone system which uses its own specialized networking infrastructure. Telephone services are offered over the Internet by packetizing the voice into packets and switching them through to the destination where the voice is played back to the user. Cellular telephony is of course another business-to-customer service, and with this service we have witnessed a variety of additional services, such as, roaming, presence, texting, and video conferencing.

Business-to-business services are not so obvious to the casual observer and are typically offered by one provider to another. Below, are some examples.

- *Networking outsourcing*: This is a service provided to clients who do not want to own and manage their own network. It is similar to data center outsourcing. A company providing this service undertakes to manage an integrated network solution for clients. Again cost and availability of know-how are factors to the decision to outsource this activity.
- *Virtual private networks (VPNs)*: This service deals with the provisioning of a backbone network that appears to be used exclusively by a client company, but in fact it is part of a larger backbone network operated by a network provider. Using various technological solutions, the same backbone network is shared by multiple client companies while at the same time it provides traffic isolation between clients, ability to maintain private addresses within a client, quality of service, and ability to grow the private network used by a client. Because of the fact that these networks are not really private but they all share the same backbone, they are called virtual private networks.
- *Content distribution:* The content displayed in a web page is typically provided by content providers who have located servers strategically so that to provide content with minimum response time.

2.3 CHARACTERISTICS OF SERVICES

In order to further understand what is a service, it is important to discuss some of its characteristics and contrast a service against the familiar notion of a manufactured product. Below, we discuss some of these characteristics. A detailed description of the service characteristics can be found in Fitzsimmons and Fitzsimmons[1].

Before we proceed, let us first identify who is the customer. A customer maybe an individual who pays in order to receive a service. For instance, a car owner requests a service from a car mechanic and pays for it. A customer could also be an organization who pays on behalf of a group of customers who receive a service. For instance, a local government pays for the education of the students of the families that leave in the area. In this case, the students are the customers who receive the service, but the local government is the one who pays for it. Another familiar example is that of an organization that pays for its employees to receive free health care. The employees are non-paying service recipients.

CO-PRODUCTION

Services are *co-produced* by the customer and the provider of the service. Specifically, the customer provides content to the service provider, such as the customer's self, customer's belongings, and customer's information. For instance, in order for a patient to be diagnosed by a doctor, the patient has to see the doctor and also describe the symptoms. So, the patient co-produces by going to the doctor and also by providing information regarding his symptoms. Similarly, when a customer goes to a restaurant, she brings herself there and also provides information as to what she would desire to eat and drink.

In order, therefore, for a service to be provided, the customer has to interact with the service provider in a variety of ways which depend on the service. This can be contrasted with manufactured goods, where a customer simply buys a product, which has been made sometime ago and which was made without the customer interacting with the manufacturer. Co-production for receiving a service takes place all the time, but we as the service recipients are not always cognizant of this activity!

SIMULTANEOUS PRODUCTION AND CONSUMPTION

A service has to be provided and consumed at the same time, since it is not something that can be stored and used sometime in the future. This is in contrast to manufactured products which can be stored and then purchased later on. If the service is not consumed while it is being offered, then it is lost. For instance, an airline flies between two cities once a day. If the seats in the airplane are not filled in before departure, then the empty seats for that flight is a lost service. These empty seats for that flight cannot be stored and re-used. At a doctor's office, if for a period of time there are no patients, then the service that the doctor can provide during that period is lost and cannot be saved and used later on. At a car rental, any car that is not rented at any time is lost service. So, in order for a service to be provided, it has to be offered and at the same time consumed, like the production of electricity. In general, major portions of a service cannot begin until the essential customer inputs are received.

SERVICES ARE PERISHABLE

Unlike production systems, a service is perishable if it is not consumed while it is being offered. As discussed above, unlike a manufactured product, a service cannot be stored for later consumption. It has to be consumed while it is being offered, or it is lost.

CUSTOMER PROXIMITY

The location where the service is provided has to be near where the customer provides the inputs. (Not the case if the input is information or belongings). For instance, in order for a patient to be examined by a doctor, the patient has to be near the doctor. Likewise, in order to use the telephone system, a user has to be near a telephone.

FRONT OFFICE – BACK OFFICE

A service can be seen as consisting of the front office which is the part of the service that faces the customer, and the back office which is whatever takes place behind the scenes that is necessary to provide the service. A good example is a restaurant. The front office is the area where the customers are seated, whereas the back office is the kitchen, the purchasing of the food, accounting, etc. In the case of the telephone system, the front office is just a telephone device, and the back office is the enormous infrastructure that is required in order to connect customers. In cloud computing, the front office is a computer and the back office is the data center that supports virtualization.

LABOR INTENSITY

A service may involve labor at varying degrees. For instance, the actual process of ordering a product using a web-based application requires no labor. (Labor is required to set up and maintain the service, but the actual process of ordering involves no human operators). On the other hand, having surgery at a hospital is labor intensive.

PRODUCTION PROCESS

The design and offering of a service can be distinguished into the following three stages: pre-production, production, and post-production. The pre-production phase involves setting up the service. The production phase involves the actual delivery of the service, and the post-production phase involves processes that take place after the service has been delivered. For instance, let us consider a web-based enterprise software, such as online publication. The pre-production phase is the one where the application software is designed, written, tested, and launched. The production phase is the phase where a user prepares and publishes a book. The post-production phase may involve a follow-up to see whether the user was satisfied by the service.

DEGREE OF CUSTOMIZATION

Service transactions can be satisfied by an automated system, such as a web-based enterprise computing system. In this case, the level of customization is minimal. On the other side of the spectrum, it can be highly customized. For instance, outsourcing a data center to a service company is highly customized requiring a close cooperation between the client and the service provider. Highly customized services are difficult to price and they cannot easily reproduced so that they can be used for other clients.

EXAMPLES

VoIP is the technology used to provide telephone services over the Internet. The list below identifies some of its characteristics.

- *Who is the customer*: Individuals and organizations who subscribe to the VoIP service
- *Co-production:* Customer must provide a phone, Internet connection, power, telephone number, dial/hang-up.
- *Simultaneous production and consumption*: The available bandwidth and VoIP hardware is used only when the customer is making a call.

- *Perishable service capacity:* Once time has passed without making a call the bandwidth during that time is lost. It cannot be stored to be used later.
- *Customer proximity:* Global proximity. Limited by availability of the Internet.
- *Front office – back office:* The front office consists of the telephone set, operators, and customer service. The back office is the entire backbone network, services, and organization that is required to provide telephone services.
- *Labor intensity:* Low, once the VoIP system is installed.
- *Production process*
  - Pre-production: Planning and installing the VoIP system
  - Production: Dialing a number, hanging up
  - Post-production: Tearing down the connection, billing, maintenance
- *Degree of customization:* Low.

Cloud computing refers to one or more data centers operated by a provider, which can be accessed over the Internet by anyone who needs computing resources. Typically, the data center is virtualized, which permits a user to request one or more virtual machine, each with a certain CPU speed and memory. The provisioning of virtual machines is on demand and the cost charged to the user is very low and it is per use time. From a user's point of view, cloud computing is a cheap alternative to buying hardware.

- *Who is the customer:* Anyone who wants computing resources.
- *Co-production:* Customer must provide a computer to access the cloud, and the software that he wants to run on the cloud.
- *Simultaneous production and consumption:* The available computing capacity of the cloud is used only when the users request virtual machines.
- *Perishable service capacity:* The available computing capacity is lost if not used. It cannot be stored to be used later.
- *Customer proximity:* Global proximity. Limited by availability of the Internet.
- *Front office – back office:* The front office consists of a web-based software that permits a user to book virtual machines and upload software. The back office consists of the data center, the network access to it, the cooling systems, the electrical backup system in case of power failure, and the organization that is required to maintain it.
- *Labor intensity:* Low, once cloud computing is installed.
- *Production process:*
  - *Pre-production:* Planning and installing the data center
  - *Production:* Uploading and running software
  - *Post-production:* Terminating virtual machines, billing, maintenance
- *Degree of customization:* Low.

2.4 STAKEHOLDERS

When designing a service it is important to identify the stakeholders. In the networking space we can identify the following stakeholders:

- *End-users:* The actual individuals who will use the service.
- *Subscriber:* This is the entity that pays for the service. As mentioned above in section 2.3, a customer maybe an individual who pays in order to receive a service, but it could also be an organization who pays on behalf of a group of customers who receive a service. For instance, a company subscribes to a network provider so that its employees can have Internet access.
- *Connectivity provider:* This entity provides networking connectivity. Large connectivity providers, such as AT&T, typically own a core network and all the access networks required to support their subscribers. Also, the delivery of data related to a service may span over several wide area networks, each operated by a different provider.
- *Service provider:* This provider hosts the execution environment for various services: video on demand, content, management of tele-conference group.
- *Service integrator (package provider):* Provides a retail service package based on services offered by the connectivity and service providers. A service integrator may own the connectivity network and some of the services, such as VoIP. It can then provide video-on-demand by entering into a contractual agreement with a content provider that owns a library of movies.

2.5 A FRAMEWORK FOR SERVICE CREATION

In order to offer a new service several steps have to be carried out, such as, marketing analysis of the potential of the proposed service, possible development of new technology that will be used for this service, launching of the service, and monitoring the quality of the service. In addition, an organization of people, processes, and technology has to be developed in order to support the service offering. Figure 2.1 gives a high-level summary of the various domains of activity involved in service creation. Logically, these domains can be divided into two parts: service definition and service delivery. The service definition has to do with all the activities related to the marketing and identification of the service and its variants. The service delivery has to do with the designing, deploying, and maintaining the service. Below, we examine briefly each domain of activity. Further details about these domains of activity can be found in Black et al[2].

There are two domains of activities related to the service definition, namely service offering and service provisioning. Service offering is concerned with the marketing and promoting of a service. Some of the issues that have to be tackled are:

- Current marketing situation and environmental trends
- Analysis of the organization's capabilities, customers, and business environment
- Products, markets, previous results, competitors, other environmental factors
- Internal *strengths* and *weaknesses*, external *opportunities* and *threats* (SWOT).

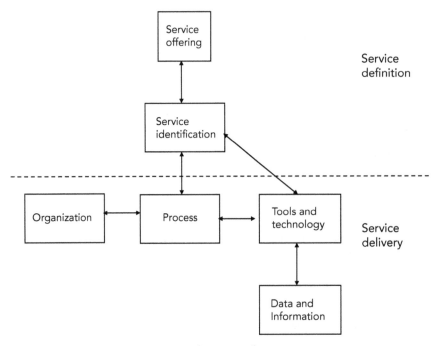

Figure 2.1: Domains of activities for service creation

- Objectives and issues
- Marketing objectives to be achieved and issues that may affect the organization's attainment of these objectives
- Target market
- Segmentation, targeting, and positioning decisions: Identify broad product markets, and segment them in order to select target markets
- Marketing strategy
- Strategy to be used in achieving the marketing objectives
- Financial plans: Expected revenues, expenses, and profits based on the marketing programs in the plan.
- Implementation controls: How progress toward objectives will be measured and how adjustments will be made to keep programs on track.

A service is not a monolithic entity, but it is made up of services, which themselves may be made up of other services. The smallest service is referred to as a *service element*. Service elements are combined to make up a *service segment*, and service segments are combined to make up a *service group*. Each service element, segment, and group has well-defined inputs and outputs, and it may be in the front office or in the back office. Examples of service composition abound. For instance, booking a vacation through one of the popular web sites involves the execution of multiple individual services, some of which are provided by other service providers. Some of these services are: compute flight schedules, display hotels in a city, display car rentals at an airport, reserve seats in a flight, reserve a hotel room, reserve a car, and authorization of a credit card. Each of these services, of course, may consist of a number of smaller services.

In addition to the hierarchical structure of a service, there may be different options available within a service. For example, Skype offers a variety of VoIP phone services, such as, computer to computer telephony, computer to a phone set, forward calls from Skype to a cell phone, and personal online number.

The service identification activity in the service offering domain, is concerned with the identification of the service elements, segments, and their hierarchical groupings to service groups, and with the *service variants* (i.e., the various service options). A service is characterized by business-oriented parameters, technical parameters, QoS, and security. Each service element is represented by a *service design*. This is a description of how a service element is delivered in practice, and it involves detailed technical data, description of inputs and outputs, flows and diagrams, and interfaces to other service elements.

The second part of service creation, service delivery, is concerned with the design, deployment, and maintenance of a service. It involves the following domains of activity: a) organization of people that will support the service, b) the design of processes that deal with how to create the service, launch it, and maintain it, c) tools and technology are necessary for the service offering, and d) databases with content required for the service offering.

The creation, delivery and maintenance of a service is supported by an organization of people, which is part of the enterprise that offers the service. These people are located at various front and back offices, and each individual has a defined set of responsibilities (role), which relies on one or more skills.

The creation and delivery of a service can be organized in terms of processes with varying degrees of complexity. Well-defined processes are necessary for a service to be successfully launched. A process is a set of activities that are undertaken in order to generate an output. Examples are: a sequence of activities executed in order to set up a video-based call, a sequence of activities executed when manufacturing a product, and a sequence of activities to process an insurance claim. A process may receive one or more inputs and generate one or more outputs. It can be very simple or very complex, and it may consist of other sub-processes. A process is depicted with diagrams which can be drawn using a graphical tool, such as Microsoft's Powerpoint, Apple's Keynote, and OpenOffice's Draw. Also, there is a variety of powerful software which in addition to providing the user with diagramming tools, they also provide other functions, such as, automatic translation of a process to executable code. The topic of depicting a process is discussed in the next Chapter.

Tools and technology involves the applications and systems necessary for creating and delivering a service. Finally, databases describe the data and information needed in the service creation and deliver. They typically contain information models, logical data models, and a physical data repository.

2.6 THE IT INFRASTRUCTURE LIBRARY (ITIL)

The *IT Infrastructure Library* (ITIL) was published by Her Majesty's Stationery Office in the UK on behalf of the Central Communications and Telecommunications Agency now within the Office of Government Commerce. It is a very popular framework that describes best practices in IT service management, and it has also been applied to networking services. The initial version of ITIL, version 1, consisted of a library of 31 books covering all aspects of IT service management. The library in the current version, version 3, has been consolidated to five core books centered around the life cycle of a service, from the initial definition and analysis of business requirements,

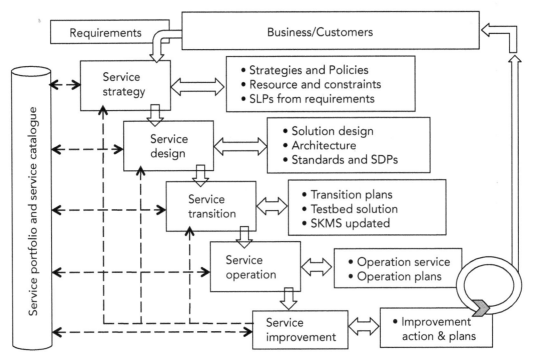

Figure 2.2: The ITIL lifecycle stages, their outcomes, and their interaction

through to migration into the live environment, live operation and continuous improvement. An overview of ITIL version 3 can be found in ITIL[3]. In this section, we review some of its basic concepts of ITIL. We note that the framework for service creation described in the previous section provides a complimentary view to ITIL.

The following stages of the service lifecycle have been identified in ITIL: service strategy, service design, service transition, service operation, and service improvement. A pictorial view of these stages, their outcomes, and their interaction is shown in figure 2.2. The service strategy is initiated from a change in the requirements. These requirements are identified in a *Service level Package* (SLP). This is passed to the service design stage where a service solution is produced together with a *Service Design Package* (SDP) that contains everything necessary to take this service through the remaining stages of the lifecycle. The SDP is passed to the service transition stage where the service is evaluated, tested, and validated. The service is then moved to the service operation phase, where it is transitioned into the live environment. The service improvement stage is concerned with the improvement of weaknesses and failures anywhere within the lifecycle stages. Below, we describe briefly the ITIL lifecycle stages.

SERVICE STRATEGY

The service strategy of any service provider must be grounded upon a fundamental understanding that its customers do not buy products, they buy the satisfaction of particular needs. Therefore, to be successful, the services provided must be perceived by the customer to deliver sufficient value in the form of outcomes that the customer wants to achieve. Achieving a deep understanding of what the customer's needs are, and when and why they occur, requires a clear understanding of exactly who is an existing or potential customer of the service provider. This, in turn, requires the service provider to understand the wider context of the current and potential market places that the service provider operates in, or may wish to operate in. The service strategy stage aims at providing answers to a host of questions, such as, what services to offer, who the services should be offered to, what is the competition in the existing and potential market places, how the customers and stakeholders will perceive value and how this value will be created, and how service performance will be measured.

SERVICE DESIGN

Service design starts with a set of business requirements handed over from the service strategy stage and ends with the development of a service solution that meets these requirements. The solution includes architectures, processes, policies and documentation, and it is described in a service design package that is handed over to the service transition stage. Below, we summarize some of the key processes and activities used in the design of a service.

SERVICE CATALOGUE

The service catalogue provides a single, consistent central source of information of all the agreed services provided by the service provider, and it is widely available to those who are approved to access it.

SERVICE LEVEL MANAGEMENT

The purpose of this activity is to ensure that the performance of all operational services is measured in a consistent and professional manner throughout the organization, and that the services and the reports produced meet the needs of the business and customers. The main information provided includes whether the *Service Level Agreements* (SLAs), the *Operational Level Agreements* (OLAs) and other support agreements have been met, and if they have not been met, what improvements in the service are required to make sure that they are met. An SLA is part of the service contract where the level of service is formally defined. For instance, in web hosting, the client may expect that the response time is less than a given value 95% of the time, the web service is available 99.999% of the time, and the mean time between two successive failures of the web server is less than a predefined value. Failing these SLA metrics may result in fines for the company hosting the web service. An OLA defines the relationships among the internal support groups of an organization working to support an SLA. The agreement describes the responsibilities of each internal support group toward other support groups, including the process and time-frame for delivery of their services.

CAPACITY MANAGEMENT

This activity deals with the capacity and performance of a service. The capacity of a service is a function of the resources allocated to it. For instance, the capacity of a web server is a function of the CPU, memory, and disk that are used to provide the service, and it is expressed in terms of the performance metrics, such as, the response time to process a request and return the results to a customer.

AVAILABILITY MANAGEMENT

This activity deals with the availability of a service, its components and other resources used in the delivery of the service. It ensures that availability targets in all areas are measured and achieved, and that they match or exceed the current and future agreed needs of the business in a cost-effective manner.

SERVICE TRANSITION

The role of the service transition stage is to deliver services into operational use. It focuses on implementing all aspects of the service including where the service has to operate in extreme or abnormal circumstances induced by errors and failures. This requires understanding of the value of the service and who it is delivered to, identification of all stakeholders within the supplier and customer areas, and adaptation and modification of the service design during the transition stage.

SERVICE OPERATION

Service operation is at the heart of day-to-day service delivery. It focuses on the execution and delivery of all processes and services in a consistent, reliable and repeatable manner. An often overlooked benefit of service operation is that it also provides validation of the service being delivered. Service operation is continuously improved due to the service improvement stage (see below).

SERVICE IMPROVEMENT

The service improvement stage is concerned with continually improving the effectiveness and efficiency of services and underlying processes. This involves the following activities: service evaluation, process evaluation, definition of improvement initiatives, and monitoring. Service evaluation requires the identification of areas where the targeted service levels are not reached. Likewise, process evaluation includes identifying areas where the targeted process metrics are not reached. The definition of improvement initiatives aims at improving services and processes based on the results of service and process evaluation. The resulting initiatives are either internal initiatives pursued by the service provider on his own behalf, or initiatives which require the customer's cooperation. Finally, monitoring is required to verify if improvement initiatives are proceeding according to plan.

PROBLEMS

1. Using section 2.3 as guidance, identify the service characteristics of VPN, POTS, and video-on-demand.

2. FastTaxReturns is an online program accessible via a browser that permits the user to prepare and file his taxes. Identify its service characteristics following section 2.3.

3. Define a service whose front office is a larger operation than its back office.

4. Identify the stakeholders in the cloud computing space.

5. Consider the framework for service creation shown in figure 2.1. For each stage identify the computer science related activities that need to be done.

6. Same as question above, but for the ITIL lifecycle shown in figure 2.2.

7. Describe the role of analytics in service creation.

8. Give an example of service composition using the SOA paradigm.

REFERENCES

[1] Fitzsimmons, J.A. and Fitzsimmons, M.J., Service Management: Operations, Strategy, Information Technology, McGraw Hill, 2006.

[2] Black, J., Draper, C., Lococo, T., Matar, F., Ward, C., "An Integration Model for Organizing IT Service Management, IBM Systems Journal, vol 46, No. 3, 2007, pp 405-422.

[3] *An Introductory Overview of ITIL® V3, The IT Service Management Forum.*

CHAPTER 3: PROCESS MODELING

3.1 INTRODUCTION

A process is a set of activities that are undertaken in order to generate an output. Examples of processes are: a sequence of activities executed in order to set up a VoIP call, a sequence of activities executed when a student submits an application to be admitted to a University, and a sequence of activities to process an insurance claim. The notion of a process is very general and one can see processes in all aspects of our lives. A process takes place in response to some stimulus. For instance, as shown in figure 3.1, when we press on our remote control key to open the car, this stimulus sets in motion a set of activities that result to the opening of the passenger door. In general, a process may receive one or more inputs and generate one or more outputs. It can be very simple or very complex, and it may consist of other sub-processes.

Processes have different complexity. A simple process follows a consistent and well-defined sequence of activities. Examples can be found in manufacturing, accounting, etc. A more complex process involves branches of different flows of activities, exceptions, and rules that are not well defined and they have to be interpreted by humans. For instance, in car repair, when fixing a problem there is a sequence of actions that have to be taken, but often several of these actions are left to the judgment of the mechanic. Finally, very complex processes demand still more initiative and creativity on the part of the human operator. They cannot be automated and it is hard to train people to do these processes. They are less well-defined, change often, and evolve as time passes. Examples are: new product development, and designing a new software system. The less complex the process, the easier it is to document it and subsequently outsource it, either offshore or onshore. Complex processes are harder to outsource since it is difficult to prepare a detailed specifications document summarizing the steps of the process.

In this Chapter, we present a set of diagrammatic representations used to depict a process. This Chapter is not a prerequisite to any of the remaining Chapters and it can be skipped.

Figure 3.1: A process

3.2 MODELING PROCESSES

Less complex processes, particularly those consisting of well-defined repetitive tasks can be represented using modeling tools for processes. By modeling we mean using diagrams to depict a process. These modeling tools should not be confused with mathematical models, such as linear programming and queueing theory, and simulation techniques, which are used to optimize resource allocation and characterize the performance of a system. These models are described in Part 5 of the book.

A process can be described using diagrams, which are often referred to as *maps, activity diagrams*, or *workflow diagrams.* These diagrams can be drawn using a simple graphical tool, such as Microsoft's Powerpoint, OpenOffice's Draw, and Apple's Keynote. In addition, there is a variety of different diagramming software with powerful additional features, such as automatic translation to executable code. This variety of sophisticated software is due to the diversified application of processes to different disciplines, such as IT and management. Examples are the *Business Process Execution Language* (BPEL), the *Business Process Modeling Notation* (BPMN), and the *Unified Modeling Language* (UML). BPEL (rhymes with people) was developed by the OASIS group and is backed by many major vendors. It is a very popular language that represents a process in XML with web service bindings. BPMN was developed by the *Business Process Management Initiative* (BPMI), and it is a graphical language with mapping to BPEL. UML was developed by the *Object Management Group* (OMG) and provides a graphical notation system for object oriented analysis and design. Both UML and BPMN have a large set of symbols that can be used to represent complex processes. These diagrams can then be used to generate code. BPMI and OMG have merged their business process management activities to provide industry standards in this area. The combined group has named itself the *Business Modeling and Integration* (BMI) *Domain Task Force* (DTF).

In order to depict a process by a diagram, we decompose it into individual activities and sub-processes, which themselves may consist of other sub-processes. An example of such a diagrammatic representation is shown in figure 3.2. The process depicts the activities involved of placing orders and subsequently manufacturing and delivering the goods. Each rectangle with rounded corners represents a sub-process which consists of a set of individual activities.

The process shown in figure 3.2 can be re-written using horizontal bands as shown in figure 3.3, referred to as *swimlanes* in BPMN. They represent the various functional or organization entities responsible for each of the

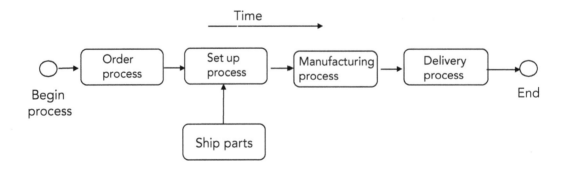

Figure 3.2: An example of a process

activities. In general, swimlanes are used to indicate which roles have responsibility for carrying the activities. The swimlanes related to the company are all adjacent, whereas the supplier's is separate. We say that the swimlanes of the company belong to one pool and that of the supplier to another pool. There is no precise definition of a pool, but in general, it is used as a container of activities that represents major participants in a process, typically separating different organizations. A participant is a buyer, a seller, a shipper, or a supplier. A pool may contain one or more lanes, and it may be open (i.e., showing internal detail) or collapsed (i.e., hiding internal detail).

In general, a process may consist of activities, which in themselves are sub-processes, as shown in figure 3.4. For simplicity, we will use the terms activity and sub-process interchangeably.

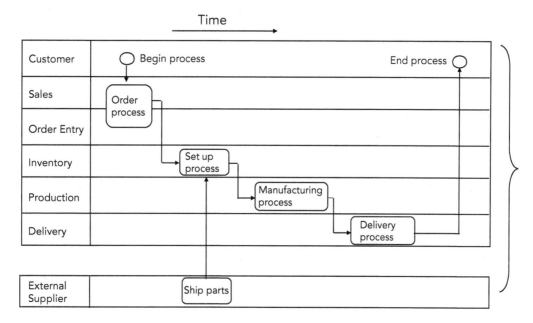

Figure 3.3: Swimlanes

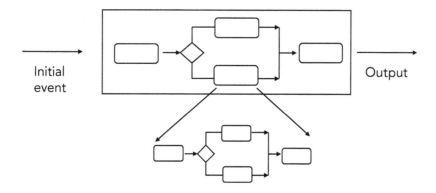

Figure 3.4: Sub-processes

As mentioned above there is a large variety of software tools that have been developed for *Business Processes* (BP), some of which have overlapping features. Below, we identify some generic groups of such software.

- *BP modeling tools:* These software tools provide a *Graphical User Interface* (GUI) through which a user can depict a process in a diagram. Additional features include: saving diagrams into a repository, simulating the process depicted by a diagram, costing, activity documentation.
- *Business rule management tools:* These are software tools for creating, storing, and using business rules.
- *Universal BP reporting:* Database capable software for storing information from BP tools.
- *BP monitoring tools:* These tools aid in creating measuring systems for business processes.
- *Business process management suites products:* These are software tools that allow the user to model processes and then automate their execution at runtime. They may also include other features, such as rules and monitoring capabilities.

3.3 PROCESS DESIGN PATTERNS

Business Process Modeling (BPM) patterns are specific combination of activities that arise commonly in business process modeling. These patterns can be used to construct more complex process models. Below, we discuss a number of patterns due to Van der Aalst et al[1] using the BPMN notation.

The patterns are grouped logically into six categories: basic patterns, advanced branch and join patterns, structural patterns, multiple instance patterns, state-based patterns, and cancellation patterns.

3.3.1 BASIC PATTERNS

Here we examine the sequence pattern, exclusive choice pattern, single merge pattern, parallel split and synchronization.

SEQUENCE PATTERN

This is a very common pattern that represents a set of activities executed in sequence, as shown in figure 3.5, where a rectangle represents an activity.

EXCLUSIVE CHOICE PATTERN

In this pattern, one of a number of activities is executed based on the result of evaluating a condition. In figure 3.6, either activity 1 or activity 2 will be executed. The diamond, known as the exclusive gateway in BPMN, indicates the decision point where a condition is evaluated at runtime to decide which activity should be executed.

An interesting variation of the exclusive gateway symbol is the case where a defaulted value is allowed. To understand this, let us consider the case in figure 3.7, and let us assume that the condition to be evaluated will result

Figure 3.5: A sequence pattern

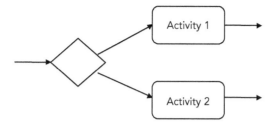

Figure 3.6: Exclusive choice pattern

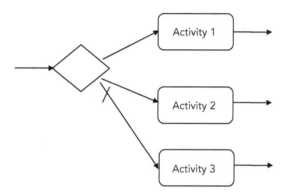

Figure 3.7: Exclusive gateway with a default flow

to executing either activity 1 or activity 2. It is possible that the modeler may not be able to predict all possible outcomes if the condition is very complicated. In this case, neither activity 1 or 2 will be executed and the process will get stuck at the exclusive gateway. To guard against such possible scenarios, a default branch is included, defined by an arrow with a strike-through line, where the flow branches out to when all the other planned cases turn out to be false.

SIMPLE MERGE PATTERN

In this pattern several flows are merged into a single flow. This is done using the exclusive gateway in the opposite way as shown in figure 3.8. When there are multiple flows into the exclusive gateway with a single outgoing flow, then there is no condition to be evaluated as described above. In the example in figure 3.9, one of the two activities will be executed and then the flow will merge through the exclusive gateway (on the right hand side of the diagram).

PARALLEL SPLIT AND SYNCHRONIZATION PATTERN

A parallel split is indicated by a diamond with the + sign, as shown in figure 3.10, and it is referred to in BPMN as the parallel gateway. In this case, both activities 1 and 2 will be launched in parallel and they will be executed independently of each other. In general, the parallel gateway provides a means to create parallel paths and therefore model parallelism. Often the parallel paths have to be synchronized, i.e., they have to be all completed before proceeding. For instance, let us assume that both activities 1 and 2 in figure 3.10 have to be synchronized. This

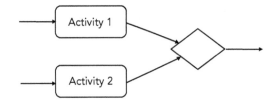

Figure 3.8: Simple merge

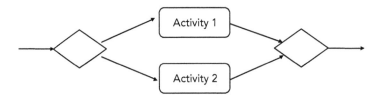

Figure 3.9: Simple merge

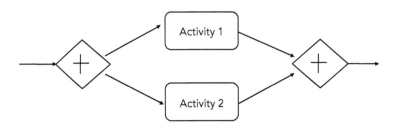

Figure 3.10: Parallel gateway splitting and merging

means that once one activity is completed, we will have to wait until the second one is also done before proceeding. This synchronization point can be modeled using the parallel gateway in the opposite direction, i.e., many flows in and one flow out.

3.3.2 ADVANCED BRANCH AND JOIN PATTERNS

These are less-well supported patterns by commercial software. We will examine the multiple choice and synchronization merge pattern, multiple merge, and the discriminator and N-out-of-M join pattern.

MULTIPLE CHOICE AND SYNCHRONIZATION MERGE PATTERN

The multiple choice pattern permits one or more parallel branches to be taken if each path satisfies a constraint evaluated at runtime. The multiple choice is indicated by the inclusive gateway, which is a diamond with a circle in it, as shown in figure 3.11. When the inclusive gateway is executed, all conditions associated with this gateway will be evaluated. Each condition that evaluates to true will result to the branch of activities to be executed. In view of this, one or more activities in figure 3.11 can be executed. (A default condition should be used to guard against unforeseen cases that will cause the process to get blocked, as explained above in the case of the exclusive gateway). The merging behavior of the inclusive gateway synchronizes those parallel branches that were activated at runtime at the splitting point of the inclusive gateway.

MULTIPLE MERGE PATTERN

In synchronizing merge, all the incoming branches have to be completed before the process continues. The multiple merge pattern allows each incoming branch to continue independently of the others. For instance, in figure 3.12, we have activities 1 and 2 executing in parallel. Connecting these activities directly to activity 3, permits the flow of execution associated with each activity to move into activity 3 without waiting on the other activity to be completed.

DISCRIMINATOR AND N-OUT-OF-M JOIN PATTERN

In this pattern, when multiple parallel paths converge at a given joint point, one of the paths is allowed to continue while the others are blocked. This is known as the discriminator, and it is a special case of N-out-of-M, where M

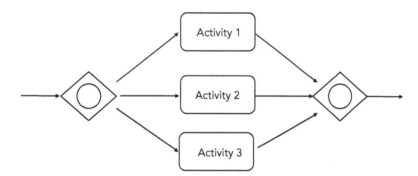

Figure 3.11: Multiple choice and synchronization merge

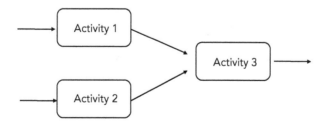

Figure 3.12: The multiple merge pattern

41

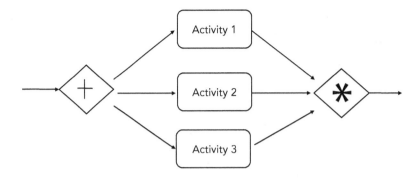

Figure 3.13: The complex gateway

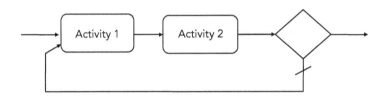

Figure 3.14: Arbitrary cycles

paths meet at the point of convergence and only the first N are let through. This pattern is notated using the complex gateway, indicated by a diamond with a star in it, as shown in figure 3.13.

3.3.3 STRUCTURAL PATTERNS

These patterns reflect practices which involve unstructured designs, such as goto-style jumps and contending termination points. There are two structural patterns: arbitrary cycles and implicit terminations.

ARBITRARY CYCLES PATTERN

This pattern repeats an activity or a set of activities by cycling back. It can be implemented using an exclusive gateway with a default flow as shown in figure 3.14.

IMPLICIT TERMINATION PATTERN

Typically a process has a single termination point, even if it has multiple branches. This pattern relaxes the restriction of drawing a single termination point by allowing a termination point for each of its branches. As shown in figure 3.15, branches can be terminated individually without the whole process being terminated. The process is terminated when all branches have been terminated. Another advantage of the individual branch terminations is that it helps reduce clutter in a process diagram. The termination symbol in BPMN is a circle.

3.3.4 MULTIPLE INSTANCES PATTERNS

These patterns deal with how multiple instances of activities are created. There are four patterns, namely with design-time knowledge, with runtime knowledge, without runtime knowledge, and with synchronization.

WITH DESIGN-TIME KNOWLEDGE PATTERN

This pattern describes how multiple instances of the same activity can be generated. The number of instances is known in advance and it is set to a fixed number. In BPMN this is indicated by an activity rectangle with three vertical parallel lines as shown in figure 3.16. If synchronization of the instantiations is required, which is the last pattern of this group, then an attribute associated with this activity rectangle has to be appropriately set.

WITH RUNTIME KNOWLEDGE PATTERN

This is similar to the pattern above, except that the number of instantiations is not known in advance but at runtime. This is indicated by an activity rectangle with a loop as shown in figure 3.17.

WITHOUT RUNTIME KNOWLEDGE PATTERN

In this case, the number of instantiations is not determined in advance, nor at runtime before the copies are to be created. Rather, the exact number is not known until some point during the execution of these instances. A combination of gateways can be used to implement the logic.

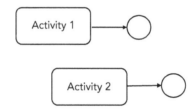

Figure 3.15: Implicit termination

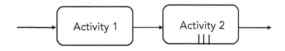

Figure 3.16: Pre-determined number of instantiations

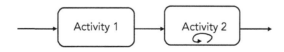

Figure 3.17: The number of instantiations is determined at runtime

3.3.5 STATE-BASED PATTERNS

These patterns apply to processes that are event-driven and spend most of their time waiting for an event to trigger the next activity. There are three state-based patterns, namely deferred choice, interleaved parallel routing, and milestone.

DEFERRED CHOICE PATTERN

The pattern deals with a process that has to wait for an outside event to occur before continuing. These events are notifications from other processes currently running or are within outside applications such as web pages. In BPMN an event gateway is used to wait for a specified event to occur, such as the arrival of a message. This gateway is indicated by a diamond with a circle and a pentagon within the circle as shown in figure 3.18. The process waits at the gateway until a message arrives. At that time, the logic associated with the gateway is executed, and only one outgoing branch will be executed. The double circle with the envelope is a message event and indicates communication with another process.

INTERLEAVED PARALLEL ROUTING PATTERN

This pattern allows several activities to be executed in sequence (not in parallel as stated in the title), but the actual order of the execution of these activities is determined at runtime. In BPMN, uses an activity rectangle with a tilde in the bottom, and within the rectangle, the activities that have to be executed are notated, as shown in figure 3.19. This symbol is referred to as an ad-hoc process.

MILESTONE

A milestone event is a point within a process when a specific event or condition has occurred. The process has to be able to identify milestone because, for instance, specific events can only occur after a milestone has occurred.

3.3.6 CANCELLATION PATTERNS

A process may have to be cancelled at any point. One way to do this is to add cancellation points at each activity of the process. A more desirable approach is to add a check or action which cancels the entire process. There are two patterns of cancellation, namely cancel activity and cancel case.

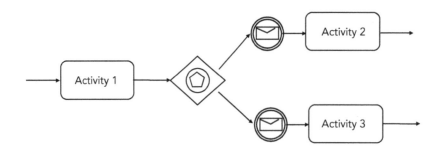

Figure 3.18: Deferred choice pattern

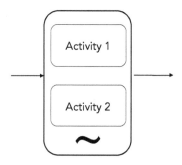

Figure 3.19: An ad-hoc process

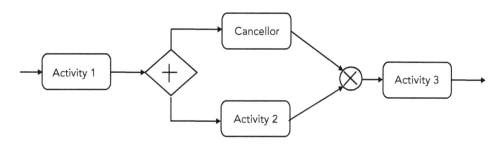

Figure 3.20: The cancel activity pattern

CANCEL ACTIVITY PATTERN

This pattern is used to stop the execution of an activity if a cancellation condition becomes true. This is implemented using a cancellation end event, depicted by a circle with a cross. As an example, let us consider activities 1, 2, and 3 shown in figure 3.20, and let us assume that activity 2 has to be cancelled if a condition becomes true. After completion of activity 1, a parallel split activates both activities 2 and "cancellor". If the cancellation trigger occurs, activity 2 is cancelled and the process moves on to execute activity 3.

CANCEL CASE PATTERN

This is an extension of the cancel activity pattern whereby an entire process is cancelled.

3.4 EXAMPLES USING BPMN

In this section, we give several examples related to the process for approving a loan, and also introduce some additional symbols. The main steps are shown in BPMN in figure 3.21. The process begins with an applicant submitting an application. The first step is a to verify the applicant's information, and if this is successful, the loan request is processed, and if approved, the funds are disbursed to the applicant.

We note that the circle on the left-hand side of the diagram indicates the beginning of the process. The circle in bold on the right-hand side of the diagram indicates the end of the process. We use the exclusive gateway, the diamond shaped symbol, to indicate which activity should be executed after the applicants information is verified. Likewise, an exclusive gateway is used after the loan is processed to indicate appropriate action based on whether

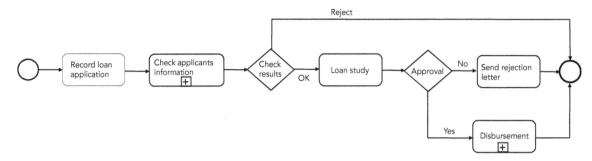

Figure 3.21: Processing a loan application

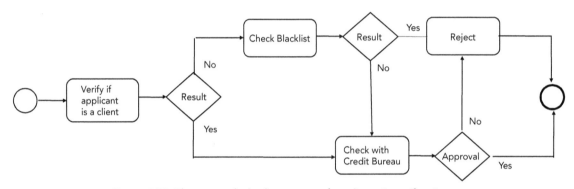

Figure 3.22: The expanded sub-process of applicant's verification

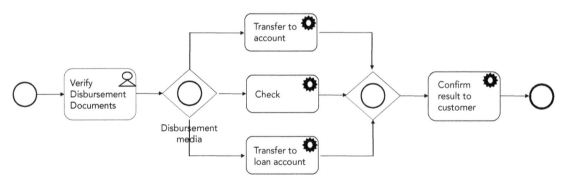

Figure 3.23: The expanded sub-process of disbursement

the loan is approved or not. In addition, we note that the activity box where the applicant's information is verified contains a plus symbol in the bottom of the box. This indicates that this activity is a collapsed sub-process. Depending on the process modeling tool, clicking on this box, will expand the sub-process diagram. The expanded sub-process is shown in figure 3.22. (We note that the collapsed sub-processes could also be included in -line with the main process in figure 3.21.)

In general, an activity could be executed either manually or automatically by a system, such as a web service, without human intervention. This can be indicated in the upper right-hand side corner of the activity box, by a star if it is an automatic activity, or by a figurine if it is a manual activity. We use this notation in the expanded sub-process of the disbursement in figure 3.23. The expanded sub-process shows the three different ways that disbursement can be carried out, that is, check, direct deposit to applicant's account, and direct deposit to the loan account. In addition, any combination of these three ways is also possible. That is, the disbursement may involve any combination of these three activities. This is indicated using the inclusive gateway, the diamond with a circle inside. All individual activities have to be completed before the process moves to confirming the disbursement to the customer. This synchronization is indicated using the inclusive gateway.

The disbursement sub-process can be further modified to allow for the process to begin at a certain time. As shown

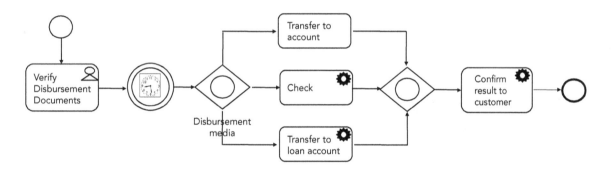

Figure 3.24: The disbursement sub-process with a time condition

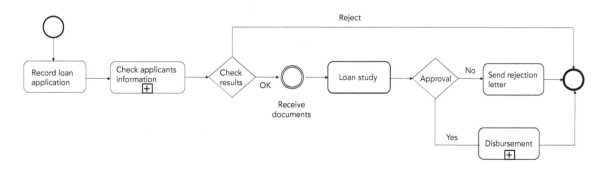

Figure 3.25: The loan application process with delayed document submission

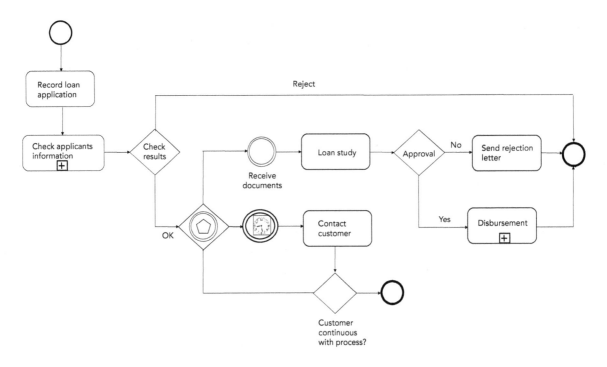

Figure 3.26: The loan application process with an event gateway

in figure 3.24, this is done using the timer start event, a circle with a clock inside, which indicates the specific day and time at which the process should start.

In the loan application process given in figure 3.21, we assumed that the client had submitted all the necessary documents at the moment the application was made. However, it is possible that some of the documents are missing and they can be submitted at a later moment. Figure 3.25 shows how the loan study activity is placed on hold until all the documents are received using the intermediate event indicated by a double circle.

The loan application process can be further enhanced to control how long it takes for the client to produce the documents. Specifically, the client is given a fixed period of time to provide the documents. If the documents are presented within this period of time then the time intermediate event is deactivated. If the documents are not presented within this period of time then the intermediate event for receiving the documents is deactivated and the customer is contacted. These activities are controlled by an event gateway, indicated by a diamond with a double circle and a pentagon inside, shown in figure 3.26. When this gateway is executed, both intermediate events are activated. Eventually, one of the two events will occur first and at that moment the process will follow the path associated with this event, while the other event will be cancelled.

As discussed above, BPMN uses swimlanes to indicate the various functional or organization entities responsible for each of the activities. Figure 3.27 shows the final version of the loan application process given in figure 3.21 with swimlanes.

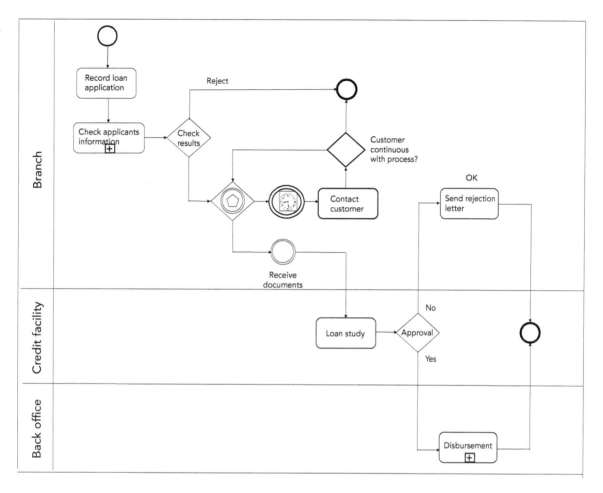

Figure 3.27: The loan application process with swimlanes

PROBLEMS

For the problems below you can use a graphical tool, such as Microsoft's Powerpoint, Apple's Keynote, and Open Office's Draw, or an open source diagramming tools for BPMN.

1. Use BPMN to map out the tasks involved in booking a trip that includes travel by air, car rental, hotel and excursions in two different locations in the same country. For this, you can use as guidance one of the well-known travel web sites. As a first step, depict the entire process at a high level showing the main aggregate groups of activities that need to be excited. Subsequently, expand each high-level activity to subprocesses. You can make your own assumptions as to the flow of the logic if some of the information required cannot be readily deduced from a travel web site.

2. Consider the service "This is my life". First, identify all the high-level functions that need to be implemented in order to provide this service. Subsequently, depict these functions by aggregate activities and show

the flow of logic among them. Expand each aggregate activity into a series of sub-processes using BPMN notation. Some of these sub-processes may have to be expanded into lower-level sub-processes.

3. *Dial-a-taxi: A networking mashup application.* A networking mashup is a service that uses other existing networking services, typically provided by operators and service providers. It is similar to a web mashup, that is a web page or application that uses data, presentation, and functionality from other web sources to create a new service. (The term mashup is also used in other areas, such as in music, where elements of two or more pre-existing pieces of music are combined to make a new song.) In the dial-a-taxi service, a number of different services are used to provide the user with a single application for calling a taxi. The flow of the logic is described below. Use BPMN to map out the flow of the activities involved in this mashup.

Helen uses a dial-a-taxi application on her smart phone to call a taxi. The application uses a location service to find Helen's location and then it displays on a map all the taxis that are near-by at that moment. In addition, each taxi is associated with different attributes, such as the estimated time of arrival at Helen's location, customer satisfaction rankings, and fare structure. Helen selects a taxi and a call is placed automatically between her and the driver. Helen informs the driver of her exact location and her destination. Seconds before the taxi arrives at the location, the taxi driver sends Helen an instant message to inform her of his pending arrival. Later, Helen is asked to rank her level of satisfaction. The implementation of this application requires the use of various services, such as, location service, display of items on a map, an application server that keeps track of the location of the taxis signed up in this service, a third-party call service so that the application server can place a call between the user and the taxi driver, instant messaging, and a web-based service for ranking satisfaction of the service. For an implementation of a dial-a-taxi service, see Banerjee and Dasgupta[2].

REFERENCES

[1] W.M.P. Van der Aalst, A.H.M. Ter Hofstede, B. Kiepuszewski, and A.P. Barrios, "Workflow Patterns", Technical Report, Eindhoven University of Technology, Eindhoven, Distributed and Parallel Databases, 14(3), pages 5-51, July 2003.

[2] N. Banerjee and K. Dasgupta, "Telecom Mashups: Enabling Web 2.0 for Telecom Services", Second international conference on ubiquitous information management and communication, ICUIMC '08.

PART 2:

QUALITY OF SERVICE AND QUALITY OF EXPERIENCE

CHAPTER 4: QUALITY OF SERVICE AND QUALITY OF EXPERIENCE

4.1 INTRODUCTION

Quality of experience (QoE) is a term that describes the experience of a user with a particular service. For instance, the telephone system has been optimized over the years so that when we make a phone call, our call is rarely blocked because of system overload, and the quality of the voice is as if this person was next to us. In this case, we have a good experience when using the system. On the other hand, if we call someone over the Internet, it is possible that we may not be able to hear the other person very well. Some of words may be cutoff and the call may be dropped. In this case, our experience may not be satisfactory. In general, our experience with the use of a service is subjective. For instance, one may not mind that the quality of a voice call over the Internet is not as good as that of the telephone system, since it is a free call.

In the case of networking services, the quality of experience is a function of the underlying network that provides the signaling to set up a service and also transports the data related to the service. If the network is slow in delivering packets to the end users, then our experience will not be very good. However, there are other factors that affect our experience with a service, such as the usability of the interfaces and devices used for the service. For instance, an older person may have difficulties operating a handheld device equipped with a small keyboard and a small screen. In this case, even if the underlying network works well, the experience of this person may not be a good one.

In general, the QoE for networking services can be organized into two groups of factors: usability factors and networking related factors. The usability factors are related to the easiness of using a device for accessing a service. Factors include the usability of the physical controls, the ergonomic design, the attributes of the device, the application/service interface itself including its functional format, progress feedback (i.e. tones to indicate how the setting up of a service is progressing), and mental effort (cognitive load). Networking related factors are responsivity, media fidelity and network availability. Responsivity deals with the network response time, and timely responses to commands. Media fidelity is related to the accuracy of received signal, echo, sound level, speech/video distortion due to errored/lost packets, and jitter. Availability expresses the percent of time the network is available to transport commands and data.

We use the term *Quality of Service* (QoS) to describe the quality of the underlying network. QoS is a well understood

	Tolerant	Conversational voice and video	Voice mail	Streaming Audio & video	Fax
Tolerance for packet loss	Intolerant	Remote app., command & control games	E-commerce Web browsing	IM FTP (foreground)	FTP (background email)
		Interactive Delay << 1 s	Responsive Delay ~ 1 s	Timely Delay ~ 10s	Background Delay >> 10 s

Tolerance for delay

Table 4.1: QoS metrics for common networking services

and studied topic within the networking community. It is expressed in term of metrics that reflect the networking related factors described above, such as, the one way end-to-end delay (hereafter referred to as the end-to-end delay), the jitter, the packet loss, rate of erroneously delivered packets, and network availability. Typically, when we talk about QoS we mainly refer to the metrics: end-to-end delay, jitter, and packet loss. Networking services tend to be more sensitive to some of these three metrics. For instance, VoIP and video on demand are sensitive to the end-to-end delay and less sensitive to packet loss. On the other extreme, file transfer is only sensitive to packet loss, and less sensitive to the time it takes to deliver a file. Table 4.1 relates various common networking services to the end-to-end delay and packet loss.

In this Chapter, we first discuss various QoS measures, and then we describe how to evaluate the QoE for audio and video using subjective and objective means.

4.2 QOS MEASURES

As mentioned above, QoS is expressed in terms of different metrics, such as, the end-to-end delay, the jitter, the packet loss, the rate of erroneously delivered packets, and network availability. In this section, we discuss the end-to-end delay, the jitter, and the packet loss.

END-TO-END DELAY

The end-to-end delay is the time it takes to deliver a packet from the transmitter to the receiver. As shown in figure 4.1, it is made up of a fixed component and a variable component. The fixed component is the sum of all fixed delays that a packet encounters from the transmitting end-device to the receiving end-device, such as, propagation delay, fixed delays induced by transmission systems, and fixed switch processing times. The variable component is the sum of all variable delays that a packet encounters from the transmitting device to the receiving device. These delays are primarily due to queueing delays in the routers along the packet's path. The end-to-end delay is measured in terms of its mean, but also it can be given as a statistical upper bound in the form of a percentile. That is, we say that the end-to-end delay is less than, say 150 ms, 95% of the time. The mean is a popular measure of the end-to-end delay but it does not capture its variability, and there-

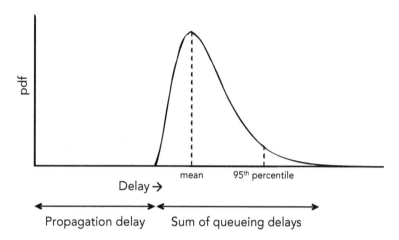

Figure 4.1: The end-to-end delay

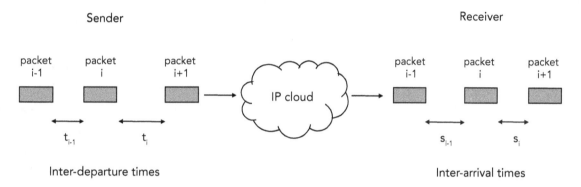

Figure 4.2: Inter-departure and inter-arrival times

fore, it is not a very useful metric. On the other hand, the delay percentile gives a better idea of the variability of the end-to-end delay and provides a bound that is valid a given percent of the time, such as, 95% and 99%. Let us now return to figure 4.1, and let us assume that the fixed propagation delay is 100 msec, and the mean and 95th percentile of the sum of all the queueing delays is 20 msec and 50 msec respectively. Then, the mean and the 95th percentile of the end-to-end delay, i.e. including the propagation delay, is 120 msec and 150 msec respectively. The 95th percentile basically tells us that only 95% of the end-to-end delay of all packets will be less than 150 msec, and only 5% will exceed this value. This information is more meaningful when designing a service and also when negotiating an SLA.

For VoIP and interactive video, the end-to-end delay (mouth to ear) has to be bounded so that there are no gaps in the conversation between two users. Such gaps, for instance, can be seen in television when someone in a far away place is being interviewed.

JITTER

Jitter is an important QoS parameter for real-time applications, such as voice and video. In these applications, the inter-arrival times between successive packets at the destination cannot be greater than a certain value, as this will cause the receiving play-out process to pause due to lack of data. In general, the inter-departure times between successive packets transmitted by the sender are not the same as the inter-arrival times at the receiver. Let us consider figure 4.2. Let t_i be the time between the end of the transmission of the ith packet and the beginning of the transmission of the $(i + 1)^{st}$ packet and let s_i be the time between the end of the arrival of the ith packet and the beginning of the arrival of the $(i + 1)^{st}$ packet. Then, the inter-departure time t_i may be less, equal, or greater than the inter-arrival time s_i. In view of this, it is possible that a string of successive packets may arrive at the destination faster or slower than they were transmitted by the source. This variability of the inter-arrival times of packets at the destination is known as jitter, and it is due to the complex interaction of the packets of a given flow with packets of other flows within the buffers of the routers.

Below we describe two simple scenarios where a string of packets may arrive faster or slower than they were transmitted by the source. In order to follow these two cases, we first have to understand how packets are queued in an output port of a router. (This topic will be examined in detail in Chapter 11.) In DiffServ and in MPLS, packets are classified into different QoS classes. These classes represent different types of services that require different QoS. For instance, there is class of service for VoIP, a different class of service for video, and a different class of service for best effort traffic. For each QoS class, there is a separate queue in the buffer of an output port of a router. Packets join one of these queues according to their class. These queues are assigned different priorities which are used by a scheduler to determine how packets from these queues are transmitted out. Typically, the VoIP queue has a higher priority than a video queue, which has a higher priority than the best effort queue. Different scheduling policies have been implemented, one of which is the static priority scheduler. In this case, the scheduler always tries to select the next packet for transmission from the highest priority queue. If that queue is empty, it then checks the second priority queue, and so on. In other words, the highest priority queue is always served first until it is empty. Then the second priority queue is served, and so on. There is no preemption of service. That is, the transmission of a packet is not interrupted if a packet of a higher priority arrives during its transmission time.

Let us now consider a string of successive packets that belong to a flow, call it flow A, with a QoS class 2 classification. (By flow we mean the traffic related to a given service transmitted between a source and a destination.) This means that the packets will join the queue for this QoS class at the output port of each router. If there is a lot of traffic coming through this queue, then it is quite possible that packets from other flows may be queued in-between the packets of flow A. As a result of this inter-leaving effect, the inder-departure time of the flow A packets from the router may get much longer than their inter-arrival times. If this persists through all the routers along the path of the flow, then the inter-arrival times of these packets at the destination will be much larger than their corresponding inter-departure times from the source.

Alternatively, they can also arrive earlier because of scheduling priorities. If we assume that the QoS class 2 has a lower priority than QoS class 1, then the scheduler will first serve the class 1 queue before it will start serving the class 2 queue (assuming a scheduler with static priorities). Therefore, if class 1 queue is very busy, it is likely that many packets from flow A will accumulate in the class 2 queue before the scheduler has a chance to start serving this queue. In this case, and assuming no inter-leaving effects, when class 2 is finally served, these packet will leave back to back at the rate of the transmitter which is typically much higher than the rate at which they were transmitted by the source. If this persists through all the routers along the path of the flow, then the inter-arrival times of these packets will be much smaller than their corresponding inter-departure times from the source.

Jitter is a well understood concept, but there is no agreed upon way of measuring it. In view of this, various measures have been proposed. These measures are associated with either the variability of the inter-arrival times of successive packets at the destination, or with the variability of the one way end-to-end delay. In the first case, jitter is expressed as the average of the successive inter-arrival times of successive packets at the destination. However, more commonly it is expressed as the percentile of the inter-arrival times of the successive packets at the destination. This is, it is an inter-arrival time so that $\gamma\%$ of the inter-arrival times are below it, where $\gamma\%$ is typically equal to 95%, 99%, and 99.9%.

Various measures of jitter have been defined based on the one way end-to-end delay, of which the following two are predominant in the industry: *Inter-Packet Delay Variation* (IPDV) and *Packet Delay Variation* (PDV), see IETF RFC 5481[1]. The IPDV is calculated by taking the difference of the one way end-to-end delay of successive packets. Let s_i and r_i be the time instances that packet i was sent and received, respectively. Then the one way end-to-end delay d_i of packet i is: $d_i = r_i - s_i$. The inter-packet delay variation between packets i and i-1 is $d_i - d_{i-1} = (r_i - s_i) - (r_{i-1} - s_{i-1}) = (r_i - r_{i-1}) - (s_i - s_{i-1})$, and it can be negative, zero, or positive. For instance, let us consider the following one way end-to-end delay values of 6 successive packets: 10, 20, 15, 25, 18, 23. Then, we have the following the IPDV values: 10, -5, 10, -7, 5. If a packet is lost, then some of the IPDV values cannot be computed. For instance, let us assume that the third packet is lost. In this case, we have the following one way end-to-end delay values 10, 20, U, 25, 18, 23, where U stands for undefined, from which we obtain the IPDV values 10, U, U, -7, 5.

The PDV is calculated by taking the difference of the one way of the end-to-end delay of each packet from the small-est one way end-to-end delay d_{min}. That is, the PDV of the ith packet is $d_i - d_{min}$. For instance, for the same set of the one way end-to-end values given above, 10, 20, 15, 25, 18, 23, we obtain the following PDV values: 0, 10, 5, 15, 8, 13, where $d_{min} = 10$. The following values are obtained when the third packet is lost: 0, 10, U, 8, 13. If the smallest end-to-end delay is equal to the propagation delay, then this difference is the sum of all the queueing delays encountered by the packet end-to-end. For instance, let us assume that the end-to-end propagation delay is 100 msec, and the observed end-to-end delay of a given packet is 180 msec. Then, the sum of all the queueing delays encountered by the packet is 80 msec.

As in the case of the end-to-end delay, the IPDV and PDV values of a set of successive packets, $d_1, d_2, \ldots, d_n$, is reported by its mean, and/or by a percentile, such as the 99th percentile.

An alternative way of calculating jitter is used in the *Real-Time Transport Protocol* (RTP), commonly used to transport VoIP and video. Let d_i be the inter-packet delay variation between packets i and $i-1$, i.e., $d_i = (r_i - r_{i-1}) - (s_i - s_{i-1})$, where s_i and r_i are the time instances that packet i was sent and received, respectively. Then the jitter J_i of packet

i is given by the following expression:

$$J_i = J_{i-1} + \frac{|d_i| - J_{i-1}}{16} = \frac{15J_{i-1} + |d_i|}{16}$$

The jitter is used to calculate the size of the *jitter buffer*, or otherwise known as the *de-jitter buffer*, used at a receiver so that a continuous playout of audio or video can be ensured. For instance, when using the ITU-T G.711 codec, audio has to be played out at the constant rate of 64 Kbps. However, the arrival of VoIP packets may vary depending upon the traffic encountered in the network. The jitter buffer delays the audio data for a short period of time, so that to ensure a continuous supply of voice data to the codec.

Sizing the jitter buffer is very simple when dealing with streaming applications, such as video-on-demand, TV over IP, and radio. Before the play-out process starts playing, it buffers 3 to 4 seconds worth of data. Then the play-out process starts reading data from the buffer, and in this way, if there is a delay in receiving packets, this delay is absorbed by the buffer. Obviously, if there are persistent delays, then the play-out process will run out of data and it will stop. Then, it will start re-buffering and once the buffer has been built to a pre-specified threshold it will start playing again. This occurs sometimes when we listen to a radio from a far away place.

Sizing the jitter buffer for VoIP is more complicated. This is because, the delay in the jitter buffer should not be too large, so that it does not affect significantly the overall end-to-end delay. On the other hand, if the delay in the jitter buffer is short, the buffer may become empty because of the variability of the inter-arrival time of VoIP packets, which will force the play out process to stop. (The same applies to interactive video, but it is not considered here). The speech gaps that occur when the buffer runs out of data maybe hidden by different concealment techniques that replace the data that are lost or not received in time. Depending upon the duration of a gap, the missing voice data are replaced by prediction from the past data, followed by silence if the condition persists more than 30 to 50 msec.

Jitter buffers can be fixed or adaptive. A fixed jitter buffer does not change in size, whereas an adaptive one changes its size depending upon how fast or slow packets arrive. Below, we examine fixed jitter buffers.

The size of a jitter buffer can be described either by the size of the buffer in bytes or by the maximum storage time, which is the time it takes to drain a full buffer. These two quantities are related through the expression:

read rate x maximum storage time = size of buffer

For instance, for the G.711 codec the read rate is 64 Kbps, and assuming a maximum storage time of 30 msec, the size of the buffer is 240 bytes. Typically, the size of a jitter buffer is expressed in terms of the maximum storage time.

We first note that if a VoIP packet experiences the minimum one way end-to-end delay, d_{min}, then its voice data could suffer the maximum delay in the jitter buffer $b_{max.}$ The sum $d_{min} + b_{max}$ should be equal to the maximum one way end-to-end delay d_{max} plus the minimum buffer delay b_{min}. That is,

$$d_{min} + b_{max} = d_{max} + b_{min}$$

Rearranging the terms, we have

$$b_{max} - b_{min} = d_{max} - d_{min}$$

That is, the range of the buffer delay is equal to the range of the one way end-to-end delay, which could be obtained using the range of the IPDV or the PDV, see IETF RFC 5481[1]. (The range of a distribution is the difference between the largest and the smallest observed values.) For instance, for the simple example given above of the one way end-to-end delay values of 6 successive packets, 10, 20, 15, 25, 18, 23, the range is $d_{max} - d_{min} = 15$. Assuming that $b_{min} = 0$, then the maximum delay applied in the jitter buffer is b_{max} equal to 15. This delay is typically referred to as the *jitter delay*. In practice, the minimum buffer time, b_{min}, may not be zero. In practice, the range $d_{max} - d_{min}$ maybe replaced by the 99th percentile of the PDV. In Cisco[2] it is recommended that the actual size of the jitter buffer should be 1.5 to 2 times the jitter delay. Since traffic condition change, the jitter is typically calculated over a short window of around 100 msec, and the size of the jitter buffer is fixed accordingly. Therefore, the jitter buffer is continuously adjusted, but it stays fixed for each window of time. This dynamic behavior of the jitter buffer should not be confused with the adaptive jitter buffer.

The first voice packet of a call that arrives finds the jitter buffer empty and it is delayed by the jitter delay, say 30 msec. After this delay, the voice data will start getting delivered to the codec. Packets that arrive when the jitter buffer is not empty are queued. If a packet finds the jitter buffer empty, it is delayed by 30 msec as above. Packets that arrive out of order are re-ordered and consumed if they arrived on time. Otherwise, they are considered as lost packets. The jitter buffer may overflow if packets arrive faster for a period of time. In this case, these packets will get lost resulting in a choppy voice signal.

PACKET LOSS

Packet loss is expressed as the percent of transmitted packets that are lost. Packets are typically lost in the buffer of a router when congestion arises. Modern packet switched networks do not have flow control at the link level, as was the case back in the 1980s with packet switched networks such X.25. In view of this, it is possible that a router may receive temporarily more packets than it can transmit out, in which case, packets loss may occur if its buffer becomes full. This problem is exacerbated in IP networks which do not use DiffServ or MPLS. Packets can also be lost during the time they are transmitted over a link if there is noise on the link. In this case, the transmitter at the receiving end of the link may fail to identify a packet. However, modern fiber optics are extremely reliable and errored transmissions are rare.

Finally, packet loss can occur at the IP layer, since packets with errored IP headers detected by the header checksum at the IP layer are discarded. If they are not detected by the checksum, they may get discarded by another IP layer procedure because a field, such as the ToS/DSCP field, is corrupted. In this case, the discarded packet are classified as lost packets. Of course it is possible that they may not get detected in which case they will get redirected based on the corrupted header. A packet with an errored header that was not discarded and/or with an errored payload, is classified as an errored packet. Errored packets are detected at the destination by a higher layer, such as TCP.

When a packet is lost, the user may or may not perceive this at the application level. For instance, in video over IP the signal is transmitted using an MPEG type of encapsulation. MPEG is a standards group in ISO that is concerned with the issue of compression and synchronization of video signals. In MPEG, successive video frames are compressed following a format like: I B B B P B B B P B B B I, where I stands for *I-frame*, B for *B-frame*, and P for *P-frame*. An intra-coded frame, or I-frame, is an encoding of a picture based entirely on the information in that frame. A predictive-coded frame, or P-frame, is based on motion compensated prediction between that frame and the previous I-frame or P-frame. A bidirectional-coded frame, or B-frame, is based on motion compensated prediction between that frame and the previous I- or P-frame or the next I- or P-frame. The encoder also can select the sequence of I, P, and B frames, which form a group of frames known as a *Group of Pictures* (GOP). The group of frames repeats for the entire duration of the video transmission. The size of the resulting frame varies significantly between frame types. I-frames are the largest while B-frames are the smallest. The size of an I-frame varies based on picture content. P- and B-frames vary depending on the motion present in the scene as well as picture content.

If a packet that contains information from any frame is lost, we may observe a slice of the image missing. If the lost packet contains I-frame information then this will most likely cause a disruption in the quality of the picture which will propagate through the set of frames belonging in the same GOP. The propagation of the error will stop once the MPEG decoder receives a new unimpaired I-frame. In general, interactive applications are tolerant of packet loss. However, moving files across requires very low packet loss since each time a packet is lost the packet will have to be retransmitted.

The above described QoS measures can be calculated by monitoring an existing network. There is a plethora of open source and proprietary monitoring tools. If the network does not exist, that is, it is currently being designed, the end-to-end delay, jitter and packet loss can be estimated using modeling techniques, such as those described in Part 5 of the book.

QoS requirements	jitter	End-to-end delay	Packet loss rate
VoIP	30 msec	≤ 150 msec	≤ 1%
Interactive video	30 msec	≤ 150 msec	≤ 1%
Streaming video	No significant requirement	up to 4 - 5 sec	≤ 5%
Peer-to-peer	No significant requirement	No significant requirement	No significant requirement

Table 4.2: QoS requirements for some services

As shown in table 4.1, networking services tend to be more sensitive to some of these metrics. For instance, conversational voice and video services are more sensitive to the end-to-end delay than streaming audio and video. In table 4.2, we give the QoS requirements for some services, see Cisco[3]. The end-to-end delay for VoIP and interactive video refers to the mouth-to-ear delay. Jitter is determined as discussed above using the IPDV or PDV values, and it is part of the end-to-end delay. We note that interactive video has the same QoS as VoIP because it also uses audio as well.

4.3 SUBJECTIVE EVALUATION OF VOICE AND VIDEO QUALITY

As discussed in the introduction to this Chapter, the QoE for networking services is affected by the QoS of the underlying network and by usability factors of the device used for accessing a service. QoS is measured objectively by monitoring the underlying network. The QoE of a user, on the other hand, is subjective and it is typically measured using subjective and objective assessment methods. Subjective evaluation is carried out by asking a number of individuals to rate numerically their perceived QoE. This is a time-consuming and expensive process and it requires special facilities. In view of this, various automated software tools have been developed that measure QoE objectively. Although they lack human input, these tests can take into account various network dependency conditions that can influence voice quality. In this section, we describe subjective evaluation methods for voice and video and in the next section we describe objective evaluation methods of voice and video.

4.3.1 EVALUATION OF VOICE QUALITY

In VoIP and video, voice codecs are typically used to compress the bandwidth of a digitized voice from the standard 64 Kbps (resulting from PCM modulation) to rates which are significantly lower. *The Mean Opinion Score* (MOS), see ITU-T P.800[4], is used to rate the perceived quality of the received audio after compression and/or transmission.

A number of listeners, chosen randomly from the normal population of telephone users, rate the heard quality of experience of test sentences read aloud by both male and female speakers over the communications medium being tested. A listener is required to give each sentence a rating from 1 to 5 using the following rating scheme:

- 5 (Excellent) - like face-to-face conversation.
- 4 (Good) - imperfections can be perceived, but sound is still clear.
- 3 (Fair) - slightly annoying.
- 2 (Poor) - annoying.
- 1 (Bad) - very annoying.

The results from the opinion scores of all the listeners are averaged out to form the MOS value. The results are further analyzed using statistical techniques such as analysis of variance.

Typical sentences used are:

- You will have to be very quiet.
- There was nothing to be seen.
- They worshipped wooden idols.
- I want a minute with the inspector.
- Did he need any money?

A MOS value of 4.0 to 4.5 is referred to as toll-quality and causes complete satisfaction. This is the normal value of the telephone system, and many VoIP services aim at it. Values dropping below 3.5 are termed unacceptable by many users. The following are the MOS values for some typical codecs.

- *Pulse Code Modulation* (PCM): This codec, described in ITU-T G.711, was released in 1972 and it is the standard codec in digital telephony. It produces a 64 Kbps data stream and has a MOS value of 4.3.
- *Internet Low Bit Rate Codec* (iLB): This is a narrowband speech codec suitable for VoIP, streaming audio, archival and messaging. It produces a 15.2 Kbps data stream with a MOS value of 4.14.
- *Adaptive Multi-Rate* (AMR): This audio codec is a patented audio data compression scheme optimized for speech coding. AMR was adopted as the standard speech codec by 3GPP and is used in GSM and UMTS. It uses link adaptation to select from one of eight different bit rates based on link conditions. It is also used to store spoken audio. It produces an 12.2 Kbps data stream, and it has a MOS value of 4.14.
- G.729: This is an audio data compression algorithm for voice that compresses digital voice in packets of 10 milliseconds duration. Because of its low bandwidth requirements, it is mostly used in VoIP. It produces an 8 Kbps data stream, and it has a MOS value of 3.92.
- G.729A is a compatible extension of G.729, but requires less computational power. This lower complexity, however, bears the cost of marginally reduced speech quality. It produces an 8 Kbps data stream, and it has a MOS value of 3.7.
- G.723.1: It is mostly used in VoIP applications due to its low bandwidth requirement. It can produce two data streams, 6.4 Kbps (MOS 3.9) and 5.3 Kbps (MOS 3.62).
- G.726: This is an ITU-T speech codec standard covering the transmission of voice at rates of 16, 24, 32, and 40 Kbps. The most commonly used data rate is 32 Kbit/s, which doubles the usable network capacity by using half the rate of G.711. It is primarily used on international trunks in the phone system, and its MOS value is 3.8.

4.3.2 EVALUATION OF VIDEO QUALITY

The quality of the perceived video may be affected by application parameters and networking parameters, as shown in figure 4.3. Application parameters are related to the encoding and decoding phases and they include factors such as: resolution, video content, encoding rate, coding scheme, and quality of source video. Typically, the higher the encoding rate, the better the quality of the video. Likewise, a good video coding algorithm and a good quality source video increases the quality of the perceived video. Networking factors, such, end-to-end delay, jitter, packet

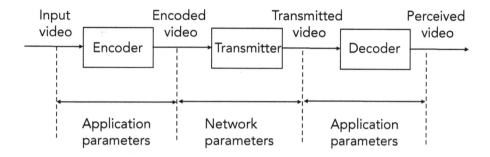

Figure 4.3: Parameters that affect the quality of perceived video

loss, and network availability, can also affect the quality of the perceived video as discussed above in section 4.2. Subjective assessment methods of the perceived quality of a video sequence can be carried out following the same idea as in MOS for audio. A number of video sequences is selected for testing, and the setting of the application and networking parameters that we want to evaluate is also selected. A number of viewers is used and each viewer rates numerically the perceived quality of the video. The average value is then calculated. The viewers should not be experts in assessing the quality of television pictures, and it is recommended that at least 15 observers are used. Two different testing methods can be used, namely *Double Stimulus Impairment Scale* (DSIC) method, and the *Double-Stimulus Continuous Quality Scale* (DSCQS) method, see ITU-R recommendation BT.500[5].

In the double stimulus impairment scale (DSIC) method, the viewer is presented with an unimpaired reference video and then with the same video impaired. Following that, the viewer is asked to vote on the second video having in mind the first video using the following scale, which is similar to the one given for voice communications: 5 (imperceptible impairments), 4 (perceptible, but not annoying), 3 (slightly annoying), 2 (annoying), and 1 (very annoying). A test session lasts up to half an hour, and it comprises a number of presentations. Each presentation may consist of the unimpaired and impaired video shown once (variant I) or twice (variant II). Variant II is more time consuming but it can be applied if the discrimination of very small impairments is required. A series of sessions is conducted, and the mean score for each test condition and test video is calculated.

The double-stimulus continuous quality-scale (DSCQS) method is useful when it is not possible to provide test conditions that exhibit the full range of the quality. Viewers are asked to view a pair of video sequences, the reference video sequence and the impaired video sequence. Each video sequence is about 10 sec, and viewers are shown each pair twice. After the second showing, viewers asked to assess the quality of each video sequence in the pair (and not the impaired one with respect to the reference as in the DSIC method above). The difference between the two scores is then used to quantify changes in the quality. The unimpaired one is included to serve as a reference, but the observers are not told which is the reference sequence. In the series of tests, the position of the reference video sequence is changed randomly. The viewers rate each video sequence by inserting a mark on a vertical scale. The scales are continuous to avoid quantizing errors, but they are divided into five equal lengths, which correspond to the five-point quality scale given above.

R-values	Speech transmission quality	User satisfaction
$90 \leq R < 100$	Best	Very satisfied
$80 \leq R < 90$	High	Satisfied
$70 \leq R < 80$	Medium	Some users dissatisfied
$60 \leq R < 70$	Low	Many users dissatisfied
$50 \leq R < 60$	Poor	Nearly all users dissatisfied

Table 4.3: R-values

Service/network scenario	R-value
ISDN subscriber to ISDN subscriber, local connection	94
Analogue PSTN subscriber to analogue PSTN subscriber, 20 msec delay (average echo path losses; no active echo control)	82
Mobile subscriber to analogue PSTN subscriber as perceived at mobile side	72
Mobile subscriber to analogue PSTN subscriber as perceived at PSTN side	64
Voice over IP connection using G.729A with voice activity detection and 2% packet loss	55

Table 4.4: Examples of speech transmission quality

In addition to the above two methods, a number of alternative methods have also been proposed, such as the *Single-Stimulus Continuous Quality Evaluation* (SSCQE), see ITU-R recommendation BT.500[5]. In one of the three methods associated with SSCDE, the viewers are allowed to dynamically rate the quality of an arbitrarily long video sequence using a slider mechanism with an associated quality scale. Thus, a series of subjective scores can be obtained, as opposed to the single MOS value in the above two methods. This can be useful for tracking rapid changes in quality. The test video sequences are presented only once.

4.4 OBJECTIVE EVALUATION OF AUDIO AND VIDEO QUALITY

Subjective voice and video quality testing is a reliable method for evaluating subjective quality. However, it is time-consuming, expensive, and requires special assessment facilities. Also, only a small sample of test conditions may be presented for assessment in a single test. In view of this, objective means of assessing quality have been developed. The quality of voice and video can be measured a) prior to transmission of the signal to the receiver, b) inside the network during the transmission, and, c) at the receiving device. The measurements obtained can be used for in-service quality monitoring and management, codec optimization, codec selection, and planning of networks and terminals for services such as VoIP, IPTV, video streaming, and mobile TV.

In this section, we describe three models, the well-known *E-model* for assessing the quality of speech, a model for assessing the quality of video-telephony, and a model for assessing the quality of IPTV. These models fall in the category of *parametric planning models,* see Takahashi et al [6], and they can be used for planning purposes. For example, transmission planners can use them to determine the necessary capacity of the network that ensures user satisfaction.

4.4.1 EVALUATION OF VOICE QUALITY – THE E-MODEL

The E-model is described in ITU-T G.107 [7] recommendation. It is used to assess the combined effect of several transmission parameters on the quality of conversational voice. The output from the E-model is a scalar quality rating value, referred to as the *R-value*. In table 4.3, we give *R*-values for different speech quality, see ITU-T G.109 [8]. Voice connections with *R*-values below 50 are not recommended. Examples of R-values for different services and networking scenarios are given in table 4.4.

R-values can be mapped into MOS using the following equation:

$$MOS(R) = \begin{cases} 1, & R < 0 \\ 1 + 0.035R + R(R-60)(100-R)7x10^{-6}, & 0 < R < 100 \\ 4.5, & R > 100 \end{cases} \tag{4.1}$$

The E-model estimates the conversational quality from mouth to ear as perceived by the user at the receive side, both as listener and talker, using different transmission impairments. It is based on the concept that transmission impairments can be transformed into psychological factors which on the psychological scale are additive. The *R*-value is calculated as follows by considering five groups of transmission impairments that affect the quality of voice.

$$R = Ro - Is - Id - Ie\text{-}eff + A \tag{4.2}$$

where

- *Ro* is the basic signal-to- noise ratio, which includes sources of noise such as the circuit noise and room noise.
- *Is* a combination of the impairments which occur more or less simultaneously with the voice signal.
- *Id* represents the impairments caused by delay. It is divided in to three factors, *Idte, Idle* and *Idd*, i.e., *Id = Idte + Idle + Idd*. The factor *Idte* gives an estimate for the impairments due to talker echo, the factor *Idle* represents impairments due to listener echo, and the factor *Idd* represents the impairment caused by the end-to-end delay *Ta*, which is independent of the echo cancelling delays. If the delays due to echo cancellation are zero

(perfect echo cancellation), then $Id = Ta$, and it is given by the following equation:

$$Id = \begin{cases} 0 \ \text{for } Ta \leq 100 \text{ ms} \\ 25\left\{\left(1+X^6\right)^{\frac{1}{6}} - 3\left(1+\left[\frac{X}{3}\right]^6\right)^{\frac{1}{6}} + 2\right\}, \ X = \dfrac{\log\left(\dfrac{Ta}{100}\right)}{\log 2} \ \text{for } Ta > 100\text{ms} \end{cases} \tag{4.3}$$

- *Ie-eff* represents impairments introduced by low bit-rate codecs and packet loss, and it is given by the following equation:

$$\textit{Ie-eff} = Ie + (95 - Ie) \cdot \frac{Ppl}{\dfrac{Ppl}{BurstR} + Bpl} \tag{4.4}$$

Ie is the equipment impairment factor due to low bit-rate codecs. It has been calculated from subjective mean opinion score test results as well as on network experience. *Ppl* is the packet-loss probability, which can be calculated as the ratio of lost packets over the total sent packets. *BurstR*, the burst ratio, reflects the burstiness of packet loss. When packet loss is random, $BurstR = 1$. Finally, *Bpl* is defined as the packet-loss robustness factor and determines the performance of the codec under different loss conditions.

Values for the *Ie* and *Bpl* can be found in Appenidx I of ITU-T G.113[9]. For instance, the value of *Ie* for the G.711 is zero and for the G.729A with voice activity detection is 11. Likewise for G.711 the *Bpl* value is 4.3 and for the G.729A with voice activity detection is 19.

- *A* is the advantage factor that allows for the compensation of impairments because of access-related advantages. This factor enables the planner to take into account the fact that customers may accept some decrease in quality for access advantage, e.g., mobility or connection into hard-to-reach regions. For example, a conventional wired access has no compensation, while a wireless access in remote areas includes a high *A* factor.

The *Ro* and *Is* factors have a low variation and default values can be used. In view of this, expression (4.2) for the *R*-value can be simplified as follows:

$$R = 93.2 - Id - \textit{Ie-eff} + A \tag{4.5}$$

This expression requires the calculation of the end-to-end delay and packet loss, since *A* is typically a constant.

4.4.2 EVALUATION OF VIDEO-TELEPHONY QUALITY
In ITU-T G.1070[10] a computational model is described that assesses the quality of point-to-point interactive videophone applications over an IP network. The model assesses the combined effects of variations in several video and speech parameters that affect QoE. A dedicated videophone terminal, such as, a desktop, or a laptop, or a

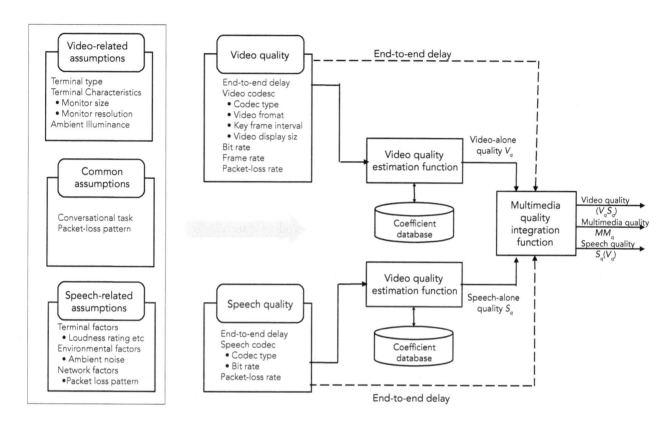

Figure 4.4: Framework for the evaluation of video-telephony quality (ITU-T G.1070)

tablet, or a smartphone, is assumed. The speech bandwidth is limited to the telephone band (300 - 3400 Hz). The model consists of the following three functions: a) a speech quality estimation using a simplified version of the E-model; b) a video quality estimation which depends on application parameters, and, c) a multimedia quality integration function. The latter function estimates the overall quality by taking into account the MOS scores provided by the speech and video estimation functions and any degradation caused by delay. (The degradation caused by the end-to-end delay is considered only in the multimedia quality integration function.) The outputs from the model are multimedia quality (MM_q), video quality influenced by speech quality ($V_q(S_q)$), and speech quality influenced by video quality ($S_q(V_q)$). A framework of this model is given in figure 4.4.

The speech quality is measured by the R-value, referred to as the quality index Q, obtained using the following simplified version of equation (4.2):

$$Q = 93.2 - Idte - Ie\text{-}eff, \tag{4.6}$$

where *Idte* represents the degradation caused by talker echo, and *Ie-eff* represents the degradation caused by speech coding and packet loss. The speech quality Sq is obtained using the following expression, which is similar to (4.1):

$$S_q = \begin{cases} 1, Q < 0 \\ 1 + 0.035Q + Q(Q-60)(100-Q)7x10^{-6}, \ 0 < Q < 100 \\ 4.5, Q > 100 \end{cases} \tag{4.7}$$

The video quality V_q is estimated using the expression:

$$V_q = 1 + I_{coding} \exp\left(-\frac{Ppl_V}{D_{PplV}}\right) \tag{4.8}$$

where I_{coding} represents the basic video quality affected by the coding distortion under a combination of video bit rate and video frame rate, Ppl_V represents the packet loss rate, and D_{PplV} is the packet loss robustness factor expressing the degree of video quality robustness due to packet loss.

The multimedia quality MM_q is expressed as follows:

$$MM_q = m_1 MM_{SV} + m_2 MM_T + m_3 MM_{SV} MM_T + m_4 \tag{4.9}$$

where MM_{SV} represents audiovisual quality, MM_T represents the audiovisual delay impairment factor, and coefficients m_1, m_2, m_3, m_4 are dependent on video display size and conversational task. MM_{SV} is expressed as a function of the speech quality S_q and the and the video quality V_q and MM_T as a function of the speech delay and the video delay. MM_q is bounded between 1 and 5. Detailed expressions for the calculation of MM_q can be found in ITU-T G.1070 [10].

4.4.3 EVALUATION OF IPTV QUALITY

Lloret et al[11] proposed a QoE expression for IPTV that consists of a network QoE, referred to as QoE_N, and a user QoE, referred to as QoE_U. QoE_N is a function of the end-to-end delay, jitter and packet loss. QoE_N is inversely proportional to the end-to-end delay, jitter and packet loss, since high values of these three parameters result to poor QoE. In addition, high values of packet loss have a big impact on the QoE . Hence, the following expression for QoE_N was proposed:

$$QoE_N = \frac{k_1}{(delay + k_3 jitter)e^{packetloss}} \tag{4.10}$$

where delay is the one-way delay, and k_1 and k_3 are two constants. k_1 takes values in [0,1] and it is expressed in msec so that the QoE_N expression is dimensionless. k_3 takes values in [0,1] and is used to give more weight to jitter than the delay (the smaller it is, the higher is its inverse).

QoE_U is a function of the synchronization time between audio and video (sync), the zapping time (zap), and *Video Quality* (VQ). The zapping time is the time elapsed from the instance the viewer presses the channel change button to the instance that the picture of the new channel is displayed along with corresponding audio. The average zapping time varies from 1 to 4 sec, depending upon the technology used. The audio to video synchronization (also known as audio video sync or lip sync) is the delay necessary to synchronize the audio and the video. This lack of synchronization may occur in the creation, mixing, transmission, reception and play-back processing of a video. A viewer does not experience lip sync when the delay is less than 160 msec. VQ varies from 2 to 10, where 2 means that the video is not perceived and 10 means that we have a video with the best quality. It is defined as VQ = 2xMOS, where MOS varies from 1 to 5. QoE_U is proportional to VQ and inversely related to the zap and sync parameters. In view of this, the following expression was proposed.

$$QoE_U = \frac{k_2 \log_{10}(VQ)}{zap + k_4 sync} \tag{4.11}$$

where k_2 is a constant expressed in msec so that the QoE_U expression is dimensionless, and it takes values in [0,1]. k_4 is a constant used to put both parameters on the same scale, and it takes values in [0,20] because sync values are in the order of hundreds of msec whereas zapping times are lower than 10 sec.

The combined expression for QoE is given below. k_1 and k_2 are used to weigh the two components QoE_N and QoE_U.

$$QoE = QoE_N + QoE_U = \frac{k_1}{(delay + k_3 jitter)e^{packetloss}} + \frac{k_2 \log_{10}(VQ)}{zap + k_4 sync} \tag{4.12}$$

PROBLEMS

1. The objective of this exercise is to generate a stream of packets between two machines, call them A and B, in order to obtain the one way end-to-end delay and jitter. In this exercise, you will connect the two machines with a cross-over Ethernet cable so that to minimize any interference from other traffic streams. In the following exercise, you will repeat the experiment by sending the stream of packets from A to B over the Internet.

    Connect two machines with a cross-over Ethernet cable, configure A with 10.0.0.1/24 and B with 10.0.0.2/24, and verify both directions of connectivity using ping. Then generate a stream of packets from A to B and collect the one way end-to-end delay x_i of each packet i, $i = 1, 2, \ldots, n$. Then, based on this information do the following:

    a. *Calculation of the end-to-end delay*: Plot out the histogram of all the one way end-to-end delays x_i, $i = 1$, $2, \ldots, n$. Calculate the mean and the 95th percentile of the one way end-to-end delay. (The 95th percentile can be calculated as follows. Sort out the x_i, $i = 1, 2, \ldots, n$, values in an ascending order. Let $y_1 \leq y_2 \leq \ldots \leq y_n$ be the sorted observations. Then, the 95th percentile is the value y_k where $k = ceiling(0.95n)$, where *ceiling(x)* is the ceiling function that maps the real number x to the smallest integer not less than x. For instance, if $n = 50$, then $k = 48$, and the percentile is the value y_{48}.)

    b. *Calculation of jitter*: As mentioned in section 4.2, there are several different definitions of jitter. Construct the difference of the one way end-to-end-delay of successive packets $d_i = |x_{i+1} - x_i|$, $i = 1, 2, \ldots, n - 1$. Plot the histogram of these differences and calculate the mean and the 95th percentile. Also, calculate the difference between the largest and smallest one way end-to-end delay.

    c. *Calculation of the packet loss*: Devise a scheme to calculate how many packets have been lost. The packet loss rate is then the number of packets lost divided by the total number of packets transmitted.

Comment on your results.

2. Carry out the same exercise as above, but now send the packets from *A* to *B* over the Internet. Do this during a peak time and also during an off-peak time. Discuss your results and also compare them with those obtained above in problem 1.

3. Use expression (4.5) to plot the *R*-values and equivalent MOS for different end-to-end delay values *Ta* and packet loss probabilities *Ppl*, assuming no echo cancellation delays, a G.729A with voice activity detection codec (*Ie* = 11, *Bpl* = 19), *BurstR* = 1, and *A* = 0. Use the range of values for the end-to-end delay and packet loss rate for VoIP given in table 4.2. Comment on your results.

REFERENCES

[1]   IETF RFC 5481, "Packet Delay Variation Applicability Statement".
[2]   Cisco, "Playout Delay Enhancement".
[3]   Cisco, "Quality of Service Design Overview".
[4]   ITU-T P.800, "Methods for Subjective Determination of Transmission Quality" 1996.
[5]   ITU-R BT.500-12, "Methodology for the Subjective Assessment of the Quality of Television Pictures".
[6]   A. Takahashi, D. Hands, and V. Barriac, "Standardization Activities in the ITU for a QoE Assessment of IPTV", IEEE Communications Magazine, February 2008, 78-84.
[7]   ITU-T G.107, "The E-model: a computational model for use in transmission planning", 2009.
[8]   ITU-T G.109, "Definition of categories of speech transmission quality", 1999.
[9]   ITU-T G.113, "Transmission impairments due to speech processing", 2007.
[10] ITU-T G.1070, "Opinion model for video-telephony applications", 2007.
[11] J. Lloret, M. Garcia, M. Atenas and A. Canovas, "A QoE management system to improve the IPTV network", Int. J. of Communication Systems, 2011, 118–138.

PART 3:

SIGNALING FOR ESTABLISHING A SERVICE

CHAPTER 5: THE SESSION INITIATION PROTOCOL (SIP)

5.1 INTRODUCTION

As mentioned in Chapter 1, services can be established using the IP multimedia subsystem (IMS). This is a signaling system that can be used by a service provider to provide multimedia services across roaming boundaries and over diverse networking technologies to subscribers. IMS is the signaling protocol used by operators for LTE. IMS relies on the *Session Initiation Protocol* (SIP), used to set up multi-media sessions. In this Chapter we present the basic features of SIP and in the next Chapter 6 we present IMS. IMS-based networking services are described in the subsequent Chapters 7 and 8.

5.2 THE SESSION INITIATION PROTOCOL (SIP)

SIP was developed as an alternative to the more complex H.323, an ITU-T series of recommendations for audio-visual communications over packet switched networks. SIP is a signaling protocol used for establishing, modifying and terminating sessions in an IP network, see IETF RFC 3261[1]. A session could be a simple two-way telephone call or it could be a collaborative multimedia conference session. SIP supports the following four functions:

- *Name translation and user location:* A user is identified by a single external visible identifier, which SIP maps to the user's current location. This ensures that the call reaches the called party wherever they are located.
- *Feature negotiation:* It provides for feature negotiation so that the participants involved in a session can agree on the features supported, recognizing the fact that not all participants can support the same level of features. For example, video may or may not be supported by a particpant.
- *Call participant management:* During a call, a participant can bring other parties onto the call or cancel connections to other users. In addition, parties could be transferred or placed on hold.
- *Call feature changes:* It allows for changing features of a session while it is in progress. For example, a call may have been set up only for voice but in the course of the call the participants may need to enable a video function; a third party joining a call may require different features to be enabled in order to participate in the call.

SIP is not integrated in other protocols, but it can be used in conjunction with other protocols, such as IMS, described in the next Chapter. SIP can run over TCP or UDP. TCP provides a reliable transport of packets, since it retransmits a packet if it is lost or corrupted and it informs the transmitter if the destination is unreachable. On the other hand, UDP does not guarantee packet delivery nor does it send a notification if a packet is not delivered.

It does check for errors if a packet is delivered using the checksum, and if the checksum fails it does not pass the packet up to the next protocol layer. In view of this, when SIP runs over UDP, it uses timers and re-transmission to make sure that a message has been reliably delivered. SIP can also use the *Transport Layer Security* (TLS) over TCP, and the *Stream Control Transmission Protocol* (SCTP) which has some advantages over TCP for message-based protocols such as SIP. The transport protocol used is indicated in the user's SIP URI, described in the following section.

5.2.1 SIP URIs

A SIP user is identified by the *Uniform Resource Identifier* (URI), the format of which is the same as an email address. (It is possible to use the same URI for both email and SIP communications.) It consists of a user name and a domain name and it has the format: `sip:alice.smith@domain.com`, where domain is the domain name of the SIP operator that Alice Smith has subscribed to. Additional information can be included in fields separated by semi-colons, such as:

`sip:alice.smith@domain.com;transport=tcp;user=ip`

The transport parameter indicates that the transport protocol used is TCP, and the user parameter indicates that the user name field left of the @ sign is a user name, as opposed to a telephone number.

The SIP URI, known as the *Address of Record* (AoR), is a public URI that can be publicized in directories, and it is used to contact a SIP user. However, in order to locate the user, her public URI has to be associated with the SIP device that she is currently using. For instance, let us assume that Alice is currently in her office logged into a computer with the IP address 152.168.1.12 under the login name alice. Then, her device is indicated as follows:

`sip:alice@152.168.1.12`

Likewise, if she is logged into a computer with the name pc1.company.com as alice, then her current device is:

`sip:alice@pc1.company.com`

The IP address of pc1.company.com is resolved through DNS queries. The SIP device currently used by a user is mapped to the user's public URI through an entity known as the *registrar* as follows. Each time Alice Smith logs into a new SIP device, she registers it with the registrar at domain.com. The registrar maps Alice's public URI `alice.smith@domain.com` to her current SIP device. A user may use a different SIP device at different times. SIP messages can be routed to different SIP devices of a user on the basis of various criteria, such as time of the day, sender, type of call, etc. For instance, Alice can program the registar to route calls to pc1.company.com at her work from 8 am to 5 pm, and then for the rest of the time to her home SIP phone. The ability to program the registrar to route calls according to different criteria is a powerful feature of SIP.

An AoR may also be a telephone number, such as +1-555-555-0000, in which case it is indicated as follows:

`sip:+15555550000@domain.com;user=phone`

where the user parameter indicates that the user name field left of the @ sign is a telephone number. If a user dials the telephone number +1-555-555-0000, then this is converted into the URI shown above. There are other variations of the SIP URI that permit to indicate phone numbers. Some phones also allow the user to dial directly an IP address. For instance dialing #152168.1.10 places a call to the IP address 152.168.1.10.

Finally, if a secure transmission is required, the scheme sips: is used which mandates that the request is forwarded to the target domain securely using the transport layer securirty (TLS), a cryptographic protocol designed to provide communication security over the Internet. The last hop from the proxy server of the target domain to the UA has to be secured according to local policies. TLS protects against attackers which try to listen on the signaling link. It does not provide real end-to-end security, since encryption is only hop-by-hop and every single intermediate proxy has to be trusted.

5.2.2 SIP USER AGENTS AND NETWORK SERVERS

The SIP architecture consists of *User Agents* (UAs) and *SIP network servers*, such as, the *proxy server*, the registrar mentioned above, and the *redirect server*. These SIP servers are distinguished only logically, and they may coexist within the same physical box. (We note that the equipment used by a user is referred to as a User Agent (UA) in SIP, and as User Equipment (UE) in IMS.)

A UA runs on an endpoint that can initiate and answer SIP calls automatically. It may be a software running on a computer, or it may be imbedded in mobile devices such as a smartphone, or a it may be a commercially available SIP phone. It comprises of a user element, the *User Agent Client* (UAC), and a server element, the *User Agent Server* (UAS). The client of a UA initiates the calls and the server of the UA answers the calls. During a session a UA will operate both as UAC and UAS. For simplicity, we do not distinguish between the client and the server of a UA in this book.

The main function of the SIP servers is to provide name resolution and user location, and to pass on messages to other servers over the IP network. SIP servers can operate in two different modes: *stateful* and *stateless*. In stateful mode the SIP server remembers the incoming requests it receives, and the responses it sends back and the outgoing requests it sends on. A server acting in a stateless mode deletes all information once it has sent a request. Stateless servers are likely to be used in the backbone of the SIP infrastructure, while stateful servers are likely to be used close to the UAs.

A proxy server is a SIP router which receives all SIP messages from UAs or from other proxy servers and routes them to their destination after it consults the registrar. Typically, the proxy server and the registrar are within the same physical box. The registrar of a domain acts as the front end to the location service for a domain, reading and writing mappings based on the contents of REGISTER requests. SIP does not mandate a particular mechanism for implementing the location service. The only requirement is that a registrar is able to read and write data to the location service, and a proxy server for that domain is capable of reading the same data.

An example of the registrar and the location service is shown in figure 5.1. In this example, we see that Alice registers alice@pc1.company.com by sending a REGISTER message to the registrar at domain.com (step 1).

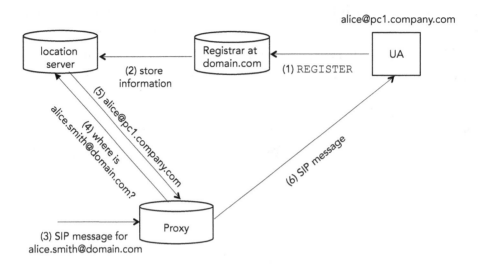

Figure 5.1: Registrar and location server

This information is then forwarded to the location server (step 2). Quite independently we see that a SIP message to `alice.smith@domain.com` is sent by a UA to its SIP proxy server (step 3). The proxy server learns from the location server which device Alice is using (steps 4 and 5), and then forwards the SIP message to Alice `alice@pc1.company.com`.

As will be seen below, a SIP session between two parties begins with an INVITE message sent from the calling party to the called party. For instance, when Bob calls Alice, his UA sends an INVITE message to the proxy server that serves Bob's UA with Alice's public URI. The proxy server forwards the INVITE message to the SIP device that Alice has currently registered, which it learns from the registrar.

An alternative solution is to forward the INVITE message to all SIP devices that belong to Alice. The proxy server can learn all the SIP devices of a user through various schemes. One way is for the user to manually enter these devices through a web page. An alternative way is to have multiple registrations for the same public URI. Forwarding the INVITE message to all the SIP devices of Alice will make all her SIP phones to ring. The remaining messages associated with setting up the session will be forwarded to the one that responded to the INVITE message, while the other devices called will receive a CANCEL message. (If two UAs respond, then the user will have to accept one and decline the other.) This feature is known as *forking* and the proxy server that can perform this feature is known as a *forking proxy*, and it can be executed either in parallel or in sequence. That is, it may send a message to all the SIP URIs of a user at the same time, or it may send it sequentially. That is, it will send the message to the first SIP URI of the user and if the user does not pick up it will send it to the next SIP URI and so on.

In some cases it is desirable to reduce the processing load on a proxy server that is responsible for routing requests by *redirecting* messages. This allows the server to push routing information for a request back to the originator and subsequently to take itself out of the loop of further messaging for this transaction. Redirection is carried by a SIP server known as the *redirect server*. As shown in figure 5.2, after receiving a request, the redirect server returns the

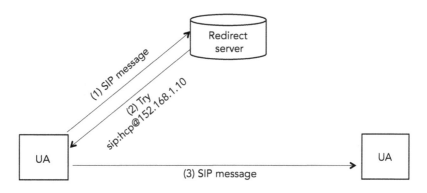

Figure 5.2: The redirection operation

SIP device of the called party to the originator. (This is obtained from the location server, not shown in figure 5.2.) Upon receipt of the URI, the originator of the request sends a new request directly to the called party. Forking can also be used, whereby the redirect server sends a list of locations to the originator.

There are other SIP servers, such as, the *Back-to-Back User Agent* (B2BUA), the *Application Layer Gateway* (ALG), the *presence service*, and SIP gateways, briefly examined below. Various application servers are examined in more detail in Chapter 7.

THE BACK-TO-BACK USER AGENT (B2BUA)

A B2BUA, in simple terms, consists of a UA client, a UA server, and some logic in-between them. This permits it to receive SIP requests, reformulate them, and then send them out as new requests. B2BUA-type of servers have many applications and they can be found in several equipment, such as, a *Branch Exchanges* (PBX) and a conference bridge. For instance, a B2BUA server can be used to implement an *anonymizer* service in which two SIP UAs can communicate without the called party knowing the calling party. To achieve this, the B2BUA reformulates an incoming request with an entirely new SIP message removing any fields that might contain information about the calling party. Any subsequent data that has to be exchanged, after a session has been set up, is done through the B2BUA. The calling party of course knows the URI of the called party, otherwise it will not be able to place a call. A B2BUA server can also be used to monitor the charge incurred by a voice call when a prepaid card is used. In this case, the call has to be dropped when the balance in the prepaid card is used up. The call is set up through a B2BUA server that monitors the cost of the call. After the B2BUA receives a request to establish a call, it opens up a new connection towards the called party and it ensures that all future messages regarding the call and data pass through itself. In this way it has a complete control of the call.

THE APPLICATION LAYER GATEWAY (ALG)

This is a SIP proxy server used to traverse a firewall. A firewall is a device typically present where a private IP network interconnects with the public Internet. It acts as a one-way gate, allowing requests to go from a private network to the Internet, and allowing the responses to these requests to return. Most requests to a private network

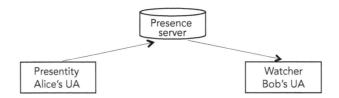

Figure 5.3: Model of the presence service

that originate in the Internet are blocked, with the exception of requests, such as, HTTP requests to a corporate public server, SMTP email transfers, and DNS queries. The interaction between a firewall and SIP depends on the transport protocol. If a UA inside a firewall uses UDP to initiate a session with a UA outside the firewall, the SIP server outside the firewall will be able to receive the SIP messages, but responses sent back will be blocked by the firewall since they are not associated with outgoing requests. However, this is not the case if TCP is used, since the firewall associates incoming responses to outgoing requests. Also, a UA outside a firewall cannot establish a session with a UA inside the firewall, since all SIP and RTP messages will be blocked. The same applies if a *Network Address Translation* (NAT) is used.

Several different solutions have been proposed to traverse a firewall or a NAT that require protocol support in the UA, such as the ALG. This is basically a SIP proxy that is trusted by the firewall. All SIP and RTP messages are directed to an ALG, which performs authentication and validation, and it also enforces policies required by a security administration. The firewall allows only SIP and RTP messages to pass through that originate or terminate at an ALG. An ALG works with NAT as well. ALGs are referred sometimes by their commercial name *Session Border Controllers* (SBC).

THE PRESENCE SERVICE

Presence is used with *Instant Messaging* (IM) which is often integrated with VoIP and other services such as white board, application sharing, and file transfer. Presence is the status of a person's current availability, such as, on-line, busy, and off-line. Rich presence conveys more information about a user's current status, that includes type of device being used and its operating system, location and local time of the user, and any other messages the user might wish to announce. Presence has been described as the dial tone of the 21st century! It replaces the dialing of a phone number or the typing of a URI with a single click on the icon of a buddy. The icon replaces multiple phone numbers of a buddy since the public address is used to locate the buddy's current URI. This helps to avoid endless futile calls that end up in leaving messages in a voice mail box. Presence enables polite and sensitive communications, since using the presence icon, we can determine if the person we want to call is available, busy, in good mood, and so on.

IETF has proposed a model for a presence service, see IETF RFC 2778[2], which consists of a *presentity*, a presence server, and a *watcher*, as shown in figure 5.3. (The word presentity is made up of the words presence and entity.) The presentity is co-located with Alice's UA and it stores and distributes Alice's presence information. The watcher is co-located with Bob's UA, and it receives information from the presence server and presents it to Bob's UA.

Alice's presence information is displayed by the watcher as a buddy. A watcher has a list of buddies for which it maintains presence information. A presentity and a watcher are two distinct clients that may co-exist within a UA, and they may be combined into a single implementation. That permits, for instance, Alice to distribute her presence information while at the same time she receives information for her own buddy list.

There are two kinds of watchers, *fetchers* and *subscribers*. A fetcher simply requests the current value of some presentity from a presence server. The subscriber receives notifications from a presence server each time the current value of a presentity changes. In section 5.5, we describe three methods, PUBLISH, SUBSCRIBE, and NOTIFY, through which the above presence model can be implemented. A presentity sends information to the presence server using the PUBLISH method; a subscriber watcher subscribes to a presence server using the method SUBSCRIBE; and, the presence server distributes presentity information using the NOTIFY method. These three methods are quite general and they can be used to implement other SIP services.

SIP GATEWAYS

A SIP gateway acts as an interface between two networks that use different signaling protocols and possibly different technologies for transporting data. For instance, a SIP to H.323 gateway connecting two IP networks terminates the SIP signaling path and converts it to that of H.323, and vice versa. However, it does not interfere with the transfer of data since both networks are IP networks. On the other hand, going from an IP network to the circuit-switched public telephone network requires signaling and data conversion. This is because the signaling protocol used by the telephone network is SS7, and its transmission technology is based on SONET/SDH. A gateway is designed to support a large number of users, such as the users in a large corporations or in a geographical area.

Gateways are typically decomposed into a *Media Gateway* (MG) and a *Media Gateway Controller* (MGC). The MGC manages the call signaling protocols, and the MG manages the media connection that carries the data. For instance, in a SIP gateway between an IP network and the public telephone network, the MGC converts SIP messages to SS7 messages and vice versa, and the MG converts IP packets to SONET/SDH and vice versa. The decomposition of a gateway to MGC and MG is transparent to SIP.

5.3 FORMAT OF A SIP MESSAGE

SIP follows the client/server model, and it is based on HTTP which is a request-response protocol. A SIP message is either a *request* from a client to a server, or a *response* from a server to a client.

An example of SIP requests and responses exchanged for setting up a session between two SIP users is shown in figure 5.4. Alice's softphone is a SIP application running on her computer, and Bob has a SIP phone. For simplicity we assume that they are both served by the same proxy server. The UA of Alice's computer sends an INVITE request message to the proxy server which then forwards it to the UA of Bob's SIP phone. The proxy server sends a 100 Trying response message to Alice's UA to indicate that it is working on routing the INVITE request message to the destination. When Bob's SIP phone receives the INVITE request message, it rings to alert Bob of the incoming call, and indicates this to the proxy server by sending a 180 Ringing response message which the proxy server forwards to Alice's UA. When Alice's UA receives the 180 Ringing response message it generates a ringing or it displays a message to indicate that Bob's phone is ringing. When Bob picks up the phone, its UA sends a 200 OK response message to the proxy which is then forwarded to Alice's UA. In response, Alice's UA sends an ACK request message to the proxy server which is forwarded to Bob's UA. At that time, the media session begins. The session is terminated when one of the two parties hangs up. A BYE request message is sent directly to the other party which responds with a 200 OK response message.

The format of a SIP request or response message is as follows:

```
Start line
A number of message headers
Empty line
Optional message body
```

The start line, each message header, and the empty line must be terminated by a carriage-return line-feed sequence (CRLF). The empty line must be present even if there are no message headers.

START LINE

The start line varies depending upon whether the message is a response or a request, but the remaining of the message is identical. The start line of a response message is referred to as the *status line*. It contains the protocol version, which is always SIP/2.0 and the status of the transaction which is given by a numerical value and also by a human-readable phrase. For instance, in the example in figure 5.4, the start line for 180 Ringing response message is:

```
SIP/2.0 180 Ringing
```

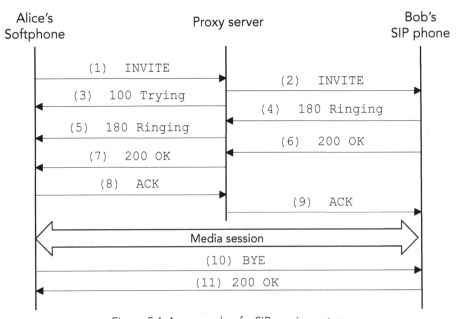

Figure 5.4: An example of a SIP session setup

The status code 180 indicates that the called party has been alerted, and the phrase `Ringing` is for human consumption, and it can be written in any language. SIP response messages are further discussed below in section 5.4.

The start line for request messages is referred to as the *request line*. It consists of a *method* name, the `Request-URI` and the protocol version SIP/2.0. The method name indicates the purpose of the request, and the `Request-URI` is the SIP URI of the called party. For instance, the start line for the `INVITE` message used in figure 5.4 is as follows:

```
INVITE sip:alice.smith@domain.com SIP/2.0
```

This message indicates that the calling party wants to invite Alice Smith whose public URI is `alice.smith@domain.com`. SIP methods are described below in section 5.5.

When describing a SIP message flow, such as the one in figure 5.4, the method names are indicated in capitals and the responses are described by their status code and phrase.

HEADER FIELDS

Header fields follow the same generic header format as in HTTP. Each header field consists of a field name followed by a colon and the field value, i.e.,

```
field name: field value
```

Arbitrary amount of whitespace on either side of the colon is allowed, though the preferred way is for no space between the field name and the colon, and a single space between the colon and the field value. For instance,

```
Subject: lunch
To: Alice Smith <sip:alice.smith@domain.com>;tag=4321
```

Some header fields may have more than one entry in a message, such as

```
Route: <sip: p1.domain1.com>
Route: <sip: p2.domain2.com>
```

These header fields can also be displayed in a single line using commas to separate the fields. The following are some of the header fields:

- `To`: It contains the URI of the destination and optionally a display name. Example:
  ```
  To: Alice Smith <sip:alice.smith@domain.com>;tag=4321
  ```
  The tag is used in identifying a session uniquely as described below.
- `From`: It contains the URI of the originator of the request. As in the `To` header field, it contains a URI and optionally a display name. Examples:
  ```
  From: Bob <sips:bob@biloxi.com>;tag=a48s
  From: sip:+12125551212@phone2net.com;tag=887s
  From: Anonymous <sip:c8oqz84zk7z@privacy.org>;tag=hyh8
  ```

- **Call-ID:** It is a unique string generated by the originator of a request, used to identify all the SIP messages associated with a single session. The unique string is generated using the current time expressed in msec and a five digit random string followed by the hostname. It must be the same for all requests and responses sent by the UAs. In addition to the Call-ID each party in the session also contributes a random identifier, unique for each call. These identifiers, called tags, are included in the To and From header fields as the session is established. Specifically, the initiator of a session generates a Call-ID and a From tag. In response, the UA answering the request generates a To tag. The combined fields: Call-ID, From tag, and To tag identify uniquely a dialog.

- **CSeq:** It contains a sequence number followed by a method name. This number is incremented for each new request sent, and it typically starts at 1 but it could start at any integer number. It is used to order transactions within a dialog, to provide a means to uniquely identify transactions, and to differentiate between new requests and request retransmissions.

- **Max-Forwards:** It serves to limit the number of hops a request can transit on the way to its destination. It consists of an integer that is decremented by one at each hop. If the Max-Forwards value reaches 0 before the request reaches its destination, it will be rejected with a 483 Too many hops error response.

- **Via:** A UA must insert this header field in a SIP request to identify the transport protocol used and its location to where the response should be sent. For instance, the location and transport protocol could be an IPv4 address using unicast UDP with assumed port number of 5060, or a domain name using TCP and port number 60202. In addition, a branch parameter is added by the UAs and proxy servers to identify a transaction created by a request. It is unique across space and time for all requests sent by a UA, except CANCEL and ACK, and it must begin with the characters z9hG4bK. Examples:

  Via: SIP/2.0/UDP 152.0.0.1:5060;branch=z9hG4bKna43f

  Via: SIP/2.0/TCP pc.domain.com;branch=z9hG4bK776sgdkse

  A proxy server that receives a request inserts its own Via header field above all the other Via header fields to indicate its own location and transport protocol, before it forwards it. These Via header fields are copied on the response message so that it traverses the same proxy servers in the opposite direction. Each proxy server removes its own Via header field and uses the next one to determine where to send the message.

- **Contact:** It gives the SIP device where the reply should be sent. In most cases, it is the SIP device address of the UA that originated the message.

- **Expires:** It is used to indicate the time interval after which the message (or content) expires. The value of this header is an integral number of seconds between 0 and $2^{32} - 1$, measured from the receipt of the request. The precise meaning of this header is method dependent. For instance, the expiration time in a REGISTER request indicates how long the client would like the registration to be valid. The expiration time in an INVITE request indicates how long the UA will wait before it receives a valid answer. It does not indicate the duration of the session that may result from the invitation. The UA generates a CANCEL request if the time indicated in the Expires header is reached and no final answer for the INVITE has been received.

- **Session-Expires** and **Min-SE:** A keepalive mechanism is used optionally to allow stateful proxies to know whether a session is alive or not. A UA maybe able to determine when a session has timed out by using session specific mechanisms, but a stateful SIP proxy that does not handle the media stream(s) for the session has no mechanism to definitively determine the state of all sessions for which it has a state. As a result, if a UA fails to send a `BYE` message or the `BYE` message gets lost, the proxy will not know that the session has ended. The keepalive mechanism adds the capability to refresh periodically a session by sending repeatedly `INVITE` requets, known as re-INVITEs, during an active session to allow UAs and proxies to determine the status of a session. The two headers `Session-Expires` and `Min-SE` (minimum session expiration) have been introduced to indicate the value of the refresh period. The `Session-Expires` header conveys the duration of the refresh period, and the `Min-SE` header conveys the minimum allowed value for the session expiration.

- `Route`: It provides routing information for requests. There are two types of routing, *strict* and *loose* routing (see also section 9.3.1). In strict routing, the path through the set of servers specified in the `Route` header field. In the loose routing, the path the request is routed through all the servers in the `Route` header field, but it may also be routed through other servers as well. A server knows if the next server in the route set supports loose routing by the designation `lr`, as shown in the example below:
  `Route: <sip: p1.domain1.com, lr>`

- `Record Route`: Typically once two UAs have established a session, subsequent messages do not go through the chain of servers used initially to establish the session. This header field is used to force routing of all subsequent requests in a session between two UAs through a proxy server. For this to happen, a server inserts its address in the `Record Route` header field which forces future requests to include a `Route` header field containing the address of the server.

- `Proxy-Authorization`: It is used by a client to identify itself (or its user) to a proxy server that requires authentication. The header field consists of credentials containing authentication information of the UA.

- `Proxy-Require`: It is used to list features and extensions that a UA requires a proxy server to support in order to process a request.

- `Subject`: It is used to indicate the subject of the media session. Its contents can be displayed during alerting to aid the user in deciding whether to accept the call. Example:
  `Subject: SIP project is due next Monday`

The first six header fields listed above are mandatory for all requests. The format of a header field is defined by the field name. Field names, field values, and parameter names are all case-insensitive. The relative order of header fields with different field names is not significant, though the header fields required for proxy processing, such as, `Via`, `Route`, `Record Route`, `Proxy-Require`, `Max-Forwards`, and `Proxy-Authorization`, should appear towards the top of the message to facilitate rapid parsing. The relative order of header field rows with the same field name is important. Additional header fields are defined below in section 5.5.

MESSAGE BODY

The message body is optional and it is separated from the header fields by an empty line. The following are some of the header fields used in a message body:

- `Content-Encoding:` It is used to indicate that the listed encoding scheme has been applied to the message body. This allows a UA to determine the decoding scheme necessary to interpret the message body. Example: `Content-Encoding: text/plain`

- `Content-Disposition:` It is used to describe the function of a message body. Some defined values are: `session, icon, alert,` and `render.`

- `Content-Language:` It indicates the language used.

- `Content-Length:` It gives the number of octets in the message body. A `Content-Length: 0` indicates no message body.

- `Content-Type:` It specifies the Internet media used in the message body, such as, *Session Description Protocol* (SDP), see section 5.6, XML dialog, XML conference info, plain text, and HTML text. Examples:

  `Content-Type: application/sdp`

  `Content-Type: application/xml+conf`

  `Content-Type: text/plain`

  `Content-Type: text/html`

- `MIME-Version:` This field is used to indicate the version of the *Multipurpose Internet Mail Extensions (MIME)* protocol used to construct the message body.

- Finally, we note that there is a compact representation of some of the header fields that can be used to save space in large messages. Specifically, a header field is represented by a single character, such as, `To` is represented by `t,` `From` by `f,` `Subject` by `s,` `Call-ID` by `i,` `contact` by `m,` and `Content-Encoding` by `e.`

5.4 SIP RESPONSE MESSAGES

A SIP response message is generated by a UA or a SIP server to reply to a request message. There are six classes of responses, each associated with a different status code, as shown in table 5.1. The first five classes were borrowed from HTTP, and the sixth one was created for SIP.

The informational class of responses 1xx, is used to indicate call progress. The following response codes have been defined:

- `100 Trying:` This response can be generated by a UA or a proxy server and it indicates that some kind of action is being taken to process a call.

- `180 Ringing:` It indicates that the `INVITE` request has been received by the UA and alerting is taking place. This response is important in the interworking of telephony protocols. When the UA answers immediately, a `200 OK` is sent without the `180 Ringing.` This is known as the *fast answer* scenario in telephony.

Response classes	Meaning
100 - 199	Informational
200 - 299	Success
300 - 399	Redirection
400 - 499	Client error
500 - 599	Server error
600 - 699	Global error

Table 5.1: SIP response classes and their meaning

- 181 Call is being forwarded: This response is used to indicate that the call has been handed off to another endpoint. It is sent when the information maybe of use to the caller. Also it provides a status of the call because a forwarding operation may result in the call taking longer to be answered.

- 182 Call queued: This response is used to indicate that the request has been queued and will be processed.

- 183 Session progress: This response indicates that information about the progress of the session may be present in a message body or media stream. Unlike the 100 Trying response, it an end-to-end response and establishes a dialog. A typical application of this response is to allow a UA to hear a ring tone, or a busy tone, or a recorded announcement in calls through gateways into the public telephone system.

The success class of responses indicate that the request has succeeded or it has been accepted. The following response codes have been defined:

- 200 OK: This is probably the most commonly used success response. It is used to accept a session invitation, in which case the message body carries the media property of the called party. It is also used in response to other requests to indicate successful completion or receipt of request. This 200 OK stops further retransmission of the request.

- 202 Accepted: It indicates that the UA has received and understood the request, but the request may not be authorized or processed by a server. It is commonly used in responses to a SUBSCRIBE request.

- 204 No notification: It is used in response to a SUBSCRIBE request that was successful but no notification with the request will be sent.

The redirection class of responses are generally sent by a SIP server, acting as a redirection server, in response to an INVITE. The UA may be programmed to send out automatically a new INVITE upon receipt of a redirection class response without the intervention of the user. The following response codes have been defined:

- 300 Multiple choices: This response contains multiple Contact header fields, each with a different location of the URI in the Request-URI field. These locations should be tried in the order of the Contact headers.

- 301 Moved permanently: It contains a Contact header field with the new permanent URI of the called party. It can be saved and used in future INVITE requests.
- 302 Moved temporarily: This is in contrast to the above response and it indicates that it cannot be cached unless an Expires header field is used.
- 305 Use proxy: It contains a URI that points to a proxy server that has authoritative information about the calling party. The caller should resend the request to the proxy for forwarding.
- 380 Alternative service: This response returns a URI that represents a service that the caller may want to use, such as a voicemail server.

The client error class of responses is used by a server or a UA to indicate that the request cannot be fulfilled as submitted. The nature of the error and how the request can be reformulated is indicated by a specific error response or by the presence of specific header fields. For instance, if no credentials are provided in the Proxy-Authorization header field in a request, a proxy server can challenge the originator to provide credentials by rejecting the request with a 407 Proxy Authentication Required status code. The proxy server populates the Proxy-Authenticate header field in the 407 Proxy Authentication Required message with information applicable to the proxy server for the requested resource. When the originator receives the 407 Proxy Authentication Required message, it resends the request with the proper credentials in the Proxy-Authenticate header. A large number of response codes have been defined for a variety of errors, such as, 400 Bad request, 401 Unauthorized, 402 Payment required, 404 Not found, 408 Requested timeout, 409 Conflict, 480 Temporarily unavailable, and 483 Too many hops.

The server error class of responses are used to indicate that the request cannot be further processed due to an error with the server. Various responses have been defined, such as: 500 Server internal error, 501 Not implemented, 502 Bad gateway, 503 Service unavailable, and 513 Message too large. Finally, the global error class indicates that the server knows that the request will fail wherever it is processed, and as a result the request should not be sent to other locations. It uses the responses: 600 Busy everywhere, 603 Decline, 604 Does not exist anywhere, and 606 Not acceptable.

5.5 SIP METHODS

SIP requests or methods are requests to a server or UA for a specific action. A UA replies with 501 Not implemented response if it receives a request that it does not support. A proxy server does not have to understand a method in order to forward it. A proxy treats an unknown method as if it is an OPTIONS method. That is, it forwards the request to the destination if it can. This allows new features and methods to be introduced without requiring software support from intermediary proxy servers. Method names are case sensitive and they are all upper case so that they can be distinguished from header fields which are upper and lower case. A list of SIP methods is given in table 5.3. Below, we describe these methods.

The REGISTER method is used by a UA to notify a SIP network of the current Contact URI. Registration is not required in order for a UA to use a proxy server for outgoing calls. It is required in order for a UA to receive incoming calls from proxy servers that serve the domain, unless a non-SIP service is used by the location service to populate the SIP's URIs and `Contact` header field of endpoints. The `Expire` header field in a `REGISTER` request is used to suggest how long the client would like to stay registered. Alternatively, this can be indicated in the expire field of the `Contact` header. The registrar selects the actual duration based on its local policies. The following header fields are mandatory in a `REGISTER`: `Via, To, From, Call-ID, CSeq,` and `Max-Forwards.` The `INVITE` method is used to establish media sessions between two UAs. A UA that originates an `INVITE` message creates a globally unique `Call-ID` that is used for the duration of the call. A `CSeq` count is also initialized and incremented for each new request related to the same `Call-ID`. The `To` and `From` headers are populated with addresses of the calling and called parties. A `From` tag is included in the `INVITE` and the receiving UA includes a `To` tag in any response. The `Expire` header field in an `INVITE` request sets a time limit on the completion of the request. That is, the originating UA must receive a final response time within the time period specified, otherwise the request is automatically cancelled. Once the session has been established, the value in the `Expire` header field has no effect. The following header fields are mandatory in an `INVITE`: `Via, To, From, Call-ID, CSeq, Contact,` and `Max-Forwards.`

The `ACK` method is used to acknowledge final responses to `INVITE` requests. Final responses to all other requests are not acknowledged. Final responses are defined as 2xx, 3xx, 4xx, 5xx, and 6xx. For 2xx responses, the `ACK` is end-to-end, but for all other final responses it is done on a hop-by-hop basis. The `CSeq` is not incremented in an `ACK` so that the UA can match it with that of the originating `INVITE`. The following header fields are mandatory in an `ACK`: `Via, To, From, Call-ID, CSeq, Contact,` and `Max-Forwards.`

Method	Description
ACK	Acknowledge the final response for INVITE
BYE	Terminates the session
CANCEL	Cancels a pending request
INFO	Transports call signaling information
INVITE	Establishes a session
MESSAGE	Carries an instant message
NOTIFY	Notifies the UA about a particular event
OPTIONS	Queries a server or a UA about its capabilities
PRACK	Acknowledge the receipt of provisional response
PUBLISH	Uploads information to a server
REFER	Instructs a server or a UA to send a request
REGISTER	Maps a public URI with a current location of the user
SUBSCRIBE	Requests to be notified about a particular event
UPDATE	Modifies the state of a session

Table 5.2: SIP methods

The BYE method is used to terminate an established media session. It is sent by a UA participating in the session, and it is never send by proxy servers and other participating third-party servers. The following header fields are mandatory in a BYE: Via, To, From, Call-ID, CSeq, and Max-Forwards. The BYE method is forwarded directly to the other UA bypassing the proxy servers, except in the case of a stateful proxy server. In this case, the request has to be routed through it so that it knows that the session has ended. For simplicity, we assume in this book that the BYE method not routed through proxy servers.

The CANCEL method is used to terminate a pending INVITE or a call attempt initiated earlier. It can be generated by UAs and proxy servers. A forking proxy uses this method to cancel pending parallel branches after a successful response has been sent back to the originating UA. The CSeq is not incremented so that proxy servers and UAs can match it with a pending INVITE. The following header fields are mandatory in a CANCEL: Via, To, From, Call-ID, CSeq, and Max-Forwards.

The SUBSCRIBE and NOTIFY methods are used to establish an asynchronous notification scheme for events. They are used for various SIP services, such as, automatic callback service based on terminal state events, buddy lists based on user presence events, and message waiting indications based on mailbox state change events. The SUB-SCRIBE method is used by a UA (subscriber) to establish a subscription for the purpose of receiving notifications via the NOTIFY method about a specific event from an entity (notifier). The NOTIFY method is used to send information to a subscriber about changes in state to which the subscriber has a subscription. The subscription request contains an Expires header with the exact duration of the subscription. The subscription can be refreshed by sending another SUBSCRIBE request before it expires. If no refresh message is received prior

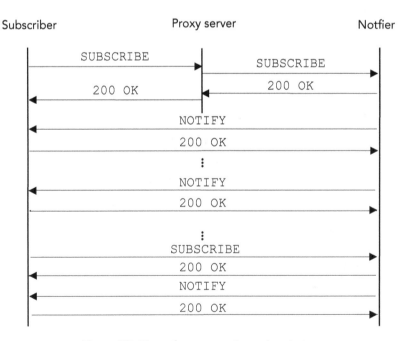

Figure 5.5: Flow of messages in a subscription

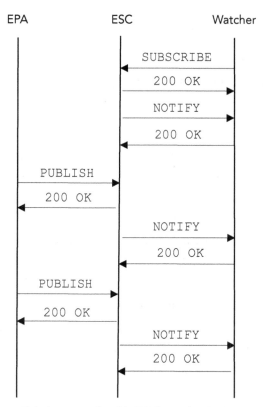

Figure 5.6: An example of PUBLISH and NOTIFY requests

its expiration time, the subscription is terminated. Unsubscribing can also be handled by sending a SUB-SCRIBE message with the Expires header set to 0. A successful unsubscription triggers a final NOTIFY message. A 200 OK response is sent to confirm receipt of a NOTIFY request. An example of the flow between a subscriber and a notifier is shown in figure 5.5. The following header fields are mandatory in a SUBSCRIBE: Via, To, From, Call-ID, CSeq, Max-Forwards, Contact, Event, and Allow-Events. The following header fields are mandatory in a NOTIFY: Via, To, From, Call-ID, CSeq, Max-Forwards, Event, Allow-Events, and Subscription-State. The header field Event is used to indicate which event package is used. (An event package defines a set of state information to be reported by a notifier to a subscriber.) The Allow-Events header field is used to list the event packages that are supported. Finally, the Subscription-State header field indicates the current state of a subscription. Values include: active, pending, or terminated.

The PUBLISH method is used to send information, such as presence state, to a server known as the *Event State Compositor* (ESC), which provides a centralized means of distributing information to a UA, referred to as watcher, that has already subscribed with ESC. A UA that publishes information is known as the *Event Publication Agent* (EPA). A UA can be an EPA and also a watcher. This model is consistent with the model of a presence service shown in figure 5.3, where an EPA is the presentity and the ESC is the presence server. An EPA sends information to an ESC using the PUBLISH request. This is similar to REGISTER in that it allows a user to create, modify, and remove state in another entity which manages this state on behalf of the user. The information received from EPAs is put together and then it is distributed to the watchers using the `NOTIFY` request. An example of the `PUBLISH` request involving one EPA and a watcher is shown in figure 5.6. The `PUBLISH` method is useful when there are multiple UAs exchanging information as it avoids each UA to have to subscribe individually to all the other UAs. The following header fields are mandatory in a `PUBLISH`: `Via, To, From, Call-ID, CSeq, Max-Forwards, Contact, Event, Allow-Events, Expires,` and `Min-Expires`. The `Min-Expires` header field conveys the minimum refresh interval supported by various soft-state elements managed by a server.

Instant Messaging (IM) is defined as the exchange of short text messages between a set of participants in near real time. IM differs from email in that instant messages are usually grouped together into brief live conversations, consisting of numerous small messages sent back and forth. As we know, the integration of IM and presence, provides a powerful communication scheme. Two different modes of IM have been defined by IETF, *pager mode* and *session mode*. In pager mode, an instant message is carried in the message body of the `MESSAGE` method as a `MIME` attachment. The following header fields are mandatory in a `MESSAGE`: `Via, To, From, Call-ID, CSeq, Max-Forwards`. The `To` header field will normally contain the address of record for the recipient of the instant message, but it may be a device address in situations where the client has current information about the recipient's location. For example, the client could be coupled with a presence system that supplies an up to date device contact for a given address of record. An instant message sent in a `MESSAGE` request is acknowledged by a `200 OK` response. The `MESSAGE` and its `200 OK` response are forwarded through the UA's proxy server. If UA 2 wants to send an instant message to UA 1 in response to the UA 1's instant message, then it will send a separate `MESSAGE` to UA 1 which will be acknowledged by UA 1 with a `200 OK,` as shown in figure 5.7. There is no explicit SIP association of the exchanged instant messages other than the user's imagination.

In session mode, instant messages are exchanged between two UAs using the *Message Session Relay Protocol* (MSRP), see IETF RFC 4975[3]. As can be seen in figure 5.8, a SIP session is established first by sending an `INVITE` request. UA 2 silently accepts the invitation without alerting the called user (i.e., no `180 Ringing` response as in figure 5.4) and displays the first message (step 9). The instant messages are exchanged between the two UAs without having to be routed through the proxy servers of the UAs using the MSRP messages SEND and `200 OK`. The session is terminated using the `SIP BYE` and `200 OK`. MSRP can also deliver a very large message, by splitting it into chunks and delivering each chunk in a separate `SEND` request.

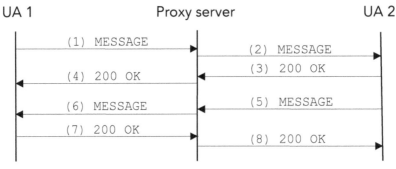

Figure 5.7: Pager mode

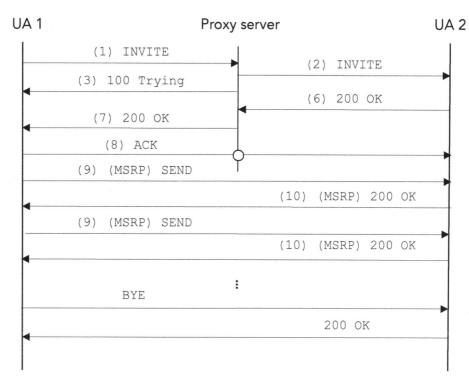

Figure 5.8:. Session mode

Most IM clients offer both modes. The pager mode makes sense when the user wishes to send a small number of short instant messages to a single or to a small number of recipients. The session model is more efficient for longer conversations since the messages are not sent through the SIP servers as in the case of the page mode. Also, by viewing IM as a media type, all of the features available in SIP signaling are available for IM.

The PRACK method is used to acknowledge receipt 1xx provisional responses, which have to be transported reliably. In cases where a provisional response has been issued, such as 180 Ringing, it is critical to determine the state of the call and in this case it is necessary to confirm receipt of the provisional response. This is done using the PRACK method. Responses 2xx, 3xx, 4xx, 5xx, and 6xx, to INVITE messages are acknowledged using the ACK message. The ACK method is used to guarantee that a response message has been received. The mandatory header fields are: Via, To, From, Call-ID, CSeq, Max-Forwards, and RAck. The header field RAck is used to indicate the sequence number of the provisional response that is being acknowledged.

The INFO method is used by a UA to send call signaling information to another UA with which it has already established a media session. It typically contains a message body, whose contents may be signaling information, a mid-call event, or some sort of stimulus. The mandatory header fields are: Via, To, From, Call-ID, CSeq, Max-Forwards, Info-Package. The Info-Package header field is used to indicate which INFO package is used.

The OPTIONS method is used to query a UA or a server about its capabilities and discover its current availability.

A UA or a proxy server responds to this method as if it was an INVITE. The mandatory header fields are: `Via`, `To`, `From`, `Call-ID`, `CSeq`, and `Max-Forwards`.

The `REFER` method is used to enable various applications, including call transfer. For instance, if Alice is in a call with Bob, and decides that Bob needs to talk to Carol, Alice can instruct her UA to send a `REFER` request to Bob's UA providing Carol's contact information. Then, assuming that Bob has given it permission, Bob's UA will attempt to call Carol using that contact. Bob's UA will then report to Alice whether it succeeded in reaching Carol. The header field `Refer-To` is used to provide the referenced URI or URL. This method can be sent either inside or outside a dialog. The mandatory header fields are: `Via`, `To`, `From`, `Call-ID`, `CSeq`, `Max-Forwards`, and `Refer-To`.

The `UPDATE` method is used to modify the state of a session without changing the state of the dialog. Possibly uses of this method include muting or placing on hold pending media streams, performing QoS, or other end-to-end attribute negotiation prior to session establishment. The mandatory header fields of this method are: `Via`, `To`, `From`, `Call-ID`, `CSeq`, `Max-Forwards`, and `Contact`.

5.6 THE SESSION DESCRIPTION PROTOCOL (SDP)

A session description contains information about a multimedia session that allows a UA to particpate in a session. It includes the IP and port number where the media data has to be sent and the codecs used to encode the voice and the images of the participants. Session descriptions are created using a standard format, and the most common format is the *Session Description Protocol* (SDP) defined in IETF RC 2327 [4]. (The term "protocol" in SDP is a misno-

Type	Meaning
v	protocol version
o	owner/creator and session identifier
s	session name
i	information about the session
u	URL containing a description of the session
e	email address
p	phone number
c	connection information - not required if included in all media
b	bandwidth information
z	time zone adjustments
k	encryption key
a	zero or more session attribute lines
t	time the session is active
r	zero or more repeat times
m	media name and transport address

Table 5.3: SDP types and their meaning

mer since it is just a textual format to describe multimedia sessions.) SDP is used in SIP and also in other signalling protocols, such as H.323 and RTP. SIP is independent of the format used to describe the session.

An SDP session description consists of a number of lines of text in the form <type> = <value>, where type is described by a one low-case character and <value> is a text string whose format depends on the <type>. Whitespace is not permitted on either side of the '=' sign. In general <value> is either a number of fields delimited by a single space character or a free format string. The <types> and their meaning are given in table 5.3.

An example of an SDP session is shown below.

```
v=0
o=alice.smith 2890844526 2890842807 IN IP4 152.168.1.10
s=Chat
i=An invitation to chat
e=asmith12@company.com
c=IN IP4 152.168.1.10
t=0 0
m=audio 49170 RTP/AVP 0
a=sendrecv
m=video 51372 RTP/AVP 31
a=sendrecv
```

The v= field gives the version of the SDP. The o= field gives the user name of the originator of the session, a session id and a session version number id, and the IP address of the machine from which the session was orginated. N stands for Internet. The s= field gives the session name, the i= field provides information about the session, and the e= field gives the caller's email address. The c= field contains the IP address of the expected data source, or data relay, or data sink. The t= value specifies the start and stop time. If the stop time is zero then this means that the session in unbounded, and if the start time is also zero, then the session is to take place at the moment the session description is received. The m= field provides a description of each media used in the session, and it has the format m=<media> <transport> <fmt list>. The <media> sub-field takes values such as audio, video, application, data, and control, and the second sub-field is the transport port to which the media stream will be sent. The third sub-field is the transport protocol used, where RTP/AVP indicates an RTP audio/video profile. This is a set of RTP parameters that describe an encoding method, identified by a profile number which is given in the fourth sub-field. For instance, 0 means 64 KHz G.711 audio encoding, and 31 means H.261 video encoding. Finally, the a= field provides additional attributes. In the above example it indicates that the streams are bidirectional, that is, both calling and called parties can send and receive.

In general, an SDP session description consists a session-level description and a several media-level descriptions. The session-level description applies to the whole session and to all the media streams. A media-level description applies to a single media stream, and there may be several media descriptions if there are more than one media

Figure 5.9: Registration of current location

stream. In the above example the seven lines above the first m= line form the session-level description. Each media-level description includes an m= line followed by optional a= lines that provide additional information.

An SDP session description is included in a SIP message as a message body encapsulated in MIME. The following is an example of MIME encapsulation.

```
Content-Disposition: multiparty/mixed; boundary="
Content-Type: application/sdp
Content-Length: 245
```

The Content-Length is expressed in bytes, the Content-Disposition indicates that the body is a session description, and the Content-Type indicates that the session description uses SDP.

5.7 EXAMPLES OF SIP MESSAGES

When Alice logs on at her computer at her work she registers her current location, alice@pc1.company.com, with the registrar. For this, Alice's UA sends a REGISTER message to the domain's registrar, as shown in figure 5.9. The value in the From header is the same as the value in the To header field unless the request is a third-party registration. The REGISTER message is as follows:

```
REGISTER sip:domain.com SIP/2.0
Via: SIP/2.0/UDP 152.0.0.1:5060; branch=z9hG4bKna43f
Max-Forwards: 70
To: <sip:alice.smith@domain.com>
From: <sip:alice.smith@domain.com>; tag=432567
Call-ID: 675438291812354765absdbohak
Cseq: 1 REGISTER
Contact: <sip:alice@pc1.company.com>
Expires: 7200
Content-Length: 0
```

The `200 OK` message is as follows:

```
SIP/2.0 200 OK
Via: SIP/2.0/UDP 152.0.0.1:5060;branch=z9hG4bKna43f; received=152.0.0.1
From: <sip:alice.smith@domain.com>; tag=432567
To: <sip:alice.smith@domain.com>;tag=37GkEhwl6
Call-ID: 675438291812354765absdbohak
Cseq: 1 REGISTER
Contact: <sip:alice@pc1.company.com>
Expires: 7200
Content-Length: 0
```

Now, let us assume that Alice wants to invite Bob. Then, as shown in figure 5.4 her UA sends an `INVITE` message to Bob, which is as follows:

```
INVITE sip:bob@domain.com SIP/2.0
Via: SIP/2.0/UDP 152.0.0.1:5060; branch=z9hG4bK776asdhds
Max-Forwards: 70
To: Bob <sip:bob@domain.com>
From: Alice <sip:alice.smith@domain.com>; tag=1928301774
Call-ID: a84b4c76e66710@pc33.atlanta.com
CSeq: 1 INVITE
Contact: <sip:alice@pc1.company.com>
Content-Type: application/sdp
Content-Length: 142
```

(SDP session description not shown)

We conclude this section, by giving an example of the pager mode of IM, shown in figure 5.7. Other examples of SIP messages can be found in IETF RFC 3665[5]. In the example given below Nick sends an IM to Michael. Nick's URI is `nick@domain.com` and he is registered at `UA1pc.domain.com`. Michael's URI is `michael@domain.com` and he is registered at `UA2pc.domain.com`. The `MESSAGE` that Nick's UA sends to its proxy server `proxy.domain.com` is as follows:

```
MESSAGE sip:michael@domain.com SIP/2.0
Via: SIP/2.0/TCP UA1pc.domain.com; branch=z9hG4bK776sgdkse
Max-Forwards: 70
From: sip:nick@domain.com;tag=49583
To: sip:michael@domain.com
```

```
Call-ID: asd88asd77a@1.2.3.4
CSeq: 1 MESSAGE
Content-Type: text/plain
Content-Length: 18
```

I am coming over.

When the proxy server receives this message it interrogates the registrar and then it forwards it to Michael's UA. The resulting message is as follows:

```
MESSAGE sip:michael@domain.com SIP/2.0
Via: SIP/2.0/TCP proxy.domain.com; branch=z9hG4bK123dsghds
Via: SIP/2.0/TCP UA1pc.domain.com; branch=z9hG4bK776sgdkse;received=1.2.3.4
Max-Forwards: 69
From: sip:nick@domain.com;tag=49394
To: sip:michael@domain.com;
Call-ID: asd88asd77a@1.2.3.4
CSeq: 1 MESSAGE
Content-Type: text/plain
Content-Length: 18
```

I am coming over.

The message received by Michael's UA is displayed, and then the following 200 OK response is generated and sent to the proxy server:

```
SIP/2.0 200 OK
Via: SIP/2.0/TCP proxy.domain.com; branch=z9hG4bK123dsghds;received=192.0.2.1
Via: SIP/2.0/TCP UA1pc.domain.com;
branch=z9hG4bK776sgdkse;received=1.2.3.4
From: sip:nick@domain.com;tag=49394
To: sip:michael@domain.com;tag=ab8asdasd9
Call-ID: asd88asd77a@1.2.3.4
CSeq: 1 MESSAGE
Content-Length: 0
```

Most of the header fields are simply reflected in the response. The proxy server receives this response, strips off the top via, and forwards the following message to the address in the next via UA1pc.domain.com:

```
SIP/2.0 200 OK
Via: SIP/2.0/TCP UA1pc.domain.com;
branch=z9hG4bK776sgdkse;received=1.2.3.4
```

```
From: sip:nick@domain.com;tag=49394
To: sip:michael@domain.com;tag=ab8asdasd9
Call-ID: asd88asd77a@1.2.3.4
CSeq: 1 MESSAGE
Content-Length: 0
```

5.8 LOCATING SIP SERVERS

In figure 5.4, we assumed that both Alice and Bob are attached to the same proxy server. In this case, the SIP messages send to each other are forwarded through the proxy server. In this section we will examine the case where the users are attached to a different proxy server, as shown in figure 5.10. This type of connectivity is known as the *SIP trapezoid*. When UA 1 wishes to communicate with UA 2, it sends an INVITE to its proxy server (proxy 1), which forwards it to the proxy server (proxy 2) of the domain of UA 2, which in turn forwards it to UA 2. Proxy 1 performs a DNS query for the domain in the requested URI specified in the INVITE message, if it does not know the SIP proxy server of UA 2. For instance, if the INVITE is destined for ua2@domain2.com, proxy 1 would do a DNS lookup on the domain2.com to discover the IP address, port, and transport protocol of proxy 2. An example of how the SIP session is set up is shown in figure 5.11.

PROBLEMS

1. What is the difference between a redirect server and a proxy server?

2. Show the SIP request and response messages exchanged in order to set up a media session using the forking operation executed in parallel, whereby user A calls user B which has two different SIP URIs.

3. Show the SIP request and response messages exchanged to set up a media session using a redirect server.

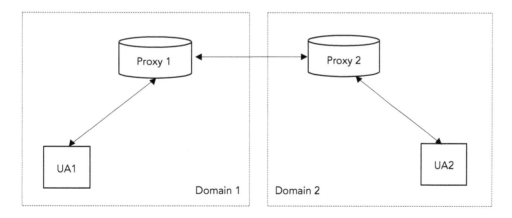

Figure 5.10: The SIP trapezoid

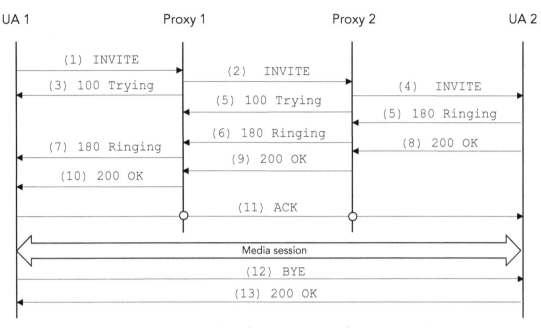

Figure 5.11: An example of SIP session setup for SIP trapezoid

4. Research the various ways the Expire header field is used in SIP.

5. Consider the following code for a REGISTER request .

```
REGISTER sip:domain.com SIP/2.0
Via: SIP/2.0/UDP 152.0.0.1:5060; branch=z9hG4bKna43f
Max-Forwards: 70
To: <sip:alice.smith@domain.com>
From: <sip:alice.smith@domain.com>; tag=432567
Call-ID: 675438291812354765absdbohak
Cseq: 1 REGISTER
Contact: <sip:alice@pc1.company.com>
Expires: 7200
Content-Length: 0
```

    a. What is the address of record for Alice?

    b. What is her contact URI?

    c. What is the IP address of her contact URI?

6. Browse through the Internet to find a free IP telephony service. Read through the instructions provided in their web site to see how you can set up your own SIP-based VoIP between two users. Use Wireshark to create a trace of the SIP messages exchanged in order to set up a VoIP session. Use the trace to better understand the material in this Chapter.

REFERENCES

[1]   IETF RFC 3261, "SIP: Session Initiation Protocol".
[2]   IETF RFC 2778, "A Model for Presence and Instant Messaging".
[3]   IETF RFC 4975, "The Message Session Relay Protocol (MSRP)"
[4]   IETF RFC 2327, "SDP: Session Description Protocol".
[5]   IETF RFC 3665, "Session Initiation Protocol (SIP) Basic Call Flow Examples".

CHAPTER 6: THE IP MULTIMEDIA SUBSYSTEM (IMS)

6.1 INTRODUCTION

The IP Multimedia Subsystem (IMS) was first proposed by 3GPP in release 5 in 2003, see 3GPP[1]. TISPAN and 3GPP2 have also contributed to the standardization of IMS, but this effort has been consolidated within 3GPP. IMS runs within the service stratum of the NGN architecture, shown in figure 6.1, which separates services and control functions from the underlying transport network that carries the data. IMS is independent of the access network, and it can be used for both wired and wireless access networks. It is the signaling protocol used in LTE.

IMS consists of a collection of servers linked by standardized interfaces that permits an operator to offer current and new services. The IMS servers are known as *Functional Elements* (FE) and they reside within the core network. Functional elements can be grouped in one router, or a single functional element can be implemented in more than one router. The signaling between the UEs and the functional elements is done using SIP. (We note that the equipment used by a user is referred to as User Equipment (UE) in IMS and as a User Agent (UA) in SIP.)

IMS can be used by an operator to provide QoS in a multimedia session. As will be seen, IMS can synchronize the establishment of a session with QoS provisioning in the transport network, so that users can have a good QoE.

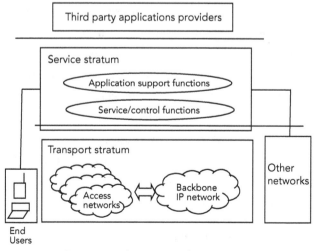

Figure 6.1: The NGN architecture

Through session establishment and QoS provision, an operator can control the access of users to the network and services so that to guarantee QoS. This is in contrast to the familiar Internet model, where the network is transparent, the services such as web services, video-on demand servers, and VoIP servers, are provided by endpoints, and users access them without QoS guarantees. IMS can also be used to charge multimedia sessions appropriately. Typically, operators charge based on the number of bytes transferred. If the operator is aware of the actual type of service that the user is using, the operator can provide different charging schemes that may be more beneficial to the user. For instance, for instant messaging it can charge a flat price per message independent of the number of bytes, and for video conferencing the operator may charge by the duration and not by the number of bytes transferred. IMS does not impose any particular business model. Rather, the operators can charge as they think fit. IMS simply provides information about the service invoked by a user, and with this information an operator can charge using a flat rate for the service, by the number of bytes transferred, by the level of QoS provided, or using some other charging scheme.

Finally, another important feature of IMS is that it enables an operator to provide integrated services. Operators may develop their own services but they also want to use third-party services and combine them with their own services. The aim of IMS is not only to provide new services, but to provide all the current and future services. In addition, users have to be able to access these services from the home networks, as well as, when they are roaming.

The objective of this Chapter is to present the basic IMS architecture. We first describe the basic IMS entities and functionalities, such as, entities for setting up a multimedia session, databases, interworking functions, and support functions. Then, we describe how a user can be identified by various identities, and give examples of the signaling involved in setting up a multimedia session in IMS. Subsequently, we describe how service provision is implemented in IMS, and we conclude the Chapter with a discussion on setting up emergency IMS sessions and SIP compression. Detailed examples of services that run on top of IMS are given in the following two Chapters.

6.2 IMS ENTITIES AND FUNCTIONALITIES

One of the fundamental characteristics of IMS is support for user mobility. In view of this, the distinction between the core and access networks becomes important in partitioning the functions necessary to support IMS. An access network links a user to a core network, and it uses one of the available technologies, such as ADSL, DOCSIS, metro Ethernet, UMTS and E-UTRAN. A core network, also known as a backbone network, is a high capacity network that provides connectivity between access networks and other core networks and also provides various services to users attached to the access networks. An example of such partitioning is shown in figure 6.2. Operator A owns the core network and the access network to which user A is attached. Operator B owns a transit network, i.e., a network that inter-connects core networks, and operator C owns a core network that serves operator's D access network in which currently user B is roaming. In this example, the IMS services reside in the core network of operator A and in the core network of operator C.

IMS also supports the concept of home and visiting networks. A home network is the core network that supports IMS services and to which an IMS user has subscribed. A visiting network is the network currently providing the

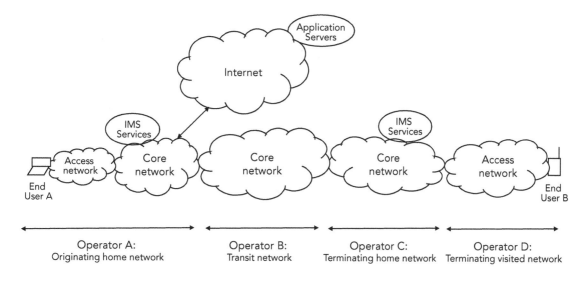

Figure 6.2: An example of access and core networks

user with IMS services. Operator A owns the home network where A's laptop is registered, while operator C owns the home network of the mobile user B who happens to be roaming in operator's D network. In the case that the session is initiated by user A, the core network of operator A is the originating home network, and the core network of operator C is the terminating home network, and the access network of operator D is terminating visited network.

IMS consists of a number of functional entities, which are organized in the following six categories.

- *Session management and routing*
- *Databases*
- *Service functions*
- *Interworking functions*
- *Support functions*
- *Charging*

Figure 6.3 shows some of the IMS entities and how they are distributed between the access and core network. The user equipment (UE) is an IMS terminal, such as, a mobile terminal attached to a packet-switched network via a wireless connection, and a computer attached via DSL. A subset of these servers, as indicated in figure 6.3, is referred to as the *IMS core*. We now proceed to describe the IMS entities in each category.

6.2.1 SESSION MANAGEMENT AND ROUTING

The following four entities, known as *Call Session Control Functions* (CSCF), have been defined for session management control and SIP routing: *Proxy CSCF* (P-CSCF), *Serving CSCF* (S-CSCF), *Interrogating CSCF* (I-CSCF), and *Emergency CSCF* (E-CSCF). These CSCF entities can be seen as the equivalent of the SIP proxy server in SIP described in the previous Chapter. They make up the core of IMS, and they are used for registration of users, session establishment, routing of SIP messages, and sending charge data for offline charging. They are located in each home network.

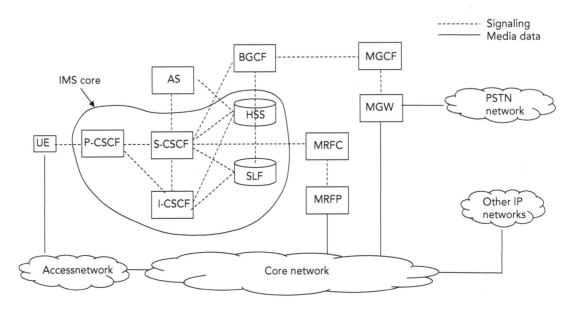

Figure 6.3: The IMS entities

The proxy CSCF (P-CSCF) is the first contact point of a UE with IMS. It acts as a proxy server for the UE and it forwards all the signaling messages between a UE and IMS. In addition, a P-CSCF performs other functions, such as, security associations with the UE for integrity protection. Verification of the correctness of signaling messages originating from a UE, and, compression and decompression of the signaling messages in order to save network bandwidth. A UE is allocated to a P-CSCF when it registers with IMS. If the UE is in its home network, then it is allocated to the P-CSCF of its home network. If it is roaming, then it is allocated to the P-CSCF of the visited network.

The serving CSCF (S-CSCF) is the focal point of IMS as it is responsible for handling registration processes, making routing decisions, maintaining session states, and service provision. Within an operator's network, different S-CSCFs may have different functionalities. In order for a user to initiate and receive an IMS service, the user has to first register with IMS. This is handled by the S-CSCSF which authenticates the user and supervises the registration process. In addition, the S-CSCF uses the user's service profile, which it downloads from the *Home Subscriber Server* (HSS) at registration time, to decide the services that the user is allowed to access. Also, the S-CSCF receives all requests originated by UEs within its home network and requests originated by UEs outside the home network for UEs within its home network, and routes them appropriately. The S-CSCF is also responsible for applying network policy rules, and it interfaces with application servers.

The interrogating CSCF (I-CSCF) is used for frowarding an intial SIP request to the S-CSCF, when the intiator does not know which S-CSCF should receive the request. For instance, a roaming UE sends its SIP registration request to its assigned P-CSCF in the visiting network, which has to be forwarded to the S-CSCF of the UE's home network. In the case that the P-CSCF does not know the S-CSCF, it forwards it to the I-CSCF of the UE's home network, which it identifies by a DNS query. Subsequently, the I-CSCF interrogates HSS, a subscribers' data base, to determine the S-CSCF assigned to the roaming user. If no S-CSCF has been assigned to the user, it allocates an S-CSCF. For scalability purposes, there may be multiple I- CSCFs within an operator's network.

The emergency CSCF (E-CSCF), not shown in figure 6.3, is dedicated to handling IMS emergency requests for police, fire station, and ambulance. The main task of E-CSCF is to select an emergency center also known as a *Public Safety Answering Point* (PSAP) where the emergency request should be delivered. Typically the selection criteria are the calling user's location and possible the type of emergency. Once the appropriate emergency center is selected, the request is forwarded to it by the E-CSCF.

6.2.2 DATABASES
There are two main databases in the IMS architecture, namely, the Home Subscriber Server (HSS) and the *Subscription Locator Function* (SLF). The HSS is the main data storage for all IMS subscribers. It contains user-related information, such as, user identities, security information, location information, roaming authorization, information about allowable services, and the S-CSCF allocated to the user. In addition, the HSS contains the *Home Location Register* (HLR), which stores details of all the SIM card issued by a mobile phone operator and the *Authentication Center* (AUC), that authenticates each SIM card that attempts to connect to the network. The HSS may consist of multiple distributed HSSs. The SLF serves as a front-end for these multiple HSSs. It may be queried by an I-CSCF during registration and session setup to get the name of the HSS containing the required subscriber-specific data. It may be also be queried by an S-CSCF during registration, and by application servers.

6.2.3 SERVICE FUNCTIONS
Service functions include application servers, the *Multimedia Resource Function Processor* (MRFC), and the *Media Resource Function Controller* (MRFP).

An *Application Server* (AS) provides a particular service, such as presence, online charging, instant messaging, IPTV, and multi-party teleconference. Application servers run on top of IMS and they are not considered to be part of the core IMS functions. The main functions of an application server are: a) processing of incoming SIP sessions requests received from IMS, b) originating SIP requests, and c) sending accounting information to a charging function. An application server may be owned by an operator, in which case it resides in the operator's home network, or it may be owned by another operator residing in that operator's network, or it may be stand alone. An application server may be dedicated to one service and a user may access one or more application servers during a sessions. Below, we give an overview of the various types of application servers accessible through IMS. Detailed examples of some of the most popular services are given in the following two Chapters.

As shown in figure 6.4, there are three different groups of application servers that are supported by IMS and they can be accessed through an S-CSCF, namely, SIP-based application servers, *Customized Applications for Mobile Network Enhanced Logic* (CAMEL) application servers, and *Parlay/Open Service Architecture* (OSA) application servers. All three groups interact with the S-CSCF through the *IMS Service Control* (ISC) interface defined by IMS.

SIP-based application servers use SIP and they are typically developed in Java, using various tools, such as SIP servlets and *Java Application Programming Interfaces* (JAIN) *Service Logic Execution Environment* (SLEE). SIP servlets were developed in order to standardize and speed up the development of services in SIP networks. They comprise

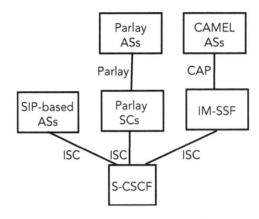

Figure 6.4: The three types of application servers

of two key features, namely, the SIP servlet container and the SIP servlet. The SIP servlet container is an application server with a built-in SIP stack that listens for incoming SIP messages. When an incoming message arrives, it triggers one or more servlets and other resources that will deal with the requested service. JAIN is a technology initiative founded by Sun Microsystems in 1998, with the goal to bring IP communication interfaces into a set of industry standards based on Java technology. A set of Java APIs were developed which can be divided into Java application interfaces and Java application containers. Application interfaces provide a mapping of telecommunication protocols to Java programming language, and application containers provide an execution environment for telecommunication services. JAIN SLEE is a standard that defines a container that provides a runtime environment for telecommunication services. It has a high performing event driven application server, an execution environment with a good concurrency model, and powerful protocol agnostic capabilities that can cover a variety of telecommunications protocols. JAIN SLEE is a specification that is a lot more complex than SIP servlets, which is more of a programming framework. SIP-based application servers are a newer development compared to the legacy CAMEL and Parlay/OSA applications.

CAMEL is a set of standards designed to work with mobile phones that allow an operator to define services over and above the standard mobile phone services. CAMEL uses the *Intelligent Network* (IN) architecture, introduced in the early 90s in order to enhance the basic telephone services offered at that time with services such as, call waiting, call screening, call portability, toll free calls, and prepaid calling. The IN architecture employs the SS7 signaling protocol used in the public telephone network to set up calls. A large number of services are supported in CAMEL, such as, call screening, call forwarding, call redirection, tones and announcements, and various charging schemes (prepaid, reverse charging, free phone, premium rate, location dependent discounts, etc.). CAMEL is particularly effective as it allows such services to be offered when a subscriber is roaming. CAMEL services are accessible from an S-CSCF through the *IP Multimedia Service Switching Function* (IM-SSF), which interacts with an S-CSCF using the ISC interface and with CAMEL using the *CAMEL Service Environment* (CAP) interface.

The Parlay/OSA suite of specifications for application servers was developed initially independently by Parlay and OSA. The Parlay group was founded in 1998 and has its origins in earlier standardization activities such as TINA-

C. The goal of the Parlay group was to specify open network APIs that would bridge capabilities from the IT domain with those of the telecommunications domain. The Parlay group started originally as a closed group consisting of five companies, but a year later it became an open group. Roughly at the same time 3GPP created the OSA group charged to define open network APIs for wireless networks. Also, in parallel, ETSI had started its own open API activities for wireline networks. In 2001, the ETSI group and the Parlay group formalized their cooperation, and eventually the three groups were consolidated in a joint working group which was responsible for the development and maintenance of the API specifications for Parlay and OSA. For all practical purposes, the Parlay and OSA specifications are identical, and from now on we shall only refer to them as the Parlay specifications.

The Parlay specifications are defined in UML, and the actual specifications are generated automatically using software tools. Three different realizations were developed from the UML specifications based on different technologies, namely, the *Common Object Request Broker* (CORBA) realization, the Java realization, and the *Web Service Definition Language* (WSDL) realization. Parlay CORBA was based on CORBA which is a heavyweight object-oriented middleware developed for client-server based communication systems. Parlay Java was developed in support of the *Java2 Enterprise Edition* (J2EE) and *Java2 Standards Edition* (J2SE), and Parlay WSDL was developed for XML-based technologies and web service deployments. Parlay WSDL was further evolved into Parlay X, which more recently has been consolidated with the OneAPI alliance.

The goal of Parlay is to provide a means for users to gain access to services available in telecommunications networks. For this, a number of interfaces have been defined, each supporting a different service. Such an interface is known as a *Service Capability Server* (SCS). As shown in figure 6.4, an SCS interacts with an S-CSCF through the ISC interface, and accesses Parlay services through Parlay APIs.

The *Multimedia Resource Function Processor* (MRFC) and the *Media Resource Function Controller* (MRFP) together provide the home network with the ability to do conferencing, play announcements, mix media streams, transcode between different codecs, obtain statistics and do any sort of media analysis. The MRFC handles SIP communications to and from the S-CSCF and controls the MRFP, which performs functions on the data plane, such as, mixing of incoming media streams for multiple parties, multimedia announcements, and media stream processing.

6.2.4 INTERWORKING FUNCTIONS

These functions are used to enable voice and video internetworking between IMS and the public telephone network.

During the establishment of a call between IMS and the public telephone network, a decision has to be made as to where to break to the circuit-switched public telephone network. For instance, to minimize costs the selection maybe done so that the call breaks into the public network as close as possible to the called party. For this, the S-CSCF sends a SIP request to the *Breakout Gateway Control Function* (BGCF) which selects the IP network where the breakout to the public telephone system will occur and also where the breakout will occur within the IP network. This could be in the same network in which the BGCF is located or in another network. If the breakout happens in the same network, then the BGCF selects the *Media Gateway Control Function* (MGCF) associated with the same network, see figure 6.3, to handle the session. If it happens in another network, then the BGCF forwards the session to the BGCF of the selected network.

The MGCF supports interworking between the IMS and the public telephone network. All incoming call control signals from a public telephone network user to an IMS user are routed to the MGCF that performs the necessary protocol conversion between SIP and ISUP of SS7, and forwards SIP requests to the appropriate server. In addition, it controls the *Media Gateway* (MGW) for conversion of the multimedia data and resource reservation in the data plane. The MGW supports interworking between the IMS and the public telephone network. It terminates the call connections from the circuit-switched network and also the media streams from the backbone network, such as, RTP streams in an IP network, and ATM connections in an ATM network, converts the media data between the two transmission technologies, i.e., packet-switched and circuit-switched, and performs transcoding and signal processing in the user plane when needed. In addition, the IMS-MGW is able to provide tones and announcements to circuit-switched users.

6.2.5 SUPPORT FUNCTIONS

The following four functions are classified as support functions: *Policy and Charging Rules Function* (PCRF), the *Interconnection Border Control Function* (IBCF), the *Security Gateway* (SEG), and the *Location Retrieval Information* (LRF).

A policy and charging rules function (PCRF) is responsible for making policy and charging rules in real-time based on subscriber activity, the requested session, network usage, and parameters such as location and time of the day. If an operator applies policy and charging rules, then during the session establishment phase of a call the P-CSCF forwards the relevant SDP information to the PCRF together with an indication of the originator. The PCRF decides whether to authorize or deny the requested session, generates charging rules, maps SDP parameters to QoS parameters and allocates bandwidth on the access link between the mobile phone and the its base. (Bandwidth allocation for a session inside a WAN is discussed in Chapter 12.) In addition, the PCRF monitors triggers. For instance, it receives reports on events, such as, user is lost and user is released, and informs the P-CSCF so that it can effect appropriate charges and release the session.

An interconnection border control function (IBCF) is used to perform interconnections between two operator domains. It enables communication between IPv6 and IPv4 IMS entities, hides network topology by removing headers that reveal the internal topology, controls transport plane functions, screens SIP signaling information, selects the appropriate signaling interconnect, and generates charging data records. The IBCF modifies SIP and SDP information in such a way so that UEs using different IP versions (IPv6 and IPv4) can communicate. It also controls the *Transition Gateway* (TrGW) which is responsible for providing interworking between IPv6 and IPv4 in the transport plane. Network topology hiding is used to hide the configuration, capacity, and topology of a network from other operators. In order to do that, an operator must place an IBCF in the routing path of the requests and responses from other IMS networks. A possible deployment of IBCF is shown in figure 6.5.

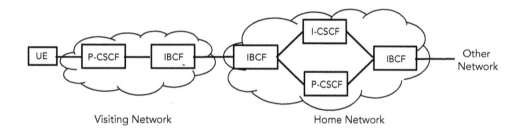

Figure 6.5: Deployment of IBCF

The security gateway (SEG) protects control-plane traffic between security domains. A security domain is a network that is managed by a single administrative authority, and it typically coincides with the boundaries of an operator's network. The SEG is placed at the border of a security domain and it enforces security policies towards other SEGs in other security domains. All inter-domain IMS traffic is routed through SEGs.

Finally, the location retrieval function (LRF) assists an emergency-CSCF (E-CSCF) to handle IMS emergency sessions by delivering location information of the UE that has initiated an IMS emergency and/or the address of the public safety answering point (PSAP) where the session should be sent. To provide location information the LRF may contain a location server or it may interface to an external location server. An LRF may provide other emergency session parameters according to local regulations.

6.2.6 CHARGING

Charging for the use of a service maybe done *offline* or *online*. Offline charging is applied to users who have a subscription and pay for their services periodically, e.g., once a month. Online charging is used for pre-paid services, such as, pre-paid calling cards and credit-based charging.

In offline charging, IMS entities, such as, P-CSCF, I-CSCF, S-CSCF, BGCF, MRFC, MGCF, and application servers, that are involved in a session, send accounting information to a *Charging Data Function* (CDF) located in the same domain. The CDF collects all the information, and builds a *Call Detail Record* (CDR), which is sent to the *Charging Gateway Function* (CGF). This gateway is needed as there may be multiple CDFs involved in a single session, since various IMS entities and application servers may send charging information to different CDFs. CGF consolidates all the charging information and passes the information to the billing system of the domain.

In online charging, only the S-CSCF, the MRFC and application servers are involved, and credit control is performed before using an IMS service. For online charging, an IMS entity needs to consult the *Online Charging System* (OCS) before allowing a user to access a service. The OCS is responsible for interacting in real time with the user's account and for controlling or monitoring the charges related to service usage. There are two different charging schemes, *Immediate Event Charging* (IEC), and *Event Charging with Unit Reservation* (ECUR). In immediate event charging, a number of credit units is immediately deducted from the user's account and the service is authorized. The service is declined when not enough credits are available. In event charging with unit reservation, a number of credit units in the user's account is first reserved before the service is authorized. After the service is over, the number of spent credit units is reported and deducted from the account. It is also possible that the OCS may receive subsequent requests from an IMS entity during the service if all granted resources have been consumed. In this case the OCS has to perform a new credit authorization. The immediate event charging scheme is appropriate when an IMS entity knows that it can deliver the requested service and the exact cost of the service. The event charging with unit reservation scheme is suitable when an IMS entity does not know beforehand if the requested service can be delivered, and/or the required number of resources for delivering the service, e.g., the duration of a multimedia session.

6.2.7 REFERENCE POINTS

We note that the IMS specifications do not describe in detail the internal functionality of the various IMS entities. Instead, the specifications provide a number of standardized interfaces, known as *reference points*, which dictate how these entities can exchange messages. The following is a partial list of reference points:

- *Gm reference point:* It is used between a UE and a P-CSCF to transport all SIP messages between a UE and a P-CSCF.
- *Mw reference point:* It is SIP based and it is used between CSCFs, i.e., P-CSCF, S-CSCF, and I-CSCF.
- *Cx:* It is used between the I-CSCF and HSS and the S-CSCF and HSS. The protocol used is DIAMETER.
- *IMS Service Control (ISC) reference point:* This is used for the exchange of SIP messages between an S-CSCF and a SIP-based application server.

For a detailed description of these interfaces see Poikselkä and G. Mayer[2].

6.3 USER IDENTIFICATION

An IMS user can be identified by various identities, such as, the *IP Multimedia Public Identity* (IMPU), the *IP Multimedia Private Identity* (IMPI), the *Globally Routable User Agent URI* (GRUU), and the *Wildcard Public User Identity*. Below, we describe these identities.

The public identity IMPU is used by a user to request communication with another user, and it can be published in phone books, web pages, and business cards. A public identity can be shared with multiple phones, so that all phones can be reached with the same identity (for example, a single phone-number for an entire family). An IMS user can initate sessions and receive sessions from both the public telephone network and the Internet. In order to be reachable form the public telephone network, the user's identity has to be in the form of a telephone number. Likewise, the public user identity of an Internet user must be in the form of user@company.com. In view of this, the public user identity is either a SIP URI or a telephone URL. The telephone URI scheme is used to express traditional E.164 numbers. Examples:

```
sip:captain.bligh@ocean.com
tel:+30 210 5550000
```

The private identity IMPI is a unique permanently allocated global identity assigned by the home network operator, used to identify the user's subscription. It is not used to identify the user himself. Therefore, it is used mainly for authentication purposes, and it can be used for administration and accounting purposes. The private identity is in the form: `private _ user@home.operator.com`.

A user may have multiple public addresses. For instance, John Smith may have the following two public identities for work: `sip:john.smith@company.com` and `tel:+1 919 5550000`. In addition, he may have the following two public identities for his personal use: `sip:john.smith@operator.com` and `tel:+1 919 1230000`. These two sets of addresses may be associated with a single subscription identified by a single private

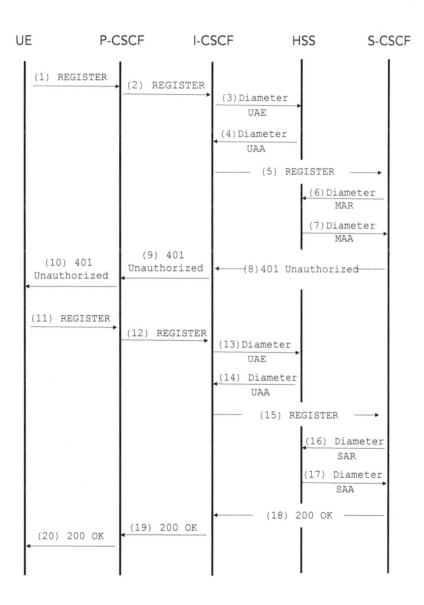

Figure 6.6: Registration of a roaming UE

identity address. The two sets of public addresses may have different treatment for incoming sessions. For instance, all incoming work-related sessions may be directed to a messaging system after 5 pm and during weekends and holidays. The two sets of addresses are maintained in two different *service profiles*, service profile 1 for his work addresses, and service profile 2 for his private addresses. The appropriate service profile is downloaded to the S-CSCF when John registers. For instance, if he registers with the work public address then service profile 1 is downloaded. Service profiles are described below in section 6.5.

The globally routable identity GRUU uses a unique combination of the user's public identity and the user's UE, and it is used to reach a particular device. There are two types of GRUU: *Public-GRUU* (P-GRUU) and *Temporary GRUU* (T-GRUU). The P-GRUU reveals the public identity and are very long lived, and the T-GRUU does not reveal the public identity and it is valid until the contact is explicitly unregistered or the current registration expires. Finally, a wildcard public user identity expresses a set of IMPUs grouped together.

6.4 SETTING UP A SESSION IN IMS

A UE has to first gain access to an access network before it can use an IMS operator. An access network is referred to as the *IP Connectivity Access Network* (IP-CAN). Examples of IP-CANs are: GPRS in GSM/UMTS networks, ADSL, and WiFi. The UE acquires an IP address, which is typically dynamically allocated by the IP-CAN operator. Subsequently, the UE has to discover the IP address of the P-CSCF that acts as the outbound/inbound SIP proxy server. All the SIP signals sent by the UE go through the P-CSCF. The P-CSCF discovery is done either through the procedure used to gain access to the IP-CAN or through DHCP. Once the P-CSCF has been discovered, the UE registers with IMS and then it can send and receive SIP messages. Registration to IMS is independent from the registration to the IP-CAN. Registration to IMS allows the IMS network to authenticate the user, establish security associations, and authorize the establishment of services.

The registration with IMS of a roaming UE is shown in figure 6.6. The UE creates a SIP REGISTER message to request the registration of a public identity of the user, and sends it to the P-CSCF of the visited network within which it is roaming. Now, in order to carry out the registration request the P-CSCF has to contact the S-CSCF of the home network of the UE. By executing a DNS procedure it obtains the SIP URI of the I-CSCF of the home network of the UE. As mentioned above in section 6.2.1, this is the entry point to an operator's IMS. The I-CSCF does not know which S-CSCF the calling UE is associated with, and sends a *Diameter User Authentication Request* (UAR) to HSS to obtain the adress of the S-CSCF. The registration request is then forwarded from the I-CSCF to the selected S-CSCF. The S-CSCF realizes that the user is not authorized, and it contacts the HSS in order to download authentication data with which it challenges the user. IMS authentication is based on a shared secret and a sequence number, which is only available in the HSS and in the *Universal Integrated Circuit Card* (UICC) of the UE. (A UICC is a smart card used in mobile terminals to ensure the integrity and security of all kinds of personal data. It is also used as storage for other applications.) The S-CSCF creates a SIP 401 Unauthorized response which includes a challenge that the UE should respond. This response is forwarded to the UE via the I-CSCF and the P-CSCF. The UE calculates a response to the challenge (sometimes known as *credentials*) and includes it in a new registration request. The sequence of messages is the same as with the first registration message. For load-balancing reasons, another I-CSCF may be used. If authentication of the credentials is successful, the S-CSCF downloads the user's profile from HSS, and it responds to the user with a `200 OK`. At this moment, the UE has registered and it can issue a request for service, such as, set up a call, and access a server.

It is the UE's responsibility to keep its registration active by refreshing periodically its registration. If the UE does not refresh its registration, then the S-CSCF removes the registration silently when the registration timer lapses. When the UE wants to unregister from the IMS it sets a registration timer to 0 and sends a `REGISTER` request.

SIP allows one public user identity to be registered at a time. Since, in IMS a user may have more than one public identity, IMS allows more than one public identity to be registered at a time through *implicit registration*. We recall from the example in section 6.3 that John Smith has the following two public identities for work:

```
sip:john.smith@company.com
tel:+1 919 5550000.
```

These two identities are maintained in the same service profile. With implicit registration, when John registers under one of these two public identities, he is automatically registered under the second one. Similarly, when one of the public user identities within the set is unregistered, all public user identities that have been implicitly registered are unregistered at the same time.

We now proceed to describe the sequence of messages involved in a basic session setup. The messages and the functional elements involved are shown in figure 6.7. We assume that the two UEs have already registered, and they are both roaming in two different visiting networks. UE 1 sends an `INVITE` request to the P-CSCF of the visited network. The P-CSCF carries out a number of operations including an inspection of the SDP offer and a check whether the requested media parameters are allowed in the network. It also adds itself in the signaling path by inserting a `Record Route` header field that contains its SIP URI. In this way all the SIP messages will go through the P-CSCF. It then sends the `INVITE` to the next hop indicated in the `Route` header, which is the S-CSCF of the home network of UE 1 that was allocated to it at registration. The S-CSCF does not know where is the called UE 2 currently. However, through the `Request-URI` it learns its SIP URI, and subsequently through DNS queries it finds the I-CSCF of the home network of UE 2. It adds itself on the signaling path and then forwards the `INVITE` request to the I-CSCF. The subsequent sequence of messages for forwarding the `INVITE` request to the S-CSCF associated with the called user is the same as the registration sequence described above. Since UE 2 has already registered, its associated S-CSCF in the home network knows the URI of the serving P-CSCF in the terminating visited network. For simplicity we assumed that the request does not have to traverse any other proxy servers, such as an I-CSCF, and it goes straight to the P-CSCF of the terminating visited network, which delivers the message to the called user. In response, a `183 Session Progress` message is issued towards the calling user. This message contains an indication whether the called UE accepted the establishment of the session with the proposed media parameters. At at that, IMS starts a resource reservation, and a `PRACK` message is issued by the calling UE 1 and sent back to the called UE 2. (This resource reservation is only in the access network, and

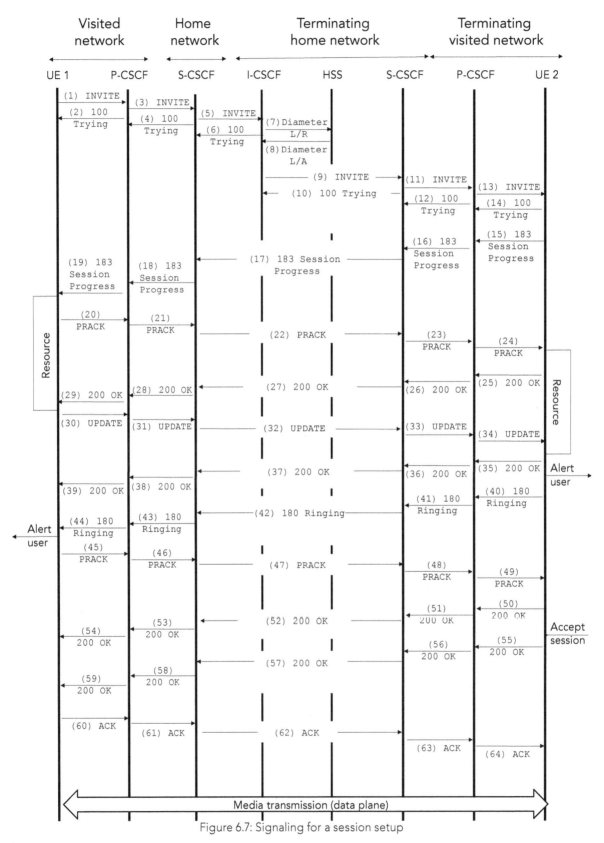

Figure 6.7: Signaling for a session setup

in particular for 2G/3G and LTE interfaces, and not in the wide area network(s) connecting the two UEs, which is the topic of Chapter 12.) When the PRACK is received, IMS starts a resource reservation within the access network of the called user, and UE 2 responds with a 200 OK. UE 1 sends an UPDATE message to UE 2, when its resource reservation is completed, upon receipt of which UE 2 generates a 200 OK. When IMS completes its resource reservation, UE 2 alerts its user and it also generates a 180 Ringing message. When UE 1 receives the 180 Ringing message, it generates a locally stored ring-back tone to indicate that UE 2 is ringing. Since the 180 Ringing message needs a response, a PRACK message is sent back to the called terminal, which responds with a 200 OK message. When the called user accepts the session, its terminal issues a 200 OK, to which UE 1 sends an ACK. This completes the INVITE session, and the media traffic begins to flow directly between UE 1 and UE 2, without the intervention of any of the IMS functional elements.

In the remaining of this section, we examine the interworking of IMS with the public telephone system. As described in section 6.2.1, IMS interworks with the circuit-switched public telephone system through the breakout gateway control function (BGCF), the media gateway control function (MGCF) and the media gateway (MGW). We recall, that there are two main issues related to setting up a call between an Internet user and a subscriber of a telephone network. The first issue is that the signaling protocols in the two networks are different, namely, SIP and SS7. The typical solution to this problem is to use a gateway whose task is to convert the signals from one protocol to the other. This is done using the MGCF, which converts SS7 signals to SIP and vice versa. The second issue has to do with the fact that the transmission of data is different in the two networks. Packet switching is used in the Internet, and SONET/SDH is used in the public telephone network. Again, this is solved using a gateway, such as the MGW, which extracts the data from SONET/SDH and forwards it in the form of IP packets, and vice versa. The MGCF operates in the control plane and the MGW in the data plane.

When a call terminates in the public telephone network, the BGCF receives a request from an S-CSCF and based on an analysis of the destination address and on agreements the operator may have for calls terminating in the public telephone network, it decides whether the call will break in the same network or in another network. If it breaks in the same network, the BGCF relays the request to one of the MGCFs in its network. Otherwise, the BGCF forwards the request to a BGCF in the selected network. Calls originating in the public telephone network and terminating in an IMS-controlled network, do not go through a BGCF because the selection of the MGCF is done by the telephone network. The session setup assuming that the call breaks in the same network where it is originated, is shown in figure 6.8. The MGCF sends and receives SS7 signals, which are not shown in the figure.

6.5 SERVICE PROVISION

As we have seen in section 6.2, a variety of application servers can be accessed from an S-CSCF. This functionality of enabling services on top of IMS is called *service provision*. The access to an application server is triggered when the S-CSCF receives a SIP request from a user. In order to serve the request, the S-CSCF needs a certain amount of information that would permit it to access the appropriate application server. This information is a collection of user-related data and it is known as *initial filter criteria*. An S-CSCF uses a user's initial filter criteria when it

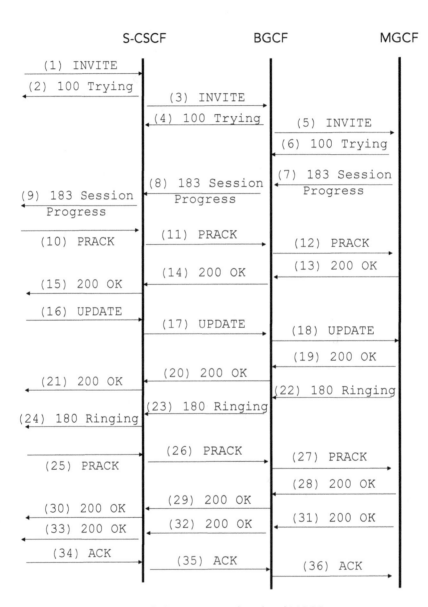

Figure 6.8: Session setup by a local MGCF

first receives a SIP request, such as, SUBSCRIBE, INVITE, and OPTIONS, that either start a dialog or is sent outside a dialog. The initial filter criteria, often referred by the initials IFC, are not used by an S-CSCF when it receives a SIP request such as, PRACK, NOTIFY, UPDATE and BYE, since they are already part of a dialog. A user's initial filter criteria are stored in the HSS in the *user profile*, which is downloaded by the S-CSCF when the user registers with IMS.

The user profile is a collection of user specific information. It contains the user's private identity to which the user's profile is applicable and one or more service profiles, as shown in figure 6.9. We recall from section 6.3, that a user's private identity can be associated with one or more public identities which are grouped in one or more service profiles. Each service profile contains one or more public user identity, a core network service authorization, and one or more initial filter criteria. The core network service authorization identifies the media services that have been authorized for use by the given public address.

An initial filter criteria is associated with a single application server, and it consists of a priority field, a trigger point, and information about the application server. The priority field is used to determine the order in which the initial filter criteria will be executed. (The lower the priority number, the higher the priority.) After the priority field there

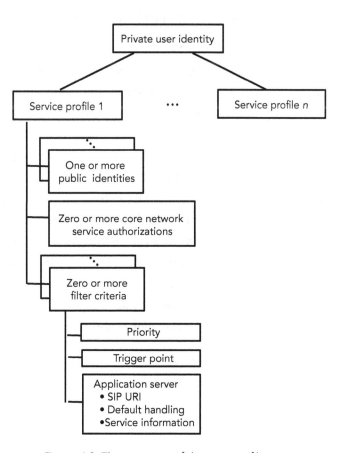

Figure 6.9: The structure of the user profile

is zero or one trigger point, which is an expression that has to be evaluated in order to determine whether a SIP request will be forwarded to the application server associated with the filter. A trigger point is made up of a collection of *Service Point Trigger* (SPT) statements. The following items can be used as service trigger points:

- *Request-URI:* It identifies a resource that the request is addressed to.
- *SIP Method:* It indicates the type of request (e.g., `INVITE` or `MESSAGE`).
- *SIP Header:* It contains information related to the request. A service point trigger could be based on the presence or absence of any SIP header or the content of any SIP header. The value of the content is a string that is interpreted as a regular expression.
- *Session Case:* It can be any one of four possible values, *originating, terminating, originating unregistered* or *terminating unregistered.* An originating case refers to when the S-CSCF is serving a calling user, and a terminating case refers to when the S-CSCF is serving the called user. The originating/terminating unregistered cases refer to originating/terminating unregistered end users.
- *Session Description:* It defines a service point trigger for the content of any SDP field within the body of a SIP Method. Regular expressions can be used to match the trigger.

For instance, the method `INVITE` in the SIP request and the `Request-URI` `sip:user@operator.com` can be used as two service trigger points to make a trigger point for accessing an application server.

The user profile is coded in XML. The following is an example of a filter criterion that routes an incoming session to `sip:vmail@ims.example.com`, a voice mail server, when the user is not registered. The SIP method is set to match `INVITE` and the session case is set to match the value of terminating unregistered (value 2). If the voice mail server cannot be contacted, then the session is terminated (value 1). The class `TriggerPoint` describes the trigger points that should be checked in order to find out if the indicated application server should be contacted or not. The absence of a `TriggerPoint` instance indicates an unconditional triggering of an application server. The attribute `ConditionTypeCNF` defines how the set of SPTs is expressed, i.e., either an ORed set of ANDed sets of SPT statements, or an ANDed set of ORed sets of SPT statements. These combinations of SPTs are termed *Disjunctive Normal Form* (DNF) and *Conjunctive Normal Form* (CNF), respectively. `ConditionTypeCNF` is a boolean that is TRUE when the `TriggerPoint` is a CNF Boolean expression, and FALSE when it is a DNF Boolean expression. The attribute `ConditionNegated` defines whether the individual SPT instance is negated. Individual SPT statements can also be negated. The attribute Group identifies the grouping of SPTs that make up the sub-expressions inside a CNF or a DNF expression. At least one group must be assigned for each SPT. In the example they all belong to group 0. For a detailed explanation of the coding rules of initial filter criteria see 3GGP [3].

```
<?xml version="1.0" encoding="UTF-8"?>
  <testDatatype xmlns:xsi="http://www.w3.org/2001/XMLSchema-instance"
  <IMSSubscription>
  <PrivateID>privatexzyjoe@ims.example.com </PrivateID>
  <ServiceProfile>
```

```
        <PublicIdentity>
                <Identity>sip:joe.doe@ims.example.com</Identity>
        </PublicIdentity>
        <PublicIdentity>
    <Identity>tel:+358503334444</Identity>
</PublicIdentity>
        <InitialFilterCriteria>
                <Priority>0</Priority>
                <TriggerPoint>
                        <ConditionTypeCNF>0</ConditionTypeCNF>
                        <SPT>
                        <ConditionNegated>0</ConditionNegated>
                        <Group>0</Group>
                        <Method>INVITE</Method>
                        </SPT>
                        <SPT>
                                <ConditionNegated>0</ConditionNegated>
                                <Group>0</Group>
                                <SessionCase>2</SessionCase>
                        </SPT>
                </TriggerPoint>
                <ApplicationServer>
                        <ServerName>sip:vmail@ims.example.com
                        </ServerName>
                        <DefaultHandling>1</DefaultHandling>
                </ApplicationServer>
        </InitialFilterCriteria>
    </ServiceProfile>
</IMSSubscription>
</testDatatype>
```

The initial filter criteria of a user are generated and stored in the HSS at the subscription time of the user to an application server. In view of this, several initial filter criteria are needed, one per application server, if the user wants to access multiple servers. Also, it is not possible to invoke an individual service or a group of services within an application server, if the server is set up to host multiple services. For this to happen, significant additional logic has to be incorporated within an application server so that it can infer which service or group of services is invoked. An alternative solution is to deploy multiple application servers, each hosting a specific combination of services likely to be invoked by a user.

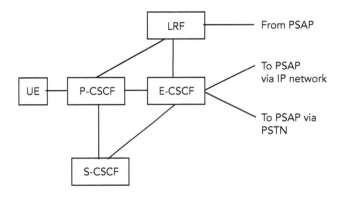

Figure 6.10: The IMS emergency call architecture

As we saw in Part 1 of this book, a service maybe composed of smaller services executed according a pre-described order, often referred to as a workflow. The initial filter criteria is a good solution when the execution of a service request involves the invocation of a single application server, but it provides a rudimentary mechanism for service composition, i.e., execution of several services according to a workflow. In view of this, the *Service Capability Interaction Manager* (SCIM) was defined by 3GPP in order to allow for more complex service coordination. SCIM enables a second level of coordinaton above the one offered by the S-CSCF, but the disadvantage is that it the execution time of a service may increase since all signaling has to go through it. In addition, its capacity has to be carefully calculated so that it does not become a bottleneck. A better solution is to set up the service execution so that service requests that do not need composition can be invoked directly through the S-CSCF. The same application servers accessed through the S-CSCF should also be integrated seamlessly in service compositions orchestrated by the SCIM.

Finally, as we saw above, a requested service is identified by the S-CSCF by examining the content of the SIP message. However, this may not be always possible, and in view of this, 3GPP has standardised a service identification scheme, referred to as the *IMS Communication Service Identification* (ICSI).

6.6 SETTING UP AN EMERGENCY IMS SESSION

The emergency service is provided by the network that a UE is currently visiting. That is, if the UE is not roaming, then the emergency service is provided by its home network. On the other hand, if it is roaming then the service is provided by the visited network.

The main components of the IMS emergency call architecture are shown in figure 6.10. When the UE detects an emergency request from a user, it initiates an emergency session request by sending an INVITE message to the P-CSCF with the Request-URI set to the emergency URI . (Prior to sending the INVITE message, the UE has to go through an emergency registration which follows the ordinary IMS registration procedure described in section 6.4 with some additions. It does not have to initiate an emergency registration if it is in its home network and has already registered with IMS.) The P-CSCF forwards the emergency session request to an emergency CSCF (E-CSCF) in the same network. As described in section 6.2, the E-CSCF is dedicated to handling IMS emergency requests for police, fire station, and ambulance. The main task of E-CSCF is to select an emergency center also known as the public safety answering point (PSAP) where the emergency request should be delivered. Typically the selection criteria are the calling user's location and the type of emergency. Once the appropriate emergency center is selected, the request is forwarded to it by the E-CSCF. The PSAP may be accessible either via the IP network or via PSTN. In the latter case, as described in section 6.2, a breakout gateway control function (BGCF) has to be selected, and interworking between the IMS and the public telephone network is carried out by the media gateway control function (MGCF) and the media gateway (MGW). The location retrieval function (LRF), as mentioned in section 6.2, handles the retrieval of location information for the UE. The LRF may interact with a separate location server or contain an integrated location server in order to obtain location information. Also, it may interact with a separate *Routing Determination Function* (RDF) or contain an integrated RDF. This is an entity which provides the proper PSAP destination address to which the emergency request should be routed.

An example of the flow of messages for setting up an emergency session is shown in figure 6.11. The UE sends an `INVITE` message with a requested emergency URI to the P-CSCF (step 1). The `INVITE` message contains location information about the UE that the UE may have. In case the UE is not able to provide any location information, the P-CSCF determines the UE's location from the LRF (steps 2 and 3). The LRF may already have the requested information, or it may request it. The means to obtaining the location information may differ depending on the access technology the UE is using to access the IMS. The `INVITE` message is forwarded to the E-CSCF (step 4), which is responsible for forwarding the request to the most appropriate PSAP. The selection of the PSAP is done based on the location of the UE and the type of the emergency, and the E-CSCF may inquire the LRF in order to obtain the correct routing address of the PSAP. Subsequently, the E-CSCF forwards the INVITE message directly to the PSAP if it is located in the IP network, or to the MGCF/MGW if it is located in the PSTN. (The specific interactions between the MGCF/MGW and PSAP are not shown.) The setup of the session is completed when the UE receives the `200 OK` message, and at that moment the media traffic begins to flow directly between the UE and the PSAP, without the intervention of any of the IMS functional elements.

6.7 SIP COMPRESSION

As we have seen in section 6.4, setting up a SIP session is a tedious process involving a large number of messages. These messages have not been optimized in terms of size, and therefore a large number of bytes are transmitted. A typical SIP message contains a large number of headers, header parameters, QoS interworking notifications, and security-related information, and it may vary from a few hundred bytes up to couple of thousand bytes or even more. Therefore, call setup procedures using SIP may take more time to be completed compared with those using existing cellular-specific signaling, which means that the end user will experience a delay in call establishment that will be unexpected and likely unacceptable. In order to minimize this delay, SIP compression is used between a UE and a P-CSCF. IMS uses the *Signaling Compression* (SigComp) architecture defined by IETF, see IETF RFC 3320 [4], which offers robust, lossless compression of application messages. SigComp runs between applications and

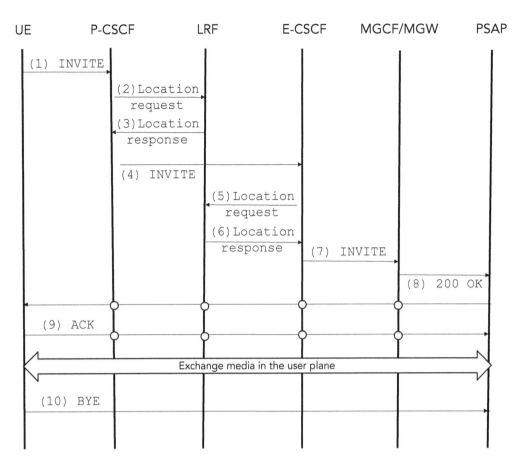

Figure 6.11: Flow of messages for setting an emergency session

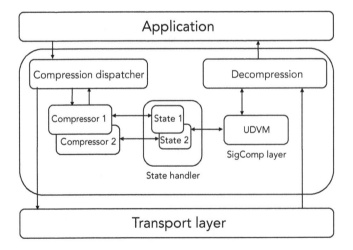

Figure 6.12: The SigComp architecture

transport-layer protocols, such as TCP, UDP, and SCTP.

The SigComp architecture consists of five entities: *compressor dispatcher, decompressor dispatcher, compressors, Universal Decompressor Virtual Machine* (UDVM), and *state handler*, see figure 6.12. The compressor dispatcher receives messages from an application, invokes a compressor, and forwards the resulting SigComp compressed messages to the destination. The decompressor dispatcher is an entity that receives SigComp compressed messages, invokes UDVM, and forwards the resulting decompressed messages to the application. A compressor is an entity that encodes application messages using a certain compression algorithm. The UDVM is used to decompress Sig-Comp compressed messages. Finally, the state handler accesses and stores state information, which is data saved for retrieval by later SigComp compressed messages.

During registration, and after a security association has been established between the UE and the P-CSCF, the UE and the P-CSCF provide details about their compression capabilities, such as memory size and processing power, and compression instructions. When a UE or a P-CSCF wants to send a compressed SIP message, it passes the message to a compressor dispatcher, which then invokes a compressor, who fetches the necessary compression states and uses a certain compression algorithm to encode the message. Subsequently, the compressor dispatcher relays the compressed message to the transport layer to be delivered to the targeted entity. On the receiving side, the decompressor dispatcher receives the message, and after some initial processing it forwards it to the UDVM, which returns the uncompressed message to the decompression dispatcher which subsequently passes the message to IMS.

PROBLEMS

1. The Cx reference point is used between I-CSCF and the HSS, and the S-CSCF and the HSS. The procedures can be divided into three main categories: location management, user data handling and user authentication. Identify and describe briefly the commands used in this interface. (For this, you need to consult the appropriate 3GPP document.)

2. Two users, Helen and Harry, are subscribers of the same home network operated by Herculean Pipes Networks. Both have registered and they are currently in the home network. Helen wants to set up a multimedia session with Harry. Draw a diagram similar to the one in figure 6.7 to show the exchange of messages for setting up a session.

3. Draw a diagram to show the interaction of the IMS entities involved in setting up a session between an IMS user and a public telephone user. Use a dotted line to indicate the signaling path and a continuous line to indicate the data plane path. Associate each hop between two interacting IMS entities with a number, and mark the hops in an ascending order that shows the way the session is set up through the IMS entities.

4. In section 6.4, we discussed how a UE registers with IMS, and figure 6.6 gives the flow of messages assuming that the UE is roaming. Construct a diagram similar to the one in figure 6.6 to show the messages involved when a roaming UE decides to de-register. (For this, you need to consult the appropriate 3GPP document.)

5. Implement an IMS testbed on your laptop! Download the FOKUS Open IMS Core (http://www.openimscore. org/) and the UCT IMS client (http://uctimsclient. berlios.de/). Install the IMS package and create two clients. (The installation is not trivial, but you should be able to find information as to how to do the installation in the Internet.) Initiate a call from one client to the other and use Wireshark to capture all the IMS messages. Construct a diagram similar to the one given figure 6.7. Note that the two UEs will be able to set up a session, but they will not be able to send voice and video to each other, unless one client is moved to another laptop.

REFERENCES

[1] 3GPP - ETSI Mobile Competence Centre, "Overview of 3GPP Release 5 - Summary of all Release 5 Features", Technical Report 2003.
[2] M. Poikselkä and G. Mayer, *The IMS: IP Multimedia Concepts and Services*, 3rd edition, Wiley (2009).
[3] 3GPP TS 29.228 V9.1.0 (2010-03), "Technical Specification Group Core Network and Terminals; IP Multimedia (IM) Subsystem Cx and Dx Interfaces; Signalling Flows and Message Contents", Release 9.
[4] IETF RFC 3320, "Signaling Compression (SigComp)".

CHAPTER 7: NETWORKING SERVICES OVER IMS

7.1 INTRODUCTION

A networking service is implemented in one or more application servers which run on top of IMS. An application server (AS) is not considered to be part of the core IMS functions. It may be owned by a subscriber's operator, in which case it resides in the operator's home network, or it may be owned by another operator residing in that operator's network, or it may be stand alone. As discussed in the previous Chapter, and shown in figure 7.1, there are three different types of application servers that can be accessed through an S-CSCF, namely, SIP-based, CAMEL, and Parlay/OSA. The three types of application servers interact with the S-CSCF through the ISC interface.

A SIP-based application server, depending upon the service, can act as an originating or a terminating UA, a proxy server, a redirect server, and a back-to-back UA (B2BUA). Below we discuss these different schemes.

A conference server may be programmed to send an `INVITE` request to a pre-defined number of people at a given time in order to set up a conference call. In this case, the application server acts as an originating UA. Likewise, an application server acts as an originating UA when it initiates a call to a user to deliver an alert, see figure 7.2. The application server sends an `INVITE` to the S-CSCF, which is forwarded to the P-CSCF and then to the UE. The UE responds with a `200 OK` to the P-CSCF, which is then forwarded back to the application server via the S-CSCF.

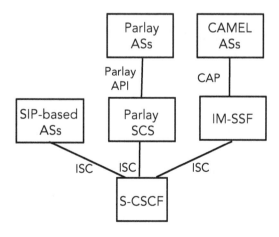

Figure 7.1: The three types of application servers

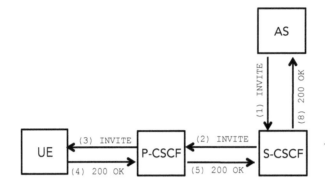

Figure 7.2: An application server acting as an originating SIP UA

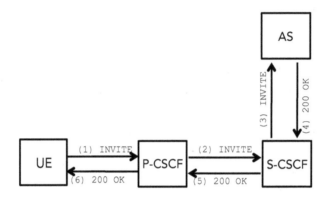

Figure 7.3: An application server acting as a terminating SIP UA

(For presentation purposes, the intermediate SIP messages between the INVITE and 200 OK are not shown. Also, all servers are assumed to be in the same home network as the UE. The same applies for the remaining examples shown figures 7.3 to 7.5.)

An application server may also act as a terminating UA, for instance, when it provides a voice mail service. In this case, as shown in figure 7.3, the UE sends an INVITE to the P-CSCF, which is forwarded to the S-CSCF, which it determines that it should be sent to the AS using the initial filter criteria. The application server behaves as a SIP UA and accepts the call by sending a 200 OK to the S-CSCF which is then forwarded to the UE via the P-CSCF. Other messages, such as SUBSCRIBE and PUBLISH are handled the same way.

An application server may be also set up to act as a SIP proxy on behalf of a UE in order to provide a service, such as, a security gateway. In this case, the application server processes the request and then proxies the request back to the S-CSCF. An example of the flow of the INVITE and 200 OK messages is shown in figure 7.4. The UE sends an INVITE (1) to the P-CSCF which is forwarded to the S-CSCF, which upon examining the initial filter criteria decides to forward it to the application server. The S-CSCF inserts in the INVITE request a Route header field that points to the application server in the first place and to the S-CSCF in the second place. This permits the application server to forward the request back to the same S-CSCF. The application server takes different decisions and actions depending on the service requested by the user, and accordingly it may add, remove, or modify the header contents contained in the SIP request. In the example in figure 7.4, the application server sends the `INVITE` message back to the S-CSCF which it then forwards it towards the called party. Eventually, a `200 OK` (6) is received which is then forwarded to the application server, and subsequently back to the UE through the S-CSCF and P-CSCF.

An application server may also be used as a SIP redirect server. In general, a SIP redirect server is used whenever a session is forwarded and the operator is not interested in being part of the session. Typical applications are call-forwarding services and call portability. The high-level signaling is shown in figure 7.5. The `INVITE` (1) request is forwarded to the S-CSCF which determines that it should use the application server and forwards the request message to it. The application server acting as a redirect server issues a `302 Moved temporarily` which is forwarded to the UE via the S-CSCF and the P-CSCF. Subsequently, the UE generates a new `INVITE` (not shown

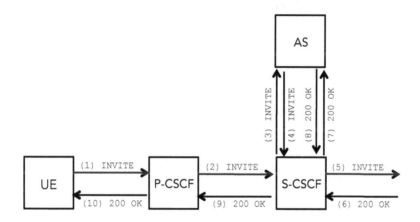

Figure 7.4: An AS acting as a SIP proxy server

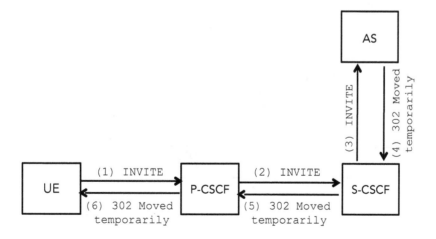

Figure 7.5: An AS acting as a redirect server

in figure 7.5) with the `Request-URI` set to the address provided in the `Contact` header field of the `302 Moved temporarily` message.

Finally, the last mode of an application server is the SIP back-to-back UA (B2BUA). We recall from section 5.2.2 that a B2BUA consists of a UA client, a UA server and some logic in-between them. In general, it performs similar actions as a SIP proxy server. It receives SIP requests, reformulates them, and sends them out as new requests. Also, it receives responses and relays them back to the originating entity.

In this Chapter, we give a high-level description of the following networking services: presence, instant messaging, conferencing, multimedia telephony, and IPTV. These services run over IMS and are implemented with SIP-based application servers. Networking services related to service continuity are described in the following Chapter.

7.2 PRESENCE

Presence has changed the way we communicate. It makes the status of a user available to others and the status of others available to the user. It may contain information such as personal status, device status, location or context, terminal capabilities, preferred contact method and services the user is willing to use to communicate with others, including voice, video, instant messaging and gaming. A presence service is embedded in many applications, such as ICQ, MSN, Yahoo! Messenger, Google Talk, Facebook chat, and Skype, that provide instant messaging, VoIP, video conferencing, and file exchange. Presence information is also a growing tool towards more effective and efficient communication within a business setting. It allows one to instantly see who is available in the corporate network, thus giving more flexibility to set up short-term meetings and conference calls. Also, it is anticipated that presence will be used in new innovative applications, such as, a phonebook for a corporation showing presence for

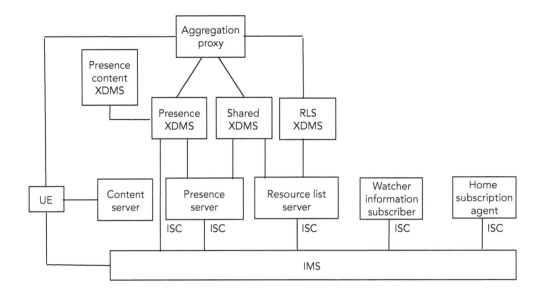

Figure 7.6: The OMA presence architecture

each subscriber, and a car driver with a GPS who can be continuously tracked and sent messages on upcoming traffic patterns that can save time and money.

The presence service was originally introduced by 3GPP, but later on the *Open Mobile Alliance* (OMA) took over the standardization of the IMS-based presence service, see OMA Presence[1]. The architecture is based on the *SIP for Instant Messaging and Presence Leveraging Extensions* (SIMPLE), a suite of specifications for presence and instant messaging developed by IETF. These specifications cover various topics such as protocols for subscription and publication, presence document formats, and protocols for managing privacy preferences, see for instance IETF RFC 3265[2], IETF RFC 3856[3] and IETF RFC 3903[4]. In this section, we review the OMA presence architecture.

The following functional entities have been defined in the presence architecture: presence source, watcher, presence server, *Resource List Server* (RLS), watcher information, and home subscription agent. These entities and various data repositories are described below. The presence architecture is shown in figure 7.6.

A presentity is a presence source that publishes presence information to be made available to interested parties known as watchers. The presentity is located in the UE or within a network entity. A watcher is an entity that subscribes to receive published presence information about a presentity or multiple presentities.

A presence server accepts, stores, and distributes presence information. The following are some of the functions it supports. It authorizes publications from presence sources, and it accepts and stores presence information published by presence sources. It composes presence information from presence sources and other information from the data repository presence XDMS (see below for a definition of XDMS). It authorizes the subscription of watchers and distributes presence information to them. Regulates the distribution of presence information and watcher information in the manner requested by watchers and watcher information subscribers.

The primary usage of a resource list server (RLS) is to allow a watcher to subscribe to a list of presentities, known as the *buddy list* or the *resource list*, with a single SUBSCRIBE message. The server subscribes the watcher to each member in the list, and when it has received presence information from all the members in the list, it sends it back to the watcher in a single NOTIFY message. A buddy list is identified by a SIP URI and it contains a list of URIs, each representing a presentity. It is created and managed by a user through a web page or some other protocol and it may contain a list of friends, co-workers, etc. In many cases, each buddy list is associated with the user who creates it and manages the set of members, and only that user is allowed to subscribe to the list. Of course, this is one mode of operation and other authorization policies can be used.

When user A subscribes to the presence of user B, the subscription needs to be authorized. This is done by the presence server as mentioned above. In addition, a user can set the authorization rules in the presence server so that a subscription request is directly approved by the user (as is often the case with social networks software). For this to happen, B's UE needs to become aware that a presence subscription has been requested. This is supported through the watcher information subscriber mechanism, see IETF RFC 3857[5]. Watcher information is an XML document that contains the set of watchers subscribed to a particular presentity and the state of their subscription. This information changes dynamically as new subscriptions are requested by users, old subscriptions expire, and subscriptions are approved or rejected by the presentity owner. The way it works is that the presence server allows B to subscribe to its own watcher information. That is, B becomes a watcher of a presentity that is its own watcher information. So, when A subscribes to B's presence, B's UE gets a notification of the change in its watcher information state. The UE alerts B of the requested authorization and then B can make a decision.

Finally, the home subscription agent controls the watcher's presence service use in the watcher's home domain. Specifically, it authorizes the watcher's presence service use in the watcher's home domain, limits the number of subscriptions of the watcher, and requests the presence server or the RLS to regulate the presence-related notification traffic based on the watcher's preferences.

Various networking services such as, presence, instant messaging, and *Push To Talk Over Cellular* (PoC), need support for users to create, change, and delete XML documents. In addition, users should be able to access these documents, search them using query requests, and also be notified of changes in the documents. For this, the *XML Configuration Access Protocol* (XCAP) is used which allows a user to read, write, and modify data stored in XML format on a server. It also maps XML document sub-trees and element attributes to HTTP URIs, so that these components can be directly accessed by HTTP. XML documents accessed and manipulated via XCAP are stored in a logical repository called the *XML Document Management Server* (XDMS). The following XDMS entitles are used in the presence architecture:

- *Presence XDMS:* This server is used to store documents related to a presentity, such as presence subscription rules.
- *Shared XDMS:* It is used to store URI lists which may be referenced from other documents.
- *Resource List Server (RLS) XDMS:* It is used to store presence buddy lists.
- *Presence content XDMS:* This server is capable of managing media files for the presence service. A presence source can store a media file in this server and then include a static URI pointing to that media file as part of the presence information it supplies to the presence server. The watcher can use the URI to obtain the media file.

XDMS entities are accessed by users through the *aggregation proxy*, which provides a single point of entry. This provides security to the XDMS entities since they are deployed behind the aggregation proxy, and it also simplifies client configuration. XDMS entities are accessed directly by the presence server.

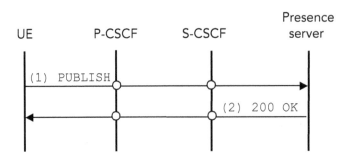

Figure 7.7: Publish presence

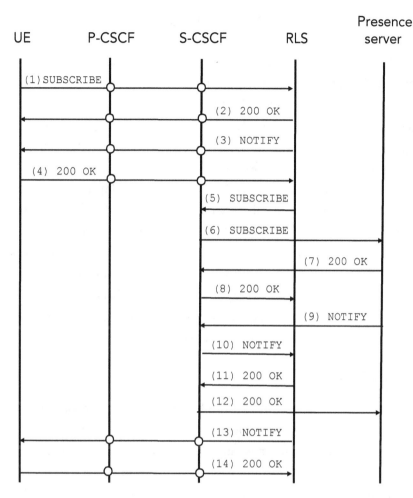

Figure 7.8: Subscription to a buddy list

In addition to the above four servers, a *content server* is used to store and retrieve MIME objects for presence. Presence sources and the presence server can store MIME objects, which can be retrieved by watchers and the presence server.

7.2.1 SIGNALING FLOWS

The SIP methods PUBLISH, SUBSCRIBE, and NOTIFY described in section 5.5 of Chapter 5, are used in the presence service. The PUBLISH method is used to send presence information to a presence server, the SUB-SCRIBE method is used by a watcher for the purpose of receiving presence information, and the NOTIFY method is used to send presence information to a subscriber. In this section, we give the flow of messages for publishing presence in a presence server and subscribing to a buddy list.

To publish and update presence information, the presence source uploads information to the presence server using the PUBLISH message. The presence server responds with a 200 OK, as shown in figure 7.7. (A circle indicates that the message is processed by the correspondig entity.)

The message flow involved when a watcher (Helen) wants to get presence information of the members in her buddy list "friends" is shown in figure 7.8. Helen's UE sends a SUBCRIBE message to the P-CSCS with the URI set to her buddy list, i.e., sip:friends@provider.com. The request is routed to the RLS whose task is to authorize Helen's subscription, extract the members of the buddy list stored in the RLS XDMS and send individual subscriptions to each member, and collect all the received status information and send it back to Helen. The RLS accepts the subscription with a 200 OK and then it sends a NOTIFY message. Assuming that the RLS does not hold any presence information about the members in the buddy list, the NOTIFY message has an empty body or it is populated with data according to local policy decisions. Subsequently, the RLS sends a SUBCRIBE message to the presence server for each member in the buddy list. In the example given in figure 7.8, we show this interaction with a single member (Nimi) who is assumed to be in the same domain as Helen. Both the RLS and the presence server that contains Nimi's presence information communicate with the same S-CSCF over an ISC interface, see figure 7.6. RLS sends a SUBCRIBE message to the presence server via the S-CSCF, to which the presence server responds with a 200 OK followed with a NOTIFY message also via the S-CSCF. When the RLS receives all the notifications from the members in the buddy list, it sends a single NOTIFY message with all the presence information back to Helen's UE. Subsequently, the RLS sends notifications to the Helen's UE each time the presence information of a member changes.

7.3 INSTANT MESSAGING

Instant messaging (IM) refers to the transfer of messages between users in near real-time. IM differs from email in that instant messages are usually grouped together into brief live conversations, consisting of numerous small messages sent back and forth. As we know, the integration of IM and presence provides a powerful communication tool. In this section, we describe the OMA Instant Messaging architecture, which is based on SIMPLE, the suite of specifications for presence and instant messaging developed by IETF.

In SIMPLE, two different modes of IM have been defined, *pager mode* and *session mode*. In pager mode, an instant message is carried in the message body of the MESSAGE method as a MIME attachment, see IETF RFC 3428 [6]. The MIME attachment typically consists of text but it may contain snippets of sounds and pictures. The Request-URI field is normally the address of record for the recipient of the instant message, but it may be a device address in situations where the client has current information about the recipient's location. For example, the client could be coupled with a presence system that supplies an up to date device contact for a given address of record. A MESSAGE request is acknowledged by a 200 OK response. Each MESSAGE and its 200 OK response are forwarded through the UA's proxy server. If UA 2 wants to send an instant message to UA 1 in response to an instant message from UA 1, then it will send a separate MESSAGE to UA 1 which will be acknowledged by UA 1 with a 200 OK, as shown in figure 5.7. There is no explicit SIP association of the exchanged instant messages other than the user's imagination.

In session mode, instant messages are exchanged between two UAs using the *Message Session Relay Protocol* (MSRP), see IETF RFC 4975 [7]. As shown in figure 5.8, a session is established first by sending an INVITE request.

UA 2 silently accepts the invitation without alerting the called user and displays the first message. The instant messages are exchanged between the two UAs without having to be routed through the proxy servers of the UAs using the MSRP messages SEND and 200 OK. The session is terminated using the BYE and 200 OK messages. MSRP can also deliver large messages by splitting them into chunks and then deliver each chunk in a different SEND message.

Most IM clients offer both modes. The pager mode makes sense when the user wishes to send a small number of short instant messages to a single or to a small number of recipients. The session model is more efficient for longer conversations since the messages are not sent through the SIP servers as in the case of the page mode. Furthermore, by viewing IM as a media type, all of the features available in SIP signaling are available for IM.

The OMA IM service, see OMA[8], depends on the OMA presence service described in the previous section, but it can operate without the presence functionality. It supports three modes of IM communication: *pager mode, large message mode*, and *IM session mode*. The first two are similar to the SIP pager and session modes in the SIMPLE architecture.

The pager mode is appropriate for a brief exchange of short messages, and the large message mode for sending a single large message typically carrying multimedia content. The MESSAGE method is used to carry the instant message as a MIME attachment. Messages sent between two users are independent and unrelated as far as signaling is concerned. However, the length of the entire MESSAGE has to be less than 1300 bytes. To allow arbitrarily large pager mode messages, the contents of the message are not inserted into the SIP message but are carried using MSRP. Specifically, in order to transmit a single instant message, a SIP session is first established between the sender and the receiver. Then, the contents of the instant message are transmitted using MSRP, and upon completion of the transmission of the entire message, the SIP session is torn down. To send a pager mode message to more than one user, the Request-URI field of the MESSAGE may point to an IM group identifier. Alternatively, a list of recipients may be carried as a MIME attachment in the body of the SIP message. An IM group URI may be part of the recipient list. The message is delivered to the whole group.

Users may send messages to other users when the recipient is offline or temporarily disconnected from the IM service (e.g., loss of wireless coverage). In these cases, the messages are received by the recipient's IM service and temporarily stored until the receiver comes back online. These are deferred messages which in the simple case are all pushed to the receiver automatically when re-connected to the IM Service. If the size of deferred messages is large or the number of deferred messages is high, the IM user may not have all deferred messages pushed automatically upon re-connection. Instead, the receiver may selectively choose which messages to retrieve by looking through a message summary. In addition, the receiver may selectively delete some deferred messages without retrieving them (e.g., based on subject or sender).

In contrast with the pager mode and the large message mode, the IM session mode is used to create a conference type of session, often called a *chat room*, hosted by the network where individual users can join and leave the group conversation over time. The IM session is established at some moment in time, continues for a finite

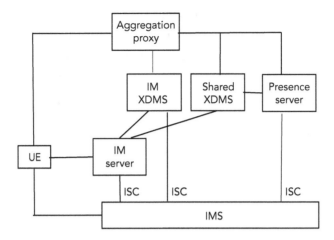

Figure 7.9: The OMA IM architecture

duration and then is dissolved. During an IM session, instant messages are carried using MSRP regardless of the size of individual messages. The SIP session is maintained for the duration of the IM session and it is not torn down after the transmission of a message is completed as in the large message mode. All messages that occur during an IM session are all related together in the context of the session. An IM conference is hosted by the IM server which acts as a conference focus to provide a central point of control. Since IM conferences usually involve a number of users, IM groups may be used to invite a number of users to join a conference. The IM group has policy information associated with it that controls the behavior of the IM conference. One policy element, for example, is the maximum number of users allowed to join the conference at one time.

The IM functional entities are shown in figure 7.9. The UE runs an IM client which performs a variety of tasks, such as, registration, initiation/participation/termination of IM sessions, sending/receiving messages, retrieving/deleting/storing messages, file transfers, and notifications of incoming messages.

The IM server carries out a variety of functions which are logically classified into four groups: *participating IM function, controlling IM function, deferred messaging IM function,* and *conversation history function.* These functions are summarized below.

- *Participating IM function:* This function offers IM access and service policies to the IM users. The following are some of its capabilities: SIP session handling, policy enforcement for incoming/outgoing IM (service authorization, IM user service profile, preferences, message size and content), execution of IM message processing configuration and settings, maintains and executes IM service settings, publishes presence information on behalf of the IM user, if the IM sever is presence enabled, charging reports.
- *Controlling IM function:* This function acts as a conference server providing centralized session handling, policy enforcement for participating groups, participants information for each group, and charging reports.
- *Deferred messaging IM function:* This function handles messages which for various reason cannot be delivered to an IM user, such as, message storing, notification about deferred messages when the user becomes

available for IM communication, IM client retrieval interface, delivery when user becomes available for IM communication, stored message security, and storage messaging charging reports.

- *History conversation functions:* The IM server stores an IM conversation upon user's request, provides IM conversation history management and retrieval functionality, limits the storage size for IM conversations allocated to the IM user, notifies the users about the size of stored IM conversation, notifies the sender about the allowed maximum IM message size.

An IM server assumes the role of participating IM function or controlling IM function depending on which set of functions it is executing in a particular active IM session. For instance, the IM server that owns or hosts the chat room assumes the controlling IM function role. UEs communicate with this server through their IM server of their IMS domain, which assumes the role of the participating IM function. Figure 7.10 gives an example where the controlling IM function is in network 2, and the two participating UEs in networks 1 and 3 communicate via their respective IM server which assumes the participating IM function role.

The IM XDMS server manages XML documents, such as, IM conversation history and deferred messages, which are specific to the IM service. Management tasks include operations such as create, modify, retrieve, and delete. The shared XDMS is used to store URI lists which may be referenced from other documents. Finally, as mentioned above in the presence section, the aggregation proxy provides a single point of entity for accessing XDMS entities.

7.3.1 SIGNALING FLOWS

In this section, we describe various signaling flows that will help understand better how various aspects of the OMA IM service are executed.

An IM client first registers with the IMS server, by sending a `REGISTER` message with the IM feature-tag `+g.oma.sip-im` in the `Accept-Contact` header. In addition, it includes the tag `+g.oma.sip-im.large-message` in the `Contact` header to indicate support for the large message mode. (The `Accept-Contact` header is part of a set of SIP extensions, see IETF RFC 3841[9], which permit a calling UA to express preferences about how a request should be handled by application servers.)

The OMA IM pager mode follows the same principles as the SIP pager mode, but it also includes additional features that add value to the service. For instance, a user maybe able to use message buddy lists, store sent messages in the network (i.e., in the IM server), create block lists and grant lists, block all messages temporarily, and get

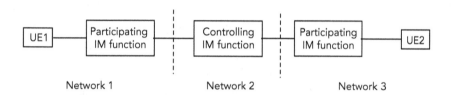

Figure 7.10: Chat server hosted in network 2

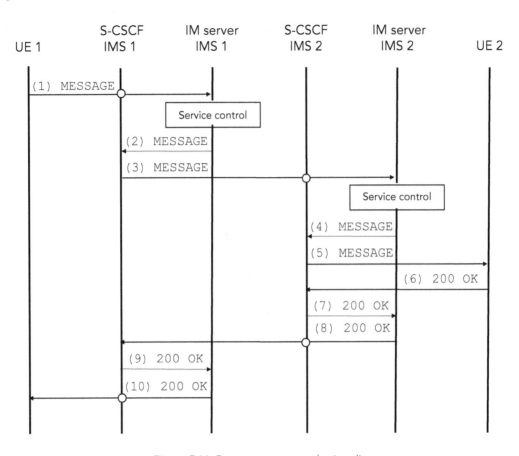

Figure 7.11: Pager message mode signaling

stored messages when being offline. In figure 7.11, we show the basic flow of messages involved when UE 1 sends an instant message to UE 2. We assume that UE 1 belongs to IMS 1 domain and UE 2 to IMS 2 domain. Only the S-CSCF and the IM server in each domain are shown. We also recall that the IM server is connected to the S-CSCF and all messages to an IM server are routed through the domain's S-CSCF. Each IM server carries out all necessary service procedures and accordingly it may reject or accept the MESSAGE request. The IM server in the IMS 2 domain may for instance reject the MESSAGE request if UE 2 has placed a block on all messages or on a specific user. In the example in figure 7.11 both IM servers accept the MESSAGE.

The OMA IM large message mode is based on MSRP. In figure 7.12 we show the basic flow of messages involved when UE 1 sends a large message to UE 2. As in the previous figure, we assume that UE 1 belongs to IMS 1 domain and UE 2 to IMS 2 domain, and only the domain S-CSCF and the IM server are shown. The user first generates an INVITE message with the Request-URI set to the intended recipient. If the message is to be sent to more than one user, then a resource list is included in the MIME body. The message is routed through the user's IMS core to the IM server (step 1), which forwards it to the recipient's IM server after it processes the message (steps 2 to 5). The recipient responds with a 200 OK message, which follows the path shown in figure 7.11, followed by an ACK from UE 1 to UE 2 which follows the same path as the INVITE message. The large message is then transmitted using the MSRP `SEND` and `200 OK` messages. The IMS core is not involved in the transmission of the MSRP messages. Also, the IM servers may or may not be in the path of the MSRP messages. An IM server may chose to be in the path for charging purposes, or it may be automatically inserted in the path due to the operator's policies. As can be seen in the example in figure 7.12, the IM servers are in the path of the MSRP messages. When the user completes transmitting a large message, it generates a `BYE` request for which it receives a `200 OK`. These messages follow the same path as the `INVITE` and `200 OK` messages.

In the OMA IM session mode a group of users participate in a messaging session which is initiated by a user. The invited group may be a *pre-defined* IM group or an *ad-hoc* IM group selected from the calling user's phone book with the help of presence information. The signaling involved is similar to the one shown in figure 7.12, but assuming multiple recipients. As mentioned above, the SIP session is maintained for the duration of the IM session and it is not torn down after the transmission of a large message is completed as in the large message mode. User UE 1 initiates a session by sending an `INVITE` request to its S-CSCF. The request includes the IM feature-tag `+g.oma.sip-im` in the `Accept-Contact` header and the tag `+g.oma. sip-im.large-message` in the `Contact` header. The `Request-URI` header contains the address of the target group, or the address of a single user, if the session is targeted to a single individual. In case of an ad-hoc group, the list of members is provided in the `MIME` body of the request. The S-CSCF executes the initial filter criteria using the special tags provided and sends the request to the IM server in its domain. Once the IM server has processed the request, it sends an individual `INVITE` request to each member in the group. Each request is sent first to the local IM server of the invited member where it gets processed and then it is forwarded to the invited member. Each

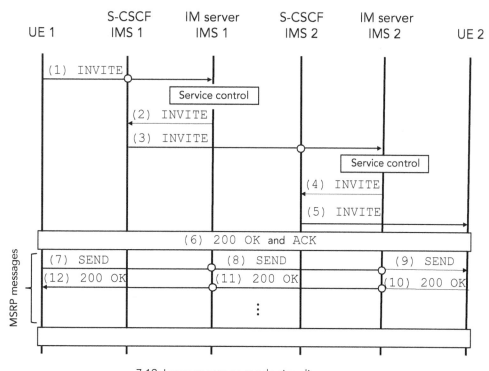

7.12: Large message mode signaling

invited member responds with a `200 OK` message which follows the opposite path back to the IM server of UE 1. An invited IM client may accept silently to participate in the session, or it may ask permission from its end user. If an invited member is offline, the request to join is rejected. When all invited members have responded, UE 1 receives a `200 OK` message from its IM server, to which it responds with an ACK message that gets propagated as the original `INVITE` request. Then the session setup is completed and all session members can send data using MSRP. A user sends a message to its IM server, which distributes it to all the recipient users via their corresponding IM server.

In addition to the above mode, a user can also participate in a chat room type of messaging session. For this, a user has to join explicitly a chat room. Chat IM sessions can go on for hours, with actual communication comprising only a small portion of the total session time. A user can participate in several chat sessions simultaneously and also the user can receive and initiate other sessions. A chat group can be a public group without any access restrictions or a private group with a pre-defined list of members. Public groups are open to anyone who knows the group identification, which is the SIP URI of the group. The group identification can be found in a chat room listing. Public IM chat groups are suitable as open discussion forums on general and specific topics (e.g., sailing, politics, travel).

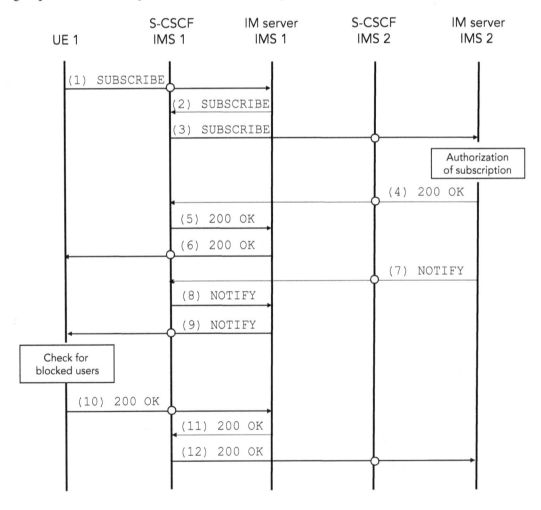

Figure 7.13: Signaling for joining a chat room

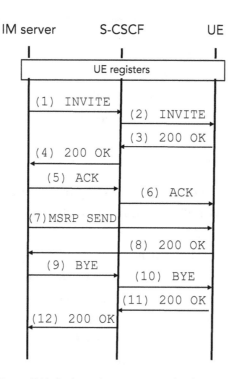

Figure 7.14: Deferred message pushed to a user

Private groups are groups where access is limited to a list pre-defined users. To join a private group, users need to know the SIP URI of the group and they also need to have the right to join the group session.

In figure 7.13 we show the signaling involved for a user UE 1 to join a chat room, that has already been set up. We assume that UE 1 belongs to domain IMS 1, and the IM server that controls the chat room, that is, it has assumed the role of the controlling IM function, belongs to the IMS 2 domain. UE 1 sends a SUBSCRIBE request to the IMS 1 , which includes the URI of the IM group in the Request-URI and an Accept-Contact header with the feature-tag +g.oma.sip-im. The message is forwarded by the S-CSCF to the participating IM server of the domain based on the feature-tag +g.oma.sip-im in the Accept-Contact header. The participating IM server does not recognize the URI as its own and sends the SUBSCRIBE request back to the S-CSCF (step 2), which it then forwards it to the IMS 2 based on the Request-URI (step 3). The S-CSCF of IMS 2 sends the SUBSCRIBE request to the IM server based on the URI in the Request-URI and the feature-tag +g.oma.sip-im in the Accept-Contact header. The controlling IM server authorizes the user to receive event information. The authorization may be based on membership in the IM group, number of IM users already subscribed to the chat room, etc. The authorization is assumed to be successful and the IM server sends a 200 OK response back to the user routed through the IMS 2 core, the IMS 1 core, and the IMS 1 IM server (steps 4 to 6). The controlling IM server collects information about all the participants in the IM session and sends a complete list of all participants to UE 1 in a NOTIFY request (steps 7 to 9). UE 1 checks whether there are blocked users in the list, and if there are it displays them to the user. It then responds back with a 200 OK message (steps 10 to 12). Whenever the membership of the chat room changes, UE 1 will receive a new `NOTIFY` request with the membership changes.

Any messages sent to an offline user are deferred and stored by its participating IM server. When the user goes online and registers with IM , the deferred messages are pushed to the user based on the user's service settings and the policies of the operator. The example shown in figure 7.14 describes how a deferred IM message is pushed to a user. As can be seen, the IM server sends the message using MSRP. It first sends an `INVITE` request to the user and after the session has been established it delivers the deferred message using the `SEND` message with the encapsulated deferred IM message and the timestamp of the time and date received.

Finally, in figure 7.15 we show the signaling flow for delivering an instant message to a group with a request for successful notification. The intermediate IMS core entities are not shown. UE 1 sends an instant message to a group in a `MESSAGE` and requests successful delivery notification (step 1). The participating IM server 1 forwards the `MESSAGE` to the controlling IM server which responds with a 200 OK (step 2). The controlling IM server sends the `MESSAGE` to the participating IM server 2 (step 3) which serves UE 2 (not shown in the diagram). IM server 2 forwards the message to UE 2 and sends the `200 OK` it receives from UE 2 to the controlling IM server (step 4). Steps 3 and 4 are repeated for the participating IM server 3 (steps 6 and 7). UE 4 that is served by the participating IM server 4 is offline. IM server 4 saves the message, marks it as a deferred message, and sends back a `202 Accepted` indicating it has received it. The controlling IM server aggregates the delivery notification responses from UE 2 and UE 3 and sends a `MESSAGE` containing a delivery notification to IM server 1, which is forwarded to UE 1. When UE 4 becomes active and registers with IMS (steps 10 and 11), the IM server 4 delivers the deferred message (step 12). UE 4 determines that a delivery notification was requested and sends a successful delivery notification message in a `MESSAGE` to IM server 4, which is forwarded back to UE 1 (steps 13 to 15).

7.4 CONFERENCING

The term conference has different meanings in different settings. In SIP it refers to a multimedia communication between many participants. This includes conferences with audio and video media streams as well as conferences and games based on instant messages. There are different conferencing models, such as, *loosely coupled, fully distributed,* and *tightly coupled.* In the loosely coupled model, there is no signaling relationship between the participants in a conference, and there is no central point of control or a conference server. Multicasting is used for distributing multimedia content to the conference participants. Participation is gradually learned through control information that is passed as part of the conference using a protocol such as the *Real-Time Control Protocol* (RTCP). Loosely coupled conferences are easily supported in SIP by using multicast addresses within its session description. In the fully distributed model, each participant transmits his media stream to the each participants via unicast using SIP, and there is no central point of control. Each pair of participants must share a common codec. Finally, in the tightly coupled model, there is a central point of control. Each participant connects to this central point, which provides a variety of conference functions, and may possibly perform media mixing functions as well. In this section, we describe the tightly coupled model defined in 3GPP [10] which is based on the IETF RFC 4353 [11]. Below, we first review the main features of the tightly coupled model as identified in IETF RFC 4353[10]

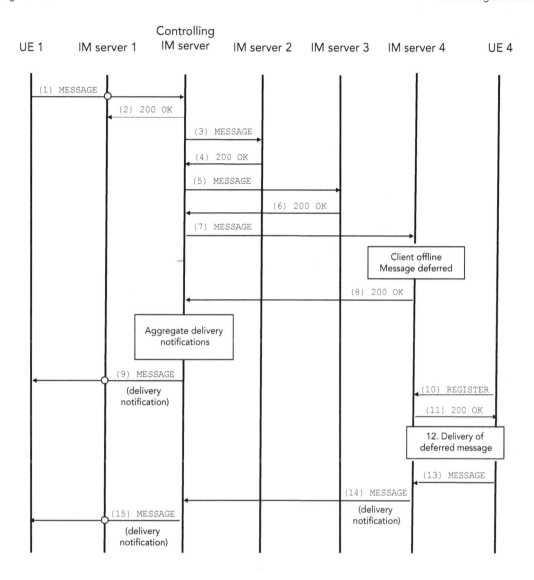

Figure 7.15: Message delivery to a group with delivery notification

and subsequently describe the 3GPP architecture.

The central point in a tightly coupled SIP conference is the *focus*. It maintains a SIP dialog with each participant in a conference and it is responsible for making sure that all the media streams in the conference are available to all the participants. It does this using one or more mixer which combines a number of input media streams to a single one which is then distributed to all the participants. A conference is uniquely identified by a SIP URI which also identifies the focus responsible for the conference. The operations of a conference are governed by a conference policy which is a set of rules associated with a certain conference. These rules include directives on the lifespan of the conference, who can and who cannot join the conference (membership policy), definitions of roles available in the conference and responsibilities associated with those roles, and policies on who is allowed to request which roles. In addition, a media conference policy is used that specifies the mixing characteristics of a conference. Conference policies are stored in a conference policy server and media conference policies are stored in a media conference policy server.

Users can gain further information about an ongoing conference by subscribing to the conference state event package defined in IETF RFC 4575 [12]. This scheme is defined for tightly couple conferences and it allows users to subscribe to a conference URI. Notifications are sent to inform the participant about the users currently online in a conference, which media these participants are using and other related information. A user subscribed to the conference state event package will also be notified whenever a participant joins or leaves the conference.

A user could be *conference-unaware* or *conference-aware*. A conference-unaware user is the simplest user that can participate in a conference. It is able to join a conference and to be invited to a conference. Any conferencing information is optionally conveyed to/from it using non-SIP means. A conference-aware user can interact with the focus in order to access enhanced call control functions, subscribe to a conference URI, and be connected to the conference notification service provided by the focus.

A user can create a conference with a known conference URI by sending an INVITE to a conferencing server. In addition, a user can create an ad hoc conference using a *conference factory* URI. Specifically, in order to create automatically an arbitrary number of ad-hoc conferences (and subsequently their focuses) using SIP, a global conference factory URI is allocated and published. A successful establishment of a call to this URI results to an automatic creation of a new conference and its focus. The URI of the new conference may be different from the conference factory URI. A conference can also be created so that the focus resides in a user.

There are many mechanisms for adding participants to a conference. Participant additions can be *first person,* where a user adds himself, or *third person* where a user adds another user. First person additions are accomplished with a standard INVITE. A user can send an INVITE request to the conference URI, and if the conference policy allows the user to join, the user is added to the conference. Third person additions with SIP are done using the REFER message. A user, say user A, sends a REFER request to another user, say user B, asking B to send an INVITE request to the conference URI. Additionally, user A can send a REFER request to the focus, asking it to send an INVITE to user B. The latter technique can be used to add a conference-unaware user.

As with additions, removals can also be first person or third person. First person departures are accomplished by sending a BYE request to the focus. This terminates the dialog with the focus and removes the participant from the conference. The focus can also remove a participant from the conference by sending it a BYE. In either case, the focus interacts with the mixer to make sure that the departed participant ceases receiving conference media, and that media from that participant are no longer mixed into the conference. Third person departures can also be done using SIP, through the REFER method.

A conference is destroyed in a variety of ways depending on its associated conference policy. For instance, the conference policy may dictate that a conference is destroyed once the last user or a specific user leaves. When a conference is destroyed while there are still participants, the focus sends a BYE to those participants before actually destroying the conference. In addition, if there are any users subscribed to the conference notification service, these subscriptions are terminated by the conference server before the conference is destroyed. Also, when a conference is destroyed, the conference policy is destroyed and the conference URI becomes invalid.

Each conference is composed of a particular set of media that the focus is managing. For example, a conference might contain a video stream and an audio stream. The set of media streams that constitute the conference can be changed by the users. When the set of media in the conference change, the focus will need to generate an INVITE to each user in order to add or remove the media stream to each participant. When a media stream is being added, a user can reject the offered media stream, in which case the user will not receive or contribute to that stream. Rejection of a stream by a user does not imply that the stream is no longer part of the conference, only that the participant is not involved in it. An INVITE can also be used by a user to add or remove a media stream.

In some conferences the concept of a *moderator* is used. The moderator is a special participant who is allowed to control certain aspects of the conference. For instance, a conference moderator can give the right to speak to a participant or withdraw it temporarily from a participant. This handling of the right to speak by a moderator is called *floor control*. In order to implement floor control, the conference moderator makes use of the *Binary Floor Control Protocol* (BFCP) which was specified in IETF RFC 4582[13]. BFCP is used directly over the media connection, i.e., between the UE of the conference moderator and the MRFP.

A *sidebar* is a sub-conference of an existing main conference. Within a sidebar some of the participants can communicate, without the other participants being aware of this. Sidebars may occur in larger conferences, when some participants want to discuss a specific issue outside the main conference.

In 3GPP [10], the focus consists of an application server (AS) and the multimedia resource function controller (MRFC), and it is referred to as the MRFC/AS. The MRFC handles SIP communications to and from the S-CSCF and controls the media resource function processor (MRFP) by means of a protocol such as Megaco/H.248. (*The Media Gateway Control Protocol* (Megaco) or H.248, was designed for control of elements in a physically decomposed multimedia gateway. It enables separation of call control from media conversion.) All the media streams on the data plane that are related to a conference are terminated at the multimedia resource function processor (MRFP). The MRFP mixes all the incoming media streams from all the participants and sends the combined media stream back to the participants. It can also provide transcoding, if the conference participants use different audio or video codecs. That is, it can translate a media stream from one codec to another.

The application server (AS), MRFC, and MRFP are shown in figure 7.16. The conference notification server in the AS accepts subscriptions from clients for the conference URI and generates notifications to them as the state of the conference changes. The state of the conference includes the participants connected to the focus and also information about the dialogs associated with them. The conference policy in the AS contains the rules that guide the operation of the focus. The rules can be simple, such as, it could be just the access list that defines the set of the allowed participants in the conference. They can also be incredibly complex, specifying time-of-day rules on participation conditioned on the presence of their participants. There is no restriction on the type of rules that can be included

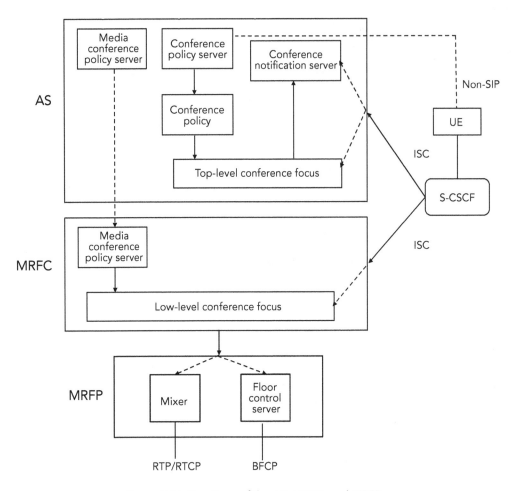

Figure 7.16: Functions of the AS, MRFC, and MRFP

in a conference policy. The conference policy server in the AS is a logical function that stores and manipulates the conference policy. This function is not specific to SIP and it may not exist. The AS does not provide media support. This is handled by the MRFC. It includes a lower-level conference focus and a conference policy which tells it to accept all invitations from the top-level focus.

7.4.1 SIGNALING FLOWS

In this section, we describe various signaling flows that will help understand better how various aspects of the conferencing service are executed.

Figure 7.17 gives the flow of messages involved when a user, UE 1, wants to create a conference using a conference-factory URI. We are not concerned with how a user can obtain a conference-factory URI, which can be done through manual pre-configuration or using a protocol such as HTTP. We assume that the MRFC/AS is in the same domain as the user. UE 1 sends an `INVITE` to the P-CSCF using a conference-factory URI. The request is forwarded to the S-CSCF which after evaluating the filter criteria of UE 1 forwards it to the conference MRFC/AS. (For presentation

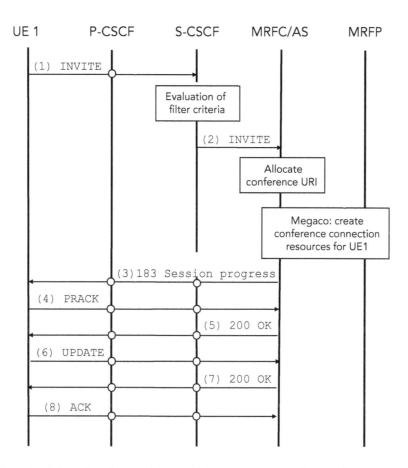

Figure 7.17: Signaling for creating a conference using a conference-factory URI

purposes, the 100 trying responses are not shown in the figure). The MRFC/AS allocates a conference URI and the MRFC initiates a Megaco interaction with the MRFP in order to create a connection point for UE 1 in MRFP and to determine media capabilities of the MRFP. The MRFC determines the complete set of codecs that MRFP is capable of supporting for this conference, and it then determines the intersection with those appearing in the SDP in the INVITE request. The media stream capabilities of MRFP are returned in a 183 Session Progress (step 3). UE 1 sends a new media request in a PRACK message, to which the MRFC/AS responds with a 200 OK. We recall from section 6.4 that a resource reservation on the access network is authorized by the P-CSCF when it receives the 183 Session Progress. When the resource reservation is completed, UE 1 sends an UPDATE message to which the MRFC/AS responds with a 200 OK followed by an ACK message from UE 1.

It is possible for UE 1 to also invite a list of users to the conference in the same INVITE message it sends to the P-CSCF (step 1). The list of the URIs of the invited participants is provided in the message body of the INVITE. The MRFC/AS invites each participant and instructs the MRFP accordingly. Finally, we note that the steps involved in setting a conference with a known URI are the same as in figure 7.17.

A user can join an existing conference whose URI is known to the user by sending an INVITE message. The steps

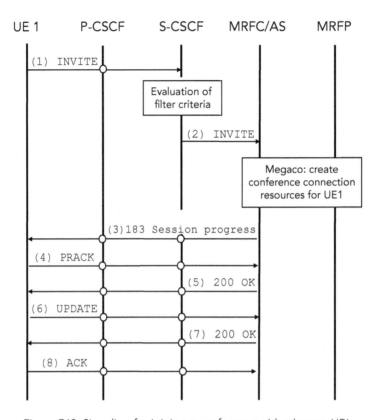

Figure 7.18: Signaling for joining a conference with a known URI

involved are similar to those in figure 7.17, and are shown in figure 7.18. We assume that the MRFC/AS is in the same domain as UE 1.

In figure 7.19 we show the signaling for the case where a user, UE 1, invites another user, UE 2, to join a conference that UE 1 just created. The two users and the MRFC/AS responsible for the conference are assumed to be on the same domain. UE 1 sends a REFER message to its P-CSCF with the To header set to the URI of UE 2 and the Refer-to header set to the conference URI. The message is forwarded to the S-CSCF, which upon evaluation of the filter criteria of UE 1 forwards it to UE 2 via its P-CSCF (step 2). UE 2 accepts the REFER message with a 202 Accepted (step 3), which is routed back to UE 1. UE 2 subsequently sends a NOTIFY message to UE 1 to indicate that the REFER message is being processed, to which UE 1 responds with a 200 OK (steps 4 and 5). UE 2 joins the conference as shown in figure 7.18, and notifies UE 1 that he has successfully joined the conference with a NOTIFY message (step 6) to which UE 1 responds with a 200 OK.

Notification messages are received by a user after it subscribes to the conference event package. This is done using the SUBSCRIBE and NOTIFICATION messages.

A user can leave a conference by sending a BYE as shown in figure 7.20. The P-CSCF de-allocates the resources allocated to UE 1, and forwards the message to the S-CSCF which it then sends it to the MRFC/AS. The conference server instructs the MRFP to release the resources reserved for UE 1 for this conference, and following the

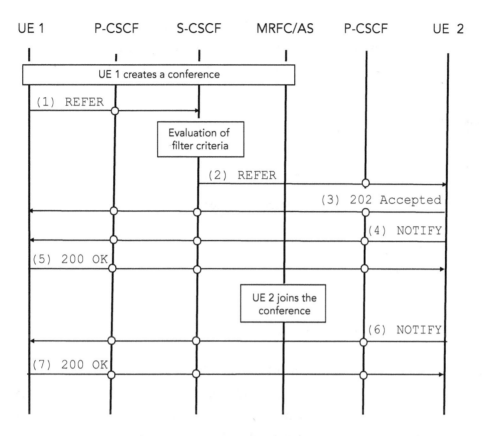

Figure 7.19: UE 1 invites UE 2 to join a conference UE 1 just created

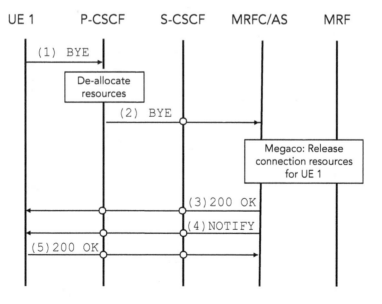

Figure 7.20: UE 1 leaves a conference

successful release of the resources, a `200 OK` is sent back to UE 1. This is followed by a `NOTIFY` message in which the MRFC/AS indicates that UE 1 has left the conference and it has been unsubscribed from its subscription to the conference event package. A `200 OK` is generated by UE 1. A user can also be dropped by the MRFC/AS as shown in figure 7.21.

7.5 MULTIMEDIA TELEPHONY

The *Multimedia Telephony* (MMTel) was standardized in 3GPP TS 24.173 [15]. It provides a number of services over IMS for fixed and mobile devices, such as:

- Bidirectional conversational transfer of speech and video
- Voice call continuity
- Fixed to mobile convergence
- Emergency call services
- Instant messaging
- File transfer
- Video clip sharing, picture sharing, audio clip sharing

MMTel allows a single SIP session to control virtually all MMTel services. For instance, one can start with a chat, then add voice, add another caller, add video, and drop any of these without losing or having to end the session. In addition, a number of supplementary services are supported through the *Telephone Application Server* (TAS), a SIP-based application server accessed via the S-CSCF over the ISC interface, such as:

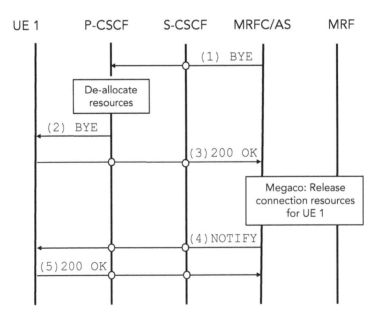

Figure 7.21: UE 1 is dropped from a conference by the MRFC/AS

- Caller ID.
- Calling party can hide its identity from the called party.
- Communication barring service: It allows users to block a request for a session.
- Message waiting indication.
- Communication diversion: A user can redirect an incoming request that fulfils certain provisioned or configured conditions to another destination.
- Communication hold: A user can suspend media components during a session and resume them at a later time.
- Control and participate in a conference involving a number of users.
- Explicit communication transfer: It enables a party involved in a communication to transfer that communication to a third party. For instance, a user who has an active communication with party A and a communication on hold with party B, can establish a new communication between A and B.
  - Advice of charge
  - Flexible alerting
  - Customized alerting tones

The signaling flows for most of the standardized MMTel services have been described in this Chapter, and also in the previous two Chapters. In this section, we describe the signaling flows for some of the supplementary services.

7.5.1 COMMUNICATION BARRING

This service allows a user to block incoming and outgoing requests for a communication session based on certain provisioned or configured conditions. In addition, it can block anonymous incoming session requests. For ex-

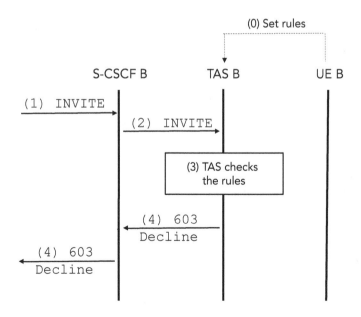

Figure 7.22: An example of an incoming barring supplementary service

ample, a user can block an originating video call attempt while roaming, block originating phone calls to specific numbers between 8am and 4pm, and block anonymous incoming messaging sessions attempts. The rules and conditions for barring communications have been standardized and the user can configure these settings on TAS using the XCAP protocol, see section 7.2. Once the rules are set, the TAS will enforce communication according to user's preferences.

In Figure 7.22, user B uses the XCAP protocol to bar all communication requests from user A (step 0). When user A makes a communication attempt towards user B (step 1), TAS blocks the request by responding with `603 Decline` (step 4), which means that the user explicitly does not wish to take part in the communication.

Figure 7.23 shows an example of an outgoing call barring. First the XCAP protocol is used to configure TAS so that to block all outgoing communication attempts towards a domain `sip:no.com` (step 0). After that, TAS declines all communication attempts to all targets in that domain.

7.5.2 COMMUNICATION DIVERSION

This service allows a user to re-direct an incoming request that fulfils certain provisioned or configured conditions to another destination. This service has the same features as the one offered by telephone operators. Figure 7.24 shows an example where user B (`B@dom.com`) wants to divert all incoming communications to user C (`C@ex.com`). First B sets up the rules in his home TAS using XCAP to divert incoming communication attempts to C. When the TAS that serves B receives an incoming communication attempt for B, it checks if B has uploaded any

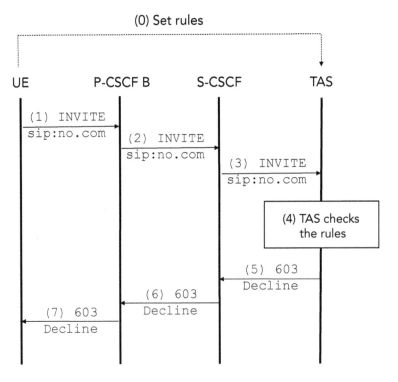

Figure 7.23: An example of an outgoing barring supplementary service

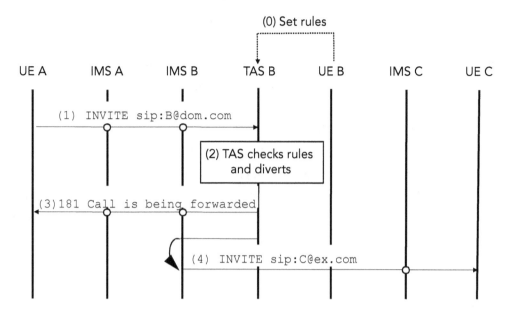

Figure 7.24: An example of the communication diversion supplementary service

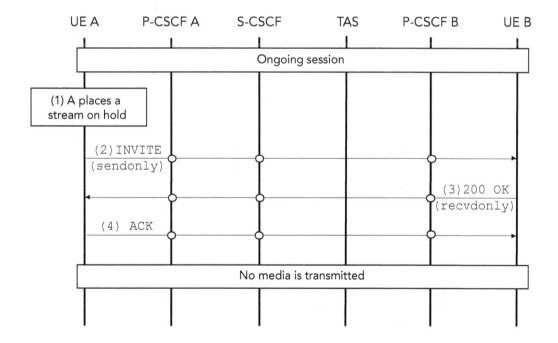

Figure 7.25: An example of putting a communication on hold

rules and based on the stored information it decides to divert the request to C. The request sent to C contains additional information showing that the call was originally targeted to B and it additionally conveys the reason for diversion (carried in the `History-Info` header). Subsequently, TAS informs the caller that the communication is being forwarded to C using the SIP Response `181 Call is being forwarded.`

7.5.3 COMMUNICATION HOLD

This service enables a user to suspend a media stream which is part of an established session, and resume it at a later time. More than one media stream can be suspended and resumed. When a user places a stream on hold, his UE sends a re-INVITE request to the other party. The attribute a in the SDP of the request is set to `sendonly` if the stream was previously a `sendrecv` media stream, or to `inactive` if the stream was previously a `recvonly` media stream. This indicates that the sender is not willing to receive the media stream from the other party.

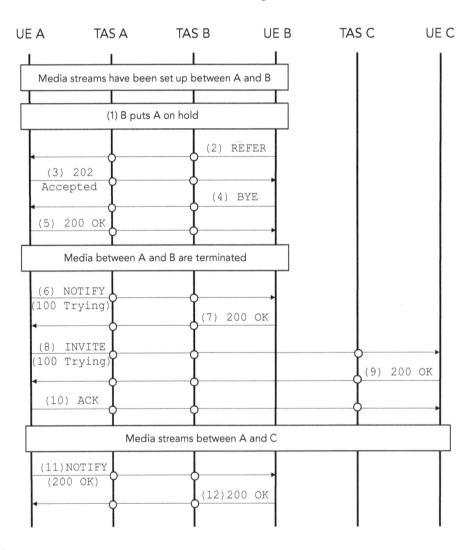

Figure 7.26: An example of a blind communication transfer

As can be seen in figure 7.25, UE B responds with a `200 OK` with `a=recvonly`. The TAS is not involved in this action, unless a notification is required to be sent (not shown in figure 7.25). When a user wants to resume the media stream, his UE sends a re-INVITE request to the other party with `a=sendrecv` if the stream was previously a `recvonly` media stream, or `a=` can be simply omitted since `sendrecv` is the default. If the stream was previously an inactive media stream, then `a=recvonly`.

7.5.4 EXPLICIT COMMUNICATION TRANSFER

This service enables a party involved in a communication to transfer the communication to a third party. The following three actors are involved in a transfer: the party that initiates the transfer of an active communication (*transferor*), the party that remains in the communication that is transferred (*transferee*), and the party to which the communication is transferred and which replaces the party that initiates the transfer (*transfer target*). A transfer may take place without first asking the transfer target whether it wants to accept the communication, or by first consulting the transfer target prior to the transfer. The first option is known as a *blind transfer*, and the second option is known as *consultative transfer*. Explicit communication transfers are handled by TAS.

In figure 7.26, we give an example of a blind transfer. We assume that users A and B have an established communication via TAS A and TAS B, and at some point of the communication session, B (transferor) wants to transfer the communication to C (transfer target). B puts the communication on hold, following the procedure described in the previous section. It then initiates the transfer of the communication by sending a REFER request to A, with the fields `To: UE A, Referred-To: UE-C,` and `Referred-By: UE-B`. The REFER request is accepted by A (step 3), and the media transfer between A and B is terminated (steps 4 and 5). Subsequently, A notifies B about the progress of the transfer (step 6), and it then initiates a new session by sending an INVITE request to C through TAS A, B, and C (step 8). When the new session has been established, A notifies B and B releases the session (steps 11 and 12).

7.6 IPTV

IPTV services include broadcast television, video on demand (VoD), and *Network Personal Video Recording* (NPVR). The latter service, otherwise known as *Network DVR* (NDVR) or *Remote Storage Digital Video Recorder* (RS-DVR), is a digital video recorder stored at the provider's central location rather than at the consumer's home.

The IPTV architecture has evolved over several years. At least three stages of evolution exist: Non-NGN based IPTV solutions, which cover most of the available solutions in the market; an NGN based IPTV architecture, which enables interaction and interworking between the IPTV application and some existing common NGN components; and, an IMS based IPTV architecture, which specifies IPTV functions supported by IMS. In this section, we describe the IMS based IPTV architecture.

An overview of the functional elements of the main IMS based IPTV architecture is shown in figure 7.27, see ETSI TS 182 027 [15]. The IPTV-enabled UE terminates the IPTV control and media signals, and displays the corre-sponding information to the user. The UE allows the user to select a program and obtain the content guides for broadcast and VoD services.

The *Service Discovery Function* (SDF) and *Service Selection Function* (SSF) are used to provide the UE with the necessary information to select an IPTV service, such as, a TV guide. In order to enable third-party content and service providers, the SDF supplies the *service attachment information,* which is a set of SSF addresses in the form of URIs and/or IP addresses. An SSF contains a list of TV channels, VoD information, and other services with connection information.

The *Service Control Function* (SCF) is a SIP application server tasked with service authorization during session initiation and session modification which includes checking the IPTV user profile in order to allow or deny access to a requested service. It also selects the relevant media functions for the delivery of the IPTV media, performs credit control, and selects appropriate advertizing content for a specific user based on the user's preferences, shopping habits, and location information.

The IPTV *Media Function* (MF) is in charge of controlling and delivering the media flows to the UE. It is split into the *Media Control Function* (MCF) and the *Media Delivery Function* (MDF). The MCF selects the MDF and controls the flow of media from MDF, monitors the status of MDF, handles interactions with the SCF, generates charging information, and controls the fetching of advertizing content and synchronizes its insertion in the IPTV stream. The MDF stores and delivers media. It can also store user specific content, such as, NPVR, time-shift TV (this is content recorded and stored to be viewed at a time more convenient), broadcast service with trick mode (VCR like commands), and user generated content. It may additionally process, encode or transcode media to different required media formats. For instance, it can change the resolution of TV depending on capabilities of the user's terminal.

The *User Profile Server Function* (UPSF) is a database that holds the user profile, which contains all the necessary information to access IPTV services. It may also hold specific data, such as, language preference and broadcast settings. It communicates with the SCF and with the IMS core. When multiple instances of UPSF exist, the IMS core and the SCF may use the services of a subscription locator function (SLF) to fetch the address of the UPSF.

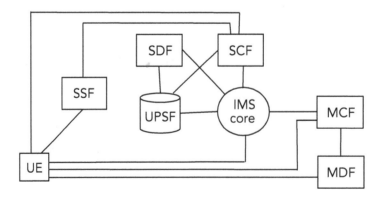

Figure 7.27: The functional elements of the IPTV over IMS architecture

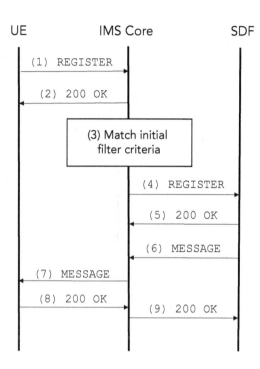

Figure 7.28: UE service attachment – push mode

7.6.1 SIGNALING FLOWS

In this section, we described the flow of messages for the following procedures: service attachment to the SDF, initiation of a broadcast session, channel switching, and termination of a broadcast session. Additional signaling flows can be found in ETSI TS 182 027 [15].

The UE first registers with IMS following the procedure described in section 6.4 and shown in figure 6.6. Subsequently, a service attachment to the SDF is performed, in order for the UE to retrieve the service attachment information, i.e., the SSF address(es) from which it can retrieve the channel and services that the user is authorized to use. The user preferences and the capabilities of the UE can be also taken into account to enable personalized service discovery. The UE can retrieve the service attachment information through the *push mode* or the *pull mode.* In the push mode, the SDF sends the SSF address to the UE when the UE registers with IMS, without the UE requesting it. In the pull mode, the UE explicitly requests the SSF address from the SDF after it registers with the IMS network. (The terms *push* and *pull* are defined with reference the network. In the push mode, the network pushes the information to the UE, whereas in the pull mode the UE pulls the information from the network.) The steps involved in the push mode are shown in figure 7.28. In steps 1 and 2, the UE registers with IMS. After registration, the S-CSCF checks the initial filter criteria and issues a REGISTER (step 4) request to SDF, which responds with a 200 OK (step 5). The SDF determines the proper SSF(s) according to the UEs capabilities, the user profile retrieved from the UPSF and also the location of the UE. It then sends a MESSAGE (step 6) containing the SSF address(es), which is forwarded to the UE. A 200 OK response is sent back to the SDF from the UE.

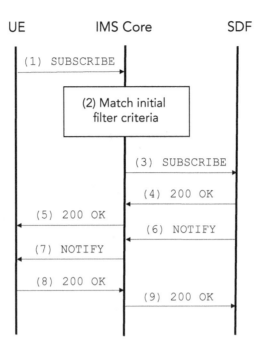

Figure 7.29: UE service attachment – pull mode

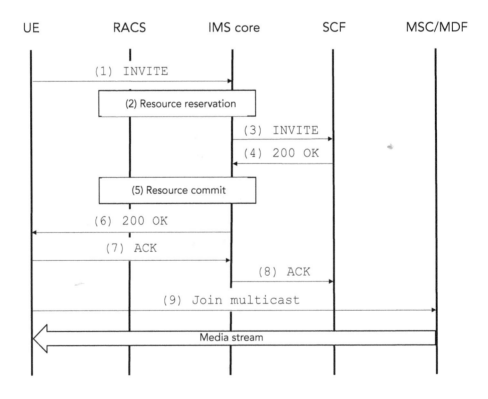

Figure 7.30: Broadcast session initiated by the UE

The UE subsequently contacts the SSF using HTTP, in order to obtain the TV channels and services data (this step is not shown in figure 7.28).

The steps involved in the pull mode are shown in figure 7.29. The UE sends a `SUBSCRIBE` request to the S-CSCF after it has registered with IMS, which checks the initial filter criteria and then forwards it to the SDF. The SDF determines the proper SSF(s) and sends back the information using the `NOTIFY` message, which is relayed by the IMS core to the UE. A `200 OK` response is sent back from the UE to the SDF. The UE subsequently contacts the SSF(s) using HTTP, to obtain the selection data (this step is not shown in figure 7.29).

The signaling flow for a UE initiated broadcast session is shown in figure 7.30. The UE issues an `INVITE` message to the P-CSCF following the selection of a broadcast channel. The P-CSCF forwards it to the S-CSCF, and it also issues a resource reservation to the *Resource Access Control System* (RACS). This architecture was standardized by TISPAN for resource and admission control on the access network and on the edge of a core network. Resource admission and control in NGN is discussed in Chapter 12. The S-CSCF forwards the `INVITE` message to the SCF based on the initial filter criteria. The SCF responds with a `200 OK`, which is forwarded to the UE by the P-CSCF after it interacts with RACS to commit the necessary resources for the broadcast media. The UE responds with an `ACK` that is forwarded to the SCF, joins an IP multicast channel and it starts receiving media. The IP multicast address is obtained from the SSF. Alternatively, the SCF can inform the UE of the MCF and MDF.

The operation for channel changing is shown in figure 7.31. The UE leaves a multicast channel and joins another multicast channel. A delay may be applied. If the user switches channel again during this delay, the flow is restarted

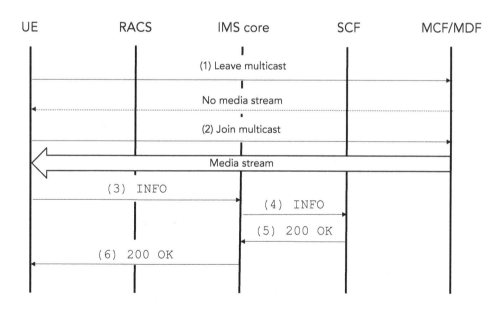

Figure 7.31: Broadcast channel switching

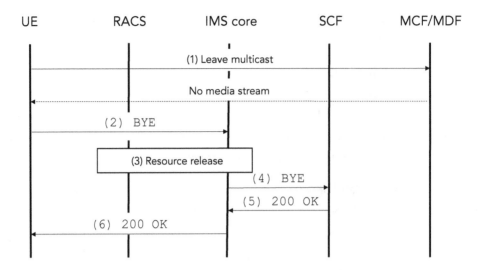

Figure 7.32: Broadcast session termination initiated by the UE

at step 1. The UE sends an INFO message to inform the SCF about which channel is being watched, to which the SCF responds with a 200 OK.

The session termination of a broadcast initiated by the UE is shown in figure 7.32. The UE leaves the multicast, and subsequently sends a BYE to the P-CSCF, which forwards it to the S-CSCF after it interacts with RACS to release all reserved resources in the transport network. The S-CSCF forwards the BYE message to the SCF which returns a 200 OK.

PROBLEMS

1. Figure 7.8 shows the signaling flow of subscription to a buddy list. In this diagram, it was assumed that the buddy list member, Nimi, is in the same domain as Helen. Draw a similar diagram to show the signaling flow in the case where a buddy list member belongs to a different IMS domain.

2. In an one-to-one IM session a participant can extend the session to an ad-hoc group session. Draw a diagram to show the signaling flow involved in extending the session.

3. Write the SIP code for the INVITE request to set up a conference in figure 7.17. (You will find useful information in 3GPP [10].)

4. Figure 7.17 shows the signaling for creating a conference using a conference-factory URI assuming that the MRFC/AS resides in the user's home network. Re-draw the signaling assuming that MRFC/AS resides in another network.

5. Draw the signaling flow for the case where a user wants to join an existing conference URI, assuming that the user is roaming and that the conference MRFC/AS resides in the user's home network.

6. Consult the document 3GPP TS 24.629 where the explicit communication transfer service is described, and draw a diagram similar to the one in figure 7.26 for the consultative transfer case.

7. Explain in your own words the role of the SDF and SSF.

8. Give two different examples of how presence can be used with IPTV services.

REFERENCES

[1]   OMA-AD Presence SIMPLE-V2, "Presence SIMPLE Architecture".
[2]   IETF RFC 3265, "Session Initiation Protocol (SIP) - Specific Event Notification".
[3]   IETF RFC 3856, "A Presence Event Package for the Session Initiation Protocol (SIP)".
[4]   IETF RFC 3903, "Session Initiation Protocol (SIP) Extension for Event State Publication".
[5]   IETF RFC 3857, "A Watcher Information Event Template-Package for the Session Initiation Protocol (SIP)".
[6]   IETF RFC 3428, "Session Initiation Protocol (SIP) Extension for Instant Messaging".
[7]   IETF RFC 4975, "The Message Session Relay Protocol (MSRP)".
[8]   OMA-TS SIMPLE_IM-V1, "Instant Messaging Using SIMPLE".
[9]   IETF RFC 3841, "Caller Preferences for the Session Initiation Protocol (SIP)".
[10] 3GPP TS 24.147 V8.4.0 (2011-12), "Technical Specification Group Core Network and Terminals; Conferencing using the IP Multimedia (IM) Core Network (CN) subsystem", Stage 3 (Release 8).
[11] IETF RFC 4353, "A Framework for Conferencing with the Session Initiation Protocol (SIP)".
[12] IETF RFC 4575, "A Session Initiation Protocol (SIP) Event Package for Conference State".
[13] IETF RFC 4582, "The Binary Floor Control Protocol (BFCP)".
[14] 3GPP TS 24.173, V11.5.0 (2013-03), "IMS Multimedia Telephony Communications Service and Supplementary Services", Stage 3 (Release 11).
[15] ETSI TS 182 027 V3.5.1 (2011-03), "Telecommunications and Internet converged Services and Protocols for Advanced Networking (TISPAN); IPTV Architecture; IPTV functions supported by the IMS subsystem".

CHAPTER 8: MULTIMEDIA SERVICE CONTINUITY

8.1 INTRODUCTION

Multimedia service continuity refers to the capability of continuing an ongoing multimedia session as the user moves across different access networks. For instance, a user with a smartphone initiates a multimedia session through the smartphone's WiFi interface, but during the multimedia session the user moves away from the range of the WiFi. In this case, the continuity service will transfer the multimedia session to the cellular interface seamlessly.

Service continuity also deals with the transfer of media components of an ongoing multimedia session from one UE to another. A typical example is the case where a user is carrying a multimedia session on his smart phone while he is walking to his office, and when he gets there he transfers the session to his desktop. There are other scenarios where the continuity service can be used. For instance, a user has an ongoing session on his smart phone with voice and video components while he is walking to his house. When the user enters his house, he transfers the voice component to an IP-enabled TV set and the video component to an IP-enabled high fidelity audio system.

3GPP has developed a set of standards for service continuity based on IMS. In addition, IETF has also proposed a solution based on SIP for the transfer of media from one device to another. 3GPP's solution is based on an application server, the *service continuity server*, accessible through the S-CSCF. It applies to practically all possible scenarios of service continuity as it arises when a mobile device moves from an LTE access network to 3G/2G access network and back, and also to transferring a session from one device to one or more other devices. IETF's solution, referred to as *SIP mobility*, on the other hand is a much simpler solution and it does not require an application server, but its applicability is restricted to session transfer between a mobile unit and stationary IP-enabled devices. In this Chapter, we first describe IETF's SIP mobility solution, and then the 3GPP service continuity architectures.

8.2 SIP MOBILITY

SIP mobility, proposed in IETF RFC 5631 [1], is used to enable the transfer of a session between a mobile device and one or more stationary IP-enabled multimedia device. Such a device could be a laptop, a PC, a hardware or a software IP phone, a video conferencing unit, an IP-enabled TV set, and an IP-enabled high fidelity audio system. For instance, a user is walking towards his office while he is on a teleconference using his smartphone. As shown in figure 8.1a, upon entering his office the user transfers the teleconference to his laptop. If the user decides to leave

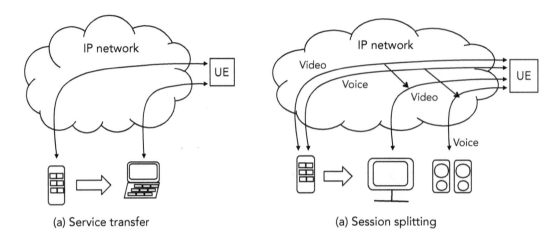

Figure 8.1: Two examples of service continuity

his office while he is still on the teleconference, he can transfer it back to his smartphone. This is known as *session retrieval*. When transferring a session, all media components may be transferred to the same device or different media components maybe transferred to different devices, as shown in figure 8.1b. In this example, a user is carrying out a multimedia session with a video and audio component. Upon entering her house, she transfers the video component to his IP-enabled TV set and the audio component to her IP-enabled high fidelity audio system.

In order to enable service continuity between devices, the user has to be aware of the devices that are available in his local area and their capabilities. This can be done using different methods, such as, bluetooth, bonjour, and the *Service Location Protocol* (SLP).

Two different solutions have been proposed for SIP mobility in IETF RFC 5631[1], namely, *Mobile Node Control* (MNC) and *Session Handoff* (SH). Below, we describe how these two methods are used for session transfer to one or more device.

8.2.1 MOBILE NODE CONTROL

The mobile node control (MNC) method uses the *Third Party Call Control,* referred to as 3pcc, to establish a session with the device(s) to which the session will be transferred. 3pcc is described in IETF RFC 3725[2], and it is commonly used by operators to set up and manage a call between two users. A common application of 3pcc is *click-to-dial.* In this case, a user while browsing through a web site clicks on an icon to talk to customer service. The web server then sets up a call between the user and a customer service representative.

The 3pcc procedure is initiated by an entity which is referred to as the *controller.* In order to set up a call between two UAs, the controller starts two separate dialogs, one for each UA, as shown in the message flow diagram in figure 8.2. The controller first sends an `INVITE` to UA 1 with no SDP offer. (The `contact` header is set to the controller's SIP address, which assures that UA 1 will respond back to the controller.) UA 1 rings the user when

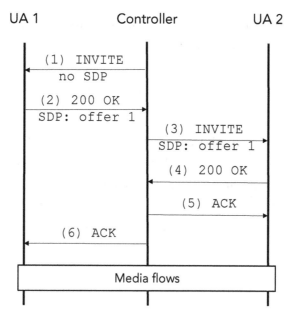

Figure 8.2: Message flow in 3pcc

it receives the SIP message, and when the user answers the phone, UA 1 sends back a `200 OK` to the controller with an SDP offer (offer 1). (The value in the `c` field in offer 1 contains the address of UA 1 where the media data should be sent to.) At that moment, the controller sends an `INVITE` to UA 2 with the SDP offer received from UA 1 (the `contact` header is set to the controller's SIP address). When the user of UA 2 answers, a `200 OK` with an SDP answer to this offer is sent back to the controller. (The value in the `c` field in the SDP offer contains the address of UA 2 where the media data should be sent to.) Assuming that UA 2 has accepted the offer from UA 1, the controller sends an `ACK` first to UA 2 and then to UA 1. The actual media session is established between UA 1 and UA 2, and the media data flows between the two addresses in the `c` field.

Let us now consider the case where a user on a mobile device wants to transfer a session with an audio and a video component to a single device. In this case, the mobile device plays the role of the controller. That is, it initiates a dialog with the local stationary device and also with the destination device with which it is currently carrying out the multimedia session. The flow of messages is the same as in figure 8.2, where UA 1 is the stationary device and UA 2 is the destination device. The SDP offer from UA 1 is given below, and it includes an audio and video medium offer, which means that both media will be transferred to the device.

```
v=0
c=IN IP4 UA1.example.com
m=audio 4400 RTP/AVP 0 8
a=rtpmap:0 PCMU/8000
a=rtpmap:8 PCMA/8000
m=video 5400 RTP/AVP 31 34
a=rtpmap:31 H261/90000
a=rtpmap:34 H263/90000
```

It is possible for the mobile device to transfer only one of the two media to UA 1. For instance, the mobile device may chose to transfer the video component to UA 1 and keep the audio component. This is done by replacing the audio media offer from the above SDP description with its own, and then attaching the new SDP offer in the re-INVITE to UA 2 (step 3 in figure 8.2). As a result, UA 2 will maintain an audio session with the mobile device and a video session with UA 1.

Let us now consider the case where a session is transferred to multiple devices. For instance, in the above example the user wants to transfer the video component to an IP-enabled TV set and the audio component to an IP-enabled audio system. The message flow is shown in figure 8.3. The mobile device establishes a new session with the audio and video devices through a separate INVITE request, and updates the existing session with the UA 2 with an SDP body that combines the offers received from the audio and video devices (step 5). The SDP offer is as follows:

```
m=audio 48400 RTP/AVP 0
c=IN IP4 audio _ dev.example.com
a=rtpmap:0 PCMU/8000
m=video 58400 RTP/AVP 34
```

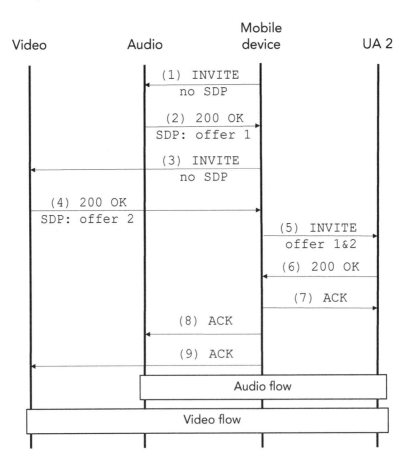

Figure 8.3: Message flow for transferring a session to multiple devices

```
c=IN IP4 video _ dev.example.com
a=rtpmap:34 H263/90000
```

UA 2 responds with its own parameters for audio and video, which the mobile unit splits and sends one to each local device in the ACK (steps 8 and 9).

The mobile device may retrieve the session by sending an INVITE request to UA 2 with its own media parameters, causing the media streams to be sent to it. Subsequently, it sends a BYE message to the local device(s) to terminate the session.

8.2.2 SESSION HANDOFF

We now proceed to describe how the second solution, the session handoff (SH), proposed for SIP mobile can be used to effect similar transfers. SH uses the REFER method, which is a request sent by a *referrer* to a *referee*, referring it to another SIP URI known as the *refer target*. In our case, the referrer is the mobile device, the referee is the device to which the session is to be transferred from the mobile device, and the refer target is the device with which the mobile device has an established multimedia session.

Figure 8.4 gives the message flow. As above, we assume that UA 1 is the local device to which the session is to be transferred from the mobile device and UA 2 is the device with which the mobile has an established session. The mobile device sends a REFER request to UA 1, referring it to invite UA 2 into a session (step 1). It informs UA

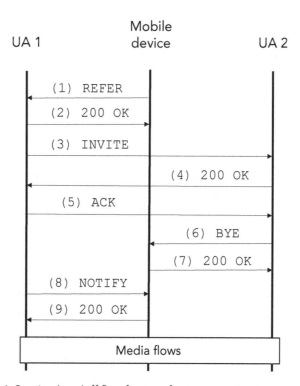

Figure 8.4: Session handoff flow for transferring a session to a single device

1 that it should initiate an audio and video session with UA 2, and that the new session with UA 2 should replace its current session. UA 1 sends a `200 OK` to the mobile device and subsequently it sends an `INVITE` to UA 2 (step 3). When the session is set up, UA 2 tears down its session with the mobile device (step 6). Also, once UA 1 has established the session with UA 2, it sends a `NOTIFY` request to the mobile device

The retrieval of the session currently on UA 1 by the mobile device is done by switching the roles of UA 1 and the mobile device in figure 8.4. That is, UA 1 is the entity that sends the `REFER` message to the mobile device. This can be initiated through an interface on UA 1. If such an interface is not available, it can be initiated from the mobile device, by sending a *nested* `REFER`, that is, a `REFER` request for another `REFER`. In this case, the second `REFER` is sent back to the mobile device.

8.3 MULTIMEDIA SERVICE CONTINUITY – THE 3GPP ARCHITECTURE

In the previous section we explored a number of service continuity scenarios that focus on the narrow case of a mobile device transferring/retrieving a session to/from other IP-enabled devices. All devices are SIP-enabled and they are interconnected through a packet-switched access network, such as WiFi. In the subsequent sections, we examine the IMS-based 3GPP architecture, designed to cover practically all possible scenarios of service continuity.

There are two types of service continuity: *access network continuity* and *device continuity*. The first type arises from the need to maintain an ongoing multimedia session as a UE moves across different access networks. The second type arises from the need to move the media of an ongoing communication session from a UE to one or more different UEs that best meets a user's communication preferences. Below, we discuss a number of different service continuity scenarios.

Three cases have been identified for access network continuity: *PS-CS session continuity, PS-PS session continuity, and PS-PS session continuity in conjunction with PS-CS continuity*. The PS-CS session continuity refers to the case where a session is transferred from a *Packet-Switched* (PS) access network to a *Circuit-Switched* (CS) access network, and vice versa. The primary application case is voice call continuity between the circuit-switched interface of 3G and WiFi, which is a packet-switched access network. We recall that 3G smartphones are equipped with a WiFi duplex interface that can operate simultaneously with the 3G interface. PS-CS call continuity allows a smartphone to switch an ongoing call between 3G and WiFi as the user roams.

The PS-PS session continuity refers to the case where a multimedia session is transferred between two different packet-switched access networks. For instance, UE 1 has established a multimedia session with another UE over a WiFi access network. During the session, UE 1 moves to an area that is better served by an LTE E-UTRAN access network, in terms of radio signal quality or in terms of other criteria. In this case, the multi-media session is transferred to E-UTRAN, which may or may not necessitate changing P-CSCFs. The "PS-PS session continuity in conjunction with PS-CS continuity" refers to the case of a multimedia session which has to use both a circuit-switched access network and a packet-switched access network simultaneously. Consider the case of a UE that has established a session with voice and data components over a packet-switched network, such as a WiFi. Later, the UE moves to a GERAN or UTRAN access network, where voice is only supported on the circuit-switched side of the air interface. In this case, the ongoing multimedia session is transferred by splitting the media into two parts, one for voice carried over the circuit-switched side and one for the data carried over the packet-switched side of the air interface.

The device continuity scenarios are similar to those examined above in the SIP mobility section, and they can be classified in the following four categories:

1. Transfer some or all media components of an ongoing multimedia session from one UE to one or more UEs.
2. Retrieve some or all media components of an ongoing multimedia session from different UEs.
3. Add new media components in an ongoing multimedia session to different UEs.
4. Remove media components of an ongoing multimedia session from different UEs.

In the first scenario a user can transfer one or more media components of an ongoing multimedia session from his device UE 1 to other UEs that he owns, say UEs 2 and 3. These two devices may be attached to a different access network with a different data rate than the one serving UE 1. For instance, UE 1 is connected to a cellular interface, whereas UEs 2 and 3 are connected to a WiFi. Also, UE 2 and 3 may have different capabilities, such as, display resolutions and codecs, which may have to be re-negotiated. In scenario 2, a user uses his device UE 1 to retrieve the voice and video components of a session currently active on devices UE 2 and UE 3 respectively.

In scenario 3, a user may add a new media component to an ongoing multimedia session carried out on a different UE. For instance, let us assume that a user has an ongoing voice session on his UE 1 device. After a while, the user adds a video component to the session through UE 1 but this component is carried out on another of his devices, UE 2. The opposite is also possible, as stated in scenario 4. That is, a user may have initially an ongoing multimedia session with a voice component on his UE 1 device and a video component on his UE 2 device. Subsequently, the user removes the video component on UE 2 using UE 1. We note that the addition or removal of media component(s) to the same device is considered a trivial case, since it can be readily supported by session re-negotiation between two peers.

When adding/removing media components to/from another UE, the user can decide which UE keeps the control. For instance, let us consider again the third scenario where a user has initially an ongoing voice session on his UE 1 device and after a while the user adds a video component on his UE 2 device using UE 1. In this case, the user has the choice of keeping UE 1 as the device for controlling the session, or transferring control to UE 2.

Service continuity should be carried out with minimal disruption. 3GPP has defined an extensive series of IMS-based standards on service continuity. In the remaining of this Chapter, we describe the voice call continuity standard between 3G and WiFi and we briefly discuss the voice call continuity standard between LTE and 2G/3G. We also describe the 3GPP service continuity architecture, which is a extension of the above two standards.

8.4 VOICE CALL CONTINUITY

Voice call continuity (VCC) is an IMS-based standard, defined in 3GPP TS 23.206 [3], which provides continuity for voice calls between 3G and WiFi. (It is also applies between 2G and WiFi, but for simplicity we shall refer only

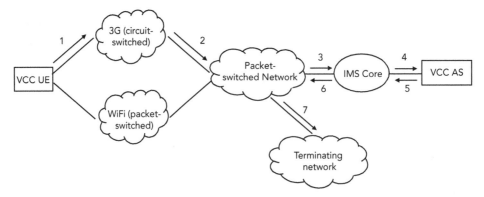

Figure 8.5: Outgoing 3G call anchored in IMS via the VCC AS

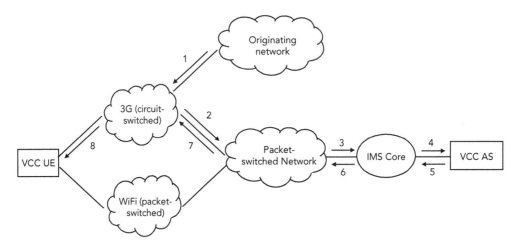

Figure 8.6: Incoming call to the 3G interface is anchored in IMS via the VCC AS

to 3G.) Mobile devices, such as smartphones and tablets, are equipped with 3G and WiFi duplex interfaces that can operate simultaneously. In order to enable VCC, these devices should have an E.164 phone number for the 3G interface and an IMS address for the WiFi interface. In 3G, voice calls are supported by the circuit-switched interface, and call continuity is automatically provided as users roam through 3G coverage areas. Voice calls are also supported by the IP packet-switched WiFi interface of the mobile device, and some WiFi-enabled devices support data continuity between access points. Voice continuity between the circuit-switched 3G and WiFi interfaces of a mobile device is enabled by the VCC architecture, which is centered around the *VCC Application server* (VCC AS). This server-based solution is in contrast to the SIP mobility solution, described above in section 8.2, which does not require a server.

In order to provide voice continuity between 3G and WiFi, the VCC AS has to be aware of all the ongoing calls that originate from a mobile device or terminate at a mobile device. This is achieved by *anchoring* all calls for which VCC service is required in the VCC AS, that is, routing these calls through the VCC AS. Calls initiated and received over the WiFi interface of a mobile device are handled by the IMS client running on the mobile device, and therefore they are automatically routed to IMS over the IP packet-switched network. Calls initiated and received over

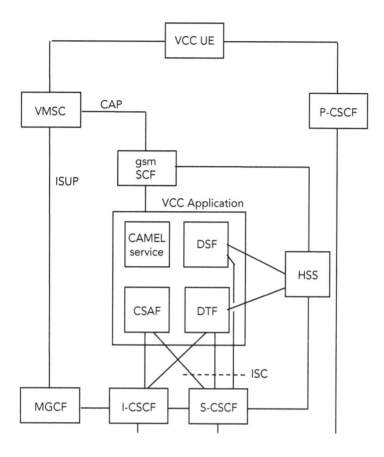

Figure 8.7: The VCC architecture

the 3G circuit-switched interface of a mobile device are handled by SS7, the signaling protocol used in telephony. Therefore, it is not possible for a call originating or terminating over a 3G interface to be handled by IMS. In view of this, the *Mobile Switching Center* (MSC) is augmented with a mechanism that routes all calls for which VCC service is required to the VCC AS. Figures 8.5 and 8.6 show how a 3G initiated or terminating call is anchored in IMS via the VCC AS.

The VCC AS is implemented as a SIP B2BUA server, and it comprises of the following functions: domain selection function (DSF), domain transfer function (DTF), *CS Adaptation Function* (CSAF), and CAMEL services hosted by GSM SCF, as shown in figure 8.7. Both DSF and DTF use the ISC reference point to communicate with S-CSCF. The DSF decides whether a call should be delivered to a called party over the 3G or the WiFi interface. For this, DSF has to determine the IMS registration status and the 3G registration status of the called party. The DTF executes transfers between the CS and PS domains as requested by VCC UEs. For this, it uses the 3rd party call control (3pcc) procedure described in section 8.2.1. It also maintains domain transfer policies, and information about the current domain being used by the requesting VCC UE, and provides domain transfer specific charging data. The CS Adaptation Function (CSAF) acts as a SIP UA on behalf of a VCC UE for 3G calls. Finally, the CAMEL service is used to provide routing functionalities to enable routing from the circuit-switched telephone network to IMS, and back. The switching of a call

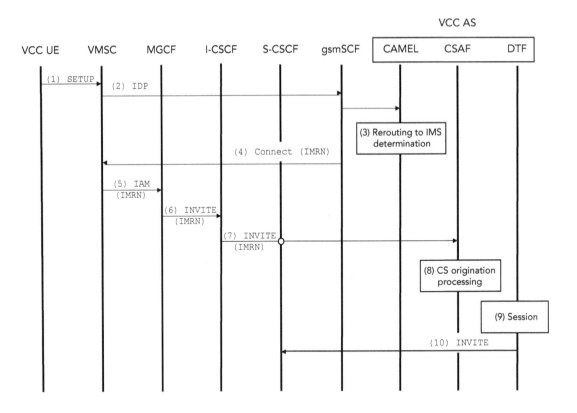

Figure 8.8: Call originates from the circuit-switched 3G interface

between domains is done through the VCC AS of the home network of the VCC UE that originates the request. Also, not all four functions are used each time, as can seen in the flow diagrams 8.8 to 8.10.

The home subscriber service (HSS) is used to store the domain through which a VCC UE can be reached. A VCC UE indicates its preferred CS or PS domain when it registers with IMS. This information is stored in the HSS, and it is used by an S-CSCF to access a VCC UE.

We now proceed to describe the VCC architecture in some detail. Figure 8.8 gives the flow of messages involved when a call is initiated by the CS domain, i.e. the circuit-switched interface of 3G. As mentioned above, in this case the MSC is augmented with a mechanism that routes all calls for which VCC service is required to the VCC AS. As can be seen in figure 8.8, in response to the SETUP request issued by the VCC UE, the *Visiting MSC* (VMSC) obtains an *IP Multimedia Routing Number* (IMRN) from the CAMEL service through the gsmSCF (steps 2 to 4), which is then used to route the call towards the user's home IMS network via an MGCF. The MGCF is necessary to translate the signals between SS7 and SIP. The IMRN is a URI used as a *Public Service Identity* (PSI). PSIs are used in IMS to identify services. They are similar to the IMS communication service identification (ICSI), see section 6.5, but they are used differently. In this case, the PSI identifies the VCC AS. Using the IMRN, the MGCF can obtain the address of an I-CSCF in the home network of the subscriber. The I-CSCF then queries the HSS and routes the request directly to the VCC AS, or via the S-CSCF (steps 6 and 7). When the INVITE arrives at the VCC AS, it is processed by the CSAF

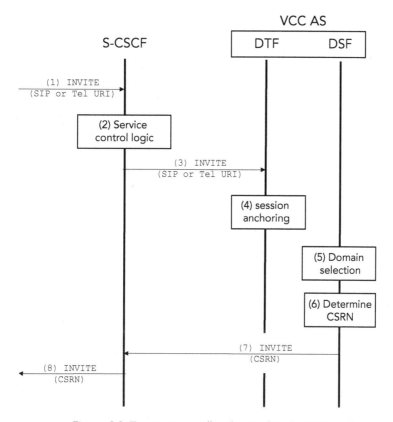

Figure 8.9: Terminating call is directed to the 3G interface

and subsequently the DTF anchors the originating session for future domain transfers (steps 8, 9, and 10). Domain transfers are implemented using the 3pcc procedure, whereby the DTF acts as the controller.

Figure 8.9 shows the steps involved when a call terminates on the circuit-switched interface of 3G. We pick up the message flow when an INVITE arrives at the home IMS of the called party (step 1). The message is processed by the S-CSCF using the initial filter criteria and then forwarded to the DTF for anchoring (step 3). Subsequently, the DSF makes a decision as to whether to use the 3G or WiFi interface of the called party. Assuming that the called party is not accessible via WiFi, DSF decides to route the call via the CS domain, and sends the INVITE back to the S-CSCF with the *CS Domain Routing Number* (CSRN). This is an identifier used by VCC to route calls to the CS domain of a VCC UE, and it can be obtained optionally in collaboration with the HSS and the CSAF. Alternatively, the INVITE back to the S-CSCF (step 7) can be send by the DTF.

The steps involved when DSF determines to route the call the WiFi interface of the called party are the same as in figure 8.9, with the exception that in step 7, DSF provides the called party's URI.

Figure 8.10 gives an example of domain transfer between 3G and WiFi. Let us assume that VCC UE 1 has established a connection with UE 2 via the WiFi interface. We assume that UE 2 is IMS capable and that it is attached to the IP network. For instance, it could be a mobile device attached to a WiFi, or a fixed device such as desktop computer served by ADSL, or cable modem, or metro Ethernet. The signaling path, indicated by the dotted line

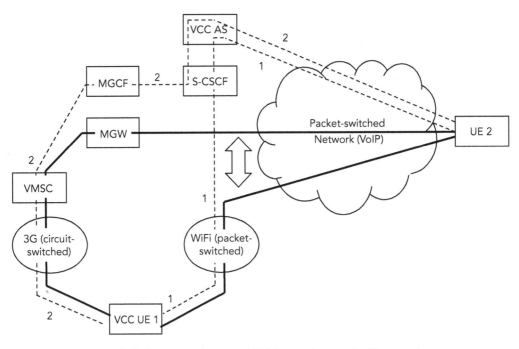

Figure 8.10: Switching domains: UE 2 is attached to the IP network

marked 1, goes through the VCC AS of the IMS in the home network of VCC UE 1. This is necessary, if we want to allow VCC UE 1 to be able to switch domains. The data path, goes through an IP packet-switched network, which is typically a dedicated network used only for VoIP. When VCC UE 1 decides to switch to the 3G interface, it requests the establishment of a new call through the 3G interface. The VCC AS realizes that VCC UE 1 is attempting to change domain, and executes the 3pcc procedure (see section 8.2.1). That is, it first establishes a connection to VCC UE 1 through 3G, then it informs UE 2 of the new location of the VCC UE 1, and finally it drops the old connection to VCC UE 1 through the WiFi interface. The signaling, indicated by the dotted line marked 2 in figure 8.10, goes through the VMSC and subsequently it gets converted to IMS signaling at the MGCF. Once the switchover has taken place, the voice is transmitted to the MGW through the circuit-switched network, where it is packetized into IP packets and subsequently transmitted to UE 2 over the IP network. The opposite happens for the voice data from UE 2 to VCC UE 1. As can be seen, the domain transfer causes the data path to change end-to-end.

Figure 8.11 gives an example of domain transfer between 3G and WiFi, where the UE 2 is either a mobile device attached to 3G or a fixed telephone attached to the telephone system. As above, the signaling path for anchoring the call at VCC AS is identified by the dotted lines numbered 1 and 2, when the VCC UE 1 is attached to a WiFi or a 3G interface respectively. When VCC UE 1 decides to switch to the WiFi interface, it requests the establishment of a new call through the WiFi interface. The VCC AS realizes that VCC UE 1 is attempting to change domain, and executes the 3pcc procedure.

We conclude this section by giving part of the flow of messages involved in the domain transfer from WiFi to 3G and vice versa in figures 8.12 and 8.13 respectively. In figure 8.12, the mobile device VCC UE wants to switch from

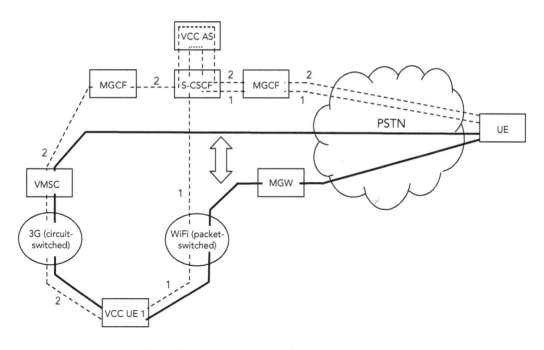

Figure 8.11: Switching domains: UE 2 is attached to the telephone system

the WiFi to 3G. It initiates a call through 3G to VMSC (step 1), which is forwarded to the MGCF with the PSI of the DTF. Subsequently, the MGCF issues an INVITE to DTF (step 3 and 4). Upon receipt of the message, the DTF completes the establishment of the call via 3G, updates the other party with the connection information of the newly established call, and releases the call through the WiFi interface of the UE. In figure 8.13, the mobile device VCC UE wants to switch from the 3G to WiFi. It initiates a call through the WiFi interface which is delivered to DTF after the S-CSCF runs the initial filter criteria. The DTF executes the 3pcc procedure (step 3).

8.5 SINGLE RADIO VOICE CALL CONTINUITY

The *Single Radio Voice Call Continuity* (SRVCC) standard, see 3GPP TS 23.217[4], deals with voice continuity between LTE (or HSPA) and the circuit-switched interface of 2G/3G. Calls over the LTE interface are set up using IMS and they are transmitted over the IP packet switching network. This is in contrast to 2G and 3G access networks, where calls are transmitted though the circuit-switched interface of the access network. Currently, LTE coverage is not ubiquitous, and therefore there is a need for switching ongoing calls between the LTE and 2G/3G access networks. The UE is assumed to be capable of transmitting and receiving on only LTE, or 3G, or 2G at any time. This type of call continuity is an example of PS-CS access transfer. As in the VCC architecture, calls have to be anchored in IMS in order to enable PS-CS access transfers. In addition, the MSC has to be enhanced with SRVCC functionality.

The standard also provides seamless video continuity from E-UTRAN to UTRAN-CS for video sessions anchored in IMS and when the UE can transmit and receive on only one access network at any given time. This part of the specification is called the *Single Radio Video Call Continuity* (vSRVCC).

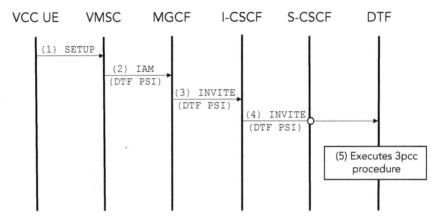

Figure 8.12: Domain transfer from WiFi to 3G

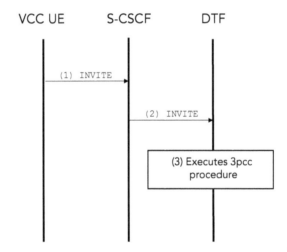

Figure 8.13: Domain transfer from 3G to WiFi

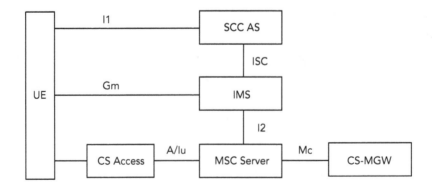

Figure 8.14: The ICS and ISC architecture

8.6 IMS SERVICE CONTINUITY AND IMS CENTRALIZED SERVICES

The call continuity standards described in the above two sections were substantially extended to provide *IMS Service Continuity* (ISC) and *IMS Centralized Services* (ICS), see 3GPP TS 23.237 [5] and 3GPP TR 23.292 [6]. (Please note that ICS is also the name of the interface used between an application server and the S-CSCF. It should be clear from the context which one is referred to.) IMS-based service continuity is provided for PS-PS access transfer, and PS-CS in conjunction with PS-CS access transfer, in addition to PS-CS access transfer addressed by the VCC and SRVCC architectures. Session transfer between UEs which have an IMS subscription under the same operator is also provided. In addition, media components can be added to or removed from an existing multimedia session. IMS centralized services provide IMS-based services, such as MMTel services, to all users irregardless of the access network to which they are attached. Basically, it enables IMS signaling to be extended to non-IMS devices, such as a mobile device connected through the 3G or 2G circuit-switched interface. The application server responsible for providing service continuity and centralized services is referred to as the *Service Centralization and Continuity Application Server* (SCC AS), and it is an evolution of the VCC AS.

The SCC AS is invoked by the S-CSCF over the ICS interface and it is responsible for anchoring the multimedia sessions and executing session transfers between different access networks. It provides the following functions: *ICS User Agent* (IUA), *CS Access Adaptation* (CAA), and *Terminating Access Domain Selection* (T-ADS).

The SCC AS acts as an IMS centralized services UA (IUA) in order to provide SIP support for setting up and controlling multimedia sessions on behalf of a UE that uses a circuit-switched interface to transport both signaling and data. The CS access adaptation (CAA) function performs adaptation of control signals exchanged between a UE that uses a circuit-switched interface and other IMS functional elements. Finally, the terminating access domain selection (T-ADS) function is used for delivery of incoming sessions to the user. The T-ADS extends the VCC DSF, i.e., not only it determines the access domain of the called party, but it also influences the selection of a UE among a set of UEs registered by the same user over the PS domain. A UE can connect to the SCC AS over three different interfaces IMS-based services, as shown in figure 8.14. A UE equipped with an IMS client and connected to a packet-switched access network, such as WiFi or LTE, can connect directly to the serving P-CSCF over the standard Gm interface, and subsequently to the SCC AS through the S-CSCF. (We recall that the Gm interface is the one used between an IMS-enabled UE and a P-CSCF.) The second option is through the I1 protocol, a transport-independent point-to-point protocol used to set up, control, and release multimedia sessions via a circuit-switched access network, see 3GPP TS 24.294 [7]. I1 runs on top of the *Unstructured Supplementary Service Data* (USSD) transport protocol, see 3GPP TS 24.090 [8]. A UE equipped with a Gm or I1 interface is referred to as an *IMS Centralized Services UE* (ICS UE). Non-ICS UEs, i.e., legacy devices connected through a circuit-switched interface can be connected to the SCC AS via its serving MSC server which is enhanced with IMS centralized services functionality and can convert SS7 signaling to SIP signaling. The MSC server interacts with IMS over the I2 interface, which is similar to the SIP interface used between CSCFs with extensions.

If an ICS UE uses the I1 interface to set up and anchor a session with the SCC AS, then it will also have to set up a circuit-switched connection over the circuit-switched access. For instance, if the ICS UE is in an area with only 3G coverage and its user wants to make a voice call, then the ICS UE will use the I1 interface to anchor the call at SCC AS, and then it will set up a call following the standard call setup procedure over the 3G circuit-switched interface. The SCC AS binds the control signaling over I1 with the signaling to set up a call over the 3G into a single IMS session for the purpose of service continuity.

A similar situation occurs when an LTE-enabled mobile device moves into a 3G area during an ongoing call. For example, let us assume that an LTE-enabled mobile device setups a call during the time it is roaming in an LTE area. In this case, the mobile device can use the Gm interface to set up and anchor the call at the SCC AS and the voice data is transmitted over the same packet-switched access network. If the mobile device enters an area where there is only 3G coverage, then the call will be transferred to the circuit-switched interface of 3G. For this to happen, a new call over the circuit-switched connection of 3G has to be established. The SCC AS has the ability to associate the control signaling received over the Gm interface with the call established via 3G, in order to initiate the procedure of a PS-CS transfer.

Service continuity is enabled using the 3pcc procedures described in section 8.2.1. For details the reader is referred to 3GPP TS 23.237 [5].

PROBLEMS

1. Figure 8.3 shows the message flow of an example where an existing session is transferred to two different devices. An extension of this scheme is the transfer of a full-duplex media service, such as video, to an input device that can only capture multimedia and to an output device that can only display multimedia, such as a camera and a video display (both are assumed to be IP-enabled devices). Show the flow of messages in a diagram and give the SDP offer that the mobile device will send to UA 2.

2. Two mobile devices, UE 1 and UE 2 are equipped with a WiFi and a 3G interface, they are VCC enabled, and they belong to different home networks. Draw a diagrams similar to those in figures 8.10 and 8.11, to show the signaling and the data paths end-to-end when both UE 1 and UE 2 switch domains.

3. Draw a diagram similar to the one in figure 8.9, assuming that the DSF routes the call to the WiFi interface of the called party.

REFERENCES

[1]   IETF RFC 5631, "Session Initiation Protocol (SIP) Session Mobility".
[2]   IETF RFC 3725, "Best Current Practices for Third Party Call Control (3pcc)in the Session Initiation Protocol (SIP)".
[3]   3GPP TS 23.206 V7.50 (2007-12), "Technical Specification Group Services and System Aspects; Voice Call

Continuity (VCC) between Circuit Switched (CS) and IP Multimedia Subsystem (IMS)", Stage 2 (Release 7).

[4] 3GPP TS 23.217 V11.8.0 (2013-03), "Single Radio Voice Call Continuity (SRVCC)", Stage 2 (Release 11).

[5] 3GPP TS 23.237 V12.2.0 (2013-03), "IP Multimedia Service Continuity", Stage 2 (Release 12).

[6] 3GPP TR 23.292 V12.1.0 (2013-03), "IP Multimedia Subsystem (IMS) Centralized Services", Stage 2 (Release 12).

[7] 3GPP TS 24.294 V10.0.0 (2013-03), "IP Multimedia Subsystem (IMS) Centralized Services (ICS) Protocol via I1 Interface", (Release 10).

[8] 3GPP TS 24.090 V11.0.0 (2012-09), "Unstructured Supplementary Service Data (USSD)", Stage 3 (Release 11).

PART 4:

QOS ARCHITECTURES IN THE TRANSPORT NETWORK

CHAPTER 9: THE MPLS AND DIFFSERV ARCHITECTURES

9.1 INTRODUCTION

In this Chapter, we describe the *Multi-Protocol Label Switching* (MPLS) and the *Differential Services* (DiffServ) architectures, two widely used schemes that can be employed to provide QoS guarantees in an IP network. MPLS and DiffServ have a different approach to the problem of providing QoS guarantees. MPLS introduces a connection-oriented structure within the IP network, that it is inherently connectionless, and DiffServ provides QoS guarantees on aggregate flows. As will be seen, DiffServ can also be employed with MPLS. Both schemes were introduced in the late 1990s, with DiffServ predating MPLS.

Below, we first describe what is a connection-oriented network and why such networks can provide QoS guarantees. Subsequently, we describe MPLS, DiffServ, and DiffServ with MPLS.

9.2 CONNECTION-ORIENTED NETWORKS

We start our discussion by first describing briefly how the routing of packets takes place within an IP network. We will assume that the IP network does not employ schemes such as DiffServ, MPLS, and deep packet inspection, that can be used to provide QoS guarantees. For presentation purposes, we will refer to this basic type of IP network, as the *classical IP network*. Let us assume that computer A sends IP packets to computer B, as shown in figure 9.1. Each IP packet consists of a header and a payload, and the header contains different fields one of which is the destination IP address of computer B. When a packet arrives at IP router 1, the header is examined and the destination address is used in the *forwarding routing table* in order to find out the next IP router to which the IP packet has to be forwarded. In our example, the next hop router is IP router 2. IP packets arriving at IP router 2 are processed the

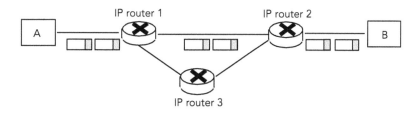

Figure 9.1: Routing IP packets

same way. That is, the destination address is looked up in the router's forwarding routing table in order to find out the next hop, which in this case is a local address.

The forwarding routing table in each IP router is constructed using a routing protocol, such as the *Open Shortest Path First* (OSPF). In simple terms, the routers exchange topological information using the OSPF protocol. This information permits each router to see the entire topology of the network. Based on this topology, each router calculates the shortest path (typically expressed in the number of hops) to each destination, and it then populates its forwarding routing table with the next hop for each destination. When a link goes down, the networking topology will change and the new topological information will be distributed to all the routers, which permits each router to re-calculate the next hop for each destination.

The advantage of this type of routing is that it is simple. However, since it minimizes the number of hops, it is difficult to guarantee any QoS measures such as end-to-end delay, jitter, and packet loss. For instance, the fact that the path that a packet follows has the smallest number of hops, does not necessarily mean that it has the shortest delay. On the other hand, if all routers have approximately the same packet loss rate, then the shortest path will result to a low end-to-end packet loss rate.

Another problem associated with the classical IP networks is that a router cannot distinguish packets and therefore it cannot give packets belonging to delay intolerant applications a higher priority for transmission out of an output port. (As will be seen later on, using priorities at the output ports of a router is important in providing QoS guarantees.) In view of this, the only way that delay sensitive applications can be served satisfactorily in a classical IP network is to under-utilize the network. This is known as over-engineering the network. In light load conditions, the queues of packets awaiting for transmission out of an output port are short, and as a result the amount of time a packet has to wait in a queue is typically negligible. This solution is expensive since the links are under-utilized (less than 20% on the average), and it does not prevent temporary occurrences of traffic congestion. An advantage of over-engineering the network, is that in the light of a link failure, traffic can be redirected over other links without saturating these links.

In order for the IP network to provide QoS guarantees without resorting to over-engineering, we need a scheme that can satisfy the following constraints. First, it guarantees that the network has sufficient bandwidth to carry a new flow from a sender to a receiver. Secondly, the end-to-end path satisfies the requested QoS metrics associated with a flow. Thirdly, it can guarantee that the packets associated with each flow can be identified within a router so that they can be scheduled for transmission out of an output port, according to their requested QoS. Such a solution can be provided by introducing a connection-based scheme in the IP network, such as MPLS.

In order to understand what is a connection, let us consider the telephone system which is probably the oldest connection-oriented network. A telephone switch, known as the *central office*, serves many thousands of subscribers. Each subscriber is connected to a central office directly via a dedicated twisted pair line known as the *local loop*. Central offices are interconnected via *Time-Division Multiplexing* (TDM) links, such as SONET/SDH links and PDH links, i.e., T1, E1, T3, and E3. Figure 9.2 shows two telephones interconnected via two central offices. For

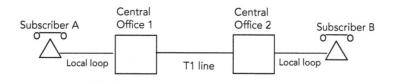

Figure 9.2: A simple telephone network

presentation purposes, let us assume that the two central offices are connected via a T1 line. Transmission on a T1 line is organized into frames, with each frame containing 24 time slots. Each time slot is 8 bits long and it carries a different voice call. The frame repeats every 128 msec, which means that a particular time slot occurs once every 128 msec, or 8,000 times per second. Since it carries 8 bits at a time, the total bit rate of a time slot as it continuously repeats frame after frame is 64 Kbps. A time slot carries a single voice call. Transmission on a T1 line is unidirectional, say from central office 1 to 2. For a bidirectional transmission between the two central offices two separate T1 lines are needed, each transmitting in opposite direction.

In order for subscriber A to talk to subscriber B, a connection has to be first established. This connection is set up by the telephone network when A lifts the receiver and dials up the digits of the called party. A signaling protocol is used to set up the connection through the central offices which are on the path from subscriber A to B. In the exmple in figure 9.2, the connection involves the dedicated line from A to central office 1, a time slot on the T1 line from central office 1 to 2, say time slot i, and the dedicated subscriber line from central office 2 to subscriber B. In the opposite direction it involves the dedicated line from B to central office 2, time slot i on the T1 line from central office 2 to 1, and the dedicated subscriber line from central office 1 to subscriber A. These resources are allocated to the phone call between subscribers A and B until one of them hangs up, at which point they are released. A telephone connection is known as a *circuit*.

We notice that we need a signaling protocol that will set up the connection and then tear it down at the end of the conversation. Setting up a connection involves calculating a path to the called party, allocating a channel on each transmission link to the connection, and alerting the called party. As mentioned above, the resources allocated to a call are used only by the two communicating parties, and they are released when the connection is terminated.

The notion of a connection is also used in the IP network. For instance, a TCP connection has to be set up before two TCP users can communicate. This type of connection, is a logical connection and it is not the same as the connection in a telephone network. The purpose of the logical connection is to synchronize the two TCP protocols, and in this case the IP routers are not aware of this connection and they do not allocate any physical resources to it, such as bandwidth, at each link. On the other hand, the purpose of establishing a circuit in a telephone network is to calculate a path to the destination and allocate physical resources to the network. If resources are not available the call will not go through. (This of course does not happen very often in a telephone system, since it has been optimized so that the probability that a call is blocked due to lack of physical resources is extremely small.)

Connections similar to the one in a telephone network have also been used in packet-switched networks since their early deployment back in the 1980s. These connections are referred to as *virtual circuits*. A virtual circuit imitates a telephone connection and it is set up and torn down using a signaling protocol. During call setup, a connection is established between the sender and the receiver prior to the transmission of packets. This is a path through the nodes of the packet-switched network which all packets will follow. Each packet consists of a header and a payload. The header contains various fields of which one or more are used to identify the connection that the packet belongs to. This information is used to route the packet through the network. Unlike the telephone system, however, the channel capacity allocated on each transmission link is not dedicated to the virtual circuit. Rather, the transmission link is shared by all the virtual circuits that pass through it.

Packet-switched networks that use virtual circuits are known as *connection-oriented* networks. Examples of such networks are: X.25, ATM, Frame Relay, and IP networks running MPLS. Connection-oriented networks are in contrast to the classical IP network, where no connections are set up between two users, and a user can transmit packets at will. Each packet is routed through the network individually using its destination address in the header. In view of this, the classical IP network is referred to as a *connectionless* network.

In MPLS, IP packets are not forwarded based on the destination address in the header. Rather, they are forwarded based on a label that is associated with a connection, known as a *Label Switched Path* (LSP). Let us consider an MPLS-enabled IP network where the routers are interconnected with gigabit Ethernet links. In this case, a special MPLS header is used which is sandwiched between the IP header and the LLC header. The MPLS header contains a label which is a short fixed-length connection identifier. An MPLS-ready IP router, which is known as a *Label Switching Router* (LSR), maintains a table of labels. When an IP packet arrives at the LSR, the label carried in the MPLS header is used in the table of labels to find the next hop. The IP packet is then switched to the appropriate destination output port of the LSR that connects to the next hop LSR. The table contains labels for only the existing connections, and therefore it is not as large as the forwarding routing table.

In order for a user to transmit over an MPLS-enabled IP network, it has to first request the establishment of a connection. This is done using a signaling protocol such as RSVP-TE, see Chapter 10. An LSR is aware of all the connections that pass through it, and therefore, it can decide whether to accept a new connection or not based on the amount of traffic that will be transmitted and the requested quality of service. The LSR allocates a portion of its bandwidth to a new connection, and it stops accepting new connections when it runs out of bandwidth or when it reaches a certain percentage of link utilization. In addition, since the IP packets are now identified by their LSP label, they can be associated with different scheduling priorities for transmission out of an output port. In this way, the packets from a delay-sensitive application can be given higher priority for transmission over packets belonging to a delay-insensitive application.

To summarize, bandwidth allocation at connection setup time and priority-based scheduling for transmitting packets out of an output port of a router are two necessary features for providing QoS guarantees. MPLS being a connection-oriented architecture provides these two features. DiffServ, on the other hand, is not a connection-

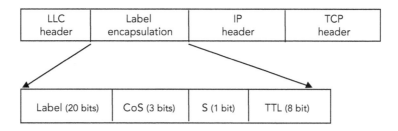

Figure 9.3: Label encapsulation

oriented scheme but it introduces a mechanism whereby QoS can be provided on aggregate flows, such as all VoIP connections. At the aggregate level, it provides bandwidth allocation and scheduling priorities at the output ports of a DiffServ-enabled router. As will be seen, DiffServ can also be used in conjunction with MPLS.

9.3 THE MPLS ARCHITECTURE

MPLS was standardized by IETF around 2000, see IETF RFC 2702[1] and IETF RFC 3031[2]. Subsequently, it was extended to *Generalized MPLS* (GMPLS) to cover all types of networks such as packet-switched, SONET/SDH, and optical networks. In this Chapter, we focus on MPLS and we will assume that the links in an IP network are point-to-point packet-over-SONET or gigabit Ethernet.

As explained above, a router forwards an IP packet according to its destination address. In MPLS, each IP packet is forwarded according to a *label* that is carried in its header. This label is associated with a destination address, and it is used to determine the output interface of an IP packet without having to look-up its destination address in the forward routing table. A label is a short fixed-length identifier that has local significance.

In IPv6, the label can be carried in the flow label field. In IPv4, however, there is no space for such a label in the IP header. In this case, the label is encapsulated and it is inserted between the LLC header and the IP header, as shown in the figure 9.3. This encapsulated label is often referred to as the *shim header*. The first field of the label encapsulation is a 20-bit field used to carry the label. The second field is a 3-bit field used for experimental purposes. For instance, it can carry a *Class-of-Service* (CoS) indication, which can be used to determine the order in which IP packets will be transmitted out of an interface. The S field is used in conjunction with the label stack, which will be discussed later on in this Chapter. Finally, the *Time-to-Live* (TTL) field contains the TTL value copied from the IP TTL field at the time the shim header was created after it is decremented by 1. Subsequently, it is decremented at each LSR hop, and it is copied back into the IP header TTL field after it is decremented by 1 when the packet exits from its LSP.

An MPLS network consists of label switching routers (LSRs) and *MPLS nodes.* An LSR is an IP router that runs the MPLS protocol. It can forward IP packets based on their labels, and it can also carry the customary IP forwarding decision by looking up the prefix of the destination IP address in the networking table. An MPLS node is an LSR but it may not necessarily have the capability to forward IP packets based on prefixes. A contiguous set of MPLS

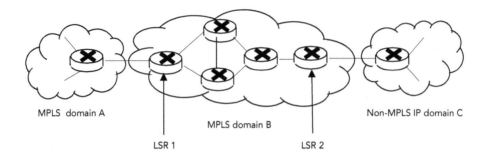

Figure 9.4: MPLS domains, LSRs, and MPLS nodes

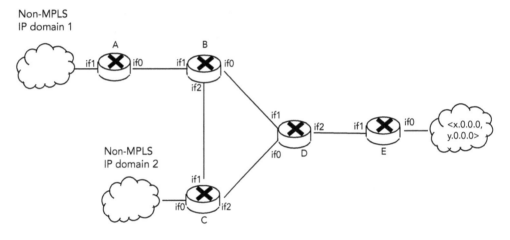

Figure 9.5: An example of multi-protocol label switching

nodes which are in the same routing or administrative domain forms an MPLS domain. Within an MPLS domain IP packets are switched using their MPLS label. An MPLS domain may be connected to other MPLS or a non-MPLS IP domains (that is, IP domains where routers use the customary forwarding decision based on prefixes). As shown in the example in figure 9.4, MPLS domain B consists of 5 routers, of which 2 are LSRs (LSR 1 and LSR 2) and the remaining 3 may be either LSRs or MPLS nodes. MPLS domain B is connected to the MPLS domain A via LSR 1, and to the non-MPLS IP domain C via LSR 2. LSRs 1 and 2 are referred to as *MPLS edge nodes*. For simplicity, we will not distinguish between LSRs and MPLS nodes and we shall refer to all the nodes within an MPLS domain as LSRs.

To see how MPLS works, let us consider an MPLS domain consisting of 5 LSRs, A, B, C, D, and E, linked with point-to-point connections as shown in figure 9.5. LSRs A and C are connected to non-MPLS IP domains 1 and 2 respectively. We assume that a new IP subnet with the prefix <x.0.0.0, y.0.0.0>, where x.0.0.0 is the base network address and y.0.0.0 is the mask, is connected to E. The flow of IP packets with this prefix from A to E is via B and D. That is, A's next-hop router for this prefix is B, B's next-hop router is D, and D's next-hop router is E. Likewise, the flow of IP packets with the same prefix from C to E is via D. That is, C's next-hop router for this prefix is D, and D's next-hop router is E. The interfaces in figure 9.5 show how these routers are interconnected. For instance, A is connected to B via if0, and B is connected to A, C, and D via if1, if2, and if0, respectively.

LSR	Incoming label	Outgoing label	Next hop	Outgoing interface
A			LSR B	if0
B	62		LSR D	if0
C			LSR D	if2
D	35		LSR E	if2
E	60		LSR E	if0

Table 9.1: FEC entry in each LFIB

When an LSR learns about the FEC associated with this new prefix <x.0.0.0, y.0.0.0>, it selects a label from a pool of free labels and it makes an entry in a table referred to as the *Label Forward Information Base* (LFIB). This table contains information regarding the incoming and outgoing labels associated with a FEC and the output interface, i.e. the FEC's next-hop router. The LSR also saves the label in its forwarding routing table, which is known as the *Forward Information Base* (FIB), in the entry associated with the FEC.

The entry in the LFIB associated with this particular FEC for each LSR is shown in table 9.1. (For presentation purposes we have listed all the entries together in a single table). We see that B has selected an incoming label equal to 62, D has selected 35, and E has selected 60. A and C have not selected an incoming label for this FEC, since they are MPLS edge routers and they do not expect to receive labeled IP packets. The remaining information in each entry gives the next-hop LSR and the output interface for the FEC. For instance, for this FEC the next-hop router for A is B and it is through if0.

An incoming label is the label that an LSR expects to find in all the incoming IP packets that belong to a FEC. For instance, in the above example, LSR B expects all the incoming IP packets belonging to the FEC associated with the prefix <x.0.0.0, y.0.0.0> to be labeled with the value 62. The labeling of these packets has to be done by the LSRs which are one-hop upstream of B. That is, they are upstream in relation to the flow of IP packets associated with this FEC. In this example, the only LSP that is upstream of B is A. In the case of D, both B and C are upstream LSRs.

In order for an LSR to receive incoming IP packets labeled with the value that it has selected, the LSR has to notify its neighbors about its label selection for a particular FEC. In the above example, LSR B sends its label to A, D, and C. A recognizes that it is upstream from B, and it uses the information to update the entry for this FEC in its LFIB. D and C are not upstream from B as far as this FEC is concerned, and they do not use this information in their LFIBs. However, they may choose to store it for future use. It is possible, for instance, that due to failure of the link between C and D, B becomes the next-hop LSR for this FEC. In this case, C will use the label advertised by B to update the entry in its LFIB.

D sends its information to B, C, and E. Since B and C are both upstream of D, they use this information to update the entries in their LFIB. Finally, E sends its information to D, which uses it to update its entry in its LFIB. As a result, each entry in the LFIB of each LSR will be modified as shown in table 9.2.

LSR	Incoming label	Outgoing label	Next hop	Outgoing interface
A		62	LSR B	if0
B	62	35	LSR D	if0
C		35	LSR D	if2
D	35	60	LSR E	if2
E	60		LSR E	if0

Table 9.2: FEC entry in each LFIB with label binding information

We note that E is the last LSR, and after that the IP packets associated with the prefix <x.0.0.0, y.0.0.0> will be forwarded to the local destination over if0 using their prefix.

Once the labels have been distributed and the entries have been updated in the LFIBs, the forwarding of an IP packet belonging to the FEC associated with the prefix <x.0.0.0, y.0.0.0> is done using solely the labels. Let us assume that A receives an IP packet from the non-MPLS IP domain 1 with a prefix <x.0.0.0, y.0.0.0>. A identifies that the packet's IP address belongs to the FEC, generates the shim header with the label value set to 62, and forwards the packet to the outgoing interface if0. When the IP packet arrives at LSR B, its label is extracted and looked up in B's LFIB. The old label is replaced by the new one, which is 35, and the IP packet is forwarded to interface if0. LSR D follows exactly the same procedure. When it receives the IP packet from B, it replaces its incoming label with the outgoing label, which is 60, and forwards it to interface if2. Finally, E strips off the shim header, and forwards the IP packet to its local destination based on its IP address. The same procedure applies for an IP packet with a prefix <x.0.0.0, y.0.0.0> that arrives at C from the non-MPLS domain 2. In figure 9.6, we show the labels allocated by the LSRs. We can see that these labels form a multipoint-to-point tree whose root is the destination LSR that serves the FEC. The distribution of labels is done using the *Label Distribution Protocol* (LDP) discussed in the following Chapter.

Label switching eliminates the CPU-intensive table look-up in the forward routing table, necessary to determine the next-hop router of an IP packet. A table look-up in the LFIB is not as time-consuming since an LFIB is considerably smaller than the forwarding routing table. Since the introduction of label switching, however, several CPU-efficient algorithms for carrying out table look-ups in the forward routing table were developed. This did not diminish the importance of label switching since it was seen as a means of introducing quality of service in the IP network.

One way that quality of service can be introduced in the network is to associate each IP packet with a priority. This priority can be carried in the 3-bit experimental field of the label encapsulation, see figure 9.3, and it is assigned by the user. Priorities can also be assigned at the point where the IP packets enter an MPLS domain, such as LSR A in figure 9.6. Labeled IP packets within an LSR are served according to their priority. An LSR and in general an IP router, maintains different QoS queues at each output interface. These queues are served using a scheduling algorithm, as discussed in Chapter 11.

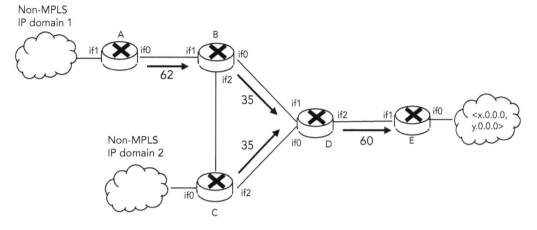

Figure 9.6: Label switched paths

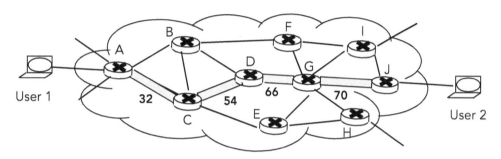

Figure 9.7: A connection in an MPLS domain

In addition to setting up multipoint-to-point trees towards a destination FEC, it is also possible to set up point-to-point connections, as shown in figure 9.7. An MPLS connection is referred to as a label switched path (LSP). For each LSP there is an ingress LSR and an egress LSR. For instance, in figure 9.7, A is the ingress LSR and J is the egress LSR.

Let us now consider how a connection is established in an MPLS domain. Let us assume that user 1 attached to LSR A in figure 9.7 wants to send a file to user 2 attached to LSR J. Before the user starts transmitting the file, a connection has to be established between LSRs A and J. The user's IP packets can be transmitted after the connection is established. The connection is torn down when the file is completely transferred. The connection is setup and torn down using a signaling protocol, such as RSVP-TE. The actual mechanics of how RSVP-TE works will be discussed in the following Chapter. At this moment, let us see how this connection is associated with the label carried in the shim header of the IP packets, and how packets are routed based on this label.

A connection is identified by a series of numbers, i.e. labels, which have local significance. That means, that each label is valid only on one hop. As we can see in figure 9.7, the LSP is routed through LSRs C, D, and G, and the labels associated with this connection are: 32, 54, 66, and 70. These labels are allocated at setup time. Each LSR

LSR	Incoming label	Outgoing label	Outgoing interface
A	-	32	to LSR C
C	32	54	to LSR D
D	54	66	to LSR G
G	66	70	to LSR J
J	70	-	to user 2

Table 9.3: Label entries for the connection shown in figure 9.7

maintains a table for each incoming port, where it associates an incoming label to an outgoing label and an output port number. Table 9.3 gives the labels entries for the connection. (For presentation purposes we have listed all the entries together in a single table, although each entry belongs to a different label table). Packets sent to LSR A from user 1 do not normally contain an MPLS header. The MPLS header with the label 32 is added by LSR A. It is then sent to LSR C, where the incoming label is looked up in the LFIB table to find the new label and the output port number. The IP packet is switched to that particular output port through the switch fabric of the LSR, and then it is transmitted out to LSR D. The same action takes place at LSR D. Finally, when it gets to LSR J, its MPLS header is removed and the packet is sent to user 2 using IP forwarding. We see that the IP packets are routed in each LSR using their incoming label and not the destination IP address.

The pair of incoming and outgoing labels at each LSR are associated with a unique connection, which permits an LSR to identify which packets belong to which connection and accordingly give them different priority for transmission out of an output port.

9.3.1 EXPLICIT ROUTING

In MPLS, a connection can be set up using the next-hop information stored in the forward routing table of an IP router. That is, the connection can be set up so that to follow the same path that a packet follows when using IP forwarding. This type of routing is known as *hop-by-hop routing*. In addition, the MPLS architecture permits the creation of a connection that follows an *explicit route* through a network which may not necessarily correspond to the hop-by-hop path. This type of routing is referred to as *explicit routing*. An explicit route is set up to satisfy a QoS criterion, such as, minimization of the end-to-end delay, maximization of throughput, etc. Such a QoS criterion may not be satisfied necessarily by the hop-by-hop routing, which typically minimizes the number of hops only. Also, explicit routing can be used to provide load-balancing, by forcing some of the traffic to follow different paths through a network, so that the utilization of the network links is as even as possible.

An explicit route is often referred to as a *constraint-based route* since it satisfies some QoS constraint(s), and the MPLS connection is known as a *Constrained-Based Routed Label Switched Path* (CR-LSP). The calculation of an explicit route is beyond the scope of MPLS. It may be calculated manually, or there may be a path computation entity which has a complete view of the network topology and current loading and which can compute routes based on a QoS criterion. Examples of such entities are: the *Resource and Admission Control Functions* (RACF) and the *Path Computation Element* (PCE) described in Chapter 12, OpenFlow[3], and OnePK[4].

An explicit route may be either *strictly explicitly routed* or *loosely explicitly routed*. In the strictly explicitly routed case, the path for the ingress LSR to the egress LSR is defined precisely. That is, all the LSRs through which the path has to pass are specified explicitly. In the loosely explicitly routed case, not all the LSRs through which the path will pass are specified. For instance, if the path has to go through a domain that belongs to a different network provider, then the actual path through this domain cannot not be specified since the domain's topology is not known to the originating network provider.

9.3.2 THE NEXT HOP LABEL FORWARDING ENTRY

So far, for presentation purposes we have assumed that an LSR maintains a single entry in its LFIB for each incoming label. In this entry, it binds the incoming label with an outgoing label and it provides the output interface to the next hop.

The MPLS architecture permits an LSR to maintain multiple entries for each incoming label. Each entry is known as the *Next Hop Label Forwarding Entry* (NHLFE), and it provides the following information: the output interface of the packet's next hop, the new label, and the operation to be performed on the packet's label. Each NHLFE entry may also contain additional information necessary in order to properly dispose of the packet. Having multiple entries for each incoming label may be useful as one can implement multi-pathing for load balance and protection. The procedure for choosing one of the NHLFE entries is beyond the scope of the MPLS architecture.

9.3.3 THE LABEL STACK

MPLS permits a packet to carry multiple labels which are organized as a stack. An example of the label stack is given in figure 9.7. Each row contains a different label encapsulation. The S bit is used to indicate whether the current label encapsulation is not the last one (S = 0), or it is the last one (S = 1). The following three operation can be performed by an LSR on the packet's label:

- Replace the label at the top of the packet's label stack with a new label.
- Pop the label stack.
- Replace the label at the top of the packet's label stack with a new label, and then push one or more new labels on to the stack.

In the examples given in figures 9.6 and 9.7, only the first two operations are used. For instance, in figure 9.7 when LSR C receives a packet from LSR A, it replaces the incoming label 32 with a new outgoing label 54 (first operation). The same happens at the LSRs D and G. The label is popped (second operation) at LSR J, which forwards the packet to user 2 by looking up its destination IP address in the forwarding routing table. The third operation is associated with stacks of labels used for MPLS tunneling. Typically, only stacks of two labels are used. An MPLS tunnel, also known as a *TE-link*, is a pre-established LSP between two LSRs in an MPLS domain, through which other LSPs of

Label (20 bits)	CoS (3 bits)	S =0	TTL (8 bits)
Label (20 bits)	CoS (3 bits)	S =0	TTL (8 bits)
⋮			
Label (20 bits)	CoS (3 bits)	S =0	TTL (8 bits)

Figure 9.8: The label stack

lesser bandwidth can be established. Below, we give an example of a TE-link and how the two-label stack is used. We note that two-label stacks are also used in *pseudowires* described in Chapter 13.

Let us consider the three MPLS domains in figure 9.9, and let us assume that a TE-link between LSRs 3 and 6 has already been established (l). TE-links are advertized by OSPF as single links, and as a result LSR 3 thinks that it is one hop away from LSR 6. Let us assume now that LSR 1 wants to establish a new LSP to LSR 8 using hop-by-hop routing. As can be seen, the shortest path from LSR 1 to LSR 8 is through the TE-link, and as a result the connection will be routed through LSR 2, the TE-link, LSR 7 and will terminate at LSR 8. Setting up the connection can be done using RSVP-TE with hop-by-hop routing as will be seen in the next Chapter.

The labels associated with this new LSP are 60, 40, the TE-link labels (32, 54, 66), 80, and 35. Multiple connections can be scheduled through this TE-link, and each connection, established from left to right in figure 9.9, is associated with a different label after it leaves LSR 6. The problem that arises in this case is that LSR 6 cannot tell which packet belongs to which connection by looking at label 66, and therefore it cannot decide how to route the packets after they leave the TE-link. (LSR 6 can of course forward the IP packets by looking up their IP address in the forwarding routing table, but this is not within the label switching framework of MPLS.) This problem is solved by introducing another label associated with the specific connection, which is carried in the bottom label of the label stack. In our example, this is label 70. LSR 2 learns this label from LSR 7 and creates a two-label stack where the bottom label is the one that LSR 6 will use to decide how to forward the IP packet and the top label is used to switch the packet through the TE-link.

The label stack on each hop and the label operation carried out at each LSR along the path is shown in figure 9.9. LSR 1 creates a shim header and populates it with label 60. The label operation at LSR 2 is: replace the label at the top of the packet's label stack (label 60) with a new label (label 40). At LSR 3, the label operations are: replace label at the top of the packet's label stack and then push one new label on to the stack. As a result of this operation, label 40 is replaced by 70, and a new label with the value 32 is pushed on top. (Label 70 is communicated to LSR 3 by LSR 6.) At LSRs 4 and 5, the packet is forwarded using the operation: replace the label at the top of the packet's label stack with a new label. As a result, the top label of the label stack is first replaced with the value 54, and then with 66. At LSR 6, the label operations are: pop the label stack and replace the label at the top of the packet's label stack

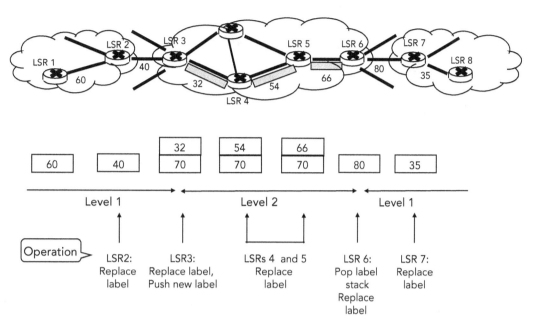

Figure 9.9: An example of an MPLS tunnel

with a new label. As a result, the top label 66 is removed from the label stack, and now label 70 is used to determine how to forward the packet. It is looked up in the LFIB to find out that the new label is 80 and the output port is the one connecting to LSR 7. Finally, LSR 7 forwards the packet to LSR 8 using the label operation: replace the label at the top of the packet's label stack with a new label. As a result, the packet arrives at LSR 8 with a label 35.

9.3.4 PENULTIMUM HOP POPPING

We recall that the operation that has to be performed on a label is stored in the LFIB. That is, in order for an LSR to decide which operation to apply, it has to read the label in the shim header of the packet, and then look it up in the LFIB in order to find out the required operation. This creates a lot of work for an egress LSR of an LSP or a TE-link. For, it first has to look up the top label of a packet's stack in the LFIB in order to learn that it has to pop it. Then, it may perform a second LFIB lookup if there is another label underneath, or it may perform an IP lookup in the forwarding routing table in order to decide how to forward the packet.

In order to ease up the workload of an egress LSR, the first LFIB lookup is avoided using *Penultimum Hop Popping* (PHP). This is a simple scheme whereby the label from the penaltimum (i.e., the last but one) LSR to the egress LSR is set to 3. For instance, in figure 9.10 we see that J is the egress LSR, and G is the penaltimum LSR of an LSP or a TE-link established between LSRs A and J. Label 3 between LSRs G and J, instructs LSR G to pop the top label before it sends the packet to the LSR J. This label is known as the *implicit NULL label*.

When the label is removed, the QoS EXP bits are lost. In some cases, this information has to be delivered to the egress LSR. This is done, by setting the label from the penaltimum LSR to the egress LSR to 0. When the egress LSR

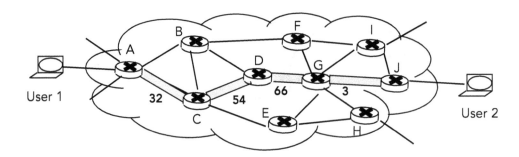

Figure 9.10: Penultimum hop popping

sees that it is a zero label it pops the label without an LFIB lookup, but it retains the EXP bits. This label is known as the *explicit NULL label.*

9.4 THE DIFFSERV ARCHITECTURE

The DiffServ architecture was proposed in 1998, IETF RFC 2474[5], and it predates MPLS by a couple of years. DiffServ is not a connection-oriented architecture such as MPLS and IntServ (reviewed in the next Chapter). Rather, it is based on the notion of controlling aggregates of flows. It is widely used by network providers.

DiffServ operates on the principle of packet classification, whereby each packet in a DiffServ-enabled IP network is classified into a traffic class. Packet marking, i.e., classification, is done at the ingress node using different parameters, such as, source address, destination address, and port numbers. A DiffServ-enabled network may also accept traffic already marked by a user. A DiffServ class is known as a *behavior aggregate*, and it is represented by a number known as the *DiffServ code point* (DSCP). The DSCP of a packet is stored in the DS field in the IP header.

Marked packets are treated differently within a DiffServ-enabled router. Typically, the queueing encountered in a router is at the output ports. In DiffServ, multiple queues are maintained at each output port, one for each DSCP, and a packet waiting to be transmitted out joins the queue associated with its own DSCP. The queues are served according to a scheduler that guarantees that higher-priority packets are transmitted out first. In addition, packets can get dropped when congestion occurs, and dropping priorities are also associated with some of the DiffServ classes of traffic. The set of controls, i.e., queue selection at an output port, scheduling priority for transmission out of the router, and packet dropping priority, is known in the DiffServ architecture as the *Per-Hop Behavior* (PHB).

In addition to marking and PHB, DiffServ polices the traffic submitted by the users at the ingress routers, the entry points of a DiffServ-enabled IP network. Customers of a network provider are not individual users, but rather companies and other organizations acting on behalf of their members. A customer enters into a service level agreement (SLA) with a network provider which is basically a contract that spells out the forwarding service the customer will receive. In the contract, it is specified how much traffic per class the customer will submit. The role of the policer at the ingress router is to guarantee that the customer does not submit more traffic than agreed upon in the SLA agreement. Excess traffic may be dropped, or it may be marked as eligible to be dropped and let into the network. If congestion occurs in a router then the marked packets are dropped.

9.4.1 THE DS FIELD

The DS field is an 8-bit field in the IP header that carries the DiffServ code points. In IPv4, the field is carried in the type of service field, and in IPv6 it is carried in the traffic class field. The type of service field in IPv4, shown in figure 9.11, consists of the 3-bit precedence field and the 5-bit type of service field. The precedence field is used for a priority marking scheme that predates DiffServ. Specifically, it is used to mark IP packets so that a scheduler in a router will know with what priority to serve them. The higher the precedence value, the more important the traffic is. This marking scheme is not part of a QoS architecture and it is not associated with SLAs. The IP precedence values and the traffic type associated with each of them are given in table 9.4.

The type of service field in IPv4 was modified for DiffServ and renamed to the DS field. As shown in figure 9.12, it consists of the 6-bit DSCP field and the 3-bit *Explicit Congestion Notification* (ECN) field. In order to maintain backwards compatibility for routers not running DiffServ, the first three bits of the DSCP field (the class selector codepoints field) correspond to the precedence field. The DSCPs are expressed in binary or in decimal, and they are given in tables 9.5 and 9.6. The following four types of DiffServ classes have been defined:

- *Expedited forwarding* (EF)
- *Assured forwarding* (AF)
- The default PHB
- Class selector (CS)

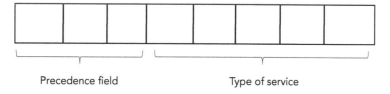

Precedence field   Type of service

Figure 9.11: The type of service field in IPv4

Binary	Name
111	Network control
110	Internet work control
101	Critical and emergency call processing
100	Flash override
011	Flash
010	Immediate
001	Priority
000	Routine

Table 9.4: Precedence values in IPv4

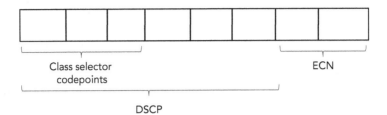

Figure 9.12: DS field

Code points	DSCP
Default/ CS0	000000
EF	101110
CS1	001000
CS2	010000
CS3	011000
CS4	100000
CS5	101000
CS6	110000
CS7	111000

Table 9.5: DSCP values

AF class	DSCP		
	Low (AFx1)	Medium (AFx2)	High (AFx3)
AF1x	AF11 = 001001	AF12 = 001010	AF13 = 001011
AF2x	AF21 = 010001	AF22 = 010010	AF23 = 010011
AF3x	AF31 = 011001	AF32 = 011010	AF33 = 011011
AF4x	AF41 = 100001	AF42 = 100010	AF43 = 100011

Table 9.6: DSCP values with drop precedence for the AF class

Applications	DiffServ class
IP routing	CS6
Voice	EF
Interactive video	AF41
Streaming video	CS4
Locally defined mission-critical data	AF31
Call signaling	AF31/CS3
Transactional data	AF21
Network management	CS2
Bulk data	AF11
Best effort	CS0
Scavenger	CS1

Table 9.7: Mapping of classes of traffic to DiffServ classes

The expedited forwarding (EF) class, given in table 9.5, is used to support applications that require low delay, low jitter, low packet loss, and assured bandwidth, such as VoIP. The assured forwarding (AF) classes, given separately in table 9.6, were designed to support data applications with assured bandwidth requirements. That is, packets will be forwarded with a high probability as long as the class rate submitted by the user does not exceed a predefined contracted rate. There are a total of 12 DSCPs within the assured forwarding class, namely AF1x, AF2x, AF3x, and AF4x, where x indicates the dropping priority which can be low (x = 1), medium (x = 2, and high (x = 3). We note that the AF class is the only class in DiffServ that can be marked for packet dropping.

The default class or CS0, given in table 9.5, is the best effort class. Because of its high use, a fair amount of bandwidth needs to be allocated to it. A similar class can be implemented through one of the AF classes. Finally, the class selector (CS) group of classes, given in table 9.5, is used to replace the classes based upon the IP precedence markings. (The first three bits correspond to the IP precedence values).

An example of how different classes of traffic can be mapped to DiffServ classes is given in table 9.7, see Cisco[6] for further details. The meaning of most of these classes of traffic is self-evident. The *locally-defined mission-critical data* class is used to provide an organization with a premium class of service for a select subset of their applications that have the highest business priority for them. For example, an enterprise may have provisioned Oracle, SAP, BEA, and DLSw+, in the transactional data class. However, the majority of their revenue may come from SAP, and therefore they may want to give this application an even higher level of preference by assigning it to a dedicated class such as the locally-defined mission-critical data class. The *transactional data* class is a combination of transactional client-server applications and interactive messaging applications. The *bulk data* class is intended for applications that are relatively non-interactive, insensitive to packet loss, and they typically span their operation over a long period of time as background occurrences. Such applications include: FTP, e-mail, backup operations, database synchronizing or replicating operations, content distribution, and any other type of background operations. Finally, the *scavenger* class has a lower priority than the best effort service. Applications assigned to this class are typically entertainment-oriented. These include: peer-to-peer media-sharing applications, such as, KaZaa, Morpheus, Grokster, Napster, and iMesh, gaming applications, such as, Doom, Quake, and Unreal Tournament, and any entertainment video applications. A discussion of the QoS and bandwidth requirements for some of the above classes is given in section 11.4.

9.4.2 EXPLICIT CONGESTION NOTIFICATION

The use of the explicit congestion notification (ECN) field in the DS field, figure 9.12, can be traced at least back to Frame Relay in the late 1980s. It was also the object of intense study in ATM networks during the 1990s. The idea behind it is that if congestion is encountered by packets in a router, the ECN field will be turned on by the router so that the receiver will know that somewhere upstream in the network congestion has occurred. The receiver can then take action to slow down the transmitter. Of course, it is possible that by the time the receiver notifies the transmitter the congestion may well have cleared up. The two-bit ECN field in the DS field was introduced to enable a similar congestion control scheme, but it has not been widely deployed.

9.5 MPLS SUPPORT FOR DIFFSERV

MPLS provides the capability to set up a connection using either the OSPF next hop routing or explicit routing. Bandwidth is allocated on each router along the path of the connection, and different classes of traffic can be defined using the EXP field. It is assumed that a policer is set up at the ingress of the MPLS domain to assure that the traffic is conformant, that is, it does not exceed the agreed upon bandwidth, and a scheduler in each router makes sure that packets are transmitted out according to their priority and requested quality of service.

MPLS does not define a policer, classes of service, and a scheduler. On the other hand, in DiffServ implementations, a scheduler, along with traffic classification, marking and metering are already available. Consequently, it makes sense to combine DiffServ with MPLS, see IETF RFC 3270[7].

DiffServ uses the 6-bit DiffServ code point (DSCP) to indicate the class of traffic, which in turn determines the per-hop behavior (PHB) for packets. In order to support DiffServ over MPLS, the DSCP has to be mapped to the 3-bit EXP field carried in the shim header. There are two options, depending upon how many PHBs the network supports.

- If the network supports up to 8 PHBs, then the mapping is straightforward, since each DSCP can be mapped into a unique EXP value. An LSP whose PHB is inferred from the EXP bits is called an *E-LSP*, where E stands for EXP inferred.
- If more than 8 PHBs are supported by the network, then they cannot be mapped into the EXP field. To resolve this issue, the label is associated with the PHB and the EXP field is used to convey the dropping priority. Thus, the PHB is determined from both the label and the EXP value. Such an LSP is know as an *L-LSP*, where L means that it is label inferred. A router associates a specific label with a PHB at connection setup.

A single E-LSP can carry traffic from different applications with different PHBs. A packet is classified to a PHB based on the EXP field. The association of the EXP values to the DiffServ code points could be done manually by configuration, or dynamically at the time the E-LSP is being set up.

An L-LSP can carry packets from a single PHB or from several PHBs as long as these PHBs are associated with the same scheduling rules, since the router will not be able to distinguish which packet belongs to which PHB. Packets in these PHBs, however, can have different dropping priority since this is signaled through their EXP field. For instance, packets belonging to the group of PHBs AF4x can be associated with the same L-LSP and they will all be treated the same way by the scheduler at each router. However, AF41, AF42 and AF43 packets can have different dropping priorities. Obviously, we cannot mix EF, AF and best effort classes onto the same L-LSP.

Bandwidth may or may not be reserved for an E-LSP or L-LSP at the time the LSP is being set up. When setting up an L-LSP with bandwidth, the requested bandwidth is allocated for the PHB that is associated with the L-LSP, and it is part of the overall bandwidth allocated for the specific PHB. When allocating bandwidth at setup time of an E-LSP, the signaled bandwidth is associated collectively for the set of PHBs carried in the EXP field.

9.6 MPLS DIFFSERV TE

Let us for a moment consider the DiffServ architecture without MPLS. As we saw above, DiffServ can control the traffic submitted by a user so that it is conformant to an agreed upon SLA. Also, a scheduler and a queueing policy at each router makes sure that the traffic associated with each DSCP gets its appropriate quality of service. However, DiffServ cannot control the total traffic that goes through a link, as there is no explicit bandwidth allocation on per link basis. In view of this, this problem is typically solved by over-engineering the network. This is an expensive solution, and still it does not provide any guarantees in the presence of link failures. MPLS on the other hand can guarantee bandwidth per connection and it can also provide protection in the presence of link failures.

Best practices dictate that the number of VoIP connections over a link should not account for more that a certain percentage of the link's total bandwidth. For instance, in the simple case where the network provider supports two types of traffic, namely VoIP and best effort, a link's capacity is divided into two groups of dedicated bandwidth, one for VoIP and the other for the best effort traffic. When a VoIP LSP is being set up, only the dedicated bandwidth to VoIP is available for allocation. If the VoIP bandwidth in a link is used up, then no more VoIP connection can be set up through that link, even if the bandwidth dedicated to best effort traffic is not used up. The same applies when the network provider supports more than two classes of traffic.

The concept of enforcing a dedicated bandwidth for each traffic class was formalized in DiffServ-aware MPLS-TE or simply DiffServ-TE, see IETF RFC 4142 [8]. Eight *Classes of Traffic* (CT), referred to as CT0 to CT7, were defined with CT7 having the highest priority and CT0 the lowest. Each class represents one or more code points, and the exact mapping of code points to CTs was not standardized. A possible mapping is to represent a group of code points that require the same scheduling behavior by the same CT. Each CT is carried by a separate LSP, referred to as *DiffServ-TE LSP*. Multiple LSPs can carry traffic from the same CT. (Multi-class LSPs have also been defined). The CT information for an LSP is transported at connection setup time.

TE-classes	(TC, priority)
TE0	(CT0,7)
TE1	(CT2,7)
TE2	(CT4,7)
TE3	(CT6,5)
TE4	(CT3,4)
TE5	(CT5,4)
TE6	(CT2,3)
TE7	(CT5,2)

Table 9.8: The eight TE classes

The interior gateway protocol, such as OSPF and IS-IS, must advertise the available bandwidth per CT. Since each LSP that carries a CT can be associated with 8 different priorities (indicated in the EXP field), we can have a total of 64 classes. For each of these classes bandwidth availability has to be advertized for each router. To minimize the volume of advertizing, only 8 classes are used derived from the eight CTs and the eight priorities. These classes are called TE-classes and they are given in table 9.8.

The percentage of the link's capacity allocated to a TE-class is called the *Bandwidth Constraint* (BC). Several BC models exist, with the most popular being the *Maximum Allocated Model* (MAM) and the *Russian Dolls Model* (RDM). In MAM a dedicated bandwidth is allocated to each TE-class. For instance, a 10 Gbps link in the example given above where the network provider uses two classes, VoIP and best effort, can be divided to 1 Gbps for VoIP and the remaining 9 Gbps for best effort. The 1 Gbps is used exclusively by VoIP LSPs and the 9 Gbps by best effort LSPs. One TE-class cannot use the bandwidth of the other TE-class, even if it is underutilized.

In the RDM case, a TE-class can share the bandwidth with other TE-classes. For instance TE7 which is the class with the strictest QoS requirements, is given a dedicated bandwidth, BC7. BC6 accommodates traffic from TE7 and TE6, BC6 from CT7, CT6, and CT5, and so on.

PROBLEMS

1. Consider the label bindings in table 9.2. How would the labels bindings change if we unplugged the link between C and D in figure 9.5?

2. Describe the difference between an explicit route and a hop-by-hop route. Under what conditions an explicit route between an ingress LSR and an egress LSR coincides with the hop-by-hop route?

3. An alternative to the unsolicited downstream scheme is the unsolicited upstream scheme, where the upstream LSR determines the label to be used on the link for a given FEC. Describe how the bindings of the labels will take place for the example in figure 9.5.

4. Consider the example of the LSP shown in figure 9.9. Let us assume that a second LSP has to be set up from LSRs 2 to 7 (over the TE-link). Show the label stack on each hop and the label operation that has to be performed at each LSR.

5. In DiffServ, best practices dictate that the number of VoIP connections over a link should not account for more that a certain percentage of the link's total bandwidth. Explain the reasoning behind this. (Hint: assume that the total traffic going through the queues of an output port, including the VoIP traffic, is less than the link's capacity.)

REFERENCES

[1] IETF RFC 2702, "Requirements for Traffic Engineering Over MPLS".
[2] IETF RFC 3031, "Multiprotocol Label Switching Architecture".
[3] OpenFlow, URL: http://www.openflow.org/documents/openflow-spec-v1.1.0.pdf.
[4] OnePK, URL: http://developer.cisco.com/web/onepk/home
[5] IETF RFC 2474, "Definition of the Differentiated Services Field (DS Field) in the IPv4 and IPv6 Headers".
[6] Cisco, "Quality of Service Design Overview".
[7] IETF RFC 3270, "MPLS Support of Differentiated Services".
[8] IETF RFC 4142, "Protocol Extensions for Support of Diffserv-aware MPLS Traffic Engineering".

CHAPTER 10: LABEL DISTRIBUTION PROTOCOLS

10.1 INTRODUCTION

MPLS requires a set of procedures for the reliable distribution of label bindings between LSRs. MPLS does not require the use of a specific label distribution protocol. In view of this, various schemes have been proposed for the distribution of labels, of which the *Label Distribution Protocol* (LDP) and the *Resource Reservation Protocol – Traffic Engineering* (RSVP–TE), are widely used.

LDP was designed specifically with a view to distributing labels for a specific FEC to the neighbors of an LSR. It can also distribute labels between two LSRs which are several hops away. LDP was extended to the *Constraint-Based Routing Label Distribution Protocol* (CR-LDP), used to set up point-to-point and point-to-multipoint LSPs. An alternative method to developing a label distribution protocol was to extend an existing protocol, such as, the *Border Gateway Protocol* (BGP), the *Protocol-Independent Multicast* (PIM), and the *Resource Reservation Protocol* (RSVP), so that it can carry labels. RSVP, originally designed for the IntServ architecture, was extended to *RSVP-Traffic Engineering* (RSVP-TE) for setting up point-to-point and point-to-multipoint LSPs. CR-LDP and RSVP-TE were competing protocols, and IETF voted to abandon CR-LDP in favor of continuing to support RSVP-TE.

In this Chapter, we describe LDP, RSVP, and RSVP-TE, starting with LDP. Subsequently, we describe RSVP-TE, which is used to set up point-to-point connections and also multicast connections (not considered in this book). In order to understand how RSVP-TE works, we first need to understand RSVP. In view of this, in section 10.3 we describe RSVP, and then in section 10.4 we describe RSVP-TE.

MPLS was developed for IP packet-switched networks that run over interfaces, such as packet-over-SONET and gigabit Ethernet. In addition, it was designed for IP packet-switched networks that run over ATM and Frame Relay. In the case of ATM, the MPLS label is carried in the VPI/VCI fields of the ATM header, and in the case of Frame Relay, the label is carried in the DLCI field of the Frame Relay header. Consequently, both LDP and RSVP-TE have extensions for the case where the underlying transport network is ATM and Frame Relay. In this Chapter, we will not consider the ATM and Frame Relay cases, and we will simply assume that the link interfaces are gigabit Ethernet or packet-over-SONET. A more complete description of this protocol is given in Perros[1].

10.2 THE LABEL DISTRIBUTION PROTOCOL (LDP)

LDP is used to distribute and maintain labels for a given FEC to the neighbors of an LSR, see IETF RFC 3037 [2], and IETF RFC 5036 [3]. As a result, a mulitpoint-to-point tree-like connection is established, as shown in figure 9.6, where the root of the tree is the destination LSR that serves the FEC, and the leaves are the ingress LSRs into the MPLS domain. Within an MPLS domain, there is one such tree of labels for each FEC.

In order for two LSRs to be able to exchange labels for a given FEC, they have first to *peer*. This peering process involves setting up a *hello adjacency* between the two LSRs over which an *LDP session* is established. Label binding messages between the two LSRs are exchanged over the LDP session. Two LSRs that use LDP to exchange label bindings are known as *LDP peers*. LDP provides a number of different LDP messages which are grouped as follows:

- *Discovery messages:* They are used to announce and maintain the presence of an LSR in the network.
- *Session messages:* They are used to establish, maintain, and terminate LDP sessions between LDP peers.
- *Advertisement messages:* They are used to create, change, and delete label bindings to FECs.
- *Notification messages:* They are used to provide advisory information and to signal error information.

LDP runs on top of TCP for reliability, with the exception of the LDP discovery messages that run over the *User Datagram Protocol* (UDP). Below, we first describe how an LDP session is set up and then describe the LDP messages and their format.

10.2.1 LABEL SPACE, LDP SESSION, AND HELLO ADJACENCY

LDP makes use of the concept of the label space, which is the set of all labels used in an LSR. Two types of label spaces have been defined: *per interface label space* and *per platform label space*. The per interface label space is used for ATM and Frame Relay interfaces. The per platform label space is a set of labels used for all interfaces other than ATM and Frame Relay interfaces, such as packet-over-SONET and gigabit Ethernet. The per platform labels are carried in the shim header shown in figure 9.3. As mentioned in the introduction, we will not consider ATM and Frame Relay interfaces, and consequently, we will assume a single per platform label space for each LSR.

An LSR label space is identified by a six-byte value, referred to as the *LDP id*. The first four bytes carry a globally unique value identifying the LSR, such as a 32-bit router id that has been assigned to the LSR by the autonomous system administrator. The last two bytes identify the label space. If the label space is per platform, then the last two bytes are set to zero.

An LDP discovery mechanism enables an LSR to discover potential LDP peers, that is, other LSRs which are directly connected to it. An LSR sends periodically *LDP link hellos* out of each interface. Hello packets are sent over UDP addressed to a well-known LDP discovery port for the "all routers on this subnet" group multicast address. An LDP link hello sent by an LSR carries the per platform label space id and possibly additional information. Receipt of an LDP link hello identifies a *hello adjacency*. For each interface, there is one hello adjacency.

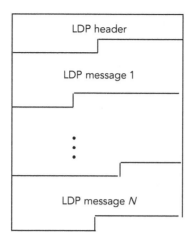

Figure 10.1: The LDP PDU format

An extended discovery mechanism can be also used for non-directly connected LSRs. This is useful when two distant LSRs may want to communicate, as in the case of pseudowires, see Chapter 13. An LSR periodically sends *LDP targeted hellos* to a specific IP address over UDP. Receipt of an LDP targeted hello identifies a hello adjacency.

The exchange of LDP link hellos between two LSRs triggers the establishment of an LDP session, over which label binding messages can be exchanged. First, a TCP session is established, and then, an LDP session is initialized, during which the two LSRs negotiate session parameters, such as, protocol version, label distribution method, and timer values. If there is a single link between two LSRs, then a single hello adjacency and a single LDP session are set up. If there are parallel links, then there are as many hello adjacencies as the number of links, but only one LDP session.

An LSR maintains a timer for each hello adjacency, which it restarts each time it receives a hello message. If the timer expires without having received a hello message from the peer LSR, the hello adjacency is deleted. The LDP session is terminated, if all hello adjacencies associated with an LDP session are deleted. In addition to this timer, an LSR also maintains a *keepAlive* timer for each session. The timer is reset each time it receives any LDP PDU from its LDP peer. If the LDP peer has nothing to send, it sends a keepAlive message. The LDP session is terminated if the timer expires without hearing from the peer LDP.

10.2.2 THE LDP PDU FORMAT

An LDP PDU consists of an LDP header followed by one or more LDP messages, which may not be related to each other, as shown in figure 10.1. The LDP header consists of the following fields:

- *Version:* A 16-bit field that contains the protocol version
- *PDU length:* A 16-bit field that gives the total length of the LDP PDU in bytes, excluding the version and PDU length fields of the LDP PDU header.

- *LDP id:* A 48-bit field with the form <32-bit router id, label space number>, that contains the label space id.

The LDP message format consists of a header followed by mandatory and optional parameters. The header and parameters are encoded using the *type-length-value* (TLV) scheme shown in figure 10.2. The following fields have been defined:

- *U (Unknown TLV bit):* It is used when an unknown TLV is received. If U = 0, a notification is returned to the message originator and the entire message is ignored. If U = 1, the TLV is silently ignored and the rest of the message is processed as if the TLV did not exist.
- *(Forward unknown TLV bit):* This bit applies only when U = 1, and the LDP message containing the unknown TLV has to be forwarded. If F = 0, the unknown TLV is not forwarded with the rest of the message. If F = 1, the unknown TLV is forwarded with the rest of the message.
- *Type:* A 14-bit field that describes how the value field is to be interpreted.
- *Length:* A 16-bit field that gives the length of the value field in bytes.
- *Value:* It contains information which is interpreted as specified in the type field. It may contain TLV encoding.

10.2.3 THE LDP MESSAGES

The LDP message format is shown in figure 10.3. The following fields have been defined:

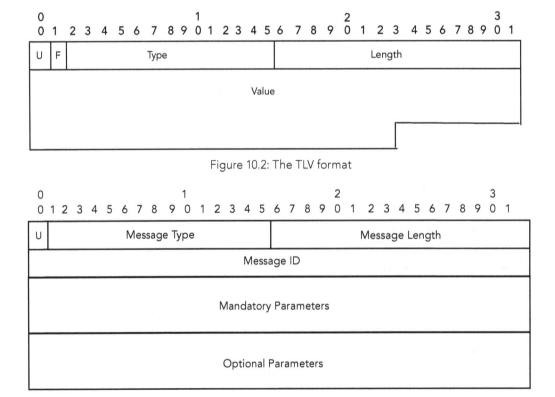

Figure 10.2: The TLV format

Figure 10.3: The LDP message format

- *U (Unknown message bit):* Upon receipt of an unknown message, if U = 0, a notification is returned to the message originator. If U = 1, the unknown message is silently ignored.

  Message type: A 15-bit field used to identify the type of message.
- *Message length:* A 16-bit field that gives the total length in bytes of the message ID field and the mandatory and optional parameters fields.
- *Message ID:* A 32-bit value used to identify this message. Subsequent messages related to this one have to carry the same message ID.

The mandatory fields will be discussed separately for each individual LDP message.

The following LDP messages have been defined: *notification, hello, initialization, keepAlive, address, address withdraw, label mapping, label request, label abort request, label withdraw, and label release.*

NOTIFICATION MESSAGE

It is used to inform an LDP peer of a fatal error or to provide advisory information regarding the outcome of processing an LDP message or the state of an LDP session. Some of the notification messages are:

- Malformed PDU or message
- Unknown or malformed TLV
- Session keepAlive timer expiration
- Unilateral session shutdown
- Initialization message events
- Events resulting from other errors

HELLO MESSAGE

LDP hello messages are exchanged as part of the LDP discovery mechanism. The format of the hello message is shown in figure 10.3, with the U bit set to zero, and the message type set to hello (0x0100). The mandatory parameters field, referred to as *the common hello parameters TLV,* is shown in figure 10.5. The following fields have been defined for the common hello parameters TLV:

- *Hold time:* It specifies the *hello hold time* in seconds. This is the time that the sending LSR will maintain its record of a hello from the receiving LSR without receipt of another hello. If hold time = 0, then the defaulted

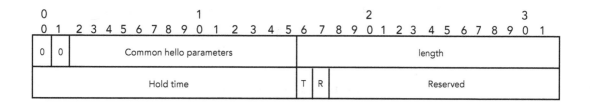

Figure 10.4: The common hello parameters TLV

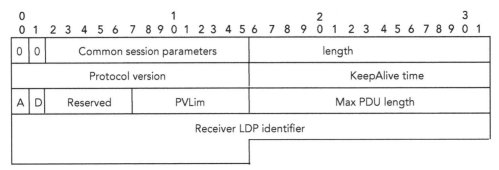

Figure 10.5: The common session parameters TLV

value is used, which is 15 sec for link hellos and 45 sec for targeted hellos. A value of 0xffff means infinite. The hold timer is reset each time a hello message is received. If it expires before a hello message is received, the hello adjacency is deleted.

- *T:* It specifies if it is a targeted hello (T = 1) or a link hello (T = 0).
- *R:* This field is known as the *request send targeted hellos.* A value of 1 indicates that the receiver is requested to send periodic targeted hellos to the source of this hello. A value of 0 makes no such request.

INITIALIZATION MESSAGE

This message is used to request the establishment of an LDP session. The format of the initialization message is shown in figure 10.3, with the U bit set to zero, and the message type set to initialization (0x0200). The format for the mandatory parameters field, referred to as the *common session parameters TLV,* is shown in figure 10.5. The following fields have been defined:

- *KeepAlive time:* It indicates the maximum number of seconds that may elapse between the receipt of two successive LDP PDUs. The keepAlive timer is reset each time an LDP PDU is received.
- *A:* It indicates the type of label advertisement. Downstream unsolicited (A = 0), or downstream on demand (A = 1). Downstream on demand is used for an ATM or a Frame Relay link. Otherwise, downstream unsolicited must be used.
- *D:* It is used to enable loop detection
- *PVLim (Path vector limit):* Gives the maximum number of LSRs recorded in the path vector used for loop detection.
- *Max PDU length:* Defaulted value of the maximum allowable length is 4096 bytes.
- *Receiver LDP identi ier:* Identifies the receiver's label space.

KEEPALIVE MESSAGE

An LSR sends keepAlive messages as part of the mechanism that monitors the integrity of an LDP session. The format of the keepAlive message is shown in figure 10.3, with the U bit set to zero, and the message type set to keepAlive (0x0201). No mandatory or optional parameters are provided.

ADDRESS AND ADDRESS WITHDRAW MESSAGES

Before sending a label mapping and a label request messages, an LSR advertises its interface addresses using the address messages. Previously advertised addresses can be withdrawn using the address withdraw message.

LABEL MAPPING MESSAGE

An LSR uses the message to advertise a mapping of a label to a FEC to its LDP peers. The format of the label mapping message has the same structure as the one shown in figure 10.3, with the U bit set to zero and the message type set to label mapping (0x0400). The mandatory parameters field consists of a FEC TLV and a label TLV.

In LDP a FEC element could be either a prefix or it could be an IP address of a destination LSR. The FEC TLV is shown in figure 10.6. LDP permits a FEC to be specified by a set of *FEC elements*, with each FEC element identifying a set of packets which may be mapped to the corresponding LSP. (This can be useful, for instance, when an LSP is shared by multiple FEC destinations all sharing the same path).

The label TLV gives the label associated with the FEC in the FEC TLV, and it is shown in figure 10.7.

LABEL REQUEST MESSAGE

An LSR sends a label request message to an LPD peer to request a mapping to particular FEC. The label request message has the format shown in figure 10.3, with the U bit set to zero, and the message type set to label request (0x0401). The mandatory parameters field contains the FEC TLV shown in figure 10.6.

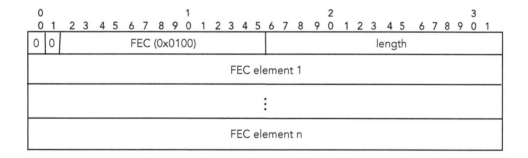

Figure 10.6: The FEC TLV

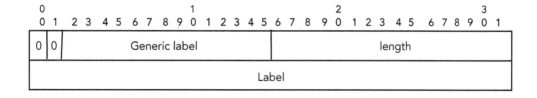

Figure 10.7: The generic label TLV

An LSR may transmit a label request message under the following conditions:

- The LSR recognizes a new FEC via its forwarding routing table; the next hop for the FEC is an LDP peer, and the LSR does not have a mapping from the next hop.
- The next hop for a given FEC changes and the LSR does not already have a mapping from the new next hop.
- The LSR receives a label request for a FEC from an upstream LDP peer; the next hop towards the FEC is an LDP peer and the LSR does not have a mapping from the next hop.

LABEL ABORT REQUEST, LABEL WITHDRAW, AND LABEL RELEASE MESSAGES

An LSR A may send a label abort message to an LDP peer LSR B to abort an outstanding label request message. This may happen, for instance, if LSR A's next hop for the FEC has changed from LSR B to a different LSR.

The label withdraw message is used by an LSR A to signal to an LDP peer LSR B that it may not continue to use a specific FEC-label mapping that LSR A had previously advertised.

Finally, the label release message is sent by LSR A to an LDP peer LSR B to signal to LSR B that LSR A no longer needs a specific FEC-label mapping previously requested of and/or advertised by the peer.

10.3 THE RESOURCE RESERVATION PROTOCOL (RSVP)

The resource reservation protocol (RSVP) was proposed as a signaling protocol for the *Integrated Service* (IntServ) architecture. RSVP is not used in MPLS. Rather, an extension of it, known as RSVP-TE, is used to set up LSPs. In order to understand RSVP-TE, we have to first understand how RSVP works. In view of this, in this section, we will describe the main features of RSVP and in the following section we will describe RSVP-TE.

The IntServ architecture was developed by IETF in the mid 1990s with a view to introducing QoS in the IP network. It supports point-to-point and many-to-many connections. In this Chapter, we focus primarily on point-to-point connections.

The following two service classes were defined in Intserv: *guaranteed service* and *controlled-load service*. The guaranteed service, provides firm bounds on the end-to-end queueing delay with no packet loss for all conforming packets. The controlled-load service provides the user with a QoS that approximates closely the QoS that a best effort service user would receive from an unloaded network. Specifically, a user may assume the following:

1. A very high percentage of transmitted packets will be successfully delivered by the network to the receiver. The percentage of packets not successfully delivered must closely approximate the basic packet error rate of the transmission links.
2. The end-to-end delay experienced by a very high percentage of the delivered packets will not greatly exceed the minimum end-to-end delay experienced by any successfully delivered packet.

In IntServ, the sender indicates to the network the traffic characteristics of the data flow that it will generate, but it is the receiver (or receivers, in case of a multiparty conference) that determines the final traffic characteristics, the desired transmission rate, and QoS. This permits an efficient handling of large groups with dynamic group membership and heterogeneous receivers. The information provided by the receiver is used by each IP router along the path to perform the following functions:

1. *Policing:* This is used to verify that the traffic transmitted by the sender conforms to the traffic descriptors specified by the receiver.
2. *Admission control:* This is used to decide whether an IP router has adequate resources to meet the requested QoS.
3. *Classification:* This is used to decide which IP packets should be considered as part of the sender's traffic and be given the requested QoS.
4. *Queueing and scheduling:* In order for an IP router to provide different quality of service to different receivers, it has to be able to queue packets into different queues in each output port and transmit packets out of these queues according to a scheduler.

(The above functions of policing, admission control, packet classification, and queueuing and scheduling, are described in detail in the next Chapter on Congestion Control.)

The IntServ architecture requires a signaling protocol for the reliable establishment and maintenance of resource reservations. As in MPLS, IntServ does not require the use of a specific signaling protocol, and it can accommodate a variety of signaling protocols, of which RSVP is the most popular one, see IETF RFC 2205[4]. RSVP was developed to support the IntServ architecture, but it can be used to carry other types of control information. This is because RSVP is not aware of the content of the protocol fields that contain traffic and policy control information used by the routers to reserve resources. RSVP was designed with a view to supporting point-to-point and connections and multiparty many-to-many connections with heterogeneous receivers.

In RSVP, the resource reservation is decided and initiated by the receiver, since only the receiver actually knows how much bandwidth it has available. This approach also permits a receiver to join or leave a multicast whenever it wants. One problem with the receiver-initiated approach is that the receiver does not know the path from the sender to itself. Therefore, it cannot request resource allocation on each router along the path since it does not know which are these routers. This problem is solved using the *Path* message that originates from the sender and travels along the unicast or multicast route to the receiver. The main purpose of the Path message is to store the *path state* information in each node along the path and to carry information regarding the sender's traffic characteristics and the end-to-end path properties. The following is some of the information contained in the Path message:

- *Phop:* This is the address of the previous hop RSVP-capable router that forwards the message. This address is stored in the path state information at each node, and it is used to send the reservation message upstream towards the sender.

- *Sender template:* This field carries the sender's IP address and optionally the UDP/TCP sender port.
- *Sender TSpec:* This defines the traffic characteristics of the data flow that the sender will generate. The format of the sender Tspec used for the IntServ architecture will be described below.
- *Adspec:* This carries One-Pass with Advertising (OPWA) information. This is information (advertisements) gathered at each node along the path followed by the Path message. This information is delivered to the receiver who can then use it to construct a reservation request or adjust appropriately an existing reservation.

Upon receipt of the Path message, the receiver sends a *Resv* message towards the sender along the reverse path that the Path message followed, as shown in figure 10.8. The following is some of the information contained in the Resv message:

- *Flowspec:* It specifies the desired QoS. It consists of the receiver TSpec, the RSpec, and the service class. The receiver TSpec is a set of traffic descriptors and it is used by the nodes along the path to reserve resources. The RSpec defines the desired bandwidth and delay guarantees. In IntServ, the service class could be either the guaranteed service or the controlled-load service. The format for the receiver TSpec and RSpec used in the IntServ architecture is described below.
- *Filter spec:* Defines the packets that will receive the requested QoS defined in the flowspec. A simple filter spec could be just the sender's IP address and optionally its UDP or TCP port.

When a router receives the Resv message, it reserves resources per the receiver's instructions and then sends the Resv message to the pervious hop router obtained from the path state information.

RSVP messages are sent in raw IP datagrams without a TCP or UDP encapsulation. (UDP encapsulation is permitted for routers that do not support raw IP datagrams).

RSVP makes use of the notion of *data flow* and *session*. A session is defined by the parameters: destination IP address, protocol id, and optionally destination port number. A data flow is simply the packets transmitted by a sender in a particular session.

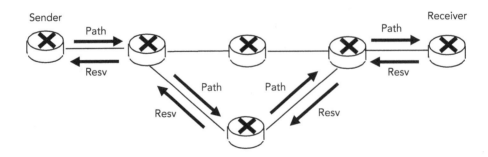

Figure 10.8: An example of the Path and Resv messages

RSVP is simplex, that is, it makes reservations for unidirectional data flows. Therefore, in order for two users A and B to communicate both ways, two separate sessions have to be established; one session from A to B, and another one from B to A.

10.3.1 RESERVATION STYLES

Three different *reservation styles*, i.e., reservation schemes, can be used with RSVP. In order to understand these schemes, let us consider the case where a number of senders transmit information to the same receiver. Each sender transmits its own data flow of packets in a session, which is defined by the receiver's IP address and protocol id. One reser-vation option is concerned with the resource reservation of these sessions. In particular, let us assume that sev-eral of these data flows pass through the same router. The router has the option to establish a separate reserva-tion for each data flow or to make a single reservation for all the data flows.

A second reservation option controls the selection of the senders. It may be *explicit* or *wildcard*. In the explicit sender selection, the receiver provides a list of senders from which it wishes to receive data. A sender cannot send packets to the receiver unless its IP address is in the explicit list. In the wildcard sender selection, any sender may transmit data to the receiver.

Based on these two reservation options the following three different styles have been defined:

1. *Wildcard-filter (WF) style*: Any sender can transmit to the session and there is a single resource reserva- tion shared by all the data flows from all upstream senders. The resource reservation is the largest of all requested reservations.
2. *Fixed-filter (FF) style:* A separate reservation is made for each particular sender specified in the explicit list of senders. Other senders identified in the explicit list which transmit in the same session do not share this reservation.
3. *Shared explicit (SE) style:* A list of senders is explicitly stated and there is a single shared reservation for all their flows.

10.3.2 SOFT STATE

RSVP takes a soft state approach to managing the reservation state in the routers and hosts. That is the state infor-mation in each router and host has to be periodically refreshed (usually about every 30 seconds) by Path and Resv messages. The state of a reservation is deleted if no matching refreshing messages arrive before a cleanup timeout interval. State may also be deleted by an explicit teardown message.

When a route changes, the next Path message will initialize the path state on the routers along the new route and the Resv message will establish a reservation on each of these routers. The state of the unused route will time out.

RSVP sends its messages as IP datagrams with no guarantee that they will get delivered. An RSVP message may never get delivered due to transmission errors or buffer overflows. This situation is taken care by the periodic refresh messages. Sending refresh messages increases the load on the network, but it eliminates the need to use a reliable protocol such as TCP which can guarantee the reliable delivery of RSVP messages.

10.3.3 THE RSVP MESSAGE FORMAT

An RSVP message consists of a common header followed by a variable number of *objects*. Each object contains a group of related parameters and it has a variable length. The common header format is shown in figure 10.9. The following fields have been defined:

- *Vers:* A 4-bit field used to indicate the protocol version number.
- *Flags:* A 4-bit field used for flags.
- *MsgType:* The message type is specified by a number carried in this 8-bit field. The following messages types and numbers have been specified:

  1 – *Path*

  2 – *Resv*

  3 – *PathErr*

  4 – *ResvErr*

  5 – *PathTear*

  6 – *ResvTear*

  7 – *ResvConf*

- *RSVP checksum:* A 16-bit checksum calculated on the entire message.
- *Send_TTL:* An 8-bit field that contains the IP time to live value.
- *RSVP length:* The total length in bytes is stored in this 8-bit field. The length includes the common header and all the objects that follow.

The object format is shown in figure 10.10. The following fields have been defined:

- *Length:* A 16-bit field used to indicate the total length in bytes of the object. It must be a multiple of 4, and at least equal to 4.
- *Class-num:* An 8-bit field used to identify the object class.
- *C-Type:* An 8-bit field used to define the object type.

The following object classes have been defined:

- *NULL:* The contents of a NULL object are ignored by the receiver.
- *SESSION:* It contains the IP destination address, the IP protocol id, and optionally a destination port. This object is required in every RSVP message.

4 bits	4 bits	8 bits	16 bits
Vers	Flags	MsgType	RSVP checksum
Send_TTL		Reserved	RSVP length

Figure 10.9: The common header format

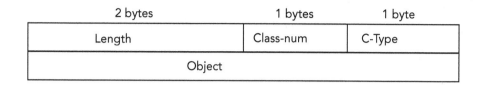

Figure 10.10: The object format

- *RSVP_HOP:* It carries the IP address of the RSVP-capable router that sent this message. The RSVP_HOP object is referred to as the PHOP (previous hop) object for messages from the sender to the receiver, and the NHOP (next hop) object for messages from the receiver to the sender.
- *TIME_VALUES:* It contains the value for the refresh period used by the creator of the message. It is required in every Path and Resv message.
- *STYLE:* It defines the reservation style plus style-specific information. It is required in every Resv message.
- *FLOWSPEC:* It carries the necessary information in an Resv message to make a reservation in a router.
- *FILTER_SPEC:* It defines which data packets should receive the QoS specified in the FLOWSPEC object. It is required in a Resv message.
- *SENDER_TEMPLATE:* It defines the sender's IP address and perhaps some additional demultiplexing information, such as a port number. It is required in a Path message.
- *SENDER_TSPEC:* It contains the traffic characteristics of the sender's data flow. It is required in a Path message.
- *ADSPEC:* It carries the one-pass with advertising (OPWA) information. As discussed above, this information is gathered at each node along the path followed by the Path message. This information is delivered to the receiver who can then use it to construct a reservation request or adjust appropriately an existing reservation
- *ERROR_SPEC:* It specifies an error in a PathErr, ResvErr, or a confirmation in a ResvConf message.
- *POLICY_DATA:* It carries information that allows a router to decide whether a reservation is administratively permitted. It may appear in a Path, Resv, PathErr, or ResvErr message. One or more POLICY_DATA objects may be used.
- *INTEGRITY:* It carries cryptographic data to authenticate the originating node to verify the contents of this RSVP message.
- *SCOPE:* It carries an explicit list of senders towards the information in the message is to be forwarded. It may appear in a Resv, ResvErr, or ResvTear message.
- *RESV_CONFIRM:* It carries the IP address of a receiver that requested a confirmation. It may appear in a Resv or ResvConf message.

Below, we describe the Path and Resv messages.

10.3.4 THE PATH MESSAGE

The Path message consists of the common header shown in figure 10.9 followed by the objects:

- INTEGRITY (optional)
- SESSION
- RSVP_HOP
- TIME_VALUES
- POLICY_DATA objects (optional)
- An optional sender descriptor consisting of the SENDER_TEMPLATE and the SENDER_TSPEC
- ADSPEC (optional)

Each sender sends a Path message for each data flow it wishes to transmit. The Path message is forwarded from router to router using the next-hop information in the routing table until it reaches the receiver. Each router along the path captures and processes the Path message. The router creates a path state for the pair {sender, receiver} defined in the SENDER_TEMPLATE and SESSION objects of the Path message. Any POLICY_DATA, SENDER_ TSPEC, and ADSPEC objects are also saved in the path state. If an error is encountered a PathErr message is sent back to the originator of the Path message.

10.3.5 THE RESV MESSAGE

When a receiver receives a Path message, it issues a Resv message which is sent back to the sender along the reverse path traveled by the Path message. We recall that the data packets follow the same path traveled by the Path message. The Resv message is a request to each node along the path to reserve resources for the data flow. It consists of the common header shown in figure 10.9 followed by the objects:

- INTEGRITY (optional)
- SESSION
- RSVP_HOP
- TIME_VALUES
- RESV_CONFIRM (optional)
- SCOPE (optional)
- POLICY_DATA objects (optional)
- STYLE
- A flow descriptor list

The RSVP_HOP contains the NHOP, that is the IP address of the router that sent the Resv message. The presence of the RESV_CONFRIM object in the Resv message is a signal to the router to send a ResvConf message to the receiver to confirm the reservation. The RESV_CONFIRM carries the IP address of the receiver.

The flow descriptor list is style dependent. For the wildcard-filter (WF) style the flow descriptor list consists of the

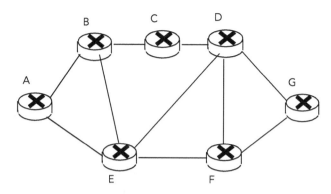

Figure 10.11: An MPLS network

FLOWSPEC object. For the Fixed-filter (FF) and shared explicit (SE) styles, it consists of the objects FLOWSPEC and FILTER_SPEC.

As mentioned above, RSVP is not aware of the content of the RSVP objects that contain the traffic information used by the routers to reserve resources. This was done purposefully so that the applicability of RSVP is not restricted to the IntServ architecture. Below, we describe the contents of the SENDER_SPEC and FLOWSPEC objects as they have been defined for the IntServ architecture.

The SENDER_TSPEC contains the traffic parameters: token bucket rate, token bucket size, peak data rate, minimum policed unit (i.e., size of smallest allowable packet), and maximum policed unit (i.e., size of maximum allowable packet).

The contents of the FLOWSPEC depend on whether the controlled-load service or the guaranteed service is requested. When requesting the controlled-load service, the FLOWSPEC consists of the receiver TSPec which contains values for the parameters: token bucket rate, token bucket size, peak data rate minimum policed unit, and maximum policed unit. These parameters are used to calculate the resource reservation in a router.

When requesting the guaranteed service, the FLOWSPEC consists of the receiver TSpec and the Rspec which carries the parameters rate and slack time. These two parameters are used to define the desired bandwidth and delay guarantee.

10.4 RESOURCE RESERVATION PROTOCOL – TRAFFIC ENGINEERING (RSVP–TE)

RSVP-TE was defined in IETF RFC 3209[5], and it is used to setup unidirectional point-to-point and multicast (not considered here) LSPs. As described in section 9.3.1 of the previous Chapter, the route can be hop-by-hop or explicit. A hop-by-hop route follows the next hop stored in the forwarding tables of each LSR, as calculated using the shortest path algorithm. An explicit route is calculated so that to satisfy a QoS criterion, such as minimizations of the end-to-end delay, and maximization of throughput. Such a QoS criterion may not be necessarily satisfied by the hop-by-hop routing, which minimizes the number of hops only. An LSP set up following an explicit route is known as a constrained-based routed label switched path (CR-LSP). The calculation of an explicit route is beyond the scope of MPLS. It may be calculated manually, or there may be a path computation entity which has a complete view of the network topology and current loading and which can compute routes based on a QoS criterion. Examples of such entities are: the *Resource and Admission Control Functions* (RACF) and the *Path Computation Element* (PCE) described in Chapter 12, OpenFlow[6], and OnePK[7].

CR-LSPs can be used in a variety of ways. For instance, they can be used in an IP network to do load balancing. That is, the traffic among its links can be evenly distributed by forcing some of the traffic over CR-LSPs which pass through links which are less utilized. CR-LSPs can also be used to create tunnels in MPLS, and introduce routes based on a QoS criterion, such as minimization of the total end-to-end delay, and maximization of throughput.

For example, let us consider the MPLS network in figure 10.11. The shortest path in terms of number of hops between the ingress LSR A and the egress LSR G is the one that passes through LSRs E and F. Using RSVP-TE we can set up a CR-LSP that satisfies a QoS criterion, such as minimize the end-to-end delay, which may be other than the shortest path. For instance, let us assume that LSRs B, C, and D are lightly utilized, so that the total end-to-end queueing delay is less than that in the shortest path. Assuming that when we factor the propagation delay, the total end-to-end delay is still less than in the shortest path, then the CR-LSP will be set up through LSRs B, C, and D, even if the number of hops is higher than the shortest path.

In keeping with the terminology used in RSVP-TE (which in fact is the same as in RSVP) we will use the terms *node, sender* and *receiver* to indicate an LSR, an ingress LSR, and an egress LSR respectively. We recall that in RSVP, a session is a data flow with a particular IP destination address and protocol id. In RSVP-TE, a session is an LSP.

RSVP-TE uses downstream-on-demand label allocation with ordered control to set up an LSP. That is, for each link, the label is provided by the downstream LSR upon request from the upstream LSR. Also, labels are allocated from the egress LSR, i.e., the receiver, towards the ingress LSR, i.e., the sender. This is implemented using the Path and Resv messages which have been augmented with new objects. For instance, a new object called the EXPLIC-IT_ROUTE, is used to carry the hops that make up the explicit path. Each hop in the path can be an individual node or an *abstract* node. An abstract node is a group of nodes whose internal topology is opaque to the sender. An abstract node is used to represent a domain that belongs to a different network provider, whose internal topology is not known. Strict or loose routing through an abstract node is permitted.

In figure 10.12, we show how an LSP is set up. The sender, i.e., the ingress node LSR A, sends a Path message to LSR B, which includes a LABEL REQUEST object. This is a new object and it indicates that a label for the path is requested. If an explicit route is used, then the EXPLICIT_ROUTE object will be also inserted in the Path message. If the LSP is set up using the next hop information in the routing table, then the EXPLICIT_ROUTE object is not included. LSR B is the next hop indicated either in the routing table for the particular IP destination address of the receiver if hop-by-hop routing is used, or the next hop indicated in the EXPLICIT_ROUTE object if explicit routing is used.

Because of the ordered control scheme, LSR B cannot issue a label to LSR A until it has received one from its downstream LSR. In view of this, it forwards the Path message to LSR C requesting a label for the path. For the same

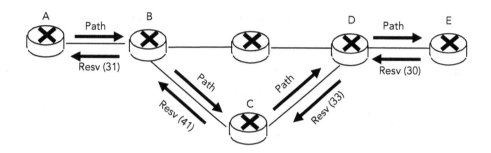

Figure 10.12: Setting up an LSP

reason, LSR C forwards it to LSR D requesting a label, and finally LSR D sends it to the ingress LSR E of the LSP requesting a label. LSR E responds with a Resv message, which is sent back to LSR D. The Resv message includes a new object called the LABEL object, which is used to carry the label. When LSR D receives the Resv message it allocates a new label, binds the two labels in the LFIB and sends the Resv message with the new label in the LABEL object to LSR C. The same procedure takes place at LSRs C and B. The LSP is established when LSR A receives the Resv message, and traffic can now flow from LSR A to E. The labels are shown in figure 10.12 in a parenthesis after the Resv message.

For bidirectional LSPs. LSR E has to issue a Path message which is forwarded by the intermediate LSRs to LSR A, which in turn responds with a Resv message. As the Resv message propagates towards LSR E, it allocates labels that will be used for traffic from LSR E to A.

RSVP-TE can reserve resources along the LSP. Bandwidth can be allocated to an LSP using standard RSVP reservations together with IntServ service classes. Resource reservation is optional, and LSPs can be set up without reserving resources. Such LSPs can be used, for instance, for best effort traffic and implement backup paths.

Other features of RSVP-TE include setup and hold priorities for an LSP, and dynamic re-route of an established LSP. Also, by adding a RECORD_ROUTE object to the Path message, the sender can receive information about the actual route that the LSP traverses.

10.4.1 SERVICE CLASSES AND RESERVATION STYLES

There is no restriction in RSVP-TE as to which IntServ service classes should be supported. RSVP-TE, however, should support the controlled-load service and the *null service*. This is a newer service where an application does not request a resource reservation on each node along the path from the sender to the receiver. Instead, a QoS policy agent in each node provides the appropriate QoS parameters to the application, as determined by a network administrator.

In the previous section, we defined the three RSVP reservation styles: wildcard-filter (WF), fixed-filter (FF), and shared explicit (SE). Of these three reservation styles, the wildcard-filter is not used in RSVP-TE. The receiver can use the FF or SE style for an LSP, and it can choose different styles for different LSPs.

When using the FF style, each LSP has its own reservation on each node along the path, and each node allocates a unique label for each sender. For instance, if an explicit route is set up using the FF style, then each node will reserve resources for the LSP and a unique label that the previous-hop node has to use when transmitting packets in this specific LSP. Now, let us consider the case where an LSP is set up using the next-hop information from the routing table. In this case, if there are multiple senders, a multipoint-to-point inverse tree will be formed. Each sender has its own path to the receiver, which is independent of the paths from the other receivers. A node in this inverse tree that handles several such paths, reserves separate resources to each path and allocates a different label for each path to be used by the previous-hop node. As a result of these actions, this inverse tree consists of multiple point-to-point independent LSPs. This also means that the same previous-hop node may use different labels to transmit traffic to the same receiver from different senders.

The SE style allows a receiver to explicitly specify the senders to be included in a reservation. There is a single reservation on each node for all senders whose path to the receiver pass through that node. Different labels are assigned to different senders, thereby creating separate LSPs.

10.4.2 THE RSVP-TE NEW OBJECTS

The following five new objects were introduced to support the functionality of RSVP-TE:

- LABEL
- LABEL_REQUEST
- EXPLICIT_ROUTE
- RECORD_ROUTE
- SESSION_ATTRIBUTE

Also, new C-Types have also been defined for the SESSION, SENDER_TEMPLATE, and FILTER_SPEC objects. We now proceed to examine the format of these new five objects.

THE LABEL OBJECT

The LABEL object is used in the Resv message to advertise a label. For the FF and SE styles, a node allocates a separate label for each sender to be used by the previous-hop node. The format of the LABEL object is shown in figure 10.13. The LABEL object class (given in the Class-num field) is 16, the object type (given in the C-Type field) is C-Type 1, and the 4-byte label field is populated with a single generic label, i.e., for the label carried in the shim header. (These labels are called generic to differentiate them from the labels used for ATM and Frame Relay.)

THE LABEL_REQUEST OBJECT

The LABEL_REQUEST object class (Class-num field) is 19, and there are three different object types (C-Type field), namely C-Type 1, C-Type 2 and C-Type 3, of which C-Type 1 is used for generic labels. Its format is shown in figure

10.14. The object contents of the C-Type 1 consist of a 16-bit reserved field, and the 16-bit L3PID field which is populated with an identifier of the layer 3 protocol that uses this path.

THE EXPLICIT_ROUTE OBJECT (ERO)

This object is used to specify the hops in the requested explicit route. Each hop could be a single node or an abstract node, i.e., a group of nodes. For simplicity, RSVP-TE refers to all the hops as abstract nodes, with the understanding that an abstract node could consist of a single node.

The EXPLICIT_ROUTE object class is 20, and only one object type has been defined, namely C-Type 1. The object contents consists of a series of variable-length sub-objects, each of which contains an abstract node. The format of the sub-object is shown in figure 10.15. The following fields have been defined:

- *L:* A 1-bit field used to indicate whether the route through an abstract node is loose or strict.
- *Type:* This 7-bit field is populated with a value that indicates the type of contents of the sub-object. The following values have been defined: 0 if the sub-object contains an IPv4 prefix, 1 if it contains an IPv6 prefix, and 32 if it contains an autonomous system number.
- *Length:* This 8-bit field is populated with the length (in bytes) of the sub-object including the L, type and length fields.

The format of the sub-objects for the IPv4 is shown in figure 10.16. The field IPv4 address contains an IPv4 prefix whose length is given in the prefix length field. The abstract node represented by this sub-object is the set of all nodes whose IPv4 address has the prefix given in the IPv4 address field. Note that a prefix length of 128 indicates a single node.

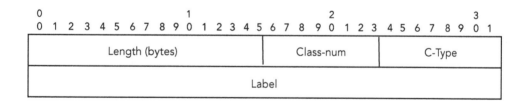

Figure 10.13: The LABEL object format

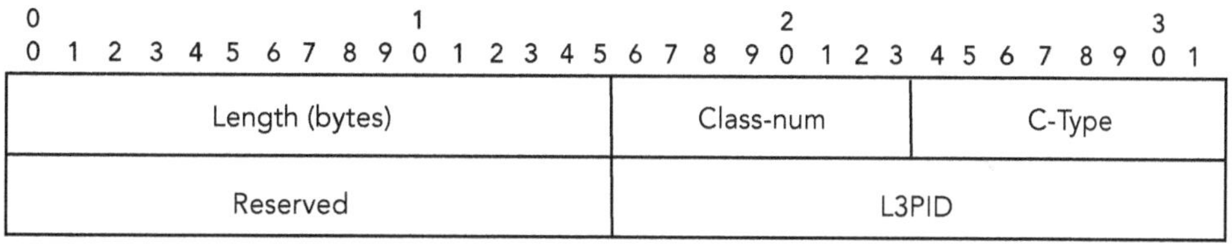

Figure 10.14: The LABEL_REQUEST object format, C_Type = 1

The sub-object format for the autonomous system is the same as the one shown in figure 10.15, with the sub-object contents consisting of a two-byte field populated with the autonomous system number. The abstract node represented by this sub-object is the set of all nodes belonging to the autonomous system.

THE RECORD_ROUTE OBJECT (RRO)

The existence of loose routes through an abstract node means that it is possible that loops can be formed particularly during periods when the underlying routing protocol is in a transient state. Loops can be detected through the RECORD_ROUTE object. In this object the IP address of each node along the path can be recorded. Also, the labels used along the path can be recorded. The RECORD_ROUTE object can be present in both Path and Rev messages.

The RECORD_ROUTE object class is 21 and there is one object type, C-Type 1. The object contents consists of a series of variable-length sub-objects organized in a last-in-first-out stack. Three different sub-objects have been defined, namely the IPv4 sub-object, the IPv6 sub-object, and the label sub-object. The first sub-object is the same as the IPv4 sub-object defined above in the EXPLICIT_ROUTE object and shown in figure 10.16 (with the exception that the reserved field has been replaced by a flags field.) The label sub-object has the structure shown in figure 10.15, and it contains the entire contents of the LABEL object.

THE SESSION_ATTRIBUTE OBJECT

This object contains setup holding priorities for an LSP, plus various flags. The setup priority is the priority used for allocating resources. The holding priority is the priority used for holding onto resources.

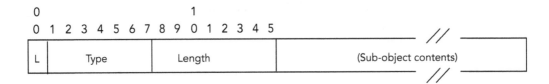

Figure 10.15: The format of a sub-object

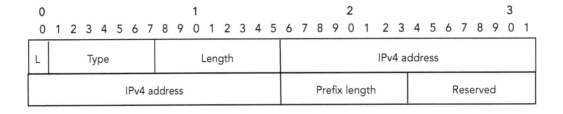

Figure 10.16: The format of the sub-object for IPv4 prefixes

10.4.3 THE RSVP-TE PATH AND RESV MESSAGES

The RSVP-TE Path and Resv message are similar to those in RSVP. The RSVP-TE Path message consists of the common header shown in figure 10.9 followed by the objects:

- INTEGRITY (optional)
- SESSION
- RSVP_HOP
- TIME_VALUES
- EXPLICIT_ROUTE (optional)
- LABEL_REQUEST
- SESSION_ATTRIBUTE (optional)
- POLICY_DATA objects (optional)
- A sender descriptor consisting of the SENDER_TEMPLATE and the SENDER_TSPEC
- ADSPEC (optional)
- RECORD_ROUTE (optional)

The RSVP-TE Resv message consists of the common header shown in figure 10.9 followed by the objects:

- INTEGRITY (optional)
- SESSION
- RSVP_HOP
- TIME_VALUES
- RESV_CONFIRM (optional)
- SCOPE (optional)
- POLICY_DATA objects (optional)
- STYLE
- A style-dependent flow descriptor list. For the Fixed-filter (FF) style it consists of the objects: FLOWSPEC, FILTER_SPEC, LABEL, RECORD_ROUTE (optional). For the shared explicit (SE) style it consists of the objects: FILTER_SPEC, LABEL, RECORD_ROUTE (optional).

10.4.4 RSVP-TE EXTENSIONS

The description of RSVP-TE given above follows the original standard published in IETF RFC 3209 [5]. Since then, there have been several extensions to the RSVP-TE protocol, some of which are discussed below.

RSVP was designed to support resource reservations for data flows defined between a sender and a receiver. As the number of data flows increases, the RSVP overhead on the network increases as well due to the continuous refreshing messages that have to be exchanged. Also, the memory required to store the path state information in each router and the amount of processing increases as well. In view of this, RSVP is not considered a protocol that scales up well. Similar problems arise in RSVP-TE, since it is based on RSVP. Several solutions have been proposed to alleviate these problems. For instance, a mechanism for reliable delivery has been proposed that reduces the need for refresh messages. This mechanism makes use of two new objects, MESSAGE_ID and MESSAGE_ID_ACK. Also, the amount of data transmitted due to refresh messages can be reduced by using the *Srefresh* message, a new summary refresh message.

In section 9.5, we discussed how MPLS can support DiffServ. The requested DiffServ codepoint is signaled using the new object DIFFSERV, see IETF RFC 3270[8]. We recall that a single E-LSP can carry traffic from different applications with different PHBs. A packet is classified to a PHB based on the EXP field. The association of the EXP values to the DiffServ code points could be done manually by configuration or dynamically at the time the E-LSP is being set up through the object DIFFSERV with C_Type = 1. The association of an L-LSP to a DiffServ code point is done using the same object DIFFSERV but with C_Type = 2.

In the same vein, in section 9.6 we described the MPLS DiffServ TE standard. The CT classes for an LSP is carried in a new class type object, the CT object. It specifies the CT from which the bandwidth reservation is requested. The following rules are used for backward compatibility:

- The CT object is present for CT1 through CT7. If the CT object is missing, CT0 is assumed.
- A node that does not understand the DiffServ-TE extensions and receives a path message with a CT object rejects the path request.

The *Generalized MPLS* (GMPLS) is an extension of MPLS and it was designed with a view to applying the MPLS label-switching technique to time-division multiplexing networks and wavelength routing optical networks, in addition to packet-switching networks. For a description of GMPLS and corresponding RSVP-TE extensions see Perros[1].

Extensions of RSVP-TE signaling for point-to-multipoint LSPs for MPLS and GMPLS were standardized in IETF RFC4875[9]. Finally, in IETF RFC 5151[10], procedures and extensions of RSVP-TE for inter-domain LSPs are given.

PROBLEMS

1. Explain the need for loosely explicit routes in RSVP-TE. Give an example of an application that requires pinning.

2. Could RSVP-TE work using unsolicited downstream label allocation with independent order? Why?

3. Explain why in RSVP the Path message contains the RSVP_HOP object.

4. Explain the difference between the fixed-filter style and the shared explicit style.

5. An explicit route through a domain is calculated using a QoS parameter, such as, end-to-end delay, jitter, and packet loss rate. For instance, if we want to minimize the total end-to-end delay, we can run the shortest path algorithm where the link cost is delay. This delay could be just the propagation delay along the link or it may also

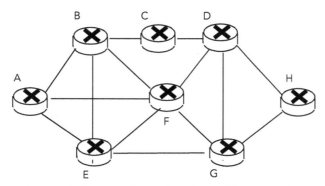

Figure 10.17: Network topology for problems 5 and 6

Link	End-to-end Delay	Jitter	Packet loss rate
A-B	10	0.1	0.01
A-E	15	0.7	0.001
A-F	30	0.03	0.0001
B-C	5	0.2	0.01
B-E	8	0.125	0.001
B-F	35	0.02	0.0001
C-D	12	0.08	0.01
D-F	15	0.07	0.001
D-G	40	0.025	0.0001
D-H	10	0.1	0.01
E-F	40	0.025	0.001
E-G	10	0.1	0.0001
F-G	8	0.125	0.001
G-H	15	0.06	0.01

Table 10.1: Delay, jitter, and packet loss rate per link (in either direction)

include a fixed queueing delay that may be encountered in the router. The following three questions are for the network shown in figure 10.17. The link costs are given in table 10.1.

a. Calculate the optimum path that minimizes the total end-to-end delay from router A to router H. (Due to the fact that the network is small, you can calculate the optimum path by brute force. That is, enumerate all possible paths and then select the one with the lowest total cost.)

b. Calculate the optimum path that minimizes the total jitter. For simplicity, we will assume that the jitter is defined as the sum of all queueing delays, and that the individual values for jitter are additive.

c. Calculate the optimum path that minimizes the total packet loss rate. This is calculated as the sum of the packet loss rates of the links along the path.

Let p_i be the packet loss rate at the ith link. Then, for a connection established over, say 1 to K links, the arrival loss rate is $\lambda p_1 + \lambda(1 - p_1)p_2 + \lambda(1 - p_1)(1 - p_2)p_3 + \ldots + \lambda(1 - p_1) \ldots (1 - p_{K-1})p_K$, where λ is the arrival rate of packets to the connection. Due to the fact that p_i is in general very small, we have that $1 - p_i$ is approximately equal to 1, and therefore, the arrival loss rate is $\lambda(p_1 + p_2 + \ldots + p_K)$. That is, the end-to-end packet loss rate is obtained by adding up al the individual packet loss rates of the links along the path of the connection.

6. In the above problem you calculated the optimum path that minimizes only a single QoS parameter. Of interest is to calculate a path that minimizes all three parameters. For this, you will use a simple scheme due to Yiltas and Perros[11], which combines the three QoS parameters of each link into a single composite parameter. This composite parameter is then used as the link cost in the shortest path algorithm.

This composite metric was motivated from the notion of the fitness function used in genetic algorithms. The idea behind the fitness value is to rank linearly the values of each QoS parameter from 1 and N, and then normalize the rankings by dividing each of them by their sum $1 + 2 + \ldots + N = N(N + 1) / 2$. Specifically, let us consider the end-to-end delay and let the set of all delays be $d_1, d_2, \ldots, d_N$, where d_i is the delay of the ith link. This sequence is first sorted in an ascending order and then the ith element of this ordered list is mapped to integer i, which is then divided by $N(N + 1) / 2$. Let us assume that the ith element of the sorted list belongs to the jth link. Then, the value $i / [N(N + 1) / 2]$ is the fitness value of this link for the delay metric. As an example, let us assume that $N = 4$, and $\{d_1, d_2, d_3, d_4\} = \{2, 4, 3, 1\}$. Then, the sorted list is $\{1(4), 2(1), 3(3), 4(2)\}$, where the value in the parenthesis indicates the link number. Then, the fitness values for the delay for link 1, 2, 3, 4 are 2 / 10, 4 / 10, 3 / 10, 1 / 10 respectively. The same procedure is used for the jitter and packet loss rate.

Let $fv(d_i)$, $fv(j_i)$, and $fv(l_i)$ be the fitness values for the end-to-end delay, jitter and packet loss rate of the ith link. Then, the composite metric cm_i for the ith link is constructed by simply adding these values, that is, $cm_i = fv(d_i) + fv(j_i) + fv(l_i)$, $i = 1, 2, \ldots, N$. The best path is then calculated using the shortest path algorithm with the above composite link cost. We note that this may not be the optimum path.

a. Use the above procedure to calculate the best path from router A to H in figure 10.17, that minimizes all three QoS parameters given in table 10.1.

b. Calculate the end-to-end delay, jitter, and packet loss rate of this path, and compare the results against the optimum solution obtained in the previous problem using one QoS parameter at a time.

REFERENCES

1   H. Perros, *Connection-Oriented Networks: SONET/SDH, ATM, MPLS, and Optical Networks*, Wiley 2005.
2   IETF RFC 3037, "LDP Applicability".
3   IETF RFC 5036, "LDP Specification".
4   IETF RFC 2205, "Resource ReSerVation Protocol (RSVP)".
5   IETF RFC 3209, "RSVP-TE: Extensions to RSVP for LSP Tunnels".
6   OpenFlow, URL: http://www.openflow.org/documents/openflow-spec-v1.1.0.pdf.

7   OnePK, URL: http://developer.cisco.com/web/onepk/home.

8   IETF RFC 3270, "Multi-Protocol Label Switching (MPLS) Support of Differentiated Services".

9   IETF RFC 4875, "Resource Reservation Protocol – Traffic Engineering (RSVP-TE) for Point-to-Multipoint TE Label
     Switched Paths (LSPs).

10   IETF RFC 5151, "Inter-Domain MPLS and GMPLS Traffic Engineering – Resource Reservation Protocol-Traffic
     Engineering (RSVP-TE) Extensions.

11   D. Yiltas and H. Perros, "QoS-based Multi-domain Routing Under Multiple QoS Metrics, IET Communications,
     Vol 5 (2011) pp 327-336.

CHAPTER 11: CONGESTION CONTROL

11.1 INTRODUCTION

Congestion control is an important component of networking, as it permits a network operator to carry as much traffic as possible, so that revenues are maximized, without affecting the quality of service offered to the users.

Two different classes of congestion control schemes have been developed, namely *preventive* congestion control and *reactive* congestion control. In preventive congestion control, as its name implies, we attempt to prevent congestion from occurring. This is done using the following two procedures: *call (or connection) admission control* (CAC), and *bandwidth enforcement*, known simply as *policing*. Call admission control is exercised at the connection level and it is used to decide whether to accept or reject a new connection. Once a new connection has been accepted, bandwidth enforcement is exercised at the packet level to assure that the source transmits on this connection within its negotiated traffic parameters.

Reactive congestion control is based on a totally different philosophy than preventive congestion control. In reactive congestion control, the network uses feedback messages to control the amount of traffic that an end-device transmits so that congestion does not arise. Probably the best example of this type of congestion is TCP.

In this Chapter, we first describe different traffic parameters used to characterize traffic and then, we discuss in detail the preventive congestion control scheme. Following that, we give examples of the QoS and bandwidth requirements of various classes of traffic, such as VoIP, video, and best effort. Finally, we conclude the Chapter with a discussion on scheduling algorithms used to determine the order in which packets are transmitted out of an output port of a router.

11.2 TRAFFIC CHARACTERIZATION

The traffic transmitted by a source can be described by various traffic parameters, such as: *peak rate, peak burst size, burstiness,* and *correlation of inter-arrival times.* Also, various probabilistic models have been used to describe the arrival process of packets. Below, we examine these traffic parameters in detail and we also briefly introduce some probabilistic models.

11.2.1 TRAFFIC DESCRIPTORS

The peak rate is the maximum amount of traffic that can be submitted by a source to a network, and it is known as the *Peak Information Rate* (PIR). It is expressed in bytes per second. The *Peak Burst Size* (PBS) is the maximum number of bytes that can be submitted by a source back-to-back at peak rate. It provides an upper bound on the packet size submitted by the user. The *Committed Information Rate* (CIR) is the amount of bandwidth, expressed in bytes per second, that the operator will allocate to the connection. The *Committed Burst Size* (CBS) is an upper bound on the packet size submitted by the user that is monitored by the operator. These four parameters are provided by the user. Typically, $PIR \geq CIR$, but $PBS = CPS$. The use of these four parameters will become obvious later on in this Chapter.

Other parameters, such as the *burstiness* of a source and the correlation of the inter-arrival times of successive packets can also be used to describe a traffic stream. However these parameters are not signaled to the network. They are mostly useful in performance evaluation studies. Burstiness is a notion that describes how transmitted packets are clumped together. Typically, a source is bursty if it transmits for a period of time and then becomes idle for another period of time. The longer the idle period, and the higher the arrival rate during the active period, the more bursty the source is. The burstiness of a source can significantly affect the packet loss rate in a router.

The correlation of the successive inter-arrival times of packets transmitted by a source can also affect the performance of a router in the same way as the burstiness. The correlation can be either positive or negative. Positive correlation means that, if an inter-arrival time is large (or small), then it is highly likely that the next inter-arrival time will also be large (or small). Negative correlation implies the opposite. That is, if an inter-arrival time is large (or small), then it is highly likely that the next inter-arrival time will be small (or large).

11.2.2 PROBABILISTIC MODELS

Probabilistic models of arrival processes are abstractions of real life arrival processes. They do not represent real life arrival processes exactly, but they capture some of the traffic parameters described above, and in view of this, they are extremely useful in performance evaluation studies. A common assumption about the arrival process of packets was that it followed the Poisson distribution. This assumption was valid back in the time when links were very slow, such as T1 links which transmit at 1.544 Mbps. The advent of high-speed networks in the late 80s, made this assumption invalid. A commonly occurring transmission pattern is depicted by the *on/off* process shown in figure 11.1. In this model, a source is assumed to transmit only during an active period, known as the *on period*.

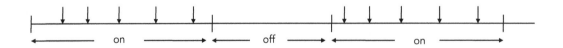

Figure 11.1: The on/off process

This period is followed by a silent period, known as the *off period*, during which the source does not transmit. This cycle of an on period followed by an off period repeats continuously until the source stops transmitting. During the on period, packets arrive with a given arrival rate λ. We assume that the arrival of a packet is instantaneous. Alternatively, we can assume that the packets arrive back-to-back during the on period, which means that the packet length is the number of bytes that arrive between two successive arrival instances in the same on period.

The on/off model captures the notion of burstiness, described above, which is an important traffic characteristic. The burstiness of a source is indicative of how packets are clumped together. There are several different ways of measuring burstiness. The simplest one is to express it as the ratio of the mean length of the on period divided by the sum of the mean on and off periods, that is

$$r = \frac{mean\ on\ period}{sum\ of\ mean\ on\ and\ off\ periods}$$

This quantity can be also seen as the fraction of time that the source is active transmitting. When r is close to 0 or to 1, the source is not bursty. The burstiness of the source increases as r approaches 0.5. Another commonly used measure of burstiness, but more complicated to calculate, is the squared coefficient of variation of the inter-arrival times defined by $Var(X) / (E(X))^2$, where X is a random variable indicating the inter-arrival times.

The length of the on and off periods of the on/off process follow an arbitrary distribution. A special case of the on/off process is the well-known *Interrupted Poisson Process* (IPP) which has been used extensively in performance studies of networks. In an IPP, the on and off periods are exponentially distributed and packets arrive during the on period in a Poisson fashion.

The IPP process can be generalized to the two-state *Markov Modulated Poisson Process* (MMPP). A two-state MMPP consists of two alternating states, state 1 and 2. Each state has an exponentially distributed duration. When the process is in state i, we have Poisson arrivals with rate λ_i, $i = 1,2$. The transitions between the two states are given by the matrix in figure 11.2. If the process is in state 1, then it shifts to state 2 with rate μ_1. Likewise, If the process is in state 2, then it shifts to state 1 with rate μ_2. Typically, the two-state MMPP model does not have a physical interpretation as the IPP model, but it is a useful model as it captures both the notion of burstiness and the correlation of the inter-arrival times. This arrival process is used in the simulation project 2 described at the end of Chapter 15, where it is further explained and it is shown how it can be used to generate arrivals. More complicated MMPPs can be also used with more than two states, but the two-state MMPP seems to be adequate for most practical problems.

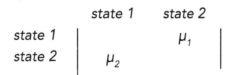

Figure 11.2: Transitions between the two periods

11.3 CONGESTION CONTROL

Congestion control procedures can be grouped into the following two categories: *reactive* control and *preventive* control. In reactive congestion control, the network uses feedback messages to control the amount of traffic that an end-device transmits so that congestion does not arise. The most well-known and successive reactive control scheme is TCP.

Preventive congestion control is widely used and it is based on a different philosophy than reactive congestion control. In preventive congestion control, as its name implies, we attempt to prevent congestion from occurring. This is achieved using the following two procedures: *call admission control* and *bandwidth enforcement.* Call admission control is exercised at the connection level and it is used to decide whether to accept or reject a new connection. Once a new connection has been accepted, bandwidth enforcement is exercised at the packet level to assure that the source transmitting on this connection is within its negotiated traffic parameters. Below, we examine these two schemes in detail.

11.3.1 CALL ADMISSION CONTROL

As we have seen from the previous Chapter, in order to establish a new point-to-point connection, a Path message is sent to the LSRs which are on the path of the connection. Each LSR has to decide whether to accept the new connection or not. If it is accepted the Path message is sent on to the next LSR, otherwise the connection is rejected. The decision to accept a new connection is fairly simple. Each connection request provides a value for *CIR* (committed information rate). This is the amount of bandwidth that has to be allocated on the outgoing link of the router through which the requested connection has to be routed. The router simply checks if the necessary bandwidth is available on the specific link, and accordingly it decides to accept or reject the request. In addition, the bandwidth allocated to each class of traffic maybe restricted to a predetermined percentage of the total bandwidth of the link. For instance, the following bandwidth constraints may apply:

- Voice: 18%
- Interactive video: 15%
- Best effort: 25%
- Bulk data: 4%
- Scavenger: 1%

(See section 9.4.1 for the definition of bulk data and scavenger traffic classes.) In this case, the decision is based on whether there is enough spare capacity for the particular class of traffic to accept the new connection. We recall that the need to maintain class-dependent bandwidth restrictions led to the MPLS DiffServ TE standard, described in Chapter 9. In general, *CIR* values are predetermined based on the application.

If *CIR = PIR*, then in the case we allocate bandwidth as if the source is transmitting continuously at peak rate. For instance, let us assume that we want to transport a TDM traffic stream, such as a T1 line, over an MPLS network. Then in this case, we know that the source will transmit continuously at 1.544 Mbps, and obviously it makes sense

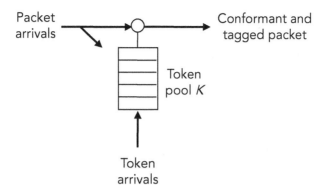

Figure 11.3: The unbuffered leaky bucket

to set $CIR = PIR$, which is 1.544 Mbps expressed in bytes per second. This type of bandwidth allocation is known as *non-statistical bandwidth allocation*, or *peak rate allocation*. Now, if the source varies its transmission rate over time, then if we set $CIR = PIR$ we are over-allocating bandwidth since we assume that the source will be transmitting continuously at peak rate. Typically, in this case, we set $CIR < PIR$, so that to take advantage of the fact that the source does not always transmit at peak rates. Now, if we have N such sources, the sum of their peak rates exceeds the total bandwidth allocated to all of them which is equal to the sum of their CIR values. This approach, known as *statistical bandwidth allocation*, works well since not all sources are likely to transmit at peak rate at the same time.

11.3.2 POLICING

Policing each source is an important function from the point of view of a network operator, since a source exceeding its traffic descriptors may affect the quality-of-service of other existing connections. Also, depending upon the pricing scheme used by the network operator, there may be loss of revenue. A source may exceed its contract due to various reasons, such as, intentional or unintentional underestimation of the required bandwidth by the user, and malfunctioning of user's equipment.

Policing of a source typically takes place at the ingress LSR of an MPLS connection. In the case of DiffServ, it takes place at the ingress router of the DiffServ-enabled network. The policing algorithms presented below are based on a popular policing mechanism known as the *leaky bucket*. As shown in figure 11.3 it consists of a token pool of size K. Each token is equivalent to a byte and tokens are generated at a given rate. The token size K is determined by the packet length, and the token generation rate is equal to PIR or CIR depending upon whether we police the PIR or the CIR of the source. Tokens are not generated during the time when the token pool is full. An arriving packet consumes as many tokens from the token pool, as its length expressed in bytes and then enters the network. The number of tokens in the token pool is then reduced by the number of consumed tokens. A packet is considered to be a *violating* packet, if it arrives at a time when the token pool is empty. Typically, violating packets are either dropped or marked and let into the network. The idea behind it, is that if the network has slack capacity, then it will route both unmarked and marked packets to its destination. However, if congestion builds up in a router, marked packets are the first to be dropped.

THE SINGLE RATE THREE COLOR MARKER (SR-TCM)

This policing scheme polices the *CIR* of a source. Two token buckets are used, namely the C and E buckets. The C token bucket is used to police the source's *CIR*. It is possible that at times the policed arrival rate may temporarily exceed *CIR*. These temporary excesses will be absorbed by the C token bucket, but in addition, the *excess* token bucket E is also used. The C bucket is filled in with tokens at the rate of *CIR* until it reaches *CBS*, its maximum capacity. Likewise, the E bucket is filled with tokens at the rate of *CIR* until it reaches *EBS*, its maximum capacity. The operation of the committed and excess token buckets is as follows:

- Initially, the token count in the committed token bucket T_C = *CBS*, and the token count on the excess token bucket T_E = *EBS*.

  Thereafter, every second, T_C and T_E are updated as follows:
    ○ T_C is incremented by *M* bytes if T_C < *CBS*, else
    ○ T_E is incremented by *M* bytes, if T_E < *EBS*
    where *CIR* = *M* bytes/sec.
- The following action is taken when a packet of size *b* arrives:
    ○ If $T_C - b \geq 0$, then there enough tokens in the committed token bucket for the packet, and $T_C = T_C - b$.
    ○ If $T_C - b < 0$ and $T_E - b \geq 0$, then there not enough tokens in the committed token bucket, but there are enough tokens in the excess token bucket, and $T_E = T_E - b$.
    ○ If $T_C - b < 0$ and $T_E - b < 0$, then there not enough tokens neither in the committed token bucket nor in the excess token bucket, and neither T_C or T_E are decremented.

We observe that if *CIR* is positive infinity, then an arriving packet will never be in excess of either token bucket counts.

An example of how this policing scheme is used is shown in figure 11.4 The top diagram gives the current contents of the excess token bucket, and the bottom one gives the current contents of the committed token bucket. The thick dotted lines in the committed token bucket show the total number of bytes of a packet that have arrived so far. The angle of this thick dotted line indicates the rate at which the packet is being transmitted. The angle of the thinner dotted line indicates the *CIR* at which the packet should be transmitted. All five packets arrive at rates higher than *CIR*. As we can see, packets 1 and 3 go through. Packet 2 arrives at a time when the committed token bucket does not have enough tokens, but there are enough tokens in the excess token bucket. As a result, the token count T_C is left unchanged, the token count T_E is reduced by the size of packet 2. Packets 4 and 5 arrive at a time when neither token buckets have enough tokens and in both cases the token counts T_C and T_E are not changed.

The three colors refer to the three possible actions that can be taken when the size of a packet is in excess of the token count in the committed token bucket and/or the excess token bucket. These actions are summarized in figure 11.5. If C has enough tokens for an incoming packet of *b* bytes, then it is decreased by *b* and the action is green. If C does not have enough tokens but E has enough tokens, then E is decreased by *b*, and the action is marked yellow. If neither buckets have *b* bytes, then the action is marked red.

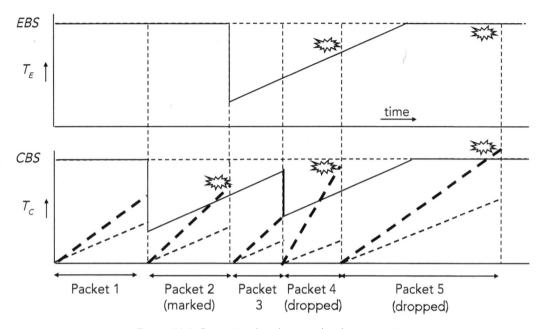

Figure 11.4: Committed and excess bucket operation

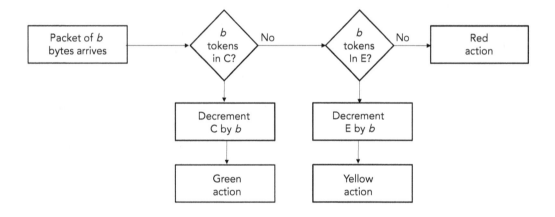

Figure 11.5: The three color rules

The green, yellow and red actions have to do with dropping and marking of a packet. The typical actions are as follows. Green action means that the packet is conformant and it should be let into the network. Yellow action means that the is not conformant, but it can be marked and let into the network. Finally, red action means that the packet is not conformant and it will be dropped.

The policer is often simplified by setting *EBS* to zero, thus becoming a two-color scheme, green and red. The red action can be either drop the violating packet or mark it and let it into the network. For instance, in DiffServ each assured forwarding (AF) class has three codepoints corresponding to three different dropping priorities. Consequently, if an AF packet is found to be violating, then it can be marked by changing its codepoint from low to medium or from low to high. Marked packets are dropped according to their dropping priority if congestion occurs in a router. However, it is not possible to mark expedited forwarding (EF) packets. This means that violating VoIP packets, typically carried in the EF class, are dropped. The same applies to packets carried in the CS classes. In the case where DiffServ runs in conjunction with MPLS and a connection has been set up as an L-LSP, then dropping priorities can be implemented for the EF and CS classes using the EXP field, see section 9.5.

THE TWO RATE THREE COLOR MARKER (TR-TCM)

This policer monitors both the *PIR* and *CIR* using two buckets, namely the P and the C. P is replenished at the rate *PIR* and C at the rate *CIR*. The maximum bucket size is *PBS* for P and *CBS* for C. In general, as described above $PIR \geq CIR$ and $BPS = CBS$. The P is replenished M times per second, where $PIR = M$ bytes/sec until it reaches its maximum capacity. Likewise, the C token bucket is replenished M' time per second, where $PIR = M'$ bytes/sec, until it reaches its maximum capacity. The logic of this policer is shown in figure 11.6. As in the case of the single rate three color marker, different actions can be applied, such as, let into the network, mark, and drop. Typically, green action means that the packet is conformant and it should be let into the network. Yellow action means that the is not conformant, but it can be marked and let into the network. Finally, red action means that the packet is not conformant and it will be dropped.

COLOR-AWARE MODE

The two algorithms presented above do not take into account the fact that the packet may have already been colored by an upstream policer. The two algorithms have also been defined to allow for pre-coloring. For instance, the single rate three color marker can be modified as follows to take into account previous markings.

- If the packet is pre-colored green and there are at least as many tokens in bucket C as the number of bytes b in the packet, then the packet is conformant, C is decreased by b, and the color of the packet does not change.
- Otherwise, if the packet is pre-colored green or yellow and there are at least b bytes in bucket E, then it is colored yellow, and E is decreased by b.
- Otherwise, it is colored red.

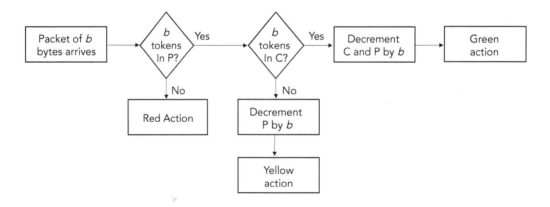

Figure 11.6: The two rate three color marker (TR-TCM)

11.4 QOS AND BANDWIDTH REQUIREMENTS

It is instructive to see how the QoS parameters and the required bandwidth are determined for various service classes. In this section, we give the QoS and bandwidth requirements for VoIP, interactive video, streaming video, and best effort, following the Cisco recommendations[1].

We note that the jitter used below is defined as the average of the differences of the end-to-end delay of successive packets. For example, if a packet requires 100 ms to traverse the network from the source user equipment to the destination user equipment and the following packet requires 125 ms to make the same trip, then the differ-ence is 25 ms. Jitter is defined here as the average of these differences calculated over a representative sample of successive arrivals.

VOIP

Packet loss causes voice clipping and skips. The packetization interval determines the size of samples contained within a single packet. Assuming a 20 msec (default) packetization interval, the loss of two or more consecutive packets results in a noticeable degradation of voice quality. In view of this, the packet loss rate has to be very low.

In addition, excessive latency can cause voice quality degradation. If the end-to-end voice delay becomes too long, the conversation begins to resemble two parties talking over a satellite link. The goal commonly used when designing networks to support VoIP is the target specified in the ITU standard G.114, which states that 150 msec of one-way end-to-end (mouth-to-ear) delay ensures user satisfaction for telephony applications. This budget should be partitioned to the various components of network delay, such as, propagation delay, queueing delays due to congestion, and delays in VoIP gateway codec and de-jitter buffer. While the ITU G.114 states that a 150 ms one-way mouth-to-ear delay budget is acceptable for high quality voice, lab testing has shown that there is a negligible difference in the voice quality mean opinion scores (MOS) when there is a 200 ms delay.

Jitter buffers (also known as play-out buffers) are used to change asynchronous packet arrivals into a synchronous stream by turning variable network delays into constant delays at the destination end systems. The role of the jitter buffer is to balance the delay and the probability of interrupted playout due to late packets. Late packets are discarded. If the jitter buffer is set either arbitrarily large or arbitrarily small, then it imposes unnecessary constraints on the characteristics of the network. A jitter buffer set too large adds to the end-to-end delay, on the expense of the end-to-end delay that the network has to support. If a jitter buffer is too small to accommodate the network jitter, then buffer overflows can occur.

QoS parameters:

- Packet loss rate ≤ 1%.
- One-way latency (mouth-to-ear) ≤ 150 ms. Up to 200 ms is still okay. (The one-way latency includes jitter.)
- Average one-way jitter ≈ 30 ms.
- Voice traffic should be marked to DSCP EF.

The standard method of transporting voice packets over the IP network requires the addition of three headers: an RTP header of 12 bytes, a UDP header of 8 bytes, and an IPv4 header of 20 bytes. These headers are added to each VoIP packet, and the resulting additional bandwidth due to these headers depends on the number of voice packets produced per second. For instance, if each voice packet carries voice samples for a duration of 20 msec, then 50 voice packets/sec are produced. This means that the total overhead due to the RTP/UDP/IP headers is 50x40x8 = 16 Kbps. (This overhead can be reduced if header compression is used.) The G.729A codec produces an 8 Kbps stream, and assuming 50 voice packets per second, this results to 24 Kbps traffic stream (8 Kbps + 16 Kbps). The actual traffic stream generated is further augmented when we account for the layer 2 overheads. For instance, a header of 32 bytes is added for 802.1Q Ethernet., and a header of 12 bytes is added for the *Point-to-Point Protocol* (PPP). For the G.729A codec at 50 packets/sec, this gives rise to a 37 Kbps and a 28 Kbps traffic stream respectively. The bandwidth generated for the G.711 and G.729A codecs (rounded to the nearest integer) is given in table 11.1. Silent suppression reduces the bandwidth of a voice stream since packets are only transmitted during the talk spurts.

The bandwidth to be allocated should be in the range of 21 to 320 Kbps depending on the codec and layer 2 overheads, in order to satisfy the above QoS requirements for the one-way end-to-end delay and jitter, see Cisco[1].

INTERACTIVE VIDEO

Interactive video traffic should be marked AF41. Excessive traffic can be marked down by a policer to AF42 or AF43. The QoS parameters are the same as G.711 since IP videoconferencing uses G.711 for audio. However, the traffic patterns of videoconferencing are radically different from voice. The QoS parameters are as follows:

- Packet loss rate ≤ 1%.
- One-way latency (mouth to ear) ≤ 150 ms. Up to 200 ms is still okay. (The one-way latency includes jitter.)
- Average one-way jitter ≈ 30 ms.

The video packets vary in size as they carry voice, video, and signaling. The overhead per packet is 40 bytes for the IP/UDP/RTP header plus layer 2 overheads. Testing shows that overheads can be upper-bounded by 20% of the video traffic stream, i.e. a 384 Kbps can be provisioned at 460 Kbps.

Codec	Voice packet duration	Bytes per voice packet	Packets /sec	B/w per call	With 802.1Q overheads	With PPP overheads
G.711	20 msec	160	50	80 Kbps	93 Kbps	85 Kbps
G.711	30 msec	240	33	75 Kbps	84 Kbps	78 Kbps
G.729A	20 msec	20	50	24 Kbps	37 Kbps	29 Kbps
G.729A	30 msec	30	33	19 Kbps	28 Kbps	22 Kbps

Table 11.1: Bandwidth requirements for VoIP

STREAMING VIDEO

Streaming video is buffered at the destination before it is played out. In view of this, it has more lenient require-ments than interactive video, because it is delay and jitter insensitive. The required bandwidth depends on the encoding format and the sampling rate of the video stream. The QoS parameters are as follows:

- Packet loss rate ≤ 5%.
- One-way latency no more than 4-5 seconds depending on codec and jitter buffer size.
- No significant jitter requirement.
- Streaming video traffic should be marked CS4.

BEST EFFORT

Best effort traffic should be marked DSCP 0. It is not uncommon to have several hundred applications with a best effort classification. In view of this, at least 25% of the link capacity should be dedicated to best effort traffic.

11.5 SCHEDULING

The queueing mechanism at an interface consists of a hardware queue and several software queues, as shown in figure 11.7. An arriving packet goes straight to the hardware queue, also known as *transmit queue*, if the hardware queue is not full. Otherwise, it joins one of the software queues, identified in figure 11.7 as Q1, Q2, . . . , Qn. The hardware queue resides in the portion of the main memory shared by the CPU and the interface, and it is served in a *First Out First In* (FIFO) manner. The software queues are implemented in the memory and they are controlled by the CPU. They have different priorities and they are served according to a scheduling algorithm. The scheduling algorithm decides the order with which the packets will be transmitted. The interface interrupts the CPU when it needs more packets to transmit. The software queues typically consist of one queue per QoS class. Per connection queueing is possible. That is, instead of maintaining a single aggregate queue with packets of the same QoS class, there are as many queues as the number of established connections for that particular QoS class.

The presence of the software queues assure that packets are not served in a FIFO manner. If the size of the hardware queue is increased, then more packets will go straight to this queue. As a result, more packets will be served in a FIFO manner, than according to their priority based on their QoS class. On the other hand, if the hardware queue is very small, then more packets are served according to their priority. However, in this case, there may be more CPU overheads required for the transfer of packets from the software queues to the hardware queue. The optimum size of the hardware queue depends on the hardware platform, software version, and layer 2 media.

A fixed amount of memory is allocated to software queues, and in addition each queue is typically bounded in size. The reason for this is that if a queue gets "hot", i.e., suddenly there is a lot of traffic destined to this queue, it is possible that the queue can increase dramatically in size and possibly affect the memory space of the other queues. For this reason, each queue may be allocated a dedicated minimum amount of memory that is used exclusively by the queue, whereas the remaining of the memory allocated to the software queues is shared by all the queues. More complex memory allocation schemes can also be used. As a result of bounding the size of the software queues, a

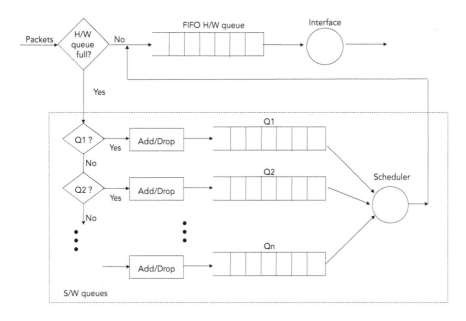

Figure 11.7: Queueing at an interface

packet that arrives at a queue maybe dropped, if the queue happens to be full at that time. This is known as *tail dropping*. Further dropping of a packet can occur after the packet has joined the queue using an algorithm such as WRED.

Tail dropping works well when we do not have marked and unmarked packets. However, if both types of packets are present, then we may be dropping unmarked packets, while there may be marked packets in the queue. A simple way to handle this is through a *threshold* scheme. In this scheme, both unmarked and marked packets are admitted as long as the total number of packets is below a threshold. Over the threshold, only unmarked packets are admitted, and the marked packets are rejected. Other mechanisms have also been proposed such as dropping from the front. This mechanism is similar to the threshold mechanism, only packets are dropped from the front. That is, when a marked packet is ready to begin its service, the total number of packets in the queue is compared against the threshold. If it is below, service begins, else the packet is dropped.

We now proceed to describe some of the scheduling algorithms used to schedule the transmission of packets.

STATIC PRIORITIES

The software queues are assigned static priorities, which dictate the order in which they are served. These priorities are called static because they do not change over time and they are not affected by the occupancy levels of the queues. In the example given in figure 11.8, we show four software queues with priorities: high, medium, normal and low. These queues are served as follows. The next packet for transmission is selected from the high priority queue. If this queue is empty, the next packet for transmission is selected from the medium priority queue. If this queue is empty, then the next packet is selected from the normal priority queue, and so on. If all queues are empty, then no packet will be selected for transmission. Thus, in essence, the high priority queue is served until it becomes empty. Then, the next priority queue is served until it becomes empty, and so on. There is no preemption of service. That is, the transmission of a packet is not interrupted if a packet of a higher priority arrives during its transmission time.

Additional scheduling rules can be introduced which take into account the current status of the queues. A typical example of such a rule is the "aging factor". If a queue, typically a low priority queue, has not been served for a period of time which is longer that a pre-specified threshold, then the queue's priority is momentarily raised so that some of its packets can be transmitted out.

EARLY DEADLINE FIRST (EDF) ALGORITHM

Let us consider the case where all packets arrive at a single queue. Each packet is assigned a deadline upon arrival. This deadline indicates the time by which the packet should depart from the queue. It is calculated by adding a fixed delay to the arrival time of the packet. This delay may vary according to the QoS class of the packet. The scheduler serves the packets according to their deadlines, so that the one with the earliest deadline gets served first. A packet that is assigned a deadline closer to its arrival time, will suffer a low delay in the queue. On the other hand, a packet that is assigned a deadline far away from the time that it arrived at the queue, may suffer a longer delay before it gets transmitted out.

Using this scheme, packets belonging to delay-sensitive applications, such as voice or video, can be served first by assigning them deadlines closer to their arrival times.

THE ROUND ROBIN SCHEDULER

This is a well known scheduling discipline where exactly one packet is served from each software queue each time. If we number the software queues from 1 to n, then they are served sequentially, as follows. If a packet from queue

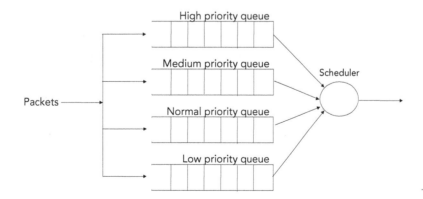

Figure 11.8: Priority software queues

i was just served, then the next queue to serve is queue $i + 1$. This sequential servicing of the queues continues until the nth queue is served, whereupon, it goes back to queue 1. If the next queue to be served, say queue i, is empty then the scheduler skips it and goes on to queue $i + 1$. In this manner, all queues share the link's bandwidth equally. However, a queue that consistently carries large packets will consume more bandwidth than the other queues.

The round robin mechanism cannot differentiate between queues since all queues are treated equally. This can be done using the *weighted round robin* scheduler, which can be set up to serve a different number of bytes from each queue. For instance, let us consider the four queues Q1, Q2, Q3, and Q4, and let us assume that we have decided that the number of bytes that should be served each time is 3000, 2000, 1000, and 500 respectively. The queues are served in a round robin manner, but the scheduler will serve as many packets from each queue such that the sum of the served bytes is at least equal to the value assigned. For instance, let us consider that Q1 contains the following packets when its turn comes up to be served: packet 1 (1400 bytes), packet 2 (1500 bytes), packet 3 (1350 bytes), and packet 4 (1200 bytes). The total count for the two packets is 2900 bytes, and therefore, the third packet will also be served. Obviously, if this happens frequently, Q1 will consume more bandwidth than allocated.

WEIGHTED FAIR QUEUEING (WFQ)

Arriving packets are classified into flows and each flow is assigned to a FIFO queue. Flows can be identified using the following fields from the IP header and the TCP or UDP header: source IP address, destination IP address, protocol number, type of service (ToS), source TCP (or UDP) port number, and destination TCP (or UDP) port number. Based on these fields, a hash value is generated. Packets with the same hash value are assigned to the same queue. If a packet is the first one for a new flow, a new queue is created and assigned to the flow.

The number of queues in the WFQ system is based on the number of active flows and it varies dynamically as new queues are created and old queues are deleted. The maximum default values of the number of queues is 256, but it can be set to take other values. If the number of the queues exceeds the maximum, then new flows are assigned to existing queues. WFQ may not be desirable when the number of flows is in the thousands.

An arriving packet is assigned a sequence number, known as the *virtual time*, which is calculated by adding the virtual time of the last packet in the same flow to the length of the arriving packet multiplied by a weight assigned to the packet. That is: new virtual time = previous virtual time + (length of the arriving packet) x weight. If there are no packets in the queue associated with the arriving packet, then the virtual time of the last departed packet is used plus progress on the current transmission (if any).

This virtual time is used by the scheduler to select the next packet for transmission. The packet with the lowest virtual time is the one to be transmitted next. The WFQ algorithms guarantees that each queue receives a percentage of the link's bandwidth. Specifically, if R is the transmission rate of the link and n is the number of non-empty queues, then WFQ queue i will receive an average of $R^*w_i / (w_1 + w_2 + \ldots + w_n)$, where w_i is the weight of the ith active non-empty queue.

The WFQ queues share a fixed amount of shared memory, known as the *hold queue*. A packet is dropped if it arrives at a time when the hold queue is full, except when a packet is assigned to an empty queue. This policy is known as *WFQ aggressive dropping.* In addition, each queue has a *Congestive Discard Threshold* (CDT), which defines an upper bound on the size of the queue. Given that the hold queue is not full, an arriving packet is dropped if its flow queue has reached its threshold. This WFQ dropping policy is known as *early dropping.* The following is an exception to this rule. If there is a packet in another queue with a virtual time higher than that of the arriving packet, then the packet with the higher virtual time is dropped.

The *Class-Based Weighted Fair Queueing* (CBWFQ) is an extension of WFQ, where the classification of packets is defined by the user. Each class is assigned to a different queue, and each queue is allocated a user-defined minimum bandwidth, which it can exceed if more bandwidth is available. As in WFQ, each queue is served in a FIFO manner, and it has a maximum size. Tail dropping is used if a packet arrives when the queue is at capacity. The minimum bandwidth allocated to each queue is used as the weight to calculate the virtual time of the packets.

Both the CBWFQ and the WFQ algorithms do not guarantee low delay and therefore they can not be used for real-time applications, such as VoIP. The *Low Latency Queueing* (LLQ) is a queueing system employed in routers by Cisco that uses a priority queue for delay sensitive traffic and CBWFQ queues for bandwidth guaranteed traffic. The strict priority queue is given priority over the other queues, and it is used for delay and jitter sensitive applications. It is allocated a maximum bandwidth, which it can exceed if more bandwidth is available. When congestion occurs, the traffic for the strict priority queue is metered and the excess traffic is dropped. The remaining of the queueing structure is the same as in CBWFQ.

PROBLEMS

1. Consider an on/off source where the on and off periods are constant and equal to 0.5 msec. During the on period, the source transmits at the rate of 20 Mbps.
   a. What is its *PIR*?
   b. What is the average transmission rate?
   c. How many bytes are transmitted during an on period?

2. Consider an LSP carrying a T1 line (1.544 Mbps).
   a. What is its *PIR*?
   b. What is its average transmission rate?

3. A call with silence suppression can be modeled by an on/off process, where the on period is 400 ms and the off period is 600 ms. From table 11.1, we see that the traffic stream generated by a G.729A codec at 50 packets per second and with PPP overheads, is 28 Kpbs.
   a. What is the total length of each VoIP packet, assuming no header compression?
   b. How many bits are transmitted during an on period?
   c. What is the average transmission rate?

4. Create a table similar to 11.1 for the following codecs:

    a. G.711, 64 Kbps uncompressed, voice packet duration 10 msec

    b. G.711, 64 Kbps uncompressed, voice packet duration 30 msec

    c. G.711, 64 Kbps uncompressed, voice packet duration 40 msec

    d. G.711, 64 Kbps uncompressed, voice packet duration 80 msec

    e. G.729A, 8 Kbps compressed, voice packet duration 10 msec

    f. G.729A, 8 Kbps compressed, voice packet duration 40 msec

    g. G.729A, 8 Kbps compressed, voice packet duration 80 msec

    h. G.723.1, 5.3 kbps compression, voice packet duration 30 msec

    i. G.723.1, 5.3 kbps compression, voice packet duration 60 msec

    j. G.723.1, 5.3 kbps compression, voice packet duration 90 msec

    k. G.723.1, 6.4 kbps compression, voice packet duration 30 msec

    l. G.723.1, 6.4 kbps compression, voice packet duration 60 msec

    m. G.723.1, 6.4 kbps compression, voice packet duration 90 msec

5. Consider the static priority queueing system shown in figure 11.8. VoIP packets join the high priority queue, and video packets join the medium priority. Let λ be the total arrival rate of packets into all the four queues, and let μ be the rate at which packets are transmitted out of these queues. From basic queueing theory, see Chapter 15, we know that this queueing system is stable, that is, the total number of packets in the queues does not go to infinity, if $\lambda < \mu$.

    a. Assume that 80% of the total arrival rate λ are VoIP packets, and the remaining 20% are video packets. Under what condition this queueing system is stable? Why?

    b. How would the end-to-end delay of the video packets in the above question change if theVoIP packets account for only 20% of the total arrival rate λ? Why?

REFERENCES

[1] Cisco, "Quality of Service Design Overview".

CHAPTER 12: THE RESOURCE AND ADMISSION CONTROL FUNCTIONS (RACF)

12.1 INTRODUCTION

In this Chapter we describe a mechanism that permits IMS and also non-IMS schemes to interact with the underlying transport network in order to guarantee the QoS of a multimedia session that is being established or modified. The underlying transport network is assumed to be QoS-enabled, that is, it runs a QoS architecture, such as MPLS or DiffServ or DiffServ with MPLS. This mechanism, known as the *Resource and Admission Control Functions* (RACF), is a concept introduced in NGN to ensure QoS for multimedia sessions. As can be seen in figure 12.1, the RACF resides in the transport stratum. It interacts with the IMS or with a non-IMS scheme and it monitors the resources used in the transport network. In this way, it can determine whether sufficient resources can be reserved so that to guarantee an appropriate level of QoS requested for a multimedia session.

In section 6.4, we described how a session is set up in IMS. The flow of messages exchanged for setting up a session is given in figure 6.7. We recall that when UE 1 receives the `183 Session Progress` message (step 20), it responds with a `PRACK` message and it starts a resource reservation. This resource reservation is only in the access network, and not in the core network(s) connecting the two UEs. Likewise, UE 2 starts a resource reservation in its own access network when it receives the `PRACK` message (step 25). T1SPA[1] developed the *Resource and Admission Control Sub-System* (RACS) for resource allocation at the access and the edge of the network. 3GPP[2] also developed a standard for resource allocation in wireless access networks. Guaranteeing QoS at the access network does not imply that there is a similar guarantee in the core network(s) interconnecting the two access networks. The RACF

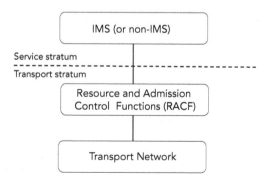

Figure 12.1: The location of RACF

architecture described in this Chapter was standardized by ITU-T Recommendation Y.2111[3], and it covers both the access and the core network. Network border control at the access-core and inter-domain boundaries is also supported by RACF.

We note that the more recently developed *Software Defined Network* (SDN) schemes, OpenFlow[4] and OnePK[5], can be used in place of the RACF or replace part of the RACF functionality. However, the RACF provides a framework which is more general than OpenFlow and OnePK, as far as QoS routing is concerned, and it can be used as a basis for developing such schemes.

In this Chapter, we first describe the RACF architecture and then in section 12.7 we discuss the issue of how QoS can be guaranteed end-to-end in a multi-domain environment. Some of the details of the RACF architecture can be skipped in the first reading, but the issues presented in section 12.7 are worth understanding.

12.2   THE RESOURCE AND ADMISSION CONTROL FUNCTIONS (RACF)

The RACF provides a real-time resource management for fixed and mobile transport technologies. It can be used with or without IMS. The functional architecture is shown in figure 12.2. The *Service Control Function* (SCF) is an abstract term used to indicate the presence of a mechanism responsible for setting up a multimedia service, and it may be the IMS architecture or a different signaling scheme. An entity within the SCF sends a QoS request to the RACF during the time that a multimedia session is being established. In the case of IMS, this entity is the P-CSCF. The RACF determines whether the requested QoS is acceptable and then it instructs the transport network, which is assumed to be QoS-enabled, to reserve bandwidth. The RACF can be shared by multiple SCFs.

The RACF consists of two types of resource and admission control functions: the *Policy Decision Functional Entity* (PD-FE) and the *Transport Resource Control Functional Entity* (TRC-FE). The PD-FE provides a single contact point to the SCF and hides the details of the transport network from the SCF, whereas the TRC-FE is service-independent and deals with the underlying transport network. This decomposition to the PD-FE and TRC-FE enables the RACF to support a variety of fixed and mobile access and core networks.

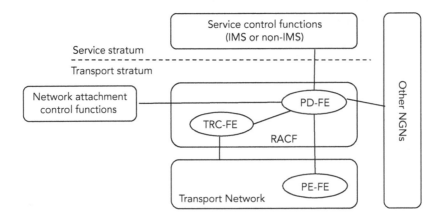

Figure 12.2: The ITU-T RACF functional architecture

The PD-FE makes the final decision regarding network resources and admission control based on network policy rules, SLAs, information provided by the SCF regarding the service that is in process of being set up, subscription information to the access network provided by the *Network Attachment Control Function* (NACF), and resource allocation results provided by the TRC-FE. The PD-FE may also interact with other entities which are external to the RACF, such as, a mobility management entity and a *Management of Performance Measurements* (MPM) entity which collects performance measurements in real-time. These entities are not shown in figure 12.2. Multiple SCFs belonging to different operators, can be supported by the same PD-FE.

The NACF is an entity outside the RACF, and it is used by a provider to carry out a number of functions related to the access of user equipment to the network. Some of the functions are: dynamic provision of IP address and user equipment configuration parameters, auto-discovery of user equipment capabilities, authentication of the user, authorization of network access and access network configuration based on user profile, and location management.

The main function of the TRC-FE is to determine whether there is sufficient bandwidth in the transport network controlled by the RACF in order to satisfy a QoS request from the SCF for a new service. If the TRC-FE determines that there is sufficient bandwidth within its network, it reserves the necessary bandwidth, updates the resource status of the network, and informs the PD-FE. The TRC-FE is null in case where no QoS is used in the network. In this case, the network is over-engineered, i.e., the capacity of the links is very big in relation of the anticipated traffic. The implementation of the TRC-FE in the various access and core networks depends on the transport technology and QoS mechanisms used.

After the PD-FE has accepted a QoS request, it sends traffic control information, filtering, marking, shaping and leaky bucket information to a functional entity in the network known as the *Policy Enforcement Functional Entity* (PE-FE). This is located at the entrance of a packet network, where policing is enforced.

Finally, the *Transport Resource Enforcement Functional Entity* (TRE-FE) shown in figure 12.2 with a dashed line, enforces policy rules as instructed by the TRC-FE at the aggregate level, e.g., VLAN, VPN and MPLS. This functional entity is for further study.

There are many different ways that a RACF can be implemented using one or more PD-FEs and one or more TRC-FEs. Multiple PD-FEs can be used within the domain of a network operator, each controlling a different sub-domain. Likewise, multiple TRC-FEs may coexist within an operator's domain, each controlling a different sub-domain. A PD-FE may contact one of these TRC-FEs, which subsequently interacts with the other TRC-FEs. A PD-FE may also contact each TRC-FE separately. Finally, the decision as to whether the requested QoS for a session can be satisfied or not may be made by a PD-FE or by the requesting SCF.

Three different examples of the implementation of the RACF architecture are given in figures 12.3 to 12.5. In the first example given in figure 12.3, the access network and the core network are under different administrative domains, that is, they are managed by different operators. Consequently there are two RACFs: RACF 1 for the access network and RACF 2 for the core network. The PD-FE of RACF 1 makes use of the NACF, but this

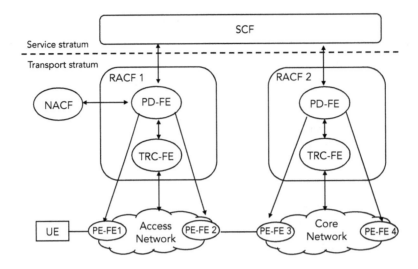

Figure 12.3: Example 1 of the RACF implementation

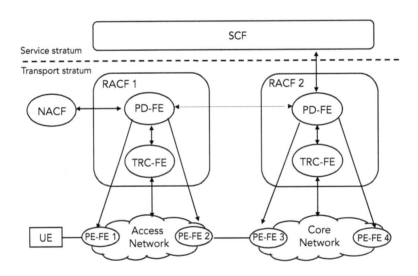

Figure 12.4: Example 2 of the RACF implementation

is not required for the PD-FE of RACF 2. We note that the two PD-FEs do not communicate with each other, and the coordination for the QoS of the session being established across the access and the core network is done by the SCF. There are two PE-FEs for each network. In the access network, PE-FE 1 polices the traffic sent by the UE, and PE-FE 2 interacts with PE-FE 3 of the core network. PE-FE 4 interacts with the PE-FE of another core network or an access network not shown in the diagram. The exact policing function performed by each PE-FE depends of course on the actual QoS scheme used in the network. Also, it is quite likely that each network may have a different set of QoS parameters, in which case the set of QoS parameters of the access network have to be mapped to the set of the QoS parameters of the core network, and vice versa for the return path. This will take place at the boundary of the two networks between PE-FE 2 and PE-FE 3.

In example 2 given in figure 12.4, the access network and the core networks are in separate administrative domains, but the SCF can only communicate with the PD-FE of the core network. In this case, the two PD-FEs communicate with each other in order to coordinate the QoS of the session being established, That is, the QoS coordination is performed at the RACF level, as opposed to the first example where it is performed at the SCF.

Finally, in the third example given in figure 12.5, the access and core networks are managed by the same operator, i.e., they are in a single administrative domain. The PD-FE controls both TRC-FEs in the access and in the core networks, and all four PE-FEs. The QoS across both networks is negotiated by the PD-FE within the RACF.

12.3 DESCRIPTION OF THE FUNCTIONAL ENTITIES

In this section, we describe the functionality of the PD-FE, the TRC-FE and the PE-FE.

The PD-FE handles QoS requests received from an SCF or another PD-FE. It makes the final policy decision based on the service information, such as, service type, flow description, bandwidth, and priority, the resource admission result from TRC-FE, and the network policy rules and transport subscription information, such as, maximum upstream and downstream capacity. If the PD-FE decides to accept a QoS request, it downloads various parameters to the PE-FE in the ingress of the network, which is responsible for policing the incoming traffic flow. Examples of these parameters are: gate control, bandwidth allocation, packet marking, and leaky bucket values, along with *Network Address and Port Translation* (NAPT) and address latching.

The PD-FE contains the following functions:

- *Final Decision Point (FDP):* This function first checks the QoS request based on service information, network policy rules and transport subscription information, and then interacts with the TRC-FE which determines whether the requested QoS request can be satisfied or not. The FDP can also indicate to the SCF if there is a loss of connectivity in the transport network.

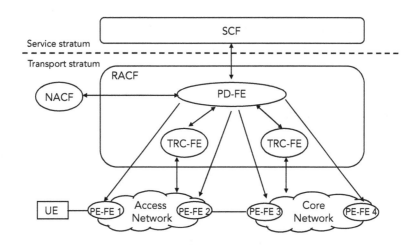

Figure 12.5: Example 3 of the RACF implementation

- *QoS Mapping – Technology Independent* (QMTI): In general, the QoS parameters and priority classes requested by a service are not the same with those of the underlying transport network. This function maps the requested QoS parameters and priority classes received from the SCF to those of the underlying network.
- *Gate Control* (GC): This function controls the opening and closing of a gate that activates an action implemented in the PE-FE. This action is applied to the IP packets based on the IPv4 5-tuple packet classifier (IP source and destination addresses, IP protocol number, source and destination ports) and to the transport interface identification information, such as VLAN or VPN number.
- *IP Packet Marking Control (IPMC)*: This function decides on the marking and remarking of packets in a flow.
- *NAPT Control and NAT Traversal* (NAPTC): This function interacts with the PE-FE and the SCF to provide the address binding information for the NAPT control and NAT traversal as needed.
- *Rate Limiting Control* (RLC): This function makes decisions on the bandwidth limits of flows for policing.
- *Firewall Working Mode Selection* (FWMS): This function selects the working mode of the firewall based on the service information. Four packet inspection modes could be identified: static packet filtering, dynamic packet filtering, tasteful inspection, and deep packet inspection.
- *Core Network Path Selection* (CNPS): This function chooses the core network ingress and/or egress path for a media flow based on the service information and technology independent policy rules in the PD-FE.
- *Network Selection (*NS): This function locates core networks that are involved to offer the requested QoS resource. It locates the PE-FEs that are involved to enforce the final admission decisions.

The TRC-FE collects and maintains resource status information of the network it controls, such as, link utilization and queue sizes in routers and switches, one-way round trip delay, and packet loss rate. On receipt of a request from the PD-FE, the TRC-FE determines whether there is sufficient bandwidth within the network, and accordingly it reserves the necessary bandwidth, updates the resource status of the network, and informs the PD-FE.

The TRC-FE provides the following basic functions:

- *QoS Mapping – Technology Dependent* (QMTD): This function maps the QoS parameters and classes received from the PD-FE to the specific QoS parameters and priority classes of the underlying network.
- *Technology Dependent Decision Point (*TDDP): This function determines if the available capacity in the network can satisfy the requested resources. For this, it uses the network topology, the state of the network usage, and subscription information in access networks. If there is available capacity, it updates the network usage to include the new request and sends a positive response to the PD-FE that the resource is available. Otherwise, it sends a negative answer.
- *Network Topology Maintenance* (NTM): This function collects and maintains the network topology information.
- *Network Resource Maintenance* (NRM): This function collects and maintains information regarding the use of its links by keeping track of the resources allocated. Alternatively, it can collect this information through in-band or out-of-band measurements. In the former case the TRC-FE obtains performance information using active probes, whereas in the latter case it obtains status information through periodic polling of routers and switches.

- *Element Resource Control (ERC):* This function controls resources at an aggregate level, such as, VLAN and VPN.

The PE-FE enforces the rules instructed by the PD-FE on a per-subscriber and per-IP flow basis. The functions of the PE-FE include:

- Opening and closing a unidirectional gate associated with a media flow in either the upstream or downstream direction. When a gate is open, all of the packets associated with the flow are allowed to pass through; when a gate is closed, all of the packets associated with the flow are blocked and dropped.
- Rate limiting and bandwidth allocation.
- Traffic classification and marking.
- Leaky bucket.
- Mapping of IP-layer QoS measures onto link layer QoS information based on predefined static policy rules.
- Network address and port translation.
- Media relay (i.e., address latching) for NAT traversal.
- Collecting and reporting resource usage information, e.g., start-time, end-time, and octets of sent data.
- Firewall based on packet filtering. Inspecting and dropping packets based on predefined static security policy rules and gates installed by PD-FE.

12.4 THE PUSH AND PULL MODES

The mechanism for allocating resources in the transport network in order to satisfy the requested QoS for a multimedia session that is currently being set up or being modified, is known as the QoS resource control mechanism or just resource control mechanism. It consists of the following three logical states:

- *Authorization:* The QoS requested resources are authorized based on policy rules. The authorized QoS limits the maximum amount of resources that can be allocated to a specified user.
- *Reservation:* The QoS requested resources are reserved based on the authorized resource and resource availability.
- *Commitment:* The QoS resources are committed for the requested media flows when the gate in the PE-FE is opened and other admission decisions, such as bandwidth allocation, have been enforced in the transport network.

As we have seen in the previous section, in order for RACF to perform resource control it requires information about the service that is being set up or being modified, the underlying transport network, and user subscription information. The RACF may control the resources in the transport network at an individual user level or at an aggregate level, such as, an LSP, a VPN, and a VLAN. Given the variety of application characteristics and performance requirements, the RACF supports the following three resource allocation schemes:

- *Single-phase scheme:* Authorization, reservation and commitment are performed in a single step. The requested resources are immediately committed upon successful authorization and reservation. The single-phase scheme minimizes the delay in allocating the resources and it is suitable for client-server-like applications.

- *Two-phase scheme:* Authorization and reservation are performed in one step, followed by commitment in a separate step. Alternatively authorization is performed in one step, followed by reservation and commitment in a separate step. The two-phase scheme is suitable for interactive applications which have stringent performance requirements and need to have sufficient resources in the transport network.
- *Three-phase scheme:* Authorization, reservation and commitment are performed in three steps sequentially. The three-phase scheme is suitable for network-hosted services in an environment where resources in the transport network are scarce.

The user equipment may have different capabilities. In view of this, the following three types have been defined:

- *Type 1:* The UE does not have QoS negotiation capabilities both at the service and transport stratum. Examples are a basic soft phone and a game console.
- *Type 2:* The UE has QoS negotiation capabilities at the service stratum only. That is, the UE can communicate with the SCF for service initiation and negotiation, but it does not have the functionality to request QoS resources from the transport network. An example of this type of equipment is the smartphone.
- *Type 3:* The UE has QoS negotiation capabilities at the service and transport stratum. That is, it can communicate with the SCF for service initiation and negotiation and it can also request QoS resources from the transport network.

In order to handle the different types of UEs and different QoS capabilities in the transport network, two different QoS control modes were proposed, namely the *push* mode and the *pull* mode. In the push mode, the RACF authorizes, reserves, and commits the requested resources in the transport network. This mode is suitable for the first two types of UE. For type 1, the SCF determines the QoS requirements of the requested service on behalf of the UE, and for type 2, it extracts them from the signaling used to set up a multimedia session. The pull mode is suitable for the type 3 UE, which has the functionality to request explicitly the reservation of resources in the transport network, using a signaling protocol such as RSVP-TE. In this case, the RACF has to pre-authorize the requested resources before the UE can send in a requests to reserve bandwidth.

In the push mode, the single-phase or two-phase resource control scheme can be used. As shown in figure 12.6, the following steps are involved:

1. The UE requests an application-specific service by sending a service request, such as a SIP `INVITE`, to the SCF. The service request may or may not contain any explicit QoS parameters.
2. The SCF determines the service QoS parameters either by deriving them from the type of the requested service or by extracting them from the service signaling message. It then requests the RACF to authorize, reserve, and commit the necessary resources in the transport network.
3. The RACF performs authorization and admission control based on policy rules, resource admission decision and transport subscription profile stored in the NACF. If the request is granted, the RACF pushes the gate control, packet marking and bandwidth allocation decisions to the PD-FE.

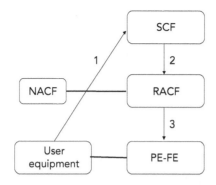

Figure 12.6: The push mode

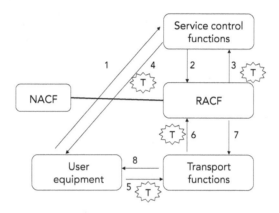

Figure 12.7: The pull mode

In the pull mode, the two-phase or three-phase resource control scheme can be used. As shown in figure 12.7, the following steps are involved:

1. The UE requests a service by sending a service request, such as, a SIP `INVITE` or an HTTP `GET`, to the SCF. The service request may or may not contain any explicit QoS parameters.

2. The SCF extracts or derives the service QoS requirements for the requested service, and sends an authorization request to the RACF that contains explicit QoS parameters.

3. The RACF checks for authorization using network policy rules. If the resources are authorized, an authorization token, see IETF RFC 3520 [6], is assigned to this service. The use of the authorization token is optional, and it is possible to perform authorization without the use of a token.

4. The token is sent to the UE.

5. The UE initiates an explicit request for resource reservation directly to the transport network using a signaling protocol. This request may also contain the authorization token.

6. On receipt of the request, the transport functions at the network edge send a request to RACF for resource reservation and admission control that may contain the authorization token as an option.

7. The RACF makes a reservation and admission control decision based on the user profile in NACF, service information, network policy rules and resource availability. If the request is granted, the RACF provides the gate control, packet marking and bandwidth allocation to the PE-FE, and informs the UE (step 8).

12.5 PROCEDURES

The RACF entities communicate with each other using well-defined interfaces, known as *reference points*. For instance, the SCF communicates with the PD-FE using the Rs reference point. The PD-FE communicates with the TRC-FE using the Rt reference point, and it communicates with the PE-FE using the Rw reference point. The Ru reference point allows the PD-FE to interact with the NACF, and the Rc reference point allows the TRC-FE to collect information about the network topology and the current level of usage of the network resources. The Rp reference point allows the interaction between TRC-FEs within the same administrative domain. These interfaces are not described in this book, and the interested reader is referred to ITU-T Recommendation Y.2111[3].

In this section, we describe the RACF signaling when a resource reservation request is issued. These messages are described using generic names, rather than the actual procedure names used in the reference points. We assume a single-phase scheme, that is, authorization, reservation and commitment are performed in a single step. We also describe the steps involved for releasing resources reserved for a session.

In figure 12.8 we give the flow of messages involved in allocating resources when the PD-FE receives a resource reservation request from the SCF (step 1). This is triggered by a service establishment event or an internal action in the SCF. The SCF determines or derives the QoS parameters, such as bandwidth and class of service, for the media flows of the service in question, and it then sends a reservation request to the PD-FE with the media flow description and its QoS parameters (step 2). The PD-FE checks if the media flow description and the required QoS resources are consistent with network policy rules held in the PD-FE and with the transport subscription information held in the NACF (step 3). It then determines the access network(s) and the core network(s) involved in the media flow, and sends an availability check request to the TRC-FE registered with the PD-FE to check resource availability in the network (step 4). If there are multiple TRC-FEs in the network, they communicate with each other to determine if the required resources are available end-to-end in the network. The TRC-FE which received the availability check request sends a response back to the PD-FE. When multiple TRC-FEs are present in the form of a distributed hierarchical structure, the top tier TRC-FE forwards the request to the other TRC-FEs and then makes the final admission decision based on the results of the admission decisions from the other TRC-FEs. The PD-FE makes the final admission decisions (step 5) based on the results of steps 3 and 4. If the media flow is not admitted, the PD-FE sends a rejection back to the SCF. Otherwise, the PD-FE determines whether this service request requires sending information to the PE-FE, and if yes, it installs the admission information in the PE-FE. The PD-FE may request the admission information to be reserved and committed immediately (single-phase scheme), or it may request the installation of admission information and await for a separate commitment later for opening the gate (two-phase scheme). The first case is the single-phase scheme described above in section 12.3, and the second case is the two-

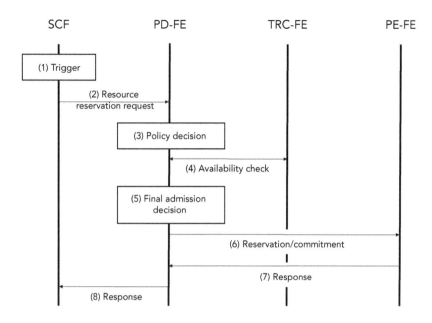

Figure 12.8: The SCF-requested resource reservation procedure

phase scheme. The PE-FE installs (and enforces) the final admission decisions sent from the PD-FE and sends a response back to the PD-FE (step 7), which then sends a response back to the SCF.

A resource modification is usually triggered by a media renegotiation event or an internal action in the SCF. The steps involved for modifying the resources allocated to a service is similar to those shown in figure 12.8.

In figure 12.9 we show the messages involved when a type 3 UE sends a QoS resource reservation request to its PE-FE using a QoS signaling protocol. In this case, the requested resource reservation is triggered by the PE-FE (step 1). It selects the right PD-FE according to binding information, and sends a resource reservation request with the flow description and its QoS parameters to the PD-FE (step 2). The PD-FE sends a resource action request to the SCF to retrieve the service information of the flow (step 3). This is a set of data provided by the SCF which has been derived from service subscription information, service QoS requirements, and service policy rules. Then, it checks if the flow description, the required QoS resources and the service information are consistent with network policy rules held in the PD-FE and the transport subscription information held in the NACF (step 4). Subsequently, the PD-FE identifies and determines which access network(s) and core network(s) are involved in the transport of the media flow, and sends an availability check request to TRC-FE (step 5). (The selection of the TRC-FE is the same as in the SCF-requested resource reservation procedure shown in figure 12.8.) The PD-FE makes the final admission decision based on the results of steps 4 and 5 (step 6), and installs the final admission policing parameters in the PE-FE (step 7). The PE-FE informs the UE using the QoS signaling protocol.

When the UE is roaming, the resource reservation request may be triggered by either the home SCF or the visiting SCF. In figure 12.10, we show the flow of messages when the resource reservation request is triggered by the visited

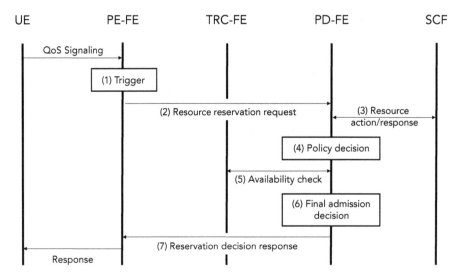

Figure 12.9: The requested resource reservation is triggered by the PE-FE

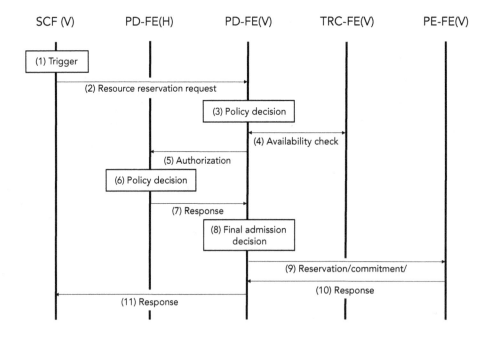

Figure 12.10: SCF-requested resource reservation for roaming UE

SCF. In this case, the visited PD-FE(V) performs the admission control based on the resources available in its own network and its own network policy rules. However, it does not have access to the user profile, and for this reason it sends an authorization request (step 5) to the home PD-FE(H). With the exception of this step, the remaining steps are similar to those for the SCF-requested resource reservation procedure shown in figure 12.8.

The SCF-invoked resource release procedure is shown in figure 12.11. This is triggered by a service termination event, a media renegotiation event, or an internal action in the SCF. The SCF first contacts the PD-FE to inform it of the resource release, which in turn contacts the PE-FE which releases the allocated resources. Subsequently, the PD-FE informs the TRC-FE so that it can update the status of the networking resources. Finally, the PD-FE informs the SCF that the networking resources have been released.

12.6 IMPLEMENTATION CONSIDERATIONS FOR THE TRC-FE

In an IP network without MPLS support, nodes forward packets based on their destination IP address. In this case, in order to use the RACF, the TRC-FE has to be specifically implemented, so that it can carry out admission control and resource allocation. One or multiple TRC-FEs can be deployed to directly manage all of the physical links within an administrative domain. A TRC-FE should maintain a *Network Topology and Resource Database* (NTRD) of a sub-domain or area within its control, where it keeps information such as, the topology of the network and the current utilization of the links. Based on the information in the NTRD, the TRC-FE can calculate a route, carry out admission control, and allocate bandwidth on each link along the route for each media flow that requires a QoS guarantee. Multiple TRC-FEs, interacting through the Rp reference point, can also be deployed in a domain.

In an IP network with MPLS support, label switching is used in order to forward packets. LSPs can be used to set up a virtual private network (see Chapter 13), and the admission control, route selection, resource allocation and label forwarding for a media flow is handled within the VPN. In this case the TRC-FE is designed so that to manage the

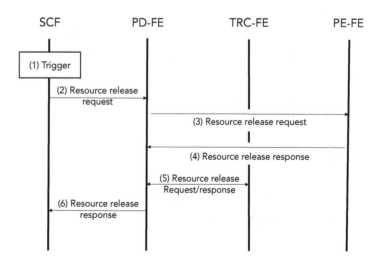

Figure 12.11: The SCF-requested resource release procedure

bandwidth of one or multiple VPNs, within an administrative domain. The TRC-FE should maintain the topology of each VPN and the current utilization level of the links within each LSP in an NTRD. Based on this information and policy rules, the TRC-FE should do route selection, admission control, and resource allocation for a media flow within its VPN. Multiple TRC-FEs, interacting through the Rp reference point, can also be deployed for a VPN.

In an Ethernet network, the TRC-FE has to maintain a link layer NTRD for the whole network. Based on the information in the NTRD, the TRC-FE instance makes admission control and resource allocation to ensure that sufficient resources are available within the Ethernet network for the admitted flows. Multiple TRC-FEs can also be deployed in a domain. Finally, in a broadband wireless network, mobile nodes handle packets through a wireless MAC protocol, which typically provides a QoS signaling mechanism. Using the TRC-FE, an admission control and resource allocation can be implemented for media flows of different applications. As above, an NTRD has to be maintained, and multiple TRC-FEs can also be deployed.

12.7 GUARANTEEING QOS END-TO-END IN A MULTI-DOMAIN ENVIRONMENT

A multimedia session may be established over multiple domains each owned and controlled by a different operator. In the example shown in figure 12.12, there are two operators A and B, each operating its own network with its own IMS, i.e., SCF, and RACF. We assume that UEs 1 and 2 belong to domains A and B respectively, and that they are currently in their own domains, i.e., they are not roaming. UE 1 initiates a multimedia session with UE 2 through its IMS, and as a result the P-CSCF of IMS A sends a resource reservation request to the PD-FE of RACF A. The PD-FE reserves the necessary resources in network A from UE 1 to the network B. It also communicates with the PD-FE of RACF B through the Ri reference point, see ITU-T Recommendation Y.2111[3], to request a resource reservation in network B, from network A to UE 2. Upon receipt of the request, the PD-FE of RACF B reserves the necessary resources in network B and informs the PD-FE of RACF A. When all resources have been allocated between the two UEs, the PD-FE of RACF A informs the P-CSCF of IMS A.

We note that the requested QoS measures, i.e., bandwidth, delay, jitter, packet loss rate, are for the entire end-to-end path and not per domain. For instance, let us assume that the 95th percentile delay, jitter, and packet loss rate requested between the two UEs in figure 12.12 are 150 msec, 30 msec, and 0.01 respectively. These values are for the end-to-end path across the two domains A and B. Consequently, in order to allow each RACF to carry out its own resource reservation, they have to be distributed over the two domains. The requested bandwidth does not pose such problems since each link along the selected route across the domains has to satisfy the same bandwidth requirement.

Another problem when establishing a connection across multiple domains, is that the QoS parameters and priority classes may vary from one domain to another. In addition, the SCF may request a priority class and QoS parameters that may not be recognized by the underlying transport network. In view of this, a mapping between different sets of QoS parameters is required. These two issues are addressed in the next two sections.

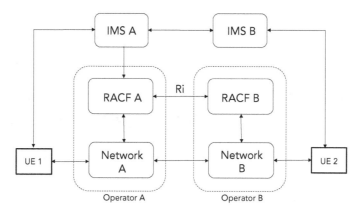

Figure 12.12: Inter-operator RACF communication when one UE is roaming

12.7.1 THE PATH COMPUTATIONAL ELEMENT

The issue of multi-domain routing subject to end-to-end QoS constraints was addressed in IETF RFC 4655[7], where an entity referred to as the *Path Computational Element* (PCE) was introduced. This entity is responsible for route selection, admission control, and resource reservation within a domain. A PCE interacts with the PCEs of other domains in order to set up a multi-domain route with end-to-end QoS constraints. Several algorithms have been proposed that permit the PCE of a domain to set up a path across multiple domains under end-to-end QoS constraints. These algorithms can be readily used in the case where each domain is controlled by a RACF. Below, we describe two such algorithms, namely, the *per-domain backward method and the per-domain tree backward* method. For further details see Geleji and Perros[8].

In order to calculate a path across multiple domains, we have to select the sequence of the domains that the path will traverse and a path within each of the domains. For presentation purposes we limit ourselves to the case where the sequence of the domains is either pre-determined through contractual agreements or the domains are physically linked in a series so that there is only one possible path for any pair of source/destination UEs.

Let us consider the three-domain network shown in figure 12.13. Domains 1 and 2 are connected via the border gateway routers BG11-BG21 and BG12-BG22. Domains 2 and 3 are connected via the routers BG24-BG32 and BG23-BG31. Each domain is controlled by its own PCE. Let us assume that PCE 1 receives a request to establish a connection between UE 1 and UE 2. In the per–domain backward method, the end-to-end path is set up in segments, one per domain, starting from the last domain that serves UE 2 and working backwards towards the first domain that serves UE 1. PCE 1 forwards the reservation request to PCE 3 which selects the cheapest path from UE 2 to domain 2 and allocates the requested resources along the path in both directions. The selection of a route so that more than one QoS metrics are minimized can be done using the simple multi-domain routing algorithm described in problem 5 of Chapter 10. We assume that the calculated path from the router that serves UE 2 to BG23 is through BG31, as indicated by the thick line. (When calculating a path from domain A to adjacent domain B, it is easier to calculate it all the way to the border routers of domain B.) PCE 3 forwards the request to PCE 2 along with the calculated path segment, which calculates the cheapest path from BG23 to a border router in domain 1. Let us

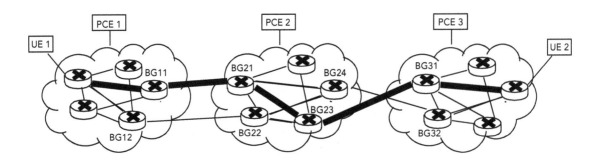

Figure 12.13: The per-domain backward method

assume that the calculated path is BG23-BG21-BG11, as indicated by the thick line. PCE 2 reserves resources along the new path segment in both directions and the two path segments are merged to form a single segment from the router that serves UE 2 to BG11. This route is forwarded to PCE 1 which calculates the cheapest path from BG11 to the router that serves UE 1, which we assume to be the one-hop path between BG11 and the router. PCE 1 reserves resources in both directions along this path, and at that time the end-to-end path has been established.

We note that this method is not optimal, though it is optimal within each domain (assuming that the routing algorithm gives optimal results). Also, it may not necessarily satisfy the requested QoS. For instance, let us assume that we want to establish a path between the two UEs so that the total end-to-end propagation does not exceed 120 msec, and the required bandwidth is 1 Gbps. Then, in order to calculate the first segment of the end-to-end path in domain 3, all links that cannot support a 1 Gbps request are eliminated from the topology and subsequently Dijkstra's algorithm is used to calculate the cheapest path using the propagation delay for each link as the cost. We do the same for domains 2 and 1. However, the resulting end-to-end path may not satisfy the delay requirement, in which case, the request to establish the path between the two UEs is rejected. It is also rejected if there are no links within a domain that can support the bandwidth request.

In the per–domain backward tree method, a tree of paths is set up backwards starting from the domain that serves UE 2 and working towards the first domain that serves UE 1, of which the best path is selected. Specifically, PCE 1 forwards the reservation request to the PCE 3 which selects the cheapest path from the router that serves UE 2 to each of the border routers of domain 2, but it does not reserve resources. In the example given in figure 12.14, we assume that the cheapest path to BG23 is through BG31, and to BG24 through BG32. This tree of paths, indicated by the thick line, is then forwarded to the PCE 2 which extends it to the border routers of domain 1. Specifically, the cheapest path is calculated from BG23 to the domain 1 border routers BG11 and BG12. We assume that these paths are: BG23-BG21-BG11 and BG23-BG22-BG12, as indicated by the thick lines. Likewise, the cheapest path is calculated from BG24 to BG11 and BG12. We assume that these paths are: BG24-BG21-BG11 and BG24-BG22-BG12, as indicated by the thick lines. Subsequently, the entire tree is trimmed so that only the shortest paths are kept from the router that serves UE 2 to BG11 and BG12. Again, no resource allocation takes place in domain 2. The tree is forwarded to PCE 1 which extends it to the router that serves UE 1. We assume that the cheapest paths are BG11-router, and BG12-router, as indicated by the thick lines. Then, it searches the tree to identify the cheapest end-to-end path and forwards the path to the PCE 3 so that it can reserve resources along the segment in domain 3. Subsequently, PCE 3 forwards the path to the PCE 2 which reserves resources along the segment in domain 2. Finally, PCE 2 forwards the path to PCE 1 which reserves resources along the segment in domain 1, and at that time the end-to-end path has been established. The establishment of the path may fail if adequate resources are not available along the segment of the path within a domain at the time when the PCE attempts to reserve resources. This method gives the optimum solution assuming that the selection of the path of domains is fixed, as is the case here.

12.7.2 MAPPING OF QOS SERVICE CLASSES

When a connection is set up over multiple domains, a mapping of the requested QoS parameters and priority classes from one domain to next is necessary if the domains are heterogeneous. The same applies if a connection spans across two different access networks, such as UMTS and a metro Ethernet network, interconnected by a wide area network. In addition, when a session is being established, the SCF may request a priority class and QoS parameters that may not be recognized by the underlying network. These are either signaled by the UEs involved in the multimedia session, or determined indirectly by the SCF. In view of this, the PD-FE, TRC-FE, and PE-FE are equipped with functionality that permits them to do QoS mapping. We recall from section 12.3 that the PD-FE contains the QoS Mapping – Technology Independent (QMTI) function, whose role is to map the QoS class and parameters of a multimedia session requested by the SCF to those of the underlying network. Likewise, a similar function, the QoS Mapping – Technology Dependent (QMTD) function, is found in the TRC-FE which maps the QoS parameters and priority class received from the PD-FE to the specific QoS parameters and classes of the underlying network. There are various ways that QoS mapping maybe enabled, the simplest one being the static binding of one QoS scheme with another. In this section, we present some of the static mappings of QoS classes.

In ITU-T Y.1541[9], 5 different QoS classes are defined, which are summarized in table 12.1. The *IP Packet Transfer Delay* (IPTD) is defined as the mean one-way end-to-end delay for all delivered packets (successful or errored). The value given in table 12.1 is an upper bound on the mean one-way end-to-end delay. The *IP packet Delay Variation* (IPDV) is defined as the difference of the one way end-to-end delay of successive packets. It is the same as the

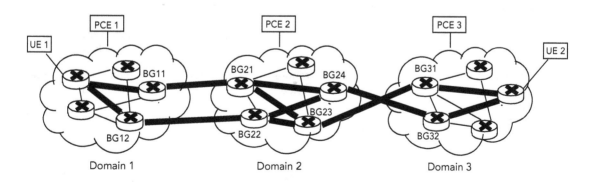

Figure 12.14: The per-domain backward tree method

inter-packet delay variation (IPDV) defined in section 4.2. The value given in the table is the $1-10^{-3}$ quantile of the IPTD minus the minimum observed value of IPTD. The *IP Packet Loss Ratio* (IPLR) and the *IP Packet Error Ratio* (IPER) are defined the same way as in section 4.2, and the values given in table 12.1 are upper bounds. Finally, U means unspecified or unbound. An evaluation interval of 1 minute is suggested.

A mapping between the ITU-T Y.1541, RSVP, DiffServ and WiMax classes for different types of applications is given in table 12.2. In addition to mapping QoS classes between two different technologies, the QoS parameters and their values of one class may also have to be mapped to those of the other class.

Class	Application type	IPTD	IPDV	IPLR	IPER
0	Real-time, jitter sensitive, high interaction (VOIP, video teleconference)	100 msec	50 msec	10^{-3}	10^{-4}
1	Real-time, jitter sensitive, interactive (VOIP, video teleconference)	400 msec	50 msec	10^{-3}	10^{-4}
2	Transaction data, highly interactive (signaling)	100 msec	U	10^{-3}	10^{-4}
3	Transaction data, interactive	400 msec	U	10^{-3}	10^{-4}
4	Low loss only (short transactions, bulk data, video streaming)	1 sec	U	10^{-3}	10^{-4}
5	Traditional applications of default IP networks	U	U	U	U

Table 12.1: The Y.1541 classes

Application type	Y.1541	IntServ	DiffServ	WiMax
VoIP, video conferencing	0 ,1	Guaranteed service	EF	Unsolicited grant service (UGS)
Audio and video streaming, highly interactive transactions, low loss applications	2, 3, 4	Guaranteed service	AF1/2/3/4	Real-time polling service (RtPS)
Email/Web browsing	5	Controlled-load service	CS0	Non-real-time polling service (NrtPS)

Table 12.2: Mappings of QoS classes

PROBLEMS

1. Refer to the example of the RACF implementation given in figure 12.3. Re-draw the RACF implementation assuming that the end-to-end topology consists of the access and the core network shown in the example followed by another core network and an access network. Assume that each access and core network belong to different operator, that is, there is one RACF per network.

2. Same as in the above problem, but now use example 3 shown in figure 12.5. Assume that the new added core and access networks are managed by a different operator, and that the QoS decision is made by the same SCF. What additional modifications are required so that the QoS decision can be made by the PD-FE contacted by the SCF?

3. Give a diagram similar to the one in figure 12.8 to show the messages involved for an SCF triggered resource reservation request for the network and RACF topology described above in problem 1.

4. For the multi-domain network shown in figure 12.13, draw a diagram similar to the one in figure 12.12 to show the inter-operator RACF communication. Assume that the home of UE 1 is domain 1 and that of UE 2 is domain 2, and that both UEs are in their home networks.

5. Consider the multi-domain network in figure 12.13. We want to establish a path between the two UEs so that the one-way end-to-end delay is less than 150 msec. We assume a high-priority connection, such as an EF connection in DiffServ, which typically suffers minimal queueing delays in the routers. In view of this, the end-to-end delay is just the end-to-end propagation delay.
    a. Assign propagation delay values to each inter-domain and intra-domain link, and then calculate by hand the end-to-end path using the per-domain backward method.
    b. Same as above, but now use the per-domain backward tree method.
    c. Assume now that you have global knowledge, and run Dijkstra's algorithm for the entire three-domain network to find the cheapest route. This is the optimum solution. Compare your results with those obtained above in questions a and b.
    d. Vary the location of the two UEs and repeat the above tasks a, b, and c.

6. Give a mapping of the QoS classes and associated QoS parameters between IEEE 802.11 and WiMax.

REFERENCES

[1] ETSI ES 282 003 V3.4.2 (2010-04), "Resource and Admission Control Sub-system (RACS); Functional Architecture".
[2] 3GPP TS 23.207 V10.0.0 (2011-03), "Technical Specification Group Services and System Aspects; End-to-End Quality of Service (QoS) Concept and Architecture", (Release 10).
[3] ITU-T Recommendation Y.2111, "Resource and Admission Control Functions in NGN".
[4] OpenFlow, URL: http://www.openflow.org/documents/openflow-spec-v1.1.0.pdf.
[5] OnePK, URL: http://developer.cisco.com/web/onepk/home.

6   IETF RFC 3520, "Session Authorization Policy Element".
7   IETF RFC 4655, "A Path Computation Element (PCE)–Based Architecture".
8   G. Geleji and H. Perros, "QoS Routing Across Multiple Autonomous Systems Using the Path Computation Elements Architecture", Annals of Telecommunications, 66 (2011), 293-306.
9   ITU-T Y.1541 (02/2006), "Network Performance Objectives for IP-based Services".

CHAPTER 13: MPLS VIRTUAL PRIVATE NETWORKS

13.1 INTRODUCTION

A *Virtual Private Network* (VPN) is used to provide a customer with networking inter-connectivity without the customer having to own the network. A customer is typically an organization which owns dispersed sites that need to be interconnected. One way of achieving this is for the customer to set up its own infrastructure, that is, install its own routers and interconnect them with privately owned or leased links. This solution tends to be expensive and it also assumes that the customer has the necessary technical know-how to set up and operate the network. An alternative solution, is to outsource the interconnectivity of the sites to a network provider. Typically, a network provider supports many such customers, and consequently the interconnectivity cost is less than what the organization would have incurred if it owned its own lines.

From the customer's point of view, the interconnectivity of its sites should take place with minimum effort. QoS should be the same as if the customer owned the infrastructure. The traffic of the customer should not be tapped by other customers and the customer's equipment should not be accessible by non-authorized users. Adding new sites and changing the bandwidth between sites should be easy, and the customer should not have to do complex routing configurations. Also, there should be no changes to the way the customer's sites have been configured, and operations that affect connectivity should be easy. On the other hand, the network provider should be able to support a large number of customers over the same infrastructure so that to maximize profits. Each customer may have a large number of sites, and a customer should be able to keep its own private addresses. The network provider sets up a network for each customer which behaves as if it belongs to the customer, but in fact it does not, since all customers share the same infrastructure, i.e., routers and links. In view of this, these "private networks" are in fact virtual private networks.

There are many different solution for VPNs in layer 1, 2, and 3. In this Chapter, we discuss layer 2 solutions based on the MPLS architecture.

13.2 VPN MODELS

In a VPN, a device that is owned by the customer which is at the edge of a customer's site is referred to as the *Customer Edge* (CE) equipment. This is in contrast to the *Provider Edge* (PE) equipment which refers to devices at the

Provider's network

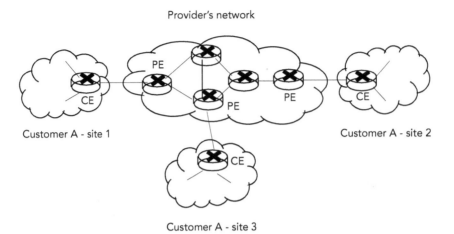

Figure 13.1: An example of the CE and PE equipment

Provider's network

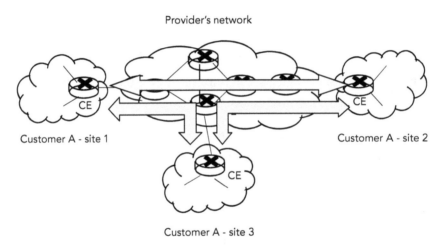

Figure 13.2: The overlay VPN model

edge of a provider's infrastructure, providing connectivity to CE devices. An example of the CE and PE equipment is shown in figure 13.1, where three different sites of a customer are interconnected via a provider's network.

We say that a VPN is a *CE-based* VPN if the intelligence and control is provided by the customer through its CE equipment. On the other hand, it is a *PE-based VPN* if the provider takes over the management of the customers' virtual backbone. Obviously, the simplest solution from the customer's point of view is a PE-based VPN.

There are two VPN models, namely the *overlay VPN model* and the *peer VPN model*. In the overlay model, a virtual backbone dedicated to the customer is overlaid on top of the provider's infrastructure. Specifically, the service provider sets up point-to-point tunnels between the customer's CEs, using various technologies, such as: ATM circuits, Frame Relay connections, IPSec, IP-over-IP tunnels, and *MPLS pseudowires.* The CEs think that they are one hop away from each other. They send topological and routing information and data packets to each other over the tunnels. The operator is unaware of the customer's internal topology and addressing. An example of the overlay model is shown in figure 13.2, which is based on the network topology given in figure 13.1. As we can see, the three CEs are interconnected pair wise by point-to-point tunnels. In the case of MPLS, these tunnels are pseudowires, which are LSPs with additional features as will be described later on in this Chapter.

This solution provides traffic isolation between customers, and prevents unauthorized users to access a customer's CEs. Also, the customer's private addresses are preserved. The disadvantages are primarily related to the management of the VPNs. For instance, the provider requires knowledge of the traffic requirements between pairs of CEs in order to provision the tunnels, which may not be precisely known. Adding a new site requires the creation of new set of tunnels to all the existing CEs, which may make the reconfiguration of a CE router in a CE-based VPN or a PE router in a PE-based VPN, quite complex. Also, in a PE-based VPN the provider may have to deal with a large number of CEs belonging to different customers.

In view of this, the overlay VPN model is good for VPNs with a small number of CEs. When the number of CEs is large, the VPN becomes a complex mesh topology that may be hard to manage. This problem is alleviated by using the peer VPN model. In this case, each CE thinks that its associated PE is part of its network, and it automatically peers with it. That is, it exchanges topological and routing information in the control plane and it sends and receives IP packets to/from its PE in the data plane. A typical PE may serve a number of different VPNs, and the problem is now shifted to that of providing isolation between the VPNs in the control and data planes within the provider's network. Adding a new customer site to the VPN only requires re-configuration between the new CE and its associated PE, and not between all the customer sites as in the overlay VPN model. Each CE advertises its reachability information for the destinations within its site to its PE, and then this information is carried to destination PEs which serve the other customer's CEs. The potential problems associated with this solution is that the provider has to make sure it provides isolation of the routing and data traffic of a customer from all the other customers. IETF RFC 4364 [1] describes a layer 3 scheme for the peer VPN model based on BGP.

13.3 PSEUDOWIRES

Pseudowires provide a layer 2 solution for the overlay VPN model. Other layer 2 solutions include Frame Relay and ATM. Layer 2 VPN schemes can be used to provide stringent QoS, and they are a significant source of revenue for network providers. *Pseudowires* (PW) allow for the transport of different types of traffic, such as, Ethernet, Frame Relay, ATM, low-rate TDM traffic (T1, T3, E1, E3), and SONET/SDH traffic over an MPLS network, see IETF RFC 3985 [2].

The basic architecture of a pseudowire is shown in figure 13.3. The customer's CE is connected to a pseudowire via a link, referred to as the *Attachment Circuit* (AC), which may be based on Frame Relay, ATM, Ethernet, MPLS, T1, SONET/SDH, etc. A pseudowire is bidirectional between the PE1 and the PE2 LSRs, and for each direction it runs over an LSP, which has to be set up before the pseudowire is established over it. Multiple pseudowires can exist between PE1 and PE2, and each LSP may carry one or more pseudowires that belong to the same customer or dif-

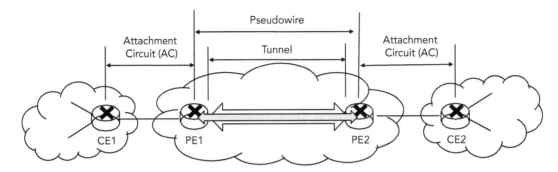

Figure 13.3: The PW architecture

ferent customers. Each customer is associated with a mesh of pseudowires interconnecting pairs of PEs that serve the customer's CEs. This mesh may become problematic to manage if the customer has a large number of sites.

The main function of a pseudowire is to encapsulate the incoming traffic from CE1 to PE1 over the attachment circuit into IP packets which are then transported over an MPLS LSP. At the egress PE2, the original traffic stream is recovered and delivered to the customer's CE2. For some of the traffic encapsulations, additional functionality may be required. The encapsulation is specific to the type of traffic carried over a pseudowire, and described in a series of IETF documents published by the *Pseudowire Emulation Edge-to-Edge* (PWE3) IETF Working Group.

Egress PE2 has to be able to associate the IP packets it receives from ingress PE1 over an LSP with a particular pseudowire. (Multiple pseudowires may run over a single LSP.) This is done using a special label, known as the *PW label*, that is carried in the packet's label stack. This label is exchanged between the two PEs at the time when the pseudowire is established.

The establishment of a pseudowire is done using the LDP downstream unsolicited mode, see IETF RFC 4447 [3]. Ingress PE1 first does a targeted hello to egress PE2, whose address is manually configured in PE1 or learned dynamically via an auto discovery procedure. The two PEs establish a hello adjacency and then a targeted session. Subsequently, PE1 sends a label mapping message to PE2, with a label TLV containing the PW label, and a FEC TLV identifying the pseudowire to which the PW label should be bound. This is a new FEC TLV that was defined for pseudowires, and the following are some of its fields.

- *PWid:* A 32-bit identifier of a pseudowire.
- *Control word bit:* This bit indicates whether a control word is used in the encapsulation of the traffic into IP packets. An example of the control word is given below for Ethernet pseudowires.
- *PW type:* A 15-bit identifier that indicates the type of the pseudowire. PW type and PWid completely identify a pseudowire. The type of the pseudowire depends on the type of data being transferred, such as, Frame Relay, ATM, Ethernet, PPP, and SONET/SDH emulation over MPLS.

The label mapping message sent by PE1 to PE2 is interpreted by PE2 as a request to set up a pseudowire from PE2 to PE1. If PE2 decides to accept this request then it sends a similar label mapping request to PE1 in order to

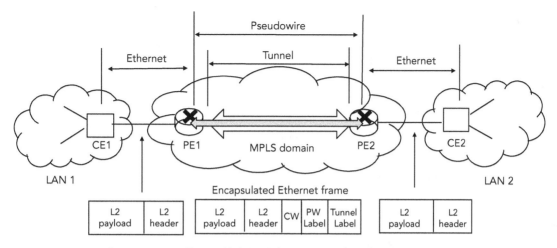

Figure 13.4: An Ethernet pseudowire

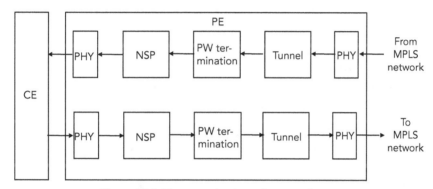

Figure 13.5: The pseudowire reference diagram

set up a pseudowire from PE1 to PE2. The two pseudowires have the same PWid and PW type, and they are bound into a single bidirectional pseudowire at each PE. (Each pseudowire runs on a unidirectional LSP.)

The IP packets associated with a pseudowire carry two labels. The top one is used by each LSR on the path of the pseudowire to forward the packet to the next LSR in the PE1 to PE2 tunnel, and the bottom carries the PW label which is used by PE2 to identify the pseudowire that the packet belongs to.

13.4 ETHERNET PSEUDOWIRES

An Ethernet pseudowire, see IETF RFC 4448 [4], allows Ethernet 802.3 frames to be carried over an MPLS network, as shown in figure 13.4. CE1 and CE2 are Ethernet switches connected to PE1 and PE2 respectively via Ethernet. PE1 receives Ethernet frames from CE1, and after encapsulation it forwards them to PE2, where the original Ethernet frames are recovered and forwarded to CE2.

Figure 13.5 gives a reference diagram of the termination point of a pseudowire within a PE. In the case of an Ethernet pseudowire, the *Native Service Processing* (NSP) function includes frame processing of the Ethernet frames, such as, stripping, overwriting or adding VLAN tags, physical port multiplexing and demultiplexing, PW-PW bridging, layer 2 encapsulation, shaping, and policing. These functions are specific to the Ethernet pseudowire, and they may not be required in other types of pseudowires. The "PW Termination" box represents the operations for setting up and maintaining the pseudowire and encapsulating and decapsulating Ethernet frames. Finally, the "Tunnel" box represents the operations related to the LSP tunnel.

The Ethernet pseudowire can be used to provide a port-to-port or VLAN-to-VLAN bidirectional connectivity over an MPLS packet-switched network. In both cases, the ingress native service processing (NSP) function strips the preamble and *Frame Check Sequence* (FCS) from the Ethernet frame and hands over the frame to the PW termination function, which adds a control word and the PW label. Subsequently, the tunnel function adds the necessary label for forwarding the IP packet over the appropriate LSP. The resulting encapsulated Ethernet frame is shown in the bottom of figure 13.4. At the egress PE, these steps are executed in the opposite order.

The control word is shown in figure 13.6. The first field is set to zero to indicate pseudowire data. The next 12-bit field is reserved, and last field is the 16-bit sequence number, which is used to detect lost, out-of-order, and duplicated packets in the MPLS network.

An Ethernet pseudowire may operate in two different modes: *raw mode* and *tagged mode*. In tagged mode, each frame must contain at least one 802.1Q VLAN tag, and the tag value is meaningful to the NSPs at the PW termination points in PE1 and PE2, which have some agreement signaled or manually configured as to how to process the tag. In raw mode, a frame may or may not contain an 802.1Q VLAN tag. If it contains a tag, then the tag is not meaningful to the NSPs, and it passes through them and the network transparently.

We can distinguish two cases when the PE receives an Ethernet frame that has a VLAN tag: *service delimiting* and non-*service delimiting*.

- *Service-delimiting tag:* In this case, the tag was placed in the frame by an equipment operated by the service provider with the purpose of distinguishing traffic that belongs to different customers. This case arises when multiple LANs from different customers are attached to the same PE.
- *Not service-delimiting tag:* This means that the tag was placed in the frame by the customer and it is not meaningful to the PE.

A tag is designated as service-delimiting or not by configuring appropriately the PE. If an Ethernet pseudowire is operating in raw mode, then service-delimiting tags are not sent over the pseudowire. In this case, if a service-delimiting tag is present when the frame is received by the PE from the attachment circuit, it is stripped from the

0	Reserved	Sequence number
4 bits	12 bits	16 bits

Figure 13.6: The control word

Tag	Service delimiting	Non service delimiting
Raw mode	1st VLAN tag removed	No operation
Tagged mode	No operation	Dummy VLAN tag added

Table 13.1: Summary of operations

frame by the NSP before the frame is sent to the PW termination function. If an Ethernet pseudowire is operating in tagged mode, every frame sent on the pseudowire must have a service-delimiting VLAN tag. If the frame as received by the PE from the attachment circuit does not have a service-delimiting VLAN tag, then the PE inserts a dummy VLAN tag before sending it on to the pseudowire. An Ethernet frame may contain more than one tag, in which case the service delimiting tag is the outermost tag. A service-delimiting tag has only local significance, that is, it is meaningful only at a particular PE-CE interface. Table 13.1 summarizes the above described operations.

13.5 VIRTUAL PRIVATE LAN SERVICE

The primary motivation for the *Virtual Private LAN Service* (VPLS) is to provide connectivity between geographically dispersed Ethernet LAN sites of a customer, as if they were connected by an Ethernet LAN. This is an important service given that Ethernet is the predominant technology for LANs. There are various ways to implement such a service. IETF RFC IETF 4761[5] describes a BGP-based solution and IETF RFC 4762[6] describes a scheme based on LDP. In this section, we describe the latter scheme.

VPLS is based on point-to-point pseudowires, each connecting a single pair of LANs. The pseudowires run on top of MPLS LSP tunnels. (Other tunnels, such as, IPsec and L2TP, can be also used.) The pseudowires are established using LDP as described in section 13.3. VPLS creates an emulated layer 2 LAN that is fully capable of learning MAC addresses and forwarding broadcast, multicast, and unicast traffic. Multiple customers can be supported from a single PE.

In figure 13.7, we give an example of two different customers interconnected using VPLS. Customer A owns three LANs and customer B also owns 3 LANs (lightly shaded). Customer A's three LANs are connected by three Ethernet pseudowires, indicated by double arrows, and customer B's LANs are connected by three Ethernet pseudowires indicated by the lightly shaded double arrows. For reliability each CE may be attached to two different PEs, not shown in figure 13.7. The set of the three PEs interconnected by customer A's pseudowires appears to customer A as a single emulated LAN. Likewise the same set of PEs interconnected by the lightly shaded pseudowires appears as a single emulated LAN to customer B.

One of the features of an Ethernet LAN is flooding. This is used to broadcast a frame and also to forward a frame to an unknown MAC address. Flooding within the emulated LAN is achieved by a PE by transmitting a frame to all the other PEs over all pseudowires. Likewise, multicasting is achieved by a PE by transmitting a multicast frame

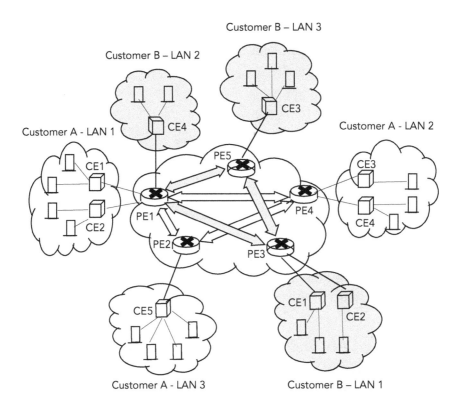

Figure 13.7: An example of VPLS

over the pseudowires associated with a specific set of MAC addresses. This is in contrast to unicasting, where a PE transmits a frame over the pseudowire associated with the specific destination MAC address.

In order to forward a frame, a PE has to learn MAC addresses, which in the VPLS case means that it has to associate MAC addresses with pseudowires. For instance, in the example given in figure 13.7, PE1 has to know that all the LAN 3 MAC addresses of customer A are served via the pseudowire PE1-PE2. Likewise, all customer B's LAN 1 addresses are served via the pseudowire PE1-PE3. The learning of MAC addresses can be achieved by manual configuration. However, it may unreasonable and perhaps infeasible to statically configure all MAC addresses. An alternative viable scheme is for a PE to learn MAC addresses dynamically in the same way that an Ethernet bridge learns. That is, a PE remembers the source MAC address of the frames received over each pseudowire. Similarly, it remembers the MAC addresses of the frames it received over an attachment circuit from each CE. Flooding is used to learn an address. For instance, let us assume that PE1, in the example given in figure 13.7, receives a frame from the PE1-PE2 pseudowire but it does not know whether to forward it to CE1 or CE2. In this case, it floods the frame to both CEs. Likewise, if PE1 receives a frame from customer's A LAN 1 and it does not know which pseudowire to use, it will flood the frame over the PE1-PE2 and PE1-PE4 pseudowires. A destination PE, in turn, will flood it to its own LANs if it does not know the address either.

A single VPLS can be associated with all the VLANs of a customer, or each customer's VLAN maybe associated with a different VPLS. In the first case, all customer's LANs share a single MAC address space and therefore MAC addresses have to be unique and non-overlapping among the customer's VLANs, so that they can be differentiated. In the second case, MAC addresses among the customer's VLANs may be overlapping, since each VLAN belongs to a different instance of VPLS.

PROBLEMS

1. Summarize the advantages and disadvantages of the overlay VPN model and the peer VPN model.

2. Explain in your own words why a PE in VPLS may not know on which pseudowire it should forward a frame.

3. Summarize the main features of the peer VPN model based on BGP, as described in IETF RFC 4364[1].

REFERENCES

[1] IETF RFC 4364, "BGP/MPLS IP Virtual Private Networks (VPNs)".
[2] IETF RFC 3985, "Pseudo Wire Emulation Edge-to-Edge (PWE3) Architecture".
[3] IETF RFC 4447, "Pseudowire Setup and Maintenance Using the Label Distribution Protocol (LDP)".
[4] IETF RFC 4448, "Encapsulation Methods for Transport of Ethernet over MPLS Networks".
[5] IETF 4761, "Virtual Private LAN Service (VPLS) Using BGP for Auto-Discovery and Signaling".
[6] IETF RFC 4762, "Virtual Private LAN Service (VPLS) Using Label Distribution Protocol (LDP) Signaling".

PART 5:
CAPACITY PLANNING OF NETWORKING SERVICES

CHAPTER 14: CAPACITY PLANNING OF NETWORKING SERVICES

14.1 INTRODUCTION

Capacity planning is the process of determining the capacity of a system so that it meets a certain performance criteria for a given demand. The capacity of a system is a function of the resources allocated to it. For instance, the capacity of a networking service is a function of the CPU, memory, disks of the various servers involved in providing the service as well as the capacity of the network that carries the data. This capacity affects performance metrics, such as, the response time (that is, the time to process a request and return the results to a customer) for a given arrival rate of requests, and availability. In order to determine, therefore, the capacity of a given networking service, we need to know the relationship between allocated resources, performance metrics, and demand. This relationship can be established if the networking service exists, since it can be measured using existing measurement tools or new ones that can be specially designed. However, if the service is new and it does not exist, then it is not possible to measure its performance. The same problem occurs, if we are considering various alternatives for expanding an existing service. Again these expanded services do not exist and therefore it is hard to measure their performance. One approach is to develop a prototype and then experiment with variations of this in order to be able to do what-if analysis and establish its performance under different resources and different loads. This approach is feasible if it is not very expensive. A more typical approach is to build a model of the networking service, and then use the model to carry out a what-if analysis. This is a faster and cheaper way to examine the performance of a networking service. This approach is not limited to networking services and in general to networking, but rather it is used in many sectors of the economy. For instance, a naval architect who is developing a new design for a boat, carries endless experiments using simulation in order to establish the boat's hydrodynamic performance. It would be unthinkable to do so using a prototype!

In the following section, we give an example of measuring the response time of an existing system. In section 14.2, we discuss various types of models that can be used to study the performance of a system that does not exist, and motivate the next two Chapters that deal with two different but complimentary modeling techniques, namely, queueing theory and simulation techniques.

14.2 MEASURING THE RESPONSE TIME OF SOLR

We describe a case study of benchmarking the performance of Solr[3], an open source Java-based full-text search service, used in a particular enterprise software that provides publishing services over the internet for self-publishers. The objective was to measure the 95th percentile of the response time of Solr for various values of RAM and CPU allocated to the *Virtual Machine* (VM) within which it ran, as a function of the arrival rate of queries, see Bouterse and Perros[1].

The software stack of Solr consisted of a virtual machine within which ran the Linux operating system, the Java runtime environment, the Jetty web server, and Solr. Jetty is an open source Java based web server that executes Solr as a java servlet. The Solr index containing the records to be searched was stored locally in the virtual disk of the Solr virtual machine, which physically resided on the local disk of the hypervisor. The virtual machine ran using the VMware ESX hypervisor. A separate testbed was created in order to benchmark the performance of Solr so that the operation of the production enterprise software was not interrupted. The testbed included the Solr virtual machine, a snapshot of the production Solr of the enterprise software, a customer request generator, and a traffic collector.

A customer request generator was configured to create a query load that recreated the loads experienced at the web front-end of the enterprise software. It was assumed that customers arrived at the web front-end according to a Poisson process with an arrival rate λ. The Tsung[2] load testing tool was used to generate customer requests. Tsung simulates user arrivals according to a Poisson process to test the scalability and performance of IP based client/server applications. The queries for the testbed were obtained by parsing a large set of real life queries submitted to the enterprise software. There were 10 results for each query, and Solr was asked to sort them in descending order.

Physically the testbed consisted of a 4948 Ethernet switch and three IBM HS20 blades, with each blade equipped with a 2x3.6 GHz processing power, 16 GB of RAM, and 2 copper 1 gigabit Ethernet interfaces. The Solr virtual machine, Tsung, and the traffic collector each ran on a separate blade. The switch provided connectivity between Tsung and Solr. In addition, a *Switched Port Analyzer* (SPAN) port was configured that duplicated the traffic flow between Tsung and Solr. The duplicated traffic was captured by the traffic collector and stored for offline analysis. A diagram of the testbed is shown in figure 14.1.

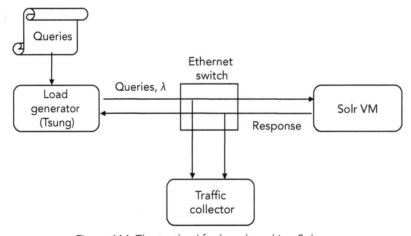

Figure 14.1: The testbed for benchmarking Solr

14.2.1 STORAGE CONSIDERATIONS

The resource reserve of the ESX-based virtual machine was set equal to the resource limit so that the CPU and RAM resources for a virtual machine did not change during an experiment. The maximum and minimum heap sizes of the Jetty web server were set in each test. Since Jetty executes Solr as a Java servlet, increasing the memory of the virtual machine without increasing the memory of the Jetty web server's heap would not allow the Solr process to take advantage of the RAM resources. The heap size is adjusted using the Xms and Xmx parameters which control the minimum and maximum heap size respectively. To reduce overhead incurred by the Java memory manager from growing and shrinking the heap size dynamically, the Xms and Xmx parameters were set to the same value for all tests. The Java VM uses a generational garbage collector, which divides the heap into generations according to the length of time a Java object or data structure is required by the application. The frequency, type, and length of garbage collection can be significantly affected by the Xmn parameter, which sets the size of the *young generation*. Typically, the Xmn value should be between one fourth and one third of the Xmx value[3]. Before each test the Xms, Xmx, and Xmn values were set and Jetty was restarted.

An additional consideration was the operating system's ability to cache the entire index into memory. The size of the index was 407 MB, and therefore the operating system at all times had at least 407 MB of free RAM to cache the index into memory. This caching was done at the disk block level and occurred transparently to Solr. The caching of the Solr index was monitored using the Linux command *free*.

Solr has three separate caches, associated with the single index searcher which provides a view of the index documents. The *filterCache* stores unordered sets of document IDs. The *queryResultCache* stores ordered sets of document IDs, which is useful for repeat queries. The *documentCache* stores Lucene document objects that have been fetched from the disk. The Solr cache sizes are defined in terms of the number of objects the cache contains. All three caches were enabled, each with a cache size of 512 MB.

14.2.2 RESULTS

A number of experiments were run to calculate the 95th percentile of the response time for different values of the CPU and RAM of the Solr virtual machine, and the query arrival rate λ. The mean response time was also calculated so that it can be contrasted against the 95th percentile values. For each experiment, the CPU, RAM, and λ were fixed, and then 3000 queries were generated at the rate of λ queries/sec. As mentioned above the arrival process of the queries was assumed Poisson. The response time for each query was captured and stored, and at the end of the experiment, the mean and the 95th percentile of the response time were calculated. At the end of each experiment, the virtual machine was turned off and reverted to the original virtual machine snapshot. This had the effect of resetting the Solr cache to the state the virtual machine was in before the experiment, thus allowing the same 3000 queries to be used in the next experiment without caching speedup advantages skewing the results.

It was observed that for various combinations of CPU and RAM of the Solr virtual machine and λ, Solr became unstable, that is, its response time became very large. As will be seen in the Chapter 15, a queue is stable when its arrival rate is less than the service rate. Otherwise, the queue is unstable and the waiting time becomes infinitely

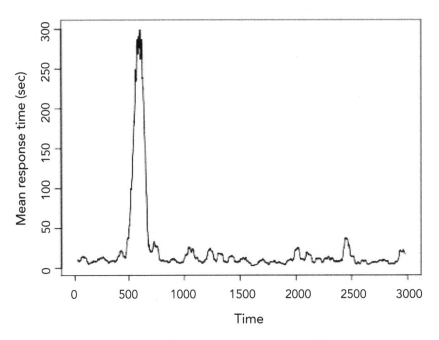

Figure 14.2: Solr mean response time – stable case

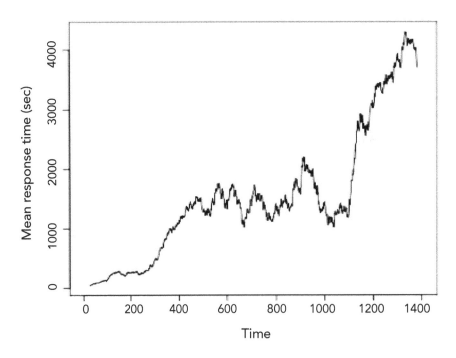

Figure 14.3: Solr mean response time – unstable case

large. Solr runs multiple threads, the number of which varies from 25 to 200, and the VM runs on two virtual cores. Consequently, it is difficult to obtain an analytic condition of stability. In view of this, the set of combinations of CPU, RAM and λ for which Solr was stable were established by trial and error. When Solr is stable it alternates between busy and idle periods. As a result, the mean response time computed over a moving window does not change very much. This is shown in figure 14.2, where the observed mean response time was computed over a moving average of 50 observations for the case when CPU = 1024 GHz, RAM = 1024 MB, and λ = 0.1/sec.

If Solr is unstable, then it is always busy, and its queues increase continuously which causes the response time to increase continuously as well. An example of this is shown in figure 14.3 assuming CPU = 1024 GHz, RAM = 1024 MB, λ = 0.333/sec and a moving window of 50 observations. Failing TCP connections and the stalling of new TCP connections are also good indicators of system instability.

In the case shown in figure 14.2, there is a spike early on. This is most likely due to the I/O latency for bringing large portions of the index into memory. In view of this, in all the experiments that were carried out, the first 1500 queries were used to make sure that the index had been cached in, and the remaining 1500 queries were used for measuring the response time. The initial 1500 queries always contained the spike in Figure 14.2.

In the first experiment, the CPU of the Solr virtual machine was set to 2048 Mhz and Xmx, Xms, and Xmn were fixed to 512 MB, 512 MB, and 128 MB respectively. The response time was measured by varying the RAM allocated to the virtual machine from 512 MB to 2048 MB in increments of 512 MB. The results are given in table 14.1. For each value of RAM we give the 95th percentile of the response time, along with the mean response time. We contrast the difference between these two values. The mean gives the average of all the observed responses, whereas the 95th percentile is a point in the tail of the distribution of the response times passed which only 5% of the observations lie. As explained in section 4.2 of Chapter 4, the percentile is a better indicator of the variability of a performance metric, such as the response time.

The results in table 14.1 pointed out to the surprising conclusion that while the CPU, λ, Xmx, Xms, and Xmn are held constant, the response time increases as the RAM of the virtual machine increases. This is counter-intuitive considering that the virtual machine as a whole has more memory. Solr appeared to perform poorly whenever the RAM of the virtual machine was greater than 1GB. This was most likely due to the configuration of the Solr virtual machine obtained from the enterprise software, and it may not be repeatable in other testbeds with a different Solr index and configuration.

CPU (MHz)	RAM (MB)	Xmx (MB)	Xms (MB)	Xmm (MB)	95th percentile (sec)	Mean (sec)
2048	512	512	512	128	6.73	2.08
2048	1024	512	512	128	7.26	2.02
2048	1536	512	512	128	15.44	4.43
2048	2048	512	512	128	17.08	4.65

Table 14.1: Varying RAM while keeping CPU, λ, Xmx, Xms, and Xmm constant

CPU (MHz)	RAM (MB)	95th percentile (sec)	Mean (sec)
2048	512	5.89	1.90
1920	512	6.81	2.12
1792	512	8.75	2.56
1664	512	10.65	3.01
1536	512	12.18	3.17
1408	512	14.42	3.76
1280	512	20.73	5.29
1152	512	21.30	5.86
1024	512	39.29	10.35

Table 14.2: Mean and 95th percentile of the response time for λ = 0.1/sec

Based on the above results, a number of different experiments were carried out where the RAM was fixed to 512 MB, which is large enough to hold the entire index in cache, the Solr caches were fixed so that they have their full effect, i.e., Xmx = Xms = 512 MB and Xmx = 128 MB, and the CPU and λ were varied as follows: CPU = [1024 MHz, 1280 MHz, 1536 MHz, 1792 MHz, 2048 MHz], λ = [0.1/sec, 0.111/sec, 0.125/sec, 0.143/sec]. For λ > 0.143/sec Solr became unstable. Given that a test simulated 3000 queries, and the inter-arrival times varied between 10 and 7 seconds, a typical experiment lasted as much as 8 hours. Detailed results can be found in[1]. A sample set of results is given in table 14.2 for λ = 0.1/sec.

14.3 PERFORMANCE MODELING

A model is a representation of a real life system. There are different types of models, and in general, they are classified into three groups: *iconic, analog,* and *symbolic*. An iconic model is an exact replica of the properties of a real life system, but in small scale. Model airplanes and maps are examples of iconic models. The air dynamics of a new design of an airplane can be studied using a small scale replica of the airplane in a tunnel. An analog model uses a physical system to represent the properties of a real life system. For instance, an ecosystem can be modeled by an electrical circuit, where energy input is represented by batteries, food flows by electric currents, and energy dissipation by amperage and voltage chambers. Symbolic models represent the properties of real life systems through the means of diagrams, mathematical equations, and computer simulation. The business process modeling tools described in Chapter 3 are symbolic models based on diagrams. Optimization models, such as linear programming, and stochastic models, such as queueing theory, are symbolic models based on mathematics. Finally, computer simulation can be used to construct a symbolic model of a system by depicting its logic in a computer program.

Symbolic models based on mathematics and computer simulation are commonly used in networking and in many other sectors of the economy, such as transportation, health, and manufacturing, in order to understand the performance of a new design before it is implemented, or improve the efficiency of an existing operation. For instance, when defining a new networking service, we first use business process diagrams in order to describe the processes involved, the tasks and sub-processes they consist of, and how these processes interact with each other. Once this has been completed, one would think that we are ready to start implementing the service. However, this is not the case since important decisions have to be made as to how to dimension the infrastructure that will support the service so that the required QoS is satisfied. For instance, let us assume that we are developing a new service that will run on a number of different servers. The main question here is how much CPU, memory, and disk capacity we should provide to each server so that the response time is less than 5 msec 95% of the time for a given number of service requests per second. How is the response time affected as the number of requests increases, and at which point it becomes unacceptable? What backup scheme should we use so that the service is available 99.999% of the time? Within the software implementation of the service, which pieces of software are likely to become bottlenecks as the traffic increases? What is the power consumption and how can it be reduced? One way to answer these questions is to build the system and then subject it to stress tests. However, this can be quite expensive. Alternatively, one can construct mathematical and simulation models of the system under study, which permit us to obtain an insight into these questions before the actual system is built.

When carrying out a performance modeling exercise, one has to follow a certain process, whose main activities are summarized below.

- *Define the problem*
- *Analyze data*
- *Create the model*
- *Validate the model*
- *Exercise the model*

First and foremost, the structure of the system under study has to be understood well, and the problem to be solved has to be defined and documented. Typically, in order to build a model one needs to have data regarding the system. This data may be available from existing records or it may be necessary to collect new data. The next step is building the model and subsequently validating it in order to make sure that it is an accurate representation of the system under study. Once an accurate model has been developed it can be then exercised in order to do what-if analysis. At any step of the modeling exercise, one may have to go back and revisit previous steps. Of course, this process is not applicable to just performance modeling studies. It is the basic process for problem solving!

Mathematical models can be classified into two groups: *deterministic models* and *stochastic models.* Deterministic models are models that do not contain the element of probability. These are primarily optimization models, such as: *linear programming, non-linear programming,* and *dynamic programming.* Stochastic models are models that contain the element of probability. Examples are: *queueing theory, stochastic processes,* and *reliability.* A simulation model may or may not contain probabilities, which means that it may be deterministic or stochastic.

In the following two Chapters, we examine queueing models and simulation techniques. These two types of models can help us study the performance of front-end and back-end networking service systems in order to determine how to dimension a service, understand how various operational parameters impact on its performance, and carry what-if analysis. Queueing models have been used successfully to model real life systems. There are numerous examples in the open literature ranging from determining the number of operators in a call center, determining where software bottlenecks may occur, determining the capacity of a telephone system, and designing manufacturing assembly lines. Simulation is probably the most commonly used technique for building models, and it is used in all sectors of the economy. Queueing models are used primarily to model a system at a high-level of abstraction. On the other hand, simulation techniques can be used easily to model a system at any level of detail. Typically, queueing models are used to do a first-cut what-if analysis. Based on this analysis a more detailed simulation model is build to study specific questions regarding the design of the system. Because of the easiness with which one can construct simulation models, one is tempted to include many features of the system under study, and as a result, the simulation model becomes extremely large and it takes a long time to run. One has to exercise restrain and a good judgment in order to develop efficient and useful simulation models.

REFERENCES

[1] B. Bouterse and H. Perros, "On the Response Time of a Solr Search Engine in a Virtualized Environment", APARM 2010, Dec. 2-4 2010, Wellington, NZ.
[2] Tsung: tsung.erlang-projects.org.
[3] Scaling Lucene and Solr. http://www.lucidimagination.com/Community/Hear-from-the-Experts/Articles/Scaling-Lucene-and-Solr

CHAPTER 15: QUEUEING MODELS

15.1 INTRODUCTION

In this Chapter, we analyze a number of simple queueing systems and show how they can be used to model networking services. This is not an in-depth presentation and the interested reader is referred to books on queueing theory for further details. A rudimentary knowledge of probability theory is required in order to understand the basic concepts. The main objective of this Chapter is to help the reader develop an intuitive feel about queueing theory and how it is used to model networking services. Therefore, any mathematical derivations can be safely skipped.

15.2 SOME BASIC CONCEPTS

Queueing theory deals with the analysis of queues (or waiting lines) where customers wait to receive a service. In our daily life, we spend a good amount of time queueing up for a service. For instance, we wait at a supermarket checkout, at a traffic light, for an elevator, at a passport control in an airport, and often we are placed on hold when calling for information. A customer waiting for service may also be a packet in the Internet, a request for a web service, paperwork waiting at somebody's desk to be processed, etc. Queueing also occurs within a software/hardware system, such as a computer system, a router, and other telecommunications systems. For instance, when streaming a video to a computer, the video is delivered in the form of packets which are reassembled at the computer to play back the video. These packets go through a number of routers, and at each router they have to wait in order to get transmitted out. Likewise, when a request is issued by a user to a web service, this request has to be executed by various software components that provide the web service. At each component there is a queue of requests waiting to be executed.

When studying a queueing system, we are typically interested in obtaining various performance measures, such as:

- *Mean waiting time:* The mean time one has to wait in a queue, including the service time, averaged out over a long period.
- *Percentile of the waiting time:* The percent of the waiting that a customer has to wait more than a given amount of time. This is a more sophisticated performance measure than the mean waiting time, as it provides a statistical bound on the waiting time.

- *Utilization of the server:* The percent of time the server is used.
- *Throughput:* The rate at which customers are processed by the server. (The rate is defined as the number of customers per unit time.)
- *Average number of customers waiting:* The mean number of customers waiting averaged out over a long period.
- *Distribution of the number of waiting customers:* This is the probability that n, $n = 1,2,\ldots$, customers wait at any time. This is a more detailed performance measure than the average number of customers.

Often when waiting in a line, we may not perceive the actual waiting time if for some reason we are distracted! In this case, the perceived waiting time is less than the actual waiting time. Queueing theory deals only with actual waiting times.

A queue is typically depicted pictorially by a circle that indicates the server and an open-ended box with vertical lines in front of the server that indicates the queue. Figure 15.1 shows four different queueing configurations of a single service station, that is, of a single point where a service is provided. These are: a single queue served by a single server, a single queue served by multiple servers, multiple queues served by a single server, and multiple queues served by multiple servers. The single queue served by a single server, commonly referred to as the *single server queue*, is the simplest and probably the most commonly encountered queueing system. The queueing system at an output port depicted in figure 11.8 is a good example of the configuration where multiple queues served by a single server. The queues contain the packets waiting to be transmitted out and the server is the transmitter. Queueing in a call center can be depicted by a single queue served by multiple servers. The queue contains the calls waiting and the servers are the people who service the calls.

Queueing systems of a single service station, such as those shown in figure 15.1, can be linked together to make up a network of queues or otherwise known as a *queueing network*. Figure 15.2, shows two different topologies obtained by linking single server queues. The tandem queueing network consists of three single server queues

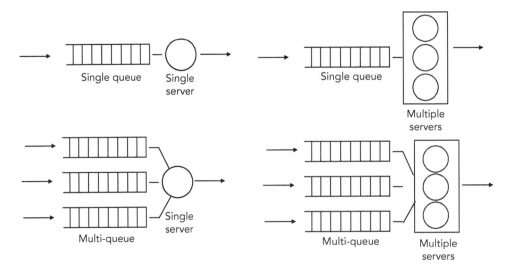

Figure 15.1: Various configurations of a single service station

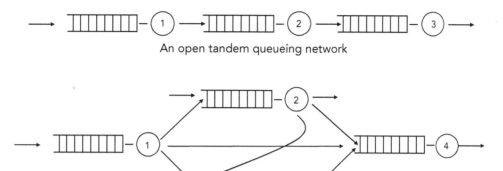

An open tandem queueing network

An open arbitrary topology of a queueing network

Figure 15.2: Two examples of open queueing networks

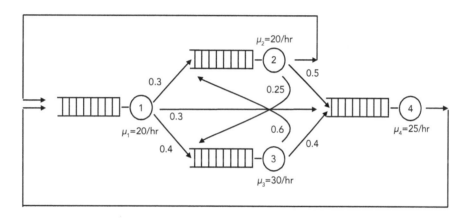

Figure 15.3: An example of a closed queueing networks

linked in series, whereas in the arbitrary topology the single server queues are linked in some arbitrary fashion. In queueing networks, each service station is typically referred to as a *node*, following the terminology from networking. We see that in the tandem queueing network, customers arrive at node 1 from outside and depart from node 3 after they receive service at each of the three nodes. In the example of the arbitrary topology, external arrivals may occur to nodes 1, 2, and 3, and customers can depart from the queueing network from nodes 2, 3, and 4. A customer may follow any of the possible paths through the network. For instance, a customer arriving at node 1, may visit nodes 2, 3, and 4 before it departs from the network. A customer arriving at node 2 may visit node 4 before it departs from the network.

The two queueing networks in figure 15.2 where customers arrive from the outside and eventually depart to the outside are called *open* queueing networks. It is also possible to have *closed* queueing networks, where a fixed number of customers constantly circulates through the nodes of the network without ever departing from it. No external customers can join a node of the network. An example of a closed network is shown in figure 15.3. Cus-

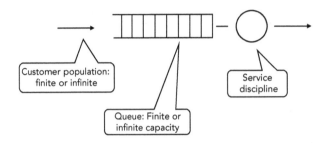

Figure 15.4: The single server queue

tomers completing their service at node 1 may join node 2,3, and 4 with probability 0.3, 0.4, and 0.3 respectively. Customers completing their service at node 2 join node 1, 3, and 4 with probability 0.25, 0.25 and 0.5 respectively. Customers completing their service at node 3 join node 2 and 4 with probability 0.6 and 0.4 respectively. Finally customers departing from node 4 are fed back to node 1.

15.3 THE SINGLE SERVER QUEUE

The single server queue, shown in figure 15.4 is the simplest queueing system. In order to analyze this queue we have to make assumptions regarding a) the population of potential customers, b) the size of the queue, c) the scheduling scheme used to decide which waiting customer will be served next, and d) the distribution of the service and inter-arrival times.

The population of customers that may visit this queueing system maybe *finite* or *infinite*. If it is infinite, then the rate at which customers arrive is not affected by how many customers are already waiting in the queue, and in view of this it is constant. For instance, if we use this queueing system to model an output port buffer of a router, then we can safely assume that the population of customers, i.e., packets, is infinite and that the rate of arrival is fixed to a certain value. If the population of customers is very small, then the rate at which they arrive decreases as more and more customers arrive at the queue, and it finally becomes zero when all the customers are in the queue. This is the case of the repairman problem discussed in Chapter 16.

In addition, the queue may be *infinite* or *finite*, meaning that it may have an infinite or finite capacity to accommodate customers waiting to receive service. Queues within a computer or a router are finite, though for simplicity they are treated as infinite queues. The server serves the waiting customers following a *scheduling* scheme. The most common one is FIFO. Other schemes are also used, such as those described in section 11.5. Finally, we need to know the distribution of the service and inter-arrival times. If we have access to real data, we can construct a histogram of the service time and of the inter-arrival time. Unfortunately, it is not possible to analyze a queueing system mathematically using histograms, unless they are approximated by a mathematical *Probability Density Function* (pdf). However, it is possible to simulate a queueing system using histograms of service and inter-arrival times as discussed in Chapter 16.

In the remainder of this section we will present some general results which are independent of the distribution of the service time and of the inter-arrival time, assuming an infinite population of customers and an infinite capacity queue. In the following five sub-sections we will obtain more detailed results for specific distributions of the service and inter-arrival times.

A queue is formed in front of a server when customers arrive faster than they can get served. The single server queue is said to be *stable* when it does not grow to become infinite over time. A stable queue goes through busy and idle periods as shown in figure 15.5. The single server queue is stable if the arrival rate is less than the service rate. The arrival rate is the mean number of arrivals per unit time, and it is equal to 1 / (mean inter-arrival time). For instance, if the mean inter-arrival is 5 minutes, then the arrival rate is 1 / 5 per minute, i.e. 0.2 per minute, or 13 per hour. Likewise, the service rate is the mean number of customers served per unit time and it is equal to 1 / (mean service time). For instance, if the mean service time is 10 minutes, then the service rate is 1 / 10 per minute, i.e., 0.1 per minute, or 6 per hour. So, the single server queue is stable if on the average fewer customers arrive than the average number of customers that the server can service if it is working all the time.

When a queue is unstable, the number of customers in the queue will grow continuously, as shown in figure 15.6. This happens when the arrival rate is greater than the service rate. Unstable queues are detrimental to the performance of a system. For instance, if a web site receives too many requests, then its queues become unstable, and as a result we have to wait for an extremely long period to get a response, or more often we get no response at all.

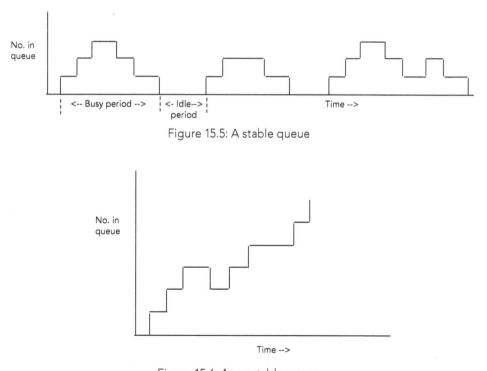

Figure 15.5: A stable queue

Figure 15.6: An unstable queue

The *throughput* of a server is defined as the average number of completed jobs per unit time. For instance, the throughput of a transmission link is the average number of transmitted packets per unit time. Let the mean service time in a single server queue be 10 minutes. If the server has always work to do, that is, there is always someone waiting in the queue to be serviced, then the number of customers it can service per hour is 6. This is the *maximum* throughput. If the queue is stable, then the throughput is equal to the rate of arrival (whatever comes in, goes out!). For instance, if the mean inter-arrival time is 20 minutes, then the arrival rate is 3 customers per hour and the throughput is 3 per hour as well. If the mean inter-arrival time is decreased to 15 minutes, then the arrival rate is 4 customers per hour and the throughput is 4 per hour as well. If the inter-arrival time is further decreased to 5 minutes, then the arrival rate is 12 customers per hour and the queue becomes unstable (or saturated). This is because on the average we have 12 arrivals per hour, whereas only 6 customers can depart per hour since this is the maximum number of customers per hour that the server can service. In this case the throughput is 6 per hour. The throughput as a function of the arrival rate is shown in figure 15.7.

The *utilization* of the server is the percent of time the server is busy, and it is equal to the (arrival rate) x (mean service time). For instance, if the arrival rate is 5 per hour and the mean service time is 6 minutes (0.1 hours), then the server's utilization is 5x0.1 = 0.5 or 50%. The utilization of a server is less than 1 when the queue is stable, and it is equal to 1 when the queue is unstable. The quantity 1 − (server utilization), is the fraction of time that the server is idle (not busy). Since, the server can only be idle when there are no customers in the queue, this quantity is also the fraction of time that the queue is empty. Obviously the fraction of time the queue is busy is the same as the fraction of time the server is busy, i.e., the server utilization.

Example: Let the mean inter-arrival be 5 minutes, that is the arrival rate is 1 / 5 = 0.2 per minute, and let the mean service time be 2 minutes. Then, we can obtain the following performance measures:

- Server utilization = 0.2x2 = 0.4 or 40% of the time.
- Percent of time the server is idle = 1 − 0.40 = 0.60, i.e. 60% of the time.
- Percent of time that there is no one in the single server queue (either waiting or being served) = 0.60 (equal to the percent of time the server is idle).

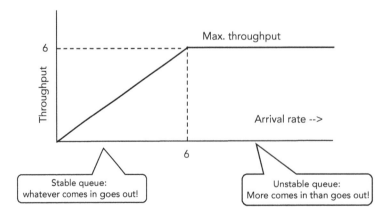

Figure 15.7: Throughput as function of the arrival rate

We now proceed to examine in more detail some well-known single server queues. (The non-mathematically in-clined reader can safely skip all the mathematical derivations.)

15.3.1 THE M/M/1 QUEUE

A commonly used probability density function for the service time and the inter-arrival time is the exponential distribution. The use of this distribution in queueing theory considerably simplifies the calculus involved when analyzing mathematically a queueing system. However, the exponential distribution suffers from the so-called *memoryless property*. This means that if the duration of an activity is exponentially distributed, then the time it takes for it to be completed is not a function of the time that has elapsed. For instance, if the inter-arrival of a bus at a bus stop for a particular bus route is assumed to be exponentially distributed, then the amount of time one has to wait for the bus does not depend on how long he has been waiting. This is contrary to our experience, where the more one waits, the more likely the bus will arrive. The pdf $f(x)$ of the exponential distribution is $f(x) = \lambda e^{-\lambda x}$, where $1/\lambda$ is the mean time between the occurrence of two successive events. In our case, $1/\lambda$ could be the mean inter-arrival time or the mean service time.

The exponential distribution is linked to the Poisson distribution, which describes the number of arrivals per unit time. As can be seen in figure 15.8, time is organized into fixed periods, each representing a unit time. The occur-rence of an event is indicated by the up-arrows, and the number of the events occurring within each unit time is also shown. If the inter-arrival time of these events is exponentially distributed with a mean $1/\lambda$, then the number of events occurring within each unit time is Poisson distributed and the probability that n events occur during a unit time is $p(n) = (\lambda^n / n!)e^{-\lambda}$. The mean number of events per unit time is λ.

Various single server queues have been analyzed under different assumptions regarding the distribution of the service and inter-arrival times, the number of servers, the capacity of the queue, the population of customers and the service scheduling discipline. These queueing system are described using the notation $A/B/s/K$, where A and B are symbols indicating the pdf of the inter-arrival and service time respectively, s is the number of servers, and K is the capacity of the queue. In this section, we will consider the simplest of these single server queues, namely the M/M/1 queue, where M stands for the exponential distribution. Specifically, we make the following assumptions: exponentially distributed inter-arrival time with rate λ, single server with an exponentially distributed service time with rate μ, infinite population of customers, infinite capacity queue, and FIFO service priority.

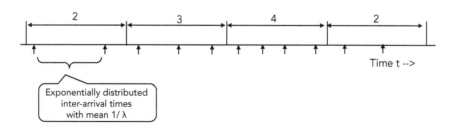

Figure 15.8: The Poisson distribution

Let us assume that λ and μ is the arrival rate and service rate respectively. We assume that the single server queue is stable, i.e., $\lambda < \mu$. Let p_n be the probability that there are n customers in the system. (By "system" we mean the queue and the space in front of the server that holds the customer who is currently in service.) The probability p_n is given by the expression:

$$p_n = \rho^n(1 - \rho), n = 0,1,\ldots \tag{15.1}$$

where ρ is known as the *traffic intensity* and is given by the expression $\rho = \lambda /\mu$. The traffic intensity is the server utilization, or the percent of time the server is busy (see previous section for the definition of utilization).

Expression (15.1) can be obtained intuitively as follows. Figure 15.9 gives the *rate diagram* of the M/M/1 queue. This is a diagram that shows how the state of the M/M/1 queue, represented by the total number of customers n in the system, changes as customers arrive and depart. For instance, assuming that we are in state $n = 1$, then the process shifts to the state $n + 1 = 2$ if an arrival occurs or it shifts to state $n - 1 = 0$ if a departure occurs. In addition, the rate diagram shows the rate at which these transitions occur. That is, how many times on the average per unit time we shift to state 3 or 1 given that we are in state 2. The rate of transition to state $n - 1$ from state $n (n > 1)$ is μ and the rate of transition to state $n + 1$ from state $n (n \geq 0)$ is λ.

The rate diagram is used to obtain the so-called *balance* equations, which are based on the observation that the total rate out of a state n is equal to the total rate into the state n, $n = 0,1,\ldots$. That is, the average number of times per unit time the process leaves state n is equal to the average number of times the process enters the same state n. We have:

$$\lambda p_0 = \mu p_1$$
$$(\lambda + \mu)p_1 = \lambda p_0 + \mu p_2$$
$$(\lambda + \mu)p_2 = \lambda p_1 + \mu p_3$$
$$\cdot$$
$$\cdot$$
$$\cdot$$
$$(\lambda + \mu)p_n = \lambda p_{n-1} + \mu p_{n+1}, n \geq 1.$$

These equations can be simplified as follows by adding two successive equations at a time:

$$\lambda p_0 = \mu p_1$$
$$\lambda p_1 = \mu p_2$$
$$\lambda p_2 = \mu p_3$$
$$\cdot$$
$$\cdot$$
$$\cdot$$
$$\lambda p_n = \mu p_{n+1}, n \geq 1.$$

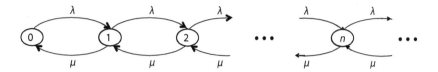

Figure 15.9: The rate diagram for the M/M/1 queue

The above equations are known as the *local balance* equations, and they can be interpreted as follows. The rate out of the state n, $n = 0,1, \ldots$, due to a customer arriving at the M/M/1 queue is equal to the rate into the same state n due to a customer departing from the M/M/1 queue. From the above equations we can easily obtain (15.1).

Various performance measures of interest can be obtained using expression (15.1). For instance, the probability that the system is empty is equal to the probability that $n = 0$, i.e., $p_0 = 1 - \rho$. The percent of time the server is idle is $1 - \rho$, and the server utilization, i.e., the percent of time the server is busy is ρ. The throughput is λ, since we have assumed that the queue is stable.

The mean number of customers L in the system is the expectation $E(X)$, where X is the number of customers in the queue. We have:

$$L = \sum_{n=0}^{\infty} n p_n = \frac{\lambda}{\mu - \lambda} \qquad (15.2)$$

The mean number of customers queueing up for service, i.e., excluding the one in service, is:

$$L_q = \sum_{n=1}^{\infty} (n-1) p_n = L - \rho$$

The mean waiting time in the system W can be obtained using Little's Law. This is a simple and very useful expression that relates the mean time spent in the system W, the mean number in the system L, and the rate of arrival λ to the system. The relation is:

$$\lambda W = L \qquad (15.3)$$

For instance, if the rate of arrival λ is 5 per unit time, and a customer spends an average of 10 units of time in the system, then the average number of customers in the system is 50.

The following is an intuitive explanation of Little's law. Seeing that a customer spends W amount of time on the average, its rate of departure is $1 / W$. Now, the mean number of customers in the system is L, and consequently the rate of departure from the system is L / W, which is equal to λ, since the system stable.

Using expression (15.2) in (15.3), we obtain the mean waiting time in the system. We have:

$$W = 1/(\mu - \lambda)\tag{15.4}$$

Using expression (15.4) we can plot W as a function of λ as shown in figure 15.10. We note that W becomes very large as λ tends to μ. This is because the queue begins to approach saturation.

Finally, the mean waiting time in the queue (excluding service time) W_q can be obtained using Little's Law, by assuming that the system is just the queue that forms in front of the server. We have:

$$W_q = \frac{L_q}{\lambda} = \frac{L - \rho}{\lambda} = \frac{1}{\mu - \lambda} - \frac{1}{\mu} = \frac{\lambda}{\mu(\mu - \lambda)}$$

Example 1: Customers arrive at a ticket counter in a Poisson fashion at the rate of 8 per hour. The time to serve a customer is exponentially distributed with mean 5 minutes, that is the service rate is 12 per hour. Then, we can calculate the following quantities:

1. The probability a customer arrives to find the ticket counter empty (i.e., it goes into service without queueing) is: $1 - \rho = 1 - \lambda / \mu = 1 - (8 / 12) = 1 / 3$.
2. The probability a customer has to wait before receiving service is: $\rho = 2 / 3$.
3. The mean number of customers in the system is: $\lambda/(\mu - \lambda) = 8 / 4 = 2$.
4. The mean time in the system is: $1/(\mu - \lambda) = 1 / 4$ hours, or 15 minutes.
5. The mean time in the queue is: $\lambda / \mu (\mu - \lambda) = 8 / (12\times4) = 1 / 6$ hours, or 10 minutes.
6. The server utilization is: $\rho = 2 / 3$, or 66.66 %.

Example 2: People waiting in line may not realize how long they have been waiting until on the average at least 5 minutes have passed. A customer upon arrival chooses one of the single server queues as shown in figure 15.12. How many single server queues we need so that the average waiting time is less than 5 minutes? The service time is exponentially distributed with mean 3 min and the arrival rate is Poisson with a rate of 30 per hour. As can be seen in table 15.1 we need four M/M/1 queues.

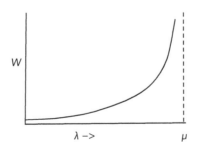

Figure 15.10: The mean waiting time as function of λ

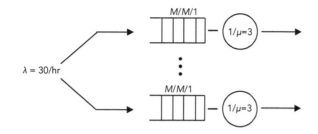

Figure 15.11: An arriving customer joins one of the queues

Number of M/M/1 queues	Arrival rate to each queue	Mean waiting in each queue
1	30	infinite
2	15	0.2 hrs (12 min)
3	10	0.1 hrs (6 min)
4	30 / 4	0.08 hrs (4.8 min)

Table 15.1: Results for example 2

Example 3: If both customers and the individual providing a service are employees of the same company, then the cost of employees waiting for service due to lost productivity and the cost of providing a server is equally important to the company. Employees arrive at the service station at the rate of 8 per hour. The cost of providing the service C_s is a function of the service rate μ, that is, $C_s = 10\mu$ per hour. The cost to the company for an employee waiting in the system is $C_w = \$50$ per hour. Assuming an M/M/1 queue what is the value of the mean service time that minimizes the total cost?

The waiting cost $C_w = 50W = 400\,[1\,/\,(\mu - 8)]$, and the total cost is $C_s + C_w$. The answer can be found in table 15.2.

15.3.2 THE M/M/S QUEUE

We consider the single server queue shown in figure 15.12, which is the same as the M/M/1 queue, only there are s servers instead of one. (Although the M/M/s queue consists of many servers, it can be still seen as a single server queue since these servers make up a single service station.) We make the following assumptions: exponentially distributed service time at each server with rate μ, exponentially distributed inter-arrival time with rate λ, infinite population of customers, infinite capacity queue, and FIFO service priority.

The queue-length probability p_n, $n = 0, 1, 2, \ldots$, that there are n customers in the system can be obtained as in the M/M/1 case. That is, we first set up the rate diagram, then write down the balance equations, and then solve the balance equations to obtain an expression for p_n, $n = 0, 1, 2, \ldots$

μ	$C_s = 10\mu$	$C_w = 400 / (\mu - 8)$	$C_s + C_w$
10	100	200	300
11	110	133.333	243.333
12	120	100	220
13	130	80	210
14	140	66.6666	206.666
15	150	57.1428	207.142
16	160	50	210
17	170	44.4444	214.444
18	180	40	220
19	190	36.3636	226.363
20	200	33.3333	233.333

Table 15.2: Results for example 3

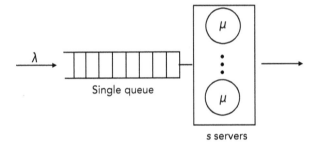

Figure 15.12: The M/M/s single

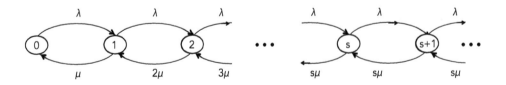

Figure 15.13: The rate diagram for the M/M/s queue

The rate diagram is shown in figure 15.13. It is similar to that of the M/M/1 queueing system as far as the arrival transitions, but the transition rates due to service completions are different due to the multiple servers. The state of the system is given by n, the total number of customers in the system. We observe that if $n \leq s$, then all n customers are in service. If $n > s$, then s customers are in service and the remaining $n - s$ are queueing up. The departure rate depends on the number of customers in service. That is, if there are n customers in service, where $n \leq s$, then the departure rate is $n\mu$. If all servers are busy, i.e., $n \geq s$, then it is $s\mu$.

Based on the rate diagram in figure 15.13, we obtain the following balance equations:

$$\lambda p_0 = \mu p_1$$
$$(\lambda + \mu)p_1 = \lambda p_0 + 2\mu p_2$$

$$\vdots$$

$$(\lambda + s\mu)p_s = \lambda p_{s-1} + (s + 1)\mu p_{s+1}$$

$$\vdots$$

$$(\lambda + s\mu)p_n = \lambda p_{n-1} + (s+1)\mu p_{n+1}, \; n > s$$

Solving the above equations, we obtain the following solution for p_n:

$$p_n = \begin{cases} \left(\dfrac{\lambda}{\mu}\right)^n \dfrac{1}{n!} p_0, & n \leq s \\[2ex] \left(\dfrac{\lambda}{\mu}\right)^n \dfrac{1}{s! s^{n-s}} p_0, & n \geq s \end{cases}$$

where p_0 is given by

$$p_0 = 1 / \left[\sum_{n=0}^{s-1} \left(\frac{\lambda}{\mu}\right)^n \frac{1}{n!} + \left(\frac{\lambda}{\mu}\right)^s \frac{1}{s!} \frac{1}{1-(\lambda/s\mu)} \right]$$

It can be shown that the mean number of customers queueing up L_q is given by the following expression:

$$L_q = \sum_{n=s}^{\infty} (n-s)p_0 = \left(\frac{\lambda}{\mu}\right)^s \frac{\lambda/s\mu}{s![1-(\lambda/s\mu)]^2} p_0$$

The remaining quantities, mean number of customers in the system L, mean waiting time in the system W, and mean queueing time W_q can be easily obtained from L_q as follows:

$$Wq = (1 / \lambda)L_q,$$
$$W = Wq + (1 / \mu),$$
$$L = \lambda Wq + (\lambda / \mu) = L_q + (\lambda / \mu).$$

The maximum service rate is $s\mu$, and the queueing system is stable when $\lambda < s\mu$. The utilization of a single server is $\lambda / s\mu$. This is because the total arrival rate is evenly serviced by the s servers. Consequently, the arrival rate serviced by a single server is λ / s, and the server utilization is $(\lambda / s)(1 / \mu) = \lambda / s\mu$. This quantity is also the probability that a single server is busy. Therefore, the expected number of busy servers is $s(\lambda / s\mu) = \lambda / \mu$.

15.3.3 THE INFINITE SERVER QUEUE

An interesting extension of the above M/M/s queue is the case where the number of servers s is infinite. In this case, each arriving customer always finds a free server, and no queue is ever formed. The number of busy servers is always equal to the number of customers in the system n. This queueing system is known as the *infinite server queue*, despite the fact that there is no queue.

Let λ and μ be the arrival rate of customers to the infinite server queue and the service rate at one server respectively. An infinite population of customers is assumed. The rate diagram is shown in figure 15.14. As can be seen, it is similar to the rate diagram in figure 15.13 for the M/M/s queue, only the departure rate is $n\mu$ for all values of n, $n \geq 1$. Based on the rate diagram in figure 15.14, we obtain the following balance equations:

$$\lambda p_0 = \mu p_1$$
$$(\lambda + \mu)p_1 = \lambda p_0 + 2\mu p_2$$
$$\cdot$$
$$\cdot$$
$$\cdot$$
$$(\lambda + n\mu)p_n = \lambda p_{n-1} + (n+1)\mu p_{n+1}, n \geq 1.$$

Solving the above equations, we obtain the following solution for p_n:

$$p_n = \left(\frac{\lambda}{\mu}\right)^n \frac{1}{n!} e^{-(\lambda / \mu)}, n = 0, 1, \ldots$$

We note that the number of customers in the system (or the number of busy servers) follows the Poisson distribution with rate λ / μ. In view of this, the number of customers in the infinite server queue is $L\lambda / \mu$. (The mean value of a random variable that follows the Poisson distribution with rate θ, is θ.)

15.3.4 A FINITE POPULATION SINGLE SERVER QUEUE

In this section we examine a single server queue under the assumption that the population of potential customers is finite. This queueing model is referred to as the *repairman* model and it is described in detail in the next Chapter.

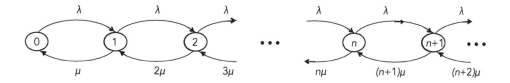

Figure 15.14: The rate diagram for the infinite server queue

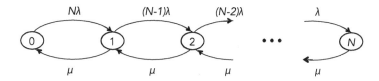

Figure 15.15: Finite population single server queue

In this section, we will only present its mathematical solution.

We assume that the total population of customers is N, and that the rate at which they arrive at the queue is given by the following function of the number of customers n in the system: $\lambda(n) = (N - n)\lambda$. When all N customers are in the system then, $\lambda(N) = 0$, that is the arrival rate is zero. The remaining assumptions are as follows: exponentially distributed inter-arrival times, single server with exponentially distributed service time with rate μ, and FIFO service discipline.

The rate diagram is given in figure 15.15. Based on the rate diagram we obtain the following balance equations:

$$N\lambda p_0 = \mu p_1$$
$$((N-1)\lambda + \mu)p_1 = N\lambda p_0 + \mu p_2$$
$$((N-2)\lambda + \mu)p_2 = (N-1)\lambda p_1 + \mu p_2$$

$$\cdot$$
$$\cdot$$
$$\cdot$$

$$\mu p_N = \lambda p_{N-1}$$

Solving the above equations, we obtain the following solution for p_n

$$p_n = \frac{N!}{(N-n)!}\left(\frac{\lambda}{\mu}\right)^n p_0, \; n = 1, 2, \ldots, N$$

where

$$p_0 = 1/ \sum_{n=0}^{N} \left[\frac{N!}{(N-n)!} \left(\frac{\lambda}{\mu} \right)^n \right] .$$

It can be shown that the mean number of customers queueing up L_q is given by the following expression:

$$L_q = \sum_{n=1}^{N} (n-1)p_n = N - \frac{\lambda + \mu}{\lambda}(1 - p_0) .$$

The remaining quantities, mean number of customers in the system L, mean waiting time in the system W, and mean queueing time W_q can be easily obtained from L_q as follows:

$$L = L_q + (1 - p_0)$$
$$W = L / \lambda'$$
$$W_q = L_q / \lambda'$$

where λ' is the average arrival rate into the system given by the following expression:

$$\lambda' = \sum_{n=0}^{N} \lambda_n p_n = \sum_{n=0}^{N} (N-n)\lambda p_n = \lambda(N-L) .$$

15.3.5 THE M/G/1 QUEUE

As mentioned in section 15.3.1, the exponential distribution simplifies significantly the calculus involved when analyzing mathematically a queueing system. However, it is a not a very realistic distribution because of the memoryless property. In this section, we present the M/G/1 queue which is similar to the M/M/1 queue except that the service time follows a general distribution, notated by the letter G. The general service time distribution is defined only by its mean and its service time. The remaining assumptions are as follows: single server, exponentially distributed inter-arrival time with rate λ, infinite population of customers, infinite capacity queue, and FIFO service priority. Below, we only give the mean number in the system, since the calculation of the probability p_n that there are n customers in the system is beyond the scope of this book.

Let λ be the rate of arrival, and let $1 / \mu$ and σ^2 be the mean and variance of the service time. Then, it can be shown that the mean number of customers is given by the following expression:

$$L = \rho + \frac{\rho^2 + \lambda^2 \sigma^2}{2(1-\rho)} \tag{15.5}$$

where ρ is the traffic intensity and it is equal to λ / μ. The above expression can be re-written as follows:

$$L = \rho + \frac{\lambda^2 E(t^2)}{2(1-\rho)}$$

where $E(t^2)$ is the second moment of the service time.

When the service time is constant, $\sigma^2 = 0$, and we have from (15.5) that $L = \rho(2 - \rho) / 2(1 - \rho)$. When the service time is exponentially distributed, expression (15.5) becomes expression (15.2). The variance of an expo-nential distribution with mean $1 / \mu$ is $(1 / \mu)^2$. Substituting this into (15.5) gives $L = \rho / (1 - \rho)$.

15.4 OPEN NETWORKS OF QUEUES

Typically, the flow of customers through a system may involve a number of different service stations. In view of this, it is not possible to model such systems by a single server queue. A network of queues is a more powerful modeling tool, as it can be used to depict the different service stations that make up the system. Networks of queues have been used extensively to model different systems, such as, computer networks, manufacturing systems, and web services.

Figure 15.16 gives an example of an open queueing network consisting of four nodes. In this example, external customers arrive at node 1 and after service completion they may join node 2, or 3, or 4 with probability 0.3, 0.4, 0.3 respectively. External customers and customers from nodes 1 and 3 arrive at node 2 and after service completion they may join node 3 with probability 0.25, or node 4 with probability 0.5, or they may depart from the network with probability 0.25. Node 3 accepts customers from outside and from nodes 1 and 2, and after service completion customers may join node 2 with probability 0.2 or node 4 with probability 0.3, or they may depart from the network with probability 0.5. Finally, node 4 accepts customers from the other three nodes and after service completion customers depart to the outside.

In general, a node in an open queueing network may receive customers from outside or from other nodes, and upon service completion, they may depart form the network or join another node with some probability. These probabilities are known as *branching probabilities*. The sum of all the branching probabilities for each node is 1. Depending upon the topology of the network and the branching probabilities, a customer may follow different paths through the network from the moment it arrives at the network to the moment it departs from it.

Looking at the example in figure 15.16, we observe that the sum of all the external arrivals, $\lambda_{01} + \lambda_{02} + \lambda_{03}$, to nodes 1,2, and 3 is 30 per hour. This is the total arrival rate to the queueing network, and it is equal to the total departure

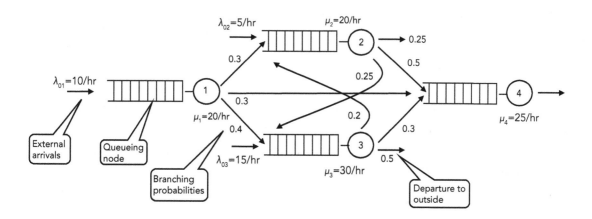

Figure 15.16: An example of an open queueing network

rate from the queueing network, assuming that all the nodes are stable. But, how do we know that each node is indeed stable? For this, we need to know the total arrival rate into each node, otherwise known as the *effective arrival rate*. This is equal to the sum of the arrival rates of all the flows routed to the node from the other nodes plus the arrival rate from a possible external flow. Let the total effective arrival rate into node i be λ_i, $i = 1, 2, 3, 4$. Assuming that each node is stable, then whatever comes in goes out and therefore the departure rate from node i is equal to the effective arrival rate λ_i. (This effective arrival rate is in fact the throughput of the node.) Consequently, we have the following equations for each node.

$$\lambda_1 = 10$$
$$\lambda_2 = 5 + 0.3\lambda_1 + 0.2\lambda_3$$
$$\lambda_3 = 15 + 0.4\lambda_1 + 0.25\lambda_2$$
$$\lambda_4 = 0.3\lambda_1 + 0.5\lambda_2 + 0.3\lambda_3$$

These equations can be solved easily to yield: $\lambda_1 = 10$, $\lambda_2 = 12.42$, $\lambda_3 = 22.10$, and $\lambda_4 = 15.845$, with a unit time being an hour. Based on these results we can verify that each node i is stable by checking that $\lambda_i < \mu_i$, $i = 1, 2, 3, 4$.

The above equations are known as the *traffic equations* and they have the following general form. Let M be the total number of nodes, λ_{0i} the external arrival rate to node i, and p_{ij} the branching probability from node i to node j, where $i = 1, 2, \ldots, M$, and $j = 1, 2, \ldots, M$. (We note that $p_{ii} \neq 0$, that is, a departing customer from node i can be fed back to itself.) Then, the traffic equations are as follows:

$$\begin{cases} \lambda_1 = \lambda_{01} + \sum_{i=1}^{M} \lambda_i p_{i1} \\ \quad\vdots \\ \lambda_M = \lambda_{0M} + \sum_{i=1}^{M} \lambda_i p_{iM} \end{cases} \tag{15.6}$$

These equations always have a unique solution, which is used to calculate the queue-length distribution of each node i.

Below, we present a solution for an open queueing network which satisfies the following assumptions:

- Single class of customers. (That is, the arrival rate, the service rate, and the branching probabilities at each node are the same for all customers.)
- M nodes.
- Customers arrive from outside at node i, $i = 1, 2, \ldots, M$, in a Poisson fashion with rate λ_{0i}. An infinite population of customers is assumed.
- After service completion at node i, $i = 1, 2, \ldots, M$, a customer may either depart to the outside with probability p_{i0} or join another node j, $j = 1, 2, \ldots, M$, with probability p_{ij}, where

$$p_{i0} + \sum_{j=1}^{M} p_{ij} = 1$$

- Each node i, $i = 1, 2, \ldots, M$, consists of s_i servers, each providing an exponentially distributed service time at the rate of μ_i.
- Each node has an infinite capacity queue, and customers are served in a FIFO manner.

The state of this queueing network is described by the vector: $(n_1, n_2, \ldots, n_M)$, where $n_i \geq 0$ is the number of customers in the ith node. (This state description is similar to the one for the M/M/1 queue, only now we have M nodes.) Let $p(n_1, n_2, \ldots, n_M)$ be the probability that the queueing network is in state $(n_1, n_2, \ldots, n_M)$. Then, for the queueing network described above it can be shown that:

$$p(n_1, n_2, \ldots, n_M) = p_1(n_1) \, p_2(n_2) \ldots p_M(n_M) \tag{15.7}$$

where $p_i(n_i)$ is the probability that there are n_i customers in node i, obtained by studying the node in isolation of the remaining nodes as an M/M/s_i queue with service rate μ_i and arrival rate λ_i, calculated by solving the traffic equations (15.6). It is assumed that the queueing network is stable, i.e., each node i is stable, $(\lambda_i < s_i \mu_i)$.

We observe that the above expression (15.7) is in the form of a product of M terms, where each term $p_i(n_i)$ consists of parameters which are related to only one node in the queueing network (as opposed to more than one node). This type of solution is known as a product-form solution, and the queueing network is said to have a product-form solution.

We demonstrate this solution using the queueing network in figure 15.16, and assuming that it satisfies the assumptions of the product-form queueing network. The idea behind this solution is that we can decompose the queueing

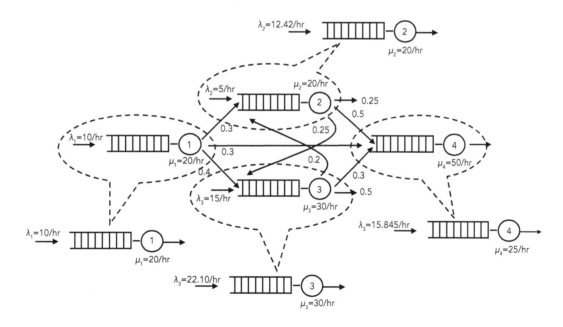

Figure 15.17: Decomposition of the queueing network to individual M/M/1 queues

network into the individual nodes and study each node in isolation assuming that the arrival rate to each node is the effective rate calculated by solving the traffic equations. The decomposition is shown in figure 15.17, where we indicate graphically how each node is analyzed in isolation. Since, $\lambda_1 = 10$ per hour, $\lambda_2 = 12.42$ per hour, $\lambda_3 = 22.10$ per hour, and $\lambda_4 = 15.845$ per hour, we have: $\rho_1 = 10 / 20 = 0.5$, $\rho_2 = 12.42 / 20 = 0.621$, $\rho_3 = 22.10 / 30 = 0.737$, and $\rho_4 = 15.845 / 25 = 0.634$. The queue-length distribution of each node considered in isolation is:

$$\begin{cases} p_1(n_1) = \rho_1^{n_1}(1-\rho_1) = 0.5 \times 0.5^{n_1} = 0.5^{n_1+1}, \ n_1 = 0,1,... \\ p_2(n_2) = \rho_2^{n_2}(1-\rho_2) = 0.379 \times 0.621^{n_2}, \ n_2 = 0,1,... \\ p_3(n_3) = \rho_3^{n_3}(1-\rho_3) = 0.263 \times 0.737^{n_3}, \ n_3 = 0,1,... \\ p_4(n_4) = \rho_4^{n_4}(1-\rho_4) = 0.366 \times 0.634^{n_4}, \ n_4 = 0,1,... \end{cases} \tag{15.8}$$

The joint probability distribution is obtained by multiplying the above probabilities. We have:

$$\begin{aligned} p(n_1,n_2,n_3,n_4) \\ = \left(0.5^{n_1+1}\right)\left(0.379 \times 0.621^{n_2}\right)\left(0.263 \times 0.737^{n_3}\right)\left(0.366 \times 0.634^{n_4}\right), \ n_1,n_2,n_3,n_4 \geq 0 \end{aligned} \tag{15.9}$$

Using expressions (15.8) we can obtain various performance measures of interest for each node, such as the probability each node is empty, the mean number of customers in each node, and the mean waiting time in each node.

In addition, using expressions (15.8) and (15.9) we can obtain results pertaining the entire queueing network, such as:

- The probability that the queueing network is empty:
  $p(0,0,0,0) = p_1(0)p_2(0)p_3(0)p_4(0) = 0.5 \times 0.379 \times 0.263 \times 0.366 = 0.018$.
- The total throughput of the network: $\lambda_{01} + \lambda_{02} + \lambda_{03} = 30$.
- The average time a customer spends in the queueing network assuming that it joins node 2 when it first arrives from the outside: This can be obtained by following all the possible paths. To simplify the calculations, let us assume that the branching probability $p_{32} = 0$, that is, customers cannot go to node 2 from node 3. Let W_i be the mean waiting time in node $i = 2, 3, 4$. Then, the mean time a customer spends in the queueing network is $W_2 + (p_{24} + p_{23}p_{34})W_4 + p_{23}W_3$. In general the average amount of time a customer spends in the queueing network, otherwise known as the mean response time, is given by the expression:

$$\frac{1}{\lambda_{01} + \lambda_{02} + \lambda_{03}}\left[\lambda_1 W_1 + \lambda_2 W_2 + \lambda_3 W_3 + \lambda_4 W_4\right]$$

- The ratio $\lambda_i / (\lambda_{01} + \lambda_{02} + \lambda_{03})$ is the percent of time a customer visits node i, and it is known as the visit ratio. The above expression for the mean response time holds for any number of nodes, where the denominator is the sum of all the external arrival rates.

We note that this type of queueing network can be analyzed using a software tool such JMT[1], discussed below in section 15.6.

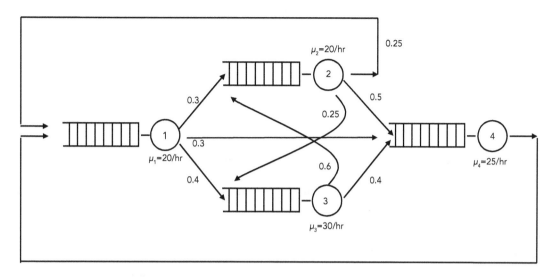

Figure 15.18: A closed queueing network

15.5 CLOSED NETWORKS OF QUEUES

In a closed network of queues, customers do not arrive from the outside nor do they depart to the outside as in open queueing networks. Instead, there is a fixed number of customers that constantly circulate through the nodes of the queueing network. In figure 15.18 we reproduce the example of the closed queueing network given in figure 15.3. Customers completing their service at node 1 may join node 2, or 3, or 4 with probability 0.3, 0.4, and 0.3 respectively. Customers completing their service at node 2 join node 1, or 3, or 4 with probability 0.25, 0.25 and 0.5 respectively. Customers completing their service at node 3 join node 2 or 4 with probability 0.6 and 0.4 respectively. Finally customers departing from node 4 are fed back to node 1.

Let us now formulate the traffic equations. Let λ_i, $i = 1, 2, 3, 4$, be the effective arrival rate to node i. Then we have:

$$\lambda_1 = 0.25\lambda_2 + \lambda_4$$
$$\lambda_2 = 0.3\lambda_1 + 0.6\lambda_3$$
$$\lambda_3 = 0.4\lambda_1 + 0.25\lambda_2$$
$$\lambda_4 = 0.3\lambda_1 + 0.5\lambda_2 + 0.4\lambda_3$$

Unlike the traffic equations in the open queueing networks which always have a single solution (assuming that the queues are stable), we observe that the above system admits an infinite number of solutions. The actual effective arrival rates cannot be determined unless we solve the queueing network. In the solution presented below it suffices to set one effective arrival rate to a fixed value and then solve for the others. For instance, we can set $\lambda_1 = 1$ and then solve for the remaining unknowns, obtaining $\lambda_2 = 0.635$, $\lambda_3 = 0.559$, and $\lambda_4 = 0.841$. We refer to these values as the relative throughputs (relative to the chosen value of λ_1).

In general, let M be the total number of nodes and p_{ij} the branching probability from node i to node j, where $i = 1, 2, \dots, M$, and $j = 1, 2, \dots, M$. (We note that $p_{ii} \neq 0$, that is, a departing customer from node i can be fed back to node i.) Then, the traffic equations are as follows:

$$\begin{cases} \lambda_1 = \sum_{i=1}^{M} \lambda_i p_{i1} \\ \quad\vdots \\ \lambda_M = \sum_{i=1}^{M} \lambda_i p_{iM} \end{cases} \tag{15.10}$$

We now present a solution for a closed queueing networks which satisfies the following assumptions:

- Single class of customers. (That is, the service rate and the branching probabilities at each node are the same for all customers.)
- M nodes.
- K customers.
- After service completion at node i, $i = 1, 2, \ldots, M$, a customer may join another node j, $j = 1, 2, \ldots, M$, with probability p_{ij}, where

$$\sum_{j=1}^{M} p_{ij} = 1$$

- Each node i, $i = 1, 2, \ldots, M$, consists of si servers, each providing an exponentially distributed service time at the rate of μ_i.
- Each node has sufficient capacity to accommodate all N customers, and customers are served in a FIFO manner.

The state of this queueing network is described by the vector: $(n_1, n_2, \ldots, n_M)$, where $n_i \geq 0$ is the number of custom-ers in the ith node, and $n_1 + n_2 + \ldots + n_M = K$. Let $p(n_1, n_2, \ldots, n_M)$ be the probability that the queueing network is in state $(n_1, n_2, \ldots, n_M)$. Then, for the queueing network described above it can be shown that:

$$p(n_1, n_2, \ldots, n_M) = \frac{1}{G} \rho_1(n_1)\rho_2(n_2)\ldots\rho_M(n_M) \tag{15.11}$$

where $\rho_i(n_i)$ is a function of the traffic intensity of node i which is dependent on the number of customers n_i in the queue. It is defined as follows. If the ith node consists of a single server, i.e., $s_i = 1$, then:

$$\rho_i(n_i) = \left(\frac{\lambda_i}{\mu_i}\right)^{n_i}, \ n_i = 0, 1, \ldots, K. \tag{15.12}$$

If the ith node consists of multiple servers, then:

$$\rho_i(n_i) = \frac{\lambda_i^{n_i}}{\prod_{j=1}^{n_i} \mu_i(j)}, \quad \text{where } \mu_i(j) = \mu_i \min(s_i, j), \, n_i = 0, 1, \ldots, K. \tag{15.13}$$

The quantities λ_i, $i = 1, 2, \ldots, M$, are the relative throughputs obtained by solving the traffic equations (15.10), as explained above. That is, we arbitrarily fix one of the λ_i's and then solve for the remaining ones.

Finally, the term G is known as the *normalizing constant*. In order that each probability $p(n_1, n_2, \ldots, n_M)$ is less than one and the sum of the probabilities of all the feasible states $(n_1, n_2, \ldots, n_M)$ for which $n_i \geq 0$, $i = 1, 2, \ldots, K$, such that $n_1 + n_2 + \ldots + n_M = K$, adds up to one, each feasible term $\rho_1(n_1)\rho_2(n_2) \ldots \rho_M(n_M)$ must be divided by G, where

$$G = \sum \rho_1(n_1)\rho_1(n_1)\ldots\rho_1(n_1) \tag{15.14}$$

summed over all $n_i \geq 0$, $i = 1, 2, \ldots, K$, such that $n_1 + n_2 + \ldots + n_M = K$. G can be calculated by enumerating all the feasible terms $\rho_1(n_1)\rho_2(n_2) \ldots \rho_M(n_M)$. However, this brute-force method is limited to very small queueing networks, and G is calculated typically using one of the several available algorithms developed expressly for the calculation of the normalizing constant, such as the *Mean Value Analysis* (MVA).

We observe that the solution given by (15.11) is also a product-form solution since it is a product of terms where each term $\rho_i(n_i)$ consists of parameters related to only one node of the network. In view of this, we say that the closed queueing network analyzed above is a *product-form queueing network*.

Once the joint probabilities $p(n_1, n_2, \ldots, n_M)$ have been calculated, we can obtain the probability $p_j(n_j)$ that there are n_j customers in the jth node by summing all the $p(n_1, n_2, \ldots, n_M)$ probabilities for all feasible combinations of n_i, $i = 1, 2, \ldots, K$, $i \neq j$, such that $n_1 + n_2 + \ldots + n_{j-1} + n_{j+1} + \ldots + n_M = K - n_M$, while keeping n_j fixed.

We demonstrate this solution using the queueing network in figure 15.18, and assuming that it satisfies the assumptions of the product-form closed queueing network. We assume that all nodes consist of a single server, the total number of customers K circulating through the network is 1, and $\mu_1 = 20$ per hour, $\mu_2 = 20$ per hour, $\mu_3 = 30$ per hour, and $\mu_4 = 25$ per hour. From the traffic equations we have already established that: $\lambda_1 = 1, \lambda_2 = 0.635, \lambda_3 = 0.559, \lambda_4 = 0.841$. Therefore, from (15.12) we have:

$$\rho_1(0) = (1 / 20)^0 = 1, \rho_1(1) = (1 / 20)^1 = 0.05$$
$$\rho_2(0) = (0.635 / 20)^0 = 1, \rho_2(1) = (0.635 / 20)^1 = 0.03175$$
$$\rho_3(0) = (0.559 / 30)^0 = 1, \rho_3(1) = (0.559 / 30)^1 = 0.01863$$
$$\rho_4(0) = (0.841 / 25)^0 = 1, \rho_4(1) = (0.841 / 25)^1 = 0.03364.$$

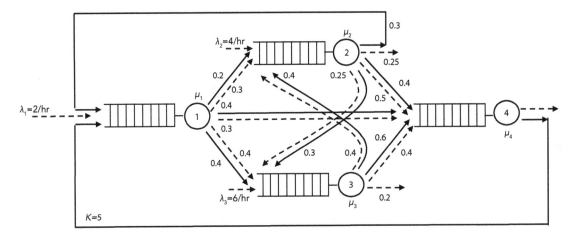

Figure 15.19: A mixed queueing network

From (15.14) we have: $G = 0.05 + 0.03175 + 0.01863 + 0.03364 = 0.13402$. Finally, we obtain:

$$p(1,0,0,0) = (1 / 0.13402)(0.05)^1 (0.03175)^0 (0.01863)^0 (0.03364)^0 = 0.3731$$
$$p(0,1,0,0) = (1 / 0.13402)(0.05)^0 (0.03175)^1(0.01863)^0 (0.03364)^0 = 0.2369$$
$$p(0,0,1,0) = (1 / 0.13402)(0.05)^0 (0.03175)^0 (0.01863)^1 (0.03364)^0 = 0.1390$$
$$p(0,0,0,1) = (1 / 0.13402)(0.05)^0 (0.03175)^0 (0.01863)^0 (0.03364)^1 = 0.2510.$$

From the above joint probability distribution we can obtain the queue-length distribution in each node. For instance, for node 1 we have that $p_1(1) = 0.3731$ and $p_1(0) = 0.6269$. The mean number of customers in node 1 is $L_1 = 0 \times p_1(0) + 1 \times p_1(1) = 0.3731$, and the throughput is $p_1(1)\mu_1 = 0.3731 \times 20 = 7.462$ per hour. Consequently, the mean time in node 1 is $0.3731 / 7.462 = 0.05$ hours.

An interesting quantity is the time T that elapses between two successive visits of a customer at node 1. It can be shown that T is equal to the sum of the mean waiting time in each node weighted by its relative throughput. That is, in our case we have: $T = \lambda_1 W_1 + \lambda_2 W_2 + \lambda_3 W_3 + \lambda_4 W_4 = 0.13216$. This quantity is also the average time it takes for a customer to traverse the network once. For a closed queueing network with M nodes it is equal to $T = \lambda_1 W_1 + \ldots + \lambda_M W_M$.

This type of queueing network can be analyzed using a software tool such JMT, described in the following section.

15.6 MIXED NETWORKS OF QUEUES

It is possible to define open and closed queueing networks over the same topology of queueing nodes using the concept of classes. For instance, let us consider four queueing nodes linked as shown in figure 15.19. Node 1 is linked to nodes 2, 3, and 4; node 2 is linked to nodes 1, 3, and 4; node 3 is linked to nodes 2 and 4; and, node 4 is linked to node 1. The actual flow of customers through these nodes depends on the class. For instance, we can define an open class where customers arrive from outside, get served at the various nodes of the queueing network and then depart to the outside. We can also define a closed class where customers constantly circulate through the nodes. The flow of the open class customers is indicated by the dotted arrows, and the flow of the closed class customers by the solid arrows. Customers from one class cannot move to the other class.

The branching probabilities depend on the class. In the case of the open class, external customers arrive at node 1 and after service completion they may join node 2, or 3, or 4 with probability 0.3, 0.4, 0.3 respectively. External customers and customers from nodes 1 and 3 arrive at node 2 and after service completion they may join node 3 with probability 0.25 or node 4 with probability 0.5, or they may depart from the network with probability 0.25. Node 3 accepts customers from outside and from nodes 1 and 2, and after service completion customers may join node 2 with probability 0.4 or node 4 with probability 0.4, or they may depart from the network with probability 0.2. Finally, node 4 accepts customers from the other three nodes and after service completion customers depart to the outside. The rate of external arrivals to nodes 1, 2, and 3 is 2 per hour, 4 per hour, and 6 per hour respectively. In the closed class, customers completing their service at node 1 may join node 2, or 3, or 4 with probability 0.2, 0.4, and 0.4 respectively. Customers completing their service at node 2 may join node 1, or 3, or 4 with probability 0.3, 0.3 and 0.4 respectively. Customers completing their service at node 3 may join node 2 or 4 with probability 0.4 and 0.6 respectively. Finally customers departing from node 4 are fed back to node 1. The number of customers K in the closed class is 5. Finally, we need to define the service time distribution and service discipline at each node for each class. For this example, we assume an exponentially distributed service time at each node with the same rate for both classes. Customers from both classes join the same queue at each node and are served in the order in which they arrive, i.e. FIFO.

This type of queueing network is often referred to as a *mixed* queueing network. It has been shown that under certain assumptions, this queueing network has a product-form solution. That is, the probability that the system is in some state is expressed as the product of terms, each containing parameters that correspond to one node only. Unlike the product-form solutions in the two previous sections, this expression is extremely complex and it can be only solved numerically. Below, we describe the assumptions under which we can obtain a product-form solution, and subsequently, we give the solution to the example described above using JMT.

We consider a queueing network of M nodes arbitrarily linked. Over this topology, we can define any number of open and closed classes. For each closed class we have to define the number of customers in the class, and for each open class we have to specify which nodes receive external arrivals and at what rate. The following three types of nodes are allowed:

- *FIFO node:* Customers from all classes join the same queue and they are served in the order in which they arrive. Multiple servers are possible and the service time is exponentially distributed with a rate which is the same for all classes. This is the type of node assumed in the example given above.
- *Infinite server node:* This node consists of an infinite number of servers. The service time can be exponentially distributed with a rate that depends on the class. It can also follow a more complex distribution, such as a mixture of exponential distributions, with parameters that depend on the class. This type of node is used typically to model situations where a customer undergoes a delay without having to queue up first. For instance,

when a packet is transmitted out of a router it undergoes a propagation delay before it reaches the next router. In addition, many packets may be in transit between the two routers. This can be modeled using an infinite server node with a mean service time equal to the propagation delay between the two routers.

- *Processor sharing node:* This is a limiting case of the well-known time-slicing discipline used in CPU scheduling. Specifically, each process receives a quantum of CPU service. If it is completed by the time the quantum expires the process departs from the system, otherwise it goes back to the end of the queue for another quantum of CPU. This repeats until the process is completed. The limiting case of this scheduling discipline is to assume that all processes are in service simultaneously each receiving a fraction of the CPU. For instance, if the CPU runs at 1 GHz and there are k processes present, then each receives $1/k$ GHz of the CPU speed. This theoretical limiting case is known as processor sharing. The service time can be exponentially distributed with a rate that depends on the class. It can also be a mixture of exponential distributions with parameters depending on the class. This type of node is used typically to model a CPU queue.

For each class we define the branching probabilities of going from node i to node j upon service completion. Customers can switch between open classes and also between closed classes, but not from an open (closed) class to a closed (open) one. Switching is done upon service completion and it is incorporated in the branching probabilities. That is, assuming that switching between class r and class q is permitted, a class r customer upon service completion at node i joins node j as class v, with probability $p_{ir,jv}$.

All interarrival times of external customers are assumed to be exponentially distributed. For each open class r there is a single arrival stream of customers with a class-dependent rate λr. The arrival rate may also depend on the total

Node	Throughput		Mean queue length		Resident time		Utilization	
	Open	Closed	Open	Closed	Open	Closed	Open	Closed
1	2.000	14.027	0.328	1.957	0.027	0.139	0.1	0.701
2	8.133	5.738	1.248	0.821	0.104	0.059	0.407	0.287
3	8.833	7.333	0.625	0.498	0.052	0.036	0.294	0.244
4	8.200	12.306	1.329	1.725	0.111	0.123	0.328	0.492

Table 15.3: Results for the queueing network in figure 15.19

K	Mean response time	Utilization			
		Node 1	Node 2	Node 3	Node 4
2	0.206	0.571	0.599	0.458	0.658
4	0.266	0.751	0.673	0.521	0.785
6	0.322	0.838	0.709	0.552	0.846
8	0.374	0.887	0.728	0.569	0.881
10	0.423	0.917	0.741	0.579	0.902

Table 15.4: Mean response time for the open class and utilization, $K = 2, 4, \ldots, 10$

number of class r customers present in the queueing network at the moment of arrival. (This permit us to model cases with a finite population of customers, as in section 15.3.4.) An arriving customer joins one of the nodes that accept external arrivals from class r probabilistically. For instance, let us assume that class r customers can join nodes i, j, and k, and let λ_r be the class-dependent arrival rate. Then, an arriving customer will join node i, or j, or k, with probability p_{roi}, p_{roj} and p_{rok} respectively. Alternatively, we can assume a separate independent stream of class r arrivals to each node i that accepts class r arrivals with a rate $\lambda_r p_{roi}$.

It is also permissible to combine all external arrivals of all open classes into a single stream whose rate may depend on the total number of customers present in the queueing network at the moment of arrival. Arriving customers join a node i as a class r customer probabilistically.

Using JMT we can analyze the example described above and shown in figure 15.19. (We note that in JMT the external arrival streams to nodes 1, 2, and 3, are modeled by a single source of arrivals with a total rate of 12 per hour. An arrival joins node 1 or 2 or 3 with probability 2 / 12, 4 / 12, and 6 / 12 respectively.) The results are presented in table 15.3. The terms "open" and "closed" refer to the open and closed classes. The "resident time" reported by JMT is the mean total time a customer spends in queue i during the entire time that it is in the queueing network, which may involve multiple visits in queue i. The sum of all the resident times for the open class is 0.294. This is the total time an open class customer spends on the average in the queueing network. Alternatively, this can be interpreted as the mean response time of the system, represented by the queueing network, for open class customers. The sum of all the resident times for the closed class is 0.357. This quantity is harder to interpret, but it gives the mean time it takes a closed class customer to traverse the queueing network once.

Using JMT we can also carry "what-if" analysis on the various parameters of the two classes. Table 15.4 gives the mean response time for the open class of customers, i.e., the total time an open class customer spends on the average in the queueing network, when K is varied from 2 to 10 by increments of 2. As expected, the mean response time increases as K increases. This is because an open class customer encounters more queueing as the number of closed class customers increases. When analyzing queueing systems it is always useful to know the server utilizations. The total utilization due to open and closed class customers of each node for the above example is also given in table 15.4. We note that for $K = 10$, nodes 1 and 4 are running at a very high utilization of over 90%.

15.7 CASE STUDY: EVALUATING THE CAPACITY OF AN ENTERPRISE SOFTWARE

In this section, we use the mixed queueing model described in the section above to model an enterprise software. Requests are submitted over the Internet, and they are either *CPU bound* or *I/O bound*. The CPU bound requests require only CPU time, whereas the I/O bound ones require data to be fetched from a disk and some CPU time. The CPU bound requests are represented by class 1, an open class of customers, and the I/O bound requests are represented by class 2, a separate open class of customers. In this example, switching between classes is not allowed and the external arrival rate of customers in each class i is λ_{0i}, $i = 1, 2$, independent of the number of class i requests already in the system.

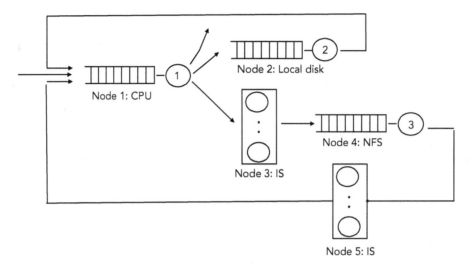

Figure 15.20: The queueing network of the enterprise software

$\lambda_{01}, \lambda_{02}$	Mean response time		CPU Utilization
	CPU bound	I/O bound	
0.001	75	350	0.530
0.002	87	373	0.597
0.003	101	402	0.663
0.004	121	437	0.727
0.005	149	482	0.789
0.006	191	544	0.848
0.007	261	639	0.902
0.008	389	802	0.948
0.009	674	1,150	0.981
0.010	1,568	2,241	0.998

Table 15.5: Results for different arrival rates

The queueing network representing this system is shown in figure 15.20. Class 1 and 2 requests arrive from the outside at node 1 which represents the CPU queue of requests to be processed by the enterprise software. This node is modeled as a processor sharing node. Upon service completion at this node, a CPU bound request departs from the queueing network, whereas an I/O bound request issues a disk I/O request to either the local disk, modeled by node 2, or to the *Network File System* (NFS), modeled by node 4. Both nodes are FIFO nodes. The NFS is accessed over the Internet, and node 3, represented by an infinite server (IS), depicts the propagation delay from the site where the enterprise software runs to the NFS. Node 5 represented also by an infinite server depicts the propagation delay from the NFS to the site of the enterprise software. An I/O bound request circulates between the CPU queue and the local disk and NFS until it is completed. We assume that completion occurs right after it completes a service at the CPU queue, where upon it departs from the queueing network.

Based on the above description, class 1 customers arrive at the CPU queue and upon service completion depart from the queueing network. A class 2 customer arrives at the CPU queue and upon service completion, it either departs from the queueing network with probability $p_{2,10}$, or it joins node 2 or node 3 with probability $p_{2,12}$ and $p_{2,13}$ respectively. Upon service completion at node 2, a class 2 customer returns to node 1 for another round of service. Upon service completion at node 3, a class 2 customer joins node 4, and then node 5, and finally it comes back to node 1. In addition to these two classes, we introduce class 3, a closed class, with 4 customers in it, which depicts various processes that run continuously in order to support the enterprise software. These processes are also I/O bound. That is, they circulate between the CPU node, the local disk node, and the NFS node. Upon completion at node 1, a class 3 customer joins node 2 or node 3 with probability $p_{3,12}$ and $p_{3,13}$ respectively. The mean CPU time required by a class 1 customer is 40 msec. (The distribution of the service time in a processor sharing node may be assumed to be either exponential or a more complex mixture of exponentials; however, it is immaterial since the solution depends only on the mean service time of the processor sharing node.) The mean time required by an I/O bound request each time it visits the CPU node is 10 msec, and the branching probabilities are: $p_{2,10} = 0.2, p_{2,12} = 0.5, p_{2,13} = 0.3$. The propagation delay is 30 msec in either direction (for both classes 2 and 3). That is, the mean service time at each infinite server is equal to 30 msec. The mean time required by a class 3 customer each time it visits the CPU node is 5 msec, and the branching probabilities are: $p_{3,12} = 0.6$ and $p_{3,13} = 0.4$. The service time at node 2 has to be exponentially distributed with the same mean for both class 2 and class 3 customers in order for the product-form solution to hold. The same holds for node 4. We assume a 10 msec mean service time at node 2 and a 5 msec mean service time at node 3.

Table 15.5 gives the mean response time (msec) of the CPU and I/O bound requests, as their arrival rates λ_{01} and λ_{02}, where $\lambda_{01} = \lambda_{02}$, are increased from 0.001/msec to 0.01/msec. The mean response time is the mean amount of time it takes the enterprise software to process a CPU or an I/O bound request. As can be seen it is higher for I/O bound requests, since they require disk I/O in addition to CPU. The utilization of the CPU node is also given in table 15.5. We note, that the mean response time for both types of requests increases rapidly as the arrival rates λ_{01}, λ_{02} get closer to 0.01, following a similar curve as the one given in figure 15.10. This is due to the fact that the utilization of the CPU node is almost 1 for $\lambda_{01} = \lambda_{02} = 0.010$/msec. The utilization of the CPU node is higher than that of the local disk and NFS nodes, not reported here, since it is doing more work than the other nodes. Consequently it is the first to saturate. The enterprise software cannot handle a higher rate of requests than 0.01 unless a faster CPU is used. Using JMT, one can experiment to find out the effects of getting a faster CPU. For instance, if the CPU speed at the CPU node is increased by 50%, then the time to execute a CPU bound request, an I/O bound request, and a class 3 job is cut down to 30 msec, 7.5 msec, and 3.75 msec respectively, and the CPU utilization drops to 0.87, and the mean response time of the CPU and I/O bound requests drops to 185 msec and 643 msec respectively for the case where $\lambda_{01} = \lambda_{02} = 0.010$/msec.

PROBLEMS

1. Consider a single server queue, and let the inter-arrival time and service time be constant. In the following two cases, is the queue stable or unstable? Why?

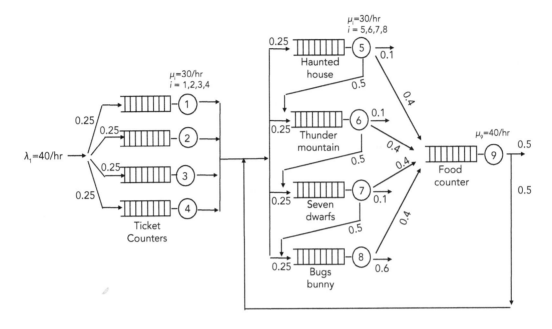

Figure 15.21: Having fun in Disneyland

a. The service time is 15 minutes and the inter-arrival time is 10 minutes

b. The service time is 10 minutes and the inter-arrival time is 15 minutes

2. How does the scheduling scheme affect the stability and throughput of a single server queue?

3. A service station has one gasoline pump. Cars wanting gasoline arrive in a Poisson fashion at the rate of 12 per hour. Customers may *balk* (i.e. leave the queue) if they find that there are cars waiting to be served. Specifically, if there are n cars already waiting at the service station (including the one currently being served), then an arriving customer will balk with probability $n / 4$, for $n = 1, 2, 3, 4$. The time required to service a car is exponentially distributed with a mean of 5 minutes.

   a. Construct the rate diagram for this queueing system

   b. Write down the balance equations

   c. Solve these equations to obtain the steady-state probability distribution of the number of cars at the station.

   d. Find the mean waiting time W for those cars that stay in the queue.

4. Show that the mean number of customers in an M/M/1/ queue remains unchanged but that the mean time spent in the system decreases by a factor of k when the arrival rate and the service rate are both increased by a factor of k. Explain this behavior.

5. Consider an M/M/s queue with mean service time 1 minute.

   a. Assume that $s = 1$. Draw L and W as a function of the arrival rate. Observe how the curve increases as the arrival rate increases.

   b. Same as in (a), but assume that $s = 2, 3, 4$.

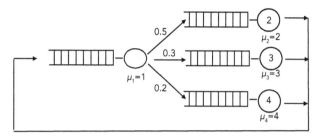

Figure 15.22: A closed queueing network

6. *Having fun in Disneyland!* A visit at Disneyland involves a fair amount of waiting in lines during the high season. One has to queue up to buy a ticket, and then once in the park, one has to queue up for each theme. Does one spend more time queueing up or enjoying the themes? That depends on the arrival rates of customers and service times (i.e., the time to see a theme). The queueing network in figure 15.21 depicts the ticket counters, four themes, and the food court. Use JMT or any other similar software to answer the following questions:

    a. Are all the queues stable?

    b. What is the utilization of each ticket counter?

    c. What is the probability that a customer will get served immediately upon arrival at the food court?

    d. What is the mean waiting time at each theme?

    e. How long would it take on the average to visit all themes once (excluding the food counter), and of that time how much one spends waiting in a queue?

    f. Average time one spends in the park.

7. Consider the closed queueing network shown in figure 15.22. Variations of this network have been used extensively to model computer systems. We assume that this queueing network satisfies all the conditions listed in section 15.5 so that it has a product-form solution. Let $K = 2$, $\mu_1 = 1$, $\mu_2 = 2$, $\mu_3 = 3$, and $\mu_4 = 4$. Calculate by hand the following:

    a. The normalizing constant G.

    b. The queue-length distribution of node 1.

    c. What is node 1's throughput?

    d. What is the average time it takes for a customer to come back to node 1?

8. Same problem as above. Use JMT or any other similar software to plot the throughput, average number of customers, mean waiting time, and utilization in each node, for $K = 1, 2, \ldots, 10$. What is the mean elapsed time between two successive visits of a customer at node 1?

REFERENCES

[1] M. Bertoli, G. Casale, and G. Serazzi, "JMT: Performance Engineering Tools for System Modeling", ACM SIGMETRICS Performance Evaluation Review, Vol 36, Issue 4, March 2009. Software available from http://jmt. sourceforge.net.

CHAPTER 16: SIMULATION TECHNIQUES

16.1 INTRODUCTION

Simulation is a popular modeling technique since it is easy to use, unlike the queueing models presented in the previous Chapter which require in-depth knowledge. Queueing theory is a useful tool for studying the response time and throughput of a networking service and also for dimensioning the underlying infrastructure so that it can handle a given number of service requests per second. However, it can only model a system at a fairly abstract level, and consequently it can be only used for first-cut analysis. More detailed analysis can be carried out using simulation, which permits the inclusion of detailed specifications that cannot be otherwise depicted in a queueing system.

A simulation model is a computer program that depicts a real system. It uses random numbers to represent the occurrence of events and it tracks the evolution of the various events that occur in the real system. Statistical techniques are used to obtain estimates of performance measures generated by a simulation model. In this Chapter, we review the basic simulation techniques used for building simulation models. A more detailed description of simulation techniques can be found in Perros[1].

There are also several simulation languages, such as, NS3, GPSS/H, SLAM II, SIMAN/ARENA, and JMT that permit a rapid development of a simulation model. The interested reader is referred to the literature for further details on simulation languages.

16.2 THE REPAIRMAN PROBLEM

We introduce the basic simulation techniques by means of an example. Specifically, we consider a queueing system, known as the *repairman problem*, which was used originally to estimate how long it takes for a broken down ma-

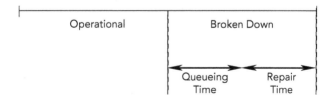

Figure 16.1: The basic cycle of a machine.

chine to be repaired. Variations of this queueing model were also used extensively to estimate the response time of computer systems. This queueing model was analyzed using queueing theory in section 15.3.4.

Let us consider a group of m identical machines. Each machine is operational for a period of time and then it breaks down. Broken down machines are served in FIFO manner by a single repairman. The total down time of a machine consists of the time it has to wait for the repairman plus the time it takes for the repairman to fix it. A machine becomes immediately operational after it has been repaired. Each machine follows the cycle shown in figure 16.1, continuously alternating between being operational and broken down.

The repairman problem is depicted by the queueing system shown in figure 16.2. The total number of operational machines plus those broken down is always equal to m. When an operational machine breaks down, it leaves the pool of operational machines and joins the repairman's queue where it waits for its turn to get serviced. Upon service completion, the machine returns to the pool of operational machines. For simplicity, we will assume that all the machines are identical. That is, they have the same operational time and the same repair time. (This can be easily changed to more complicated cases where each machine has its own operational and repair times.) We will set up a simulation model of the queueing system in figure 16.2 with a view to estimating how long a machine is down.

The first and most important step in building a simulation model, is to identify the *events* whose occurrence alter the *status* of the system. The status of a system is depicted by a number of variables whose value completely characterize the system under study at any time. In this problem, the main status variable is n, the number of broken down machines, i.e., those waiting in the queue plus the one being repaired. If $n = 0$, then we know that the queue is empty, the repairman is idle, and all the machine are operational. If $n = 1$, then the queue is empty, the repairman is busy, and $m - 1$ machines are operational. If $n > 1$, then the repairman is busy with a machine, there are $n - 1$ broken down machines in the queue, and $m - n$ machines are operational.

There are only two events whose occurrence will cause n to change value. These are:
1. A machine breaks down, i.e., an arrival occurs to the queue.
2. A machine is fixed, i.e., a departure occurs from the queue.

The flowcharts given in figures 16.3 and 16.4 show what happens when these events occur.

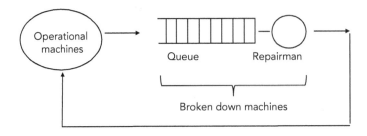

Figure 16.2: The repairman problem.

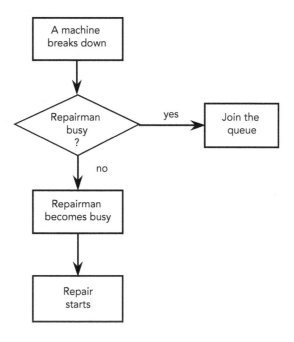

Figure 16.3: An arrival event.

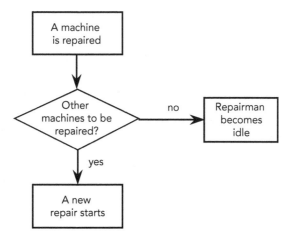

Figure 16.4: A departure event.

In order to incorporate the above two basic events in the simulation model, we need a set of variables, known as *clocks*, which keep track of the time instants at which an arrival or a departure will occur in the future. Each machine is associated with its own clock which shows the time at which the machine will break down, i. e., it will arrive at the repairman's queue. In addition, we require another clock associated with the repairman which shows the time at which the repair of a machine will be completed, i.e., it will cause a departure event to occur. In addition to these clocks, it is a good practice to maintain a *master clock*, which simply shows the current time in the simulation. (This is just a variable defined within the simulation program, and it has nothing to do with the computer's clock.)

The heart of the simulation model centers around the manipulation of the events that change the state of the system. In our case, at any instance, we have as many arrival events as the number of operational machines plus a departure event if the repairman is busy. Unlike in real life, in a simulation we always know ahead of time when these events will occur in the future! These times are stored in the associated clocks of the events. For instance, if there are 3 operational machines and the repairman is busy, then the clock of each operation machine will show the time in the future at which the machine will break down and there will be an arrival. Also, the clock of the repairman will show the time in the future when the repair will be completed and there will be a departure. The event associated with the clock with the smallest value is the next one to occur in the future. Once this event has been determined, the master clock is advanced to this time instance, and appropriate action takes place accordingly to whether it is an arrival or a departure. This logic for the simulation is shown figure 16.5.

If the next event is a machine break down, then we branch out to the left of the flowchart. If the server, i.e., the repairman, is busy, then the machine joins the repairman's queue, and we go back to the beginning to find the next event. Otherwise, repair work on the machine starts immediately, and we have to determine when the service, i.e.,

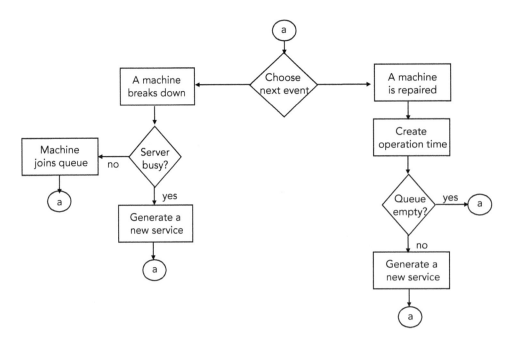

Figure 16.5: Event manipulation.

the repair, will be completed and a departure will occur. Let us assume that the repair time of a machine is constant equal to 5 units of time. Then, a departure will occur 5 units of time later. The departure clock is updated appropriately, and we go back to the beginning to find the next event.

If the next event is a departure, then we exit to the right of the flowchart. The machine becomes operational which means that we have to decide when it will break down again. Let us assume that the operational time is constant and equal to 10 units of time. Then the clock associated with the machine that indicates the time at which it will break down is updated accordingly. If there are no other machines waiting to be repaired, then the repairman becomes idle, and we go back to the beginning to find the next event. Otherwise, a new service begins, the departure clock is updated appropriately, and we go back to the beginning to find the next event.

We are now ready to carry out the hand simulation shown in table 16.1. Let us assume that we have 3 machines, and let $CL1$, $CL2$, and $CL3$ be the arrival event clock of machine 1, 2, and 3, respectively. These clocks indicate the time at which each machine will break down. Also, Let $CL4$ be the clock associated with the departure event, MC the master clock, n the number of broken down machines (including the one currently being repaired), and R the state of the repairman ($R = 1$ if busy, $R = 0$ if idle). We assume that at time zero all three machines are operational and that $CL1 = 1$, $CL2 = 4$, $CL3 = 9$. Looking at the clocks, we see that machine 1 will break down at time 1, machine 2 at time 4 and machine 3 at time 9. Consequently, the next event is the break down of machine 1. We advance the master clock to 1, i.e., $MC = 1$, and then schedule a service time with a completion time equal to $MC + 5 = 6$. Checking the clocks again, we see that machine 1 will be repaired at time 6, machine 2 will break down at time 4, and machine 3 will break down at time 9. We advance the master clock to the next event, which is the breakdown of machine 2. We set $MC = 4$, and since the repairman is busy, machine 2 is queued in the repairman's queue. No other action is required at that moment. This logic is repeated by checking the clocks to find the next event, and so on. This process continues for ever until a stopping rule is satisfied and the simulation is ended.

As can be seen, we only check the system at times when events occur. The time in-between events is of no interest to the simulation since nothing happens and the status of the system does not change.

MC	CL1	CL2	CL3	CL4	n	R
0	1	4	9	-	0	idle
1	-	4	9	6	1	busy
4	-	-	9	6	2	busy
6	16	-	9	11	1	busy
9	16	-	-	11	2	busy
11	16	21	-	16	1	busy
16	-	21	26	21	1	busy

Table 16.1: Hand simulation for the repairman problem

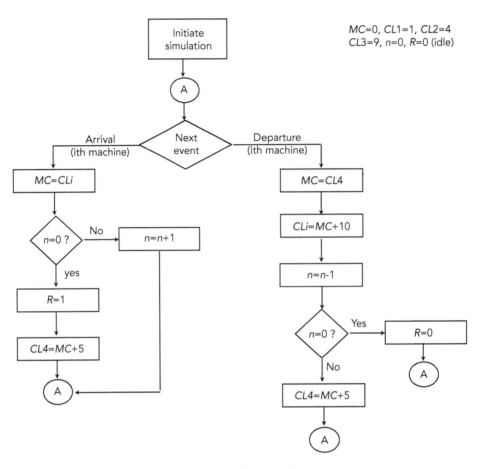

Figure 16.6: A flowchart of the simulation program

We note that at time 16 in the hand simulation we have two events that occur at the same time: machine 1 will break down, and machine 3 will be repaired and become operational. We can execute these two events in an arbitrary order. That is, we can take care of the break down first and then the completion of the repair, or the other way round. In this particular simulation model, the order at which we will execute the two events is immaterial, but this may not be the case in general. This problem of more than one clock having the same value only occurs when the clocks take integer values. It does not occur when the clocks take real values as two clock values will never be the same.

The above hand simulation can be easily implemented on a computer. An outline of the logic of the simulation program is given in figure 16.6. The actual implementation of this program is left as an exercise (see simulation project 1, at the end of this Chapter).

16.3 GENERATING RANDOM NUMBERS
In the example above we assumed that the operational times and repair times are all constant. These assumptions were made in order to simplify the problem. In real life, the time a machine is operational varies. Also, the repair

time varies depending upon parts availability and the type and severity of failure. The variability of the opera-tional times and repair times, and in general of any variable used in a simulation, is typically represented by an empirical or a theoretical probability distribution. In view of this, in order to make a simulation model more real-istic, one should be able to use numbers from a given theoretical or empirical distribution generated in a random way. We distinguish between generating random numbers which are uniformly distributed in [0,1], known as *pseudo-random numbers*, and random numbers which follow an empirical or theoretical distribution, known as *random variates or stochastic variates*. In this section, we first discuss how to generate pseudo-random numbers and then present the inverse transformation method for generating random variates.

16.3.1 PSEUDO-RANDOM NUMBERS

There is no such a thing as a *single* random number. Rather, we speak of a *sequence* of random numbers that follow a specified theoretical or empirical distribution. There are two main approaches to generating random numbers. In the first approach, a physical phenomenon is used as a source of randomness from where random numbers can be generated. Random numbers generated in this way are called *true random numbers*. A true random number generator requires a completely unpredictable and non-reproducible source of randomness. Such sources can be found in nature, or they can be created from hardware and software. For instance, the elapsed time between emissions of particles during radioactive decay is a well-known randomized source. Also, the thermal noise from a semiconductor diode can be used as a randomized source. Finally, sampling a human computer interaction pro-cesses, such as keyboard or mouse activity of a user, can give rise to a randomized source.

The second approach to generating random numbers, which is the most popular approach, is to use a mathemati-cal algorithm. Efficient algorithms have been developed that can be easily implemented in a computer program to generate a string of random numbers. These algorithms produce numbers in a deterministic fashion. That is, given a starting value, known as the *seed*, the same sequence of random numbers can be produced each time as long as the seed remains the same. Despite the deterministic way in which random numbers are created, these numbers appear to be random since they pass a number of statistical tests designed to test various properties of random numbers. In view of this, these random numbers are referred to as *pseudo-random numbers*.

An advantage of generating pseudo random numbers in a deterministic fashion is that they are reproducible, since the same sequence of random numbers is produced each time we run a pseudo-random generator with the same starting value. This is helpful when debugging a simulation program, as we typically want to reproduce the same sequence of events in order to verify the accuracy of the simulation.

Pseudo-random numbers and random variates are typically generated on demand. That is, each time a random number is required, the appropriate generator is called which returns a single random number. Consequently, there is no need to generate a large set of random numbers in advance and store them in an array for future use as in the case of true random numbers.

In general, an acceptable method for generating random numbers must yield sequences of numbers or bits that are: uniformly distributed, statistically independent, reproducible, and non-repeating for any desired length. Several algorithms have been proposed for pseudo-random number generation, such as, the *congruential* method, the *Tausworthe* generators, the *lagged Fibonacci* generators, and the *Mersenne twister*. Below, we examine the congrunetial method.

The congrunetial method is a very popular method and most of the pseudo-random number generators in programming languages are based on some variation of this method. The advantage of the congruential method is that it is very simple, fast, and it produces pseudo-random numbers that are statistically acceptable for computer simulation. The congruential method uses the following recursive relationship to generate random numbers:

$$x_{i+1} = ax_i + c \ (\text{mod } m)$$

where x_i, a, c and m are all non-negative numbers. Given that the previous random number was x_i the next random number x_i+1 can be generated as follows. Multiply x_i by a and then add c. Then, compute the modulus m of the result. That is, divide the result by m and set x_{i+1} equal to the remainder of this division. For example, if $x_0 = 0$, $a = c = 7$, and $m = 10$ then we can obtain the following sequence of numbers: 7, 6, 9, 0, 7, 6, 9, 0, . . . The initial value x_0, required to get the generator started is known as the seed. The seed value does not affect the long-term behavior of the simulation model after a small set of numbers has been generated.

The method using the above expression is known as the mixed congruential method. A simpler variation of this method is the multiplicative congruential method. This method utilizes the relation $x_{i+1} = ax_i$ (mod m). The numbers generated by a congruential method are between 0 and $m - 1$. Uniformly distributed random numbers between 0 and 1 can be obtained by simply dividing the resulting x_i by m.

The number of successively generated pseudo-random numbers after which the sequence starts repeating itself is called the *period*. If the period is equal to m, then the generator is said to have a *full period*. It is important to note that one should not use any arbitrary values for a, c and m. Systematic testing of various values for these parameters have led to generators which have a full period and which are statistically satisfactory. Such generators can be found in all programming languages and in statistical and mathematical software packages.

16.3.2 RANDOM VARIATES
Random variates are generated using pseudo-random numbers in a variety of ways. In this section, we present the *inverse transformation* method which is one of the most commonly used techniques.

The inverse transformation method is applicable only to cases where the cumulative density function can be inverted. Assume that we wish to generate random variates from the pdf $f(x)$. Let $F(x)$ be its cumulative density function. We note that $F(x)$ is defined in the region [0,1]. We explore this property of the cumulative density function to obtain the following simple generator. We first generate a pseudo-random number r which we set equal to $F(x)$. That is, $F(x) = r$. The quantity x is then obtained by inverting $F(x)$. That is, $x = F^{-1}(r)$, where $F^{-1}(r)$ indicates

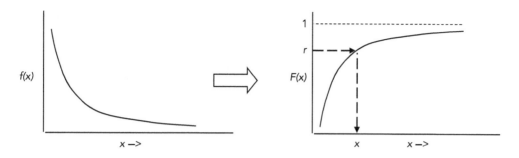

Figure 16.7: The inverse transformation method

the inverse transformation of $F(x)$. A pictorial explanation of this method is given in figure 16.7.

As an example, let us assume that we want to generate random variates with probability density function $f(x) = 2x, 0 \le x \le 1$. We first calculate the cumulative density function $F(x)$. We have

$$F(x) = \int_0^x 2t\,dt = x^2$$

Now, let r be a pseudo-random number. Then, we have

$$2x = r$$

or

$$x = \sqrt{r}.$$

SAMPLING FROM A UNIFORM DISTRIBUTION

The probability density function of the uniform distribution is $f(x) = 1 / (a - b)$, $a < x < b$, and its cumulative density function is:

$$F(x) = \int_a^x \frac{1}{b-a}dt = \frac{x-a}{b-a}$$

The inverse transformation method for generating random variates is as follows. Generate a pseudo-random number r. Then,

$$r = F(x) = \frac{x-a}{b-a}$$

or

$$x = a + (b - a)r.$$

SAMPLING FROM AN EXPONENTIAL DISTRIBUTION.

The probability density function $f(x)$ of an exponential distribution is $f(x) = ae^{-ax}$, $a > 0$, where $x \ge 0$, and its cumulative density function is $F(x) = 1 - e^{-ax}$. The procedure is as follows. Generate a pseudo-random number r. Then

$$r = F(x) = 1 - e^{-ax},$$

or

$$1 - r = e^{-ax},$$

or

$$x = -(1/a) \log_e(1 - r).$$

It can be simplified to

$$x = -(1/a) \log_e(r),$$

since $1 - r$ is also a pseudo-random number.

SAMPLING FROM A DISCRETE-TIME PROBABILITY DISTRIBUTION

Let X be a discrete random variable with probability $p(X = i) = p_i$, and let $p(X \leq i) = P_i$ be its cumulative probability. An example of a cumulative distribution is shown in figure 16.8. Random variates from this probability distribution can be easily generated using the inverse transformation method as follows. Let r be a pseudo-random number, and let us assume that it falls between P_2 and P_3. Then, the random variate x is equal to 3. In general, $x = i$ if $P_{i-1} < r \leq P_i$. This method is based on the fact that $p_i = P_i - P_{i-1}$ and that since r is a random number, it will fall in the interval $(P_i, P_{i-1}]$ $p_i\%$ of the time.

As an example, let us consider the well-known newsboy problem. Let X be the number of newspapers sold by a by a newsboy per day, which from historical data has the following distribution.

X	1	2	3	4	5
f(x)	0.20	0.20	0.30	0.15	0.15

The cumulative probability distribution is:

X	1	2	3	4	5
F(x)	0.20	0.40	0.70	0.85	1

Random variates can be generated as follows:

1. Sample a pseudo-random number r.
2. Locate the interval within which r falls in order to determine the random variate x.

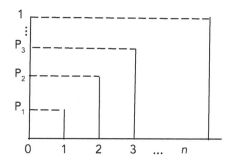

Figure 16.8: A cumulative distribution

- If $0.85 < r \le 1.00$ then $x = 5$
- If $0.70 < r \le 0.85$ then $x = 4$
- If $0.40 < r \le 0.70$ then $x = 3$
- If $0.20 < r \le 0.40$ then $x = 2$
- Otherwise   then $x = 1$.

SAMPLING FROM A CONTINUOUS-TIME PROBABILITY DISTRIBUTION

Let us assume that the empirical observations of a random variable X can be summarized into the histogram shown in figure 16.9. From this histogram, we obtain the set of values $(x_i, f(x_i))$, where x_i is the midpoint of the ith interval, and $f(x_i)$ is the height of the ith rectangle. Using this set of values we can construct approximately the cumulative probability distribution as shown in figure 16.10, where:

$$F(x_i) = \sum_{k=1}^{x_i} f(x_k)$$

The cumulative distribution is assumed to be monotonically increasing within each interval $[F(x_{i-1}), F(x_i)]$, for $i = 1, 2, \ldots, 6$.

Now, let r be a pseudo-number and let us assume that $F(x_{i-1}) \le r \le F(x_i)$. Then, using linear interpolation, the random variate x can be obtained as follows:

$$x = x_{i-1} + (x_i - x_{i-1}) \frac{r - F(x_{i-1})}{F(x_i) - F(x_{i-1})}$$

This approach can be also used to generate random variates from a known continuous probability distribution $f(x)$. We first obtain a set of values $(x_i, f(x_i)$ as shown in figure 16.11. This set of values is then used in place of the exact probability density function. (This is known as "discretizing" the probability density function.) Using this set of values we can proceed to construct the cumulative probability distribution and then obtain random variates as de-

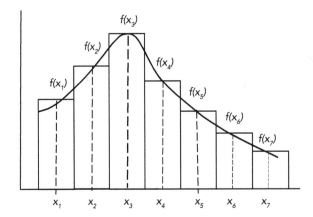

Figure 16.9: Histogram of a random variable X.

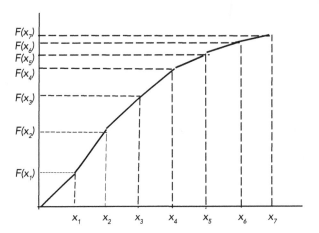

Figure 16.10: The cumulative distribution.

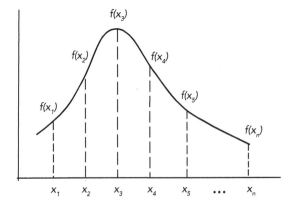

Figure 16.11: Discretizing a probability density function

scribed above. The accuracy of this approach depends on the number of the x_i points. Obviously, the more points, the more accurate the discretization process is.

16.4 SIMULATION DESIGNS

The term simulation design is used to describe a method for tracking the occurrence of events in a simulation. There are three different simulation designs. The first two designs are: *event-advance* and *unit-time advance*, and they are both event-based but utilize different ways to advance the time. The third design is *activity-based*. The event-advance and unit-time advance designs are the most popular simulation designs. In this section, we review these two designs.

16.4.1 EVENT-ADVANCE DESIGN

This is the design employed in the example of the repairman model described above in section 16.1. The basic idea behind this design is that the status of the system changes each time an event occurs, and during the time that elapses between two successive events, the system's status remains unchanged and consequently it does not have to be monitored. In order to implement this idea, each event is associated with a clock. The value of this clock gives the time instance in the future that this event will occur. Upon completion of processing an event, all possible events that will occur in the future are checked in order to find the one with the smallest clock value. It then advances the master clock to this particular time when the next event will occur. It takes the appropriate action associated with this event, and then repeats the process of finding the next event, and so on. The simulation, therefore, moves through time by only visiting the time instances at which events occur. In view of this it is known as *event-advance design*.

The basic logic of the event-based design is summarized in figure 16.12. We note that a conditional event is an event that gets triggered because of the occurrence of another event. For instance, in the repairman model, an arrival at the repairman's queue may cause a service event to be scheduled, if the repairman is idle at that time. The service event in this case is a conditional event.

Let us assume that a simulation model is currently at time t. The collection of all events scheduled to occur in the future is known as the *future event list*. For each event scheduled to occur in the future, the list contains the following information:

- Time of occurrence (i.e., value of the event's clock)
- Type of event

The event type is used in order to determine what action should be taken when the event occurs. For instance, using the event type we can determine which procedure to call.

The next event is located by finding the event in the future event list with the lowest clock value. If there are just a few events then the next event can be located by comparing the clocks. However, when simulating complex systems, the number of events may be very large and in this cases we need an efficient algorithm to find the next event since this operation may well account for a large percentage of the total computation involved in running a simulation program. The efficiency of this algorithm depends on how the event list is stored in the computer. An event list

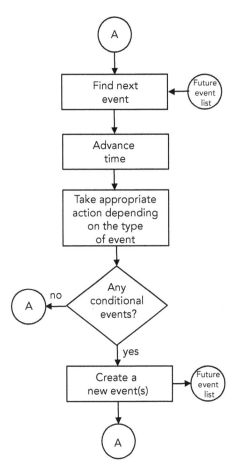

Figure 16.12: The event-advance simulation design

should be stored in such a way so as to lend itself to an efficient execution of the following operations.

- Locate the next future event time and the associated event type.
- Delete an event from the list after it has occurred.
- Insert newly scheduled events in the event list.

Different data structures can be used to store an event list, such as a simple sequential array, a linked list, and a heap.

16.4.2 UNIT-TIME ADVANCE DESIGN

In the event-advance simulation, the master clock is advanced from event to event. Alternatively, the master clock can be advanced in small fixed increments of time, each increment being equal to one unit of time. That is, each time the master clock is advanced by a unit time and all event clocks are compared with the current value of the master clock. If any of these clocks is equal to the current value of the master clock, then the associated event has just occurred and appropriate action has to take place. If no clock is equal to the current value of the master clock,

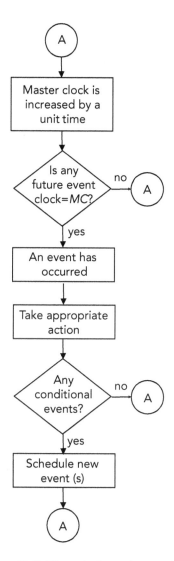

Figure 16.13: The unit-time advance design

then no event has occurred and no action has to take place. In either case, the master clock is again increased by a unit time and the cycle is repeated. In view of this particular way of advancing the master clock, this simulation design is known as the *unit-time advance design*. The basic logic of this design is summarized in the flowchart given in figure 16.13.

When all the event clocks in a simulation are defined as integer variables, the unit time can be easily determined so that each event clock is an integer multiple of it. In this case, an event occurs when its clock value becomes equal to the current value of the master clock, as shown in case a of figure 16.14.

However, in many simulations the event clocks are represented by real variables, and they will never be equal

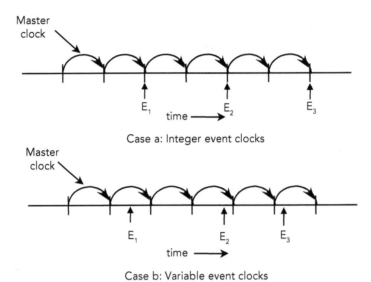

Case a: Integer event clocks

Case b: Variable event clocks

Figure 16.14: Relation between event clocks and the master clock.

to the master clock. In this case, events occur in between two successive time instants of the master clock as shown in case b of figure 16.14. The exact time of occurrence of an event E is known in the simulation since its clock value is known. However, the logic of the simulation is typically based on the master clock, and as far as the simulation is concerned, en event occurs at the master clock value which is the nearest to the event clock value, either before or after the event depending upon how the logic of the computer program has been set up. This introduces inaccuracies when estimating time parameters related to the occurrence of events. Another inaccuracy that might arise is due to the possibility of having multiple events occurring during the same unit of time, in which case, we may not know precisely the order with which they occurred.

In general, a unit time should be small enough so that at most one event occurs during the period of a unit of time. However, if it is too small, the simulation program will spend most of its time in non-productive mode, i.e., advancing the master clock and checking whether an event has occurred. Several heuristic and analytic methods have been proposed for choosing a unit time. A simple heuristic rule is to set the unit time equal to one-half of the smallest random variate generated. (This can be determined by exercising the random variate generators separately, prior to running the simulation.) Alternatively, one can carry out several simulation runs, each with a different unit time, in order to observe its impact on the computed results. For instance, one can start with a small unit time. Then, it can be slightly increased, and if it is found to have no effect on the computed results, it can be further increased, and so on.

16.5 STATISTICAL ESTIMATION

After the simulation model has been built and debugged, and it can be used to generate data from which various performance measures can be obtained. To start a simulation we have to provide a seed for the pseudo-random generator and also we have to assume that the system is in a given state. For instance, in the hand simulation in table 16.1, we assumed that at time zero all three machines are operational and that $CL1 = 1$, $CL2 = 4$, $CL3$

= 9. The assumptions regarding the initial state of a simulation are known as the *initial conditions*. Obviously, the behavior of the system will be affected by the initial conditions. However, if we let the simulation run for a long period, its statistical behavior will eventually become independent of the initial conditions. In general, the initial conditions affect the behavior of the system for only an initial period of time. Thereafter, the simulation behaves statistically in the same way whatever the initial conditions. During this initial period, the simulation is said to be in a *transient state*, and after this period is over, the simulation is said to be in a *steady state*. Typically, a simulation model is used to study the steady-state behavior of a system. In this case, the simulation has to run long enough so that to get away from the transient state and also obtain good statistical estimates.

Most of the performance measures that one would like to estimate are related to the probability distribution of a random variable X which is observed through the simulation. Typically, we are not interested in the entire probability distribution, but rather in the mean and the standard deviation of X. Also, percentiles of the probability distribution of X are of interest. For instance, from the management point of view, one may be interested in the 95th percentile of X, which is a value such that only 5% of observations are greater than it. Percentiles often are more meaningful than the mean. Below, we discuss how to estimate the mean and its confidence intervals. The calculation of percentiles is discussed in the simulation project 2 at the end of this Chapter.

Let us consider a random variable X observed through a simulation, such as the down time of a machine, and let x_1, $x_2, \ldots, x_n$ be n successive observations of X. Then,

$$\bar{X} = \frac{1}{n}\sum_1^n x_i$$

is the unbiased estimate of the true population mean, i.e., the expectation of the random variable X. The confidence interval is estimated as follows. If the observations $x_1, x_2, \ldots, x_n$ are independent of each other, then the standard deviation is given by:

$$s = \sqrt{\frac{1}{n-1}\sum_1^n \left(\bar{X} - x_i\right)^2}$$

and, therefore, we obtain the confidence interval

$$\left(\bar{X} - 1.96\frac{s}{\sqrt{n}}, \ \bar{X} + 1.96\frac{s}{\sqrt{n}}\right)$$

The confidence interval tells us that the true population mean lies within the interval 95% of the time. That is, if we ran the same simulation experiment 100 times, each time with a different seed for the pseudo-random number generator so that to create a different sequence of events, then on the average, 95% of these times the true population mean will be within the interval. Therefore, the smaller the confidence interval, the better the estimate.

If the successive observations $x_1, x_2, \ldots, x_n$ are not independent, as is often the case, then the above expression for the standard deviation does not hold. In this case, there are various ways that can be used to calculate the standard deviation, one of which is the *batch means* method. This is a very easy method to use. The n observations are divided into k batches of equal number of b observations, as follows:

$$| \; x_1, \; x_2, \ldots, x_b \; | \; x_{b+1}, x_{b+2}, \ldots, x_{2b} \; | \; \ldots \; | \; x_{(k-1)b+1}, x_{(k-1)b+2}, \ldots, x_{kb} \; |$$

$$\text{batch 1} \qquad \text{batch 2} \qquad\qquad\qquad \text{batch k}$$

(We assume that $n = kb$.) Batch 1 contains observations x_1, x_2, ..., x_b, batch 2 contains observations x_{b+1}, x_{b+2}, ... , x_{2b}, and so on. The observations in batch 1 which are close to batch 2 are likely to be correlated with the observations in batch 2 which are close to batch 1. Also, the observations in batch 2 which are close to batch 3 are likely to be correlated with those in batch 3 which are close to batch 2, and so on. Let Y_i be the mean of the observations in batch i, $i = 1, 2, \ldots, k$. If we choose b to be large enough, then the sequence of $Y_1, Y_2, \ldots, Y_k$, can be shown that it is approximately uncorrelated. Therefore, we can treat these means as being independent and calculate their mean and standard deviation. We have

$$\bar{Y} = \frac{1}{k} \sum_1^k Y_i$$

and

$$s = \sqrt{\frac{1}{k-1} \sum_1^k \left(\bar{Y} - Y_i \right)^2}$$

from which we can calculate the confidence interval of the mean as above.

As a rule of thumb, the error $1.96(s / n^{1/2})$ has to be less than 10% of the value of the mean. This permits us to decide how long the simulation should be. If the observations are independent from each other, we run the simulation for an initial value n and calculate the confidence interval. If the error is not less than 10% of the mean, then we run the simulation for a larger sample of observations and check again. We keep repeating this process until we are satisfied that the above condition holds. If the batch means method is used, then we keep increasing the batch size until the condition is satisfied.

16.6 VALIDATION

Validation of a simulation model is a very important issue that is often neglected. How accurately does a simulation model (or, for that matter, any kind of model) reflect the operations of a real life system under study? How confident can we be that the obtained simulation results are accurate and meaningful?

The following checks can be carried out in order to validate a simulation model.

1. *Check the pseudo-random number generator.* A battery of statistical tests can be carried out to make sure that the pseudo-random number generator used in the simulation program creates numbers that are uniformly distributed in [0,1] and statistically independent.

2. *Check the stochastic variate generators.* Similar statistical tests can be carried out for each stochastic variate

generator used in a simulation model.

3. *Check the logic of the simulation program.* This is a rather difficult task. One way of going about it is to print out the status variables, the future event list, and other relevant data structures each time an event takes place. Then, can check by hand whether the data structures are updated appropriately. This is a rather tedious task. However, using this method one can discover logical errors and also get a good feel about the simulation model.

4. *Relationship validity.* Verify that the assumptions you made when building the simulation model are same as in the system under study.

5. *Output validity.* There are various ways that the validity of the output can be confirmed. A simple method is to consider special cases for which you can predict qualitatively the behavior of the results. For instance, in the repairman model, if we assume that the repair time is extremely small, then the waiting time for the repairman is almost zero, and the total down time of a machine is close to zero as well. This can be confirmed by running the simulation with different decreasing service times and observe the down time go to zero.

Other validity tests can be carried out by obtaining graphs of a particular measure of interest for different values of the input parameters and then try to interpret these graphs intuitively.

PROBLEMS

1. Consider the multiplicative congruential method for generating random digits. Assuming that $m = 10$, determine the length of the cycle for each set of values of a and x_0 given below.

   a. $a = 2, x_0 = 1, 3, 5.$
   b. $a = 3, x_0 = 1, 2, 5.$

2. Use the inverse transformation method to generate random variates with the probability density function:

$$f(x) = \begin{cases} 3x^2, & 0 \le x \le 1 \\ 0, & \text{otherwise} \end{cases}$$

3. Apply the inverse transformation method to obtain a formula that yields the value of a random variate x given a pseudo-random number r. (Note that $f(x)$ below has to be normalized.)

$$f(x) = \begin{cases} 5x, & 0 \le x \le 4 \\ x - 2, & 4 \le x \le 10 \end{cases}!$$

4. Redo the hand simulation of the repairman model, shown in table 16.1, using the event-based design,

with a unit time equal to 1

REFERENCES

1   H.G. Perros, *Computer Simulation Techniques*: The Definitive Introduction. URL: http://www4.ncsu.edu/~hp//
    simulation.pdf

SIMULATION PROJECT 1: THE REPAIRMAN PROBLEM

The objective of this project is to develop a computer program to simulate the repairman problem described in this Chapter. The project is divided into four tasks, as described below.

TASK 1:

Write a computer program using a high-level language to simulate the hand simulation in table 16.1. Each time an event occurs, print out a line of output to show the current value of the clocks and of the other status parameters (as in the hand simulation). Run your simulation until the master clock is equal to 20. Check by hand whether the simulation advances from event to event properly, and whether it updates the clocks and the other status parameters correctly.

TASK 2:

Change your simulation program so that the operational time and the repair time of a machine are exponentially distributed with the same means as before. Make sure that the clocks are defined as real variables. Run your simulation model as before. Each time an event occurs, print out a line of output to show the new value of the clocks and the other relevant parameters. Check by hand whether the logic of the simulation is correct.

TASK 3:

- First remove all the print statements that print out a line of output each time an event occurs. Set up a data structure to collect information regarding the amount of time each machine spends being broken down, i.e., waiting in the repairman's queue and also being repaired.
- Run your simulation for 3100 observations (i.e., repairs). Discard the first 100 observations to account for the transient state. Based on the remaining 1000 observations, calculate the mean and the standard deviation of the time a machine is broken down and then calculate the confidence interval.
- The calculation of the standard deviation may not be correct due to the presence of autocorrelation. Implement the batch means method in your program and run your program for 31 batches, where a batch is equal to 100 observations. Disregard the first batch, and use the other 30 batch means to construct a confidence interval of the mean time a customer is broken down. Compare the results with those obtained above without

the batch means method.

- Check if the error $1.96(s / n)^{1/2}$ is less or equal to 10% of the mean. If not, increase the batch size and re-run your simulation. Continue until the above condition is met.

TASK 4:

- Run a series of experiments where each time you reduce the mean repair time and observe that the waiting time in the repairman's queue is also reduced.
- Confirm that the exact solution for the mean time a machine is broken down given in section 15.3.4 is within the confidence interval of the mean time a customer is broken down obtained above in task 3.

SIMULATION PROJECT 2: ESTIMATION OF THE 95TH PERCENTILE OF THE END-TO-END DELAY AND BANDWIDTH ALLOCATION UNDER END-TO-END DELAY PERCENTILE BOUNDS

Typically bandwidth allocation is done so that the packet loss rate at an IP router is less than a predefined percentage. However, this type of bandwidth allocation does not necessarily guarantee that the end-to-end delay of packets is bounded. The objective of this project, is to determine how much bandwidth should be allocated at each router for a connection so that the end-to-end delay is statistically bounded. That is, say, 95% of the time it is less than a predefined number.

There are two steps in this simulation project. First, you will develop a simulation model of a connection traversing five routers in order to estimate the one-way end-to-end delay of the packets transmitted over the connection. Subsequently, you will use this simulation model to determine the required bandwidth that has to be allocated at each router so that a given percentile of the end-to-end delay is less than a given value.

1. PROJECT DESCRIPTION

We will assume that a connection is modeled by the tandem queueing network shown in figure 16.15 consisting of 5 nodes. Each node is a single server queue representing an output buffer of a router. The server (shown as a circle) represents the transmitter that transmits the packets out of the router. Each queue is assumed to have infinite capacity, that is, packets cannot get lost. The transmitter transmits packets in the order in which they come in, that is, FIFO. A packet joins the first queue, where it waits for its turn to be served, i.e., transmitted out, and following service completion it moves up to the next queue and so on until it eventually departs.

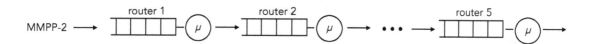

Figure 16.15: The 5-node tandem queueing network

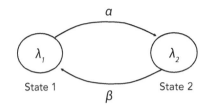

Figure 16.16: A two-state MMPP (MMPP-2)

THE ARRIVAL PROCESS

Typically, in high speed networks packets arrive in a bursty fashion, and often the successive inter-arrival times are correlated. We represent this type of arrival by a two-state Markov modulated Poisson process (MMPP-2). This is a doubly stochastic process where the rate of a Poisson process is defined by the state of a two-state continuous-time Markov process, see figure 16.16. More specifically, the arrival process can find itself in two different states, i.e., state 1 and 2. In each state packets arrive in a Poisson fashion at a rate that depends on the state. The arrival process stays in state 1 for an exponentially distributed amount of time with a mean $1 / \alpha$. During this time, arrivals of packets occur with a Poisson process with parameter λ_1. After the time it spends in state 1 is finished, it moves to state 2 where it also spends an exponentially distributed amount of time with mean $1 / \beta$. During this time, the arrival process is a Poisson process with parameter λ_2. Subsequently, it moves back to state 1 and the process repeats again.

THE SERVICE TIME

In this queueing network, the service time in all five servers is exponentially distributed and it has the same mean $1 / \mu$ for all queues.

2. THE SIMULATION STRUCTURE

Your program should prompt the user for the following inputs:

1. The parameters of the arrival process: α, β, λ_1, λ_2.
2. The exponential service mean time $1 / \mu$.
3. The total number of simulated departures.

You program will stop when the number of customers departed from the network reaches the total number of simulated departures specified at input.

For each arrival customer, your program should keep track of the total time it spends in the queueing network, which represents the end-to-end delay. This is the time elapsing from the moment a customer arrives at the first queue to the moment the same customer departs from the last queue.

GENERATION OF THE INTER-ARRIVAL AND SERVICE TIMES

In the simulation, you have to generate random numbers that follow the exponential distribution with a given mean. For this, you need a pseudo-random number generator, typically available in most programming languages. For debugging purposes, always use the same seed, so that to recreate the same sequence of events. In view of this, you should use a random number generator that you can seed yourself. (Some of them are automatically seeded.) Make sure you read the rules of the random number generator as to what type of number it will accept as a seed.

A random value from an exponential distribution with a given mean can be generated by the expression:

$$- \textit{(mean of exponential distribution)} * log_e(r), \qquad\qquad (16.1)$$

where r is a pseudo-random number in $[0,1]$. Each time you need a new exponential random variate you should use a new pseudo-random number.

EVENTS

In our simulation, we have the following events:

1. End of state 1
2. Completion of an arrival during state 1
3. End of state 2
4. Completion of an arrival during state 2
5. Arrival at a queue
6. Service completion at a queue

The occurrence of one event may trigger the occurrence of one or more events, as explained below.

Start your simulation assuming that the arrival process is in state 1 and all the queues are empty. In order to get the simulation going you need to pre-generate the duration time of state 1 and also the time that the first arrival will occur. When the first packet arrives it will join the first queue and since the system is empty it will start to receive service, and for this, the time at which the service is completed has to be generated. After the packet completes its service it will move to the next queue, and so on. In the meantime other packets will arrive and they will start making their way through the queues.

In order to track the simulation we use a master clock (MC). Each event is associated with a time of completion in the future. The MC helps us decide which event will be executed next. The simulation logic is described below, but first let us take a look at the events and what action to take each time an event occurs.

- *End of state 1:* We will assume at the beginning of the simulation that the arrival process is in state 1. For this we have to generate an exponential time t of the duration the process stays in state 1 using expression (16.1) with a mean $1 / \alpha$. Then, the time this event will occur in the future is $MC + t$, where MC is the current clock time. When this time is reached, the event "end of state 1" has occurred and the process shifts to state 2. At that moment, we have to calculate how long the process will stay in state 2. For this, you should generate an exponential value t using expression (16.1) with a mean $1/\beta$. Then, the event "end of state 2" will occur at $MC + t$, where MC is the current time. In general, each time the event "end of state 1" occurs, we have to calculate how long the process will stay in state 2 and then compute the time when the event "end of state 2" will occur.

- *End of state 2:* When this time is reached, the process shifts to state 1 and for this we have to decide how long the process will stay in state 1. Generate an exponential value t using expression (16.1) with a mean $1/\alpha$. The time the event "end of state 1" will occur is $MC + t$, where MC is the current time.

- *Arrivals during state i:* Each time the process shifts to a new state, we generate a new inter-arrival time t of a packet using expression (16.1) with mean $1/\lambda_i$, where i is the current state of the arrival process. Its time of occurrence is $MC + t$, where MC is the current time.

  Each time an arrival occurs we will immediately generate a new inter-arrival time t with the same mean and mark its time of occurrence $MC + t$, where MC is the current time. If the "end of the state" event occurs before the arrival of the packet, then this arrival is discarded.

  When a new packet is generated, it joins the first queue. If the server queue is idle, we generate a service time t using expression (16.1) with a mean $1/\mu$. The service completion time is $MC + t$, where MC is the current time. If the server is busy, the packet will join the queue and no further action will be taken.

- *Service completion at queue i:* The packet moves to the next queue $i + 1$. If the server is empty, we generate a service time t using expression (16.1) with a mean $1/\mu$. The service completion time is $MC + t$, where MC is the current time. If the server is busy, the packet joins the queue and no further action is taken. Also, if there are packets waiting in queue i, then the next packet will start its service and for this we have to generate a new service time t at queue i using expression (16.1) with a mean $1/\mu$. The service completion time is $MC + t$, where MC is the current time.

SIMULATION LOGIC

The main simulation logic is very simple. After completing servicing an event, check all the future events to see which of them will occur next. Advance the clock to the time of the next event and service the event according to the logic described above.

Since, the arrival process is either in state 1 or 2, the maximum number of events that can be scheduled to occur in the future at any time is 7. These events are: service completion event at queue 1, 2, 3, 4, and 5, end of state 1 or 2 of the arrival process, arrival of a packet. Associate each event with the time that it is scheduled to occur in the future, and also where to jump to in the code to service this event. The event list can be implemented in a static array or in a linked list as described in Perros[1].

3. STATISTICAL ANALYSIS

For each new arrival, your simulation has to store the arrival time. When the packet departs from the last queue, calculate the time it spent in the entire queueing network and store it in an array for further processing. This is the end-to-end delay of the packet.

THE 95TH PERCENTILE OF THE END-TO-END DELAY TIME

Based on the observations stored in the array calculate the 95th percentile as follows. Given a random variable with a probability distribution, the 95th percentile is the value of this random variable such that only 5% values of this random variable are greater than itself. Let X be a random variable indicating the end-to-end delay time in the queueing network, and let x_i be the end-to-end delay time of the ith packet. Then the 95th percentile of the end-to-end delay is a value T such that $\text{Prob}[X \le T] = 0.95$. Now, suppose that the total number of observations is n, i.e., $x_1, x_2, \ldots, x_n$. To calculate the percentile T, you have to sort them out in ascending order. Let $y_1 \le y_2 \le \ldots \le y_n$ be the sorted observations. Then, the 95th percentile T is the value y_k where $k = \text{ceiling}(0.95n)$, where $\text{ceiling}(x)$ is the ceiling function that maps the real number x to the smallest integer not less than x. For instance, if $n = 50$, then $k = 48$, and the percentile is the value y_{48}.

THE CONFIDENCE INTERVAL OF THE 95TH PERCENTILE OF THE END-TO-END DELAY TIME

A confidence interval provides an indication of the error associated with an estimate, which in this case is the 95th percentile. To calculate the confidence interval you will have to obtain 30 different percentiles of the end-to-end delay time for the same input values. An easy way to do this is to use the batch means method. Let us assume a batch size of 1000 departures. Run your simulation for the first 1000 departures in batch 1 and calculate the 95th percentile of their end-to-end delay time. Store this number in an array. Continue the simulation for the next 1000 departures in batch 2 without changing anything in your simulation, and compute and store their 95th percentile. Repeat this until you have simuated 30 batches. Now, let $T_1, T_2, T_3, \ldots, T_n$ be the calculated percentiles where $n = 30$. Then, the mean of the percentiles is:

$$T_{mean} = \frac{1}{n}\sum_1^n T_i$$

and the standard deviation s is:

$$s = \sqrt{\frac{\sum_1^n (T_{mean} - T_i)^2}{n-1}}$$

The confidence interval at 95% confidence is given by:

$$\left(T_{mean} - 1.96\frac{s}{\sqrt{n}}, T_{mean} + 1.96\frac{s}{\sqrt{n}} \right)$$

Inputs	Values	Distribution
MMPP2: α	0.3	Exponential
MMPP2: β	0.5	Exponential
MMPP2: λ_1	3	Exponential
MMPP2: λ_2	4	Exponential
Service rate μ	5	Exponential
Total departures	30100	
Total number of batches	30	

Table 16.2: Input values

Accurate simulation results require that the confidence interval is very small. That is, the error $1.96(s / n^{1/2}) \sim 0.10T_{mean}$. If the error is not small enough, increase the batch size from 1000 arrivals to 1100, and run the simulation again for 30 batches. Keep increasing the batch size until the error is within the limits.

When you start the simulation, you will assume that there are no customers in the queueing network, i.e. the system is empty. The initial behavior of the simulation will be affected by this "system empty" assumption as well as by the seed of the pseudo-random number generator. In order to eliminate the effects of these initial conditions, you should run the simulation for 100 departures first. After that "warming up" period, start the batch method described above.

4. RESULTS

TASK 1: PERCENTILE CALCULATION
Run your simulation to obtain the 95th percentile of the end-to-end delay of the packets and its confidence interval. The input values are given in table 16.2. If your program is correct, the confidence interval of T_{mean} should contain the value 5.75!

TASK 2: BANDWIDTH ESTIMATION
Run your simulation for different values of the service rate μ, which represents the bandwidth allocated to the connection, so that the 95th percentile of the end-to-end delay T_{mean}, is less or equal to 4. For this you will need to start with your current value of μ and then keep changing it (up to two decimal points) until you find your optimum value. Repeat the experiment for the 80th, 85th, 90th and 99th percentile.

Summarize your findings in a graph with the optimum value of μ on the vertical axis and the percentile on the horizontal axis. Discuss your results. Why does the graph has this particular shape? Can you spot any trends in the graph?

INDEX

INDEX